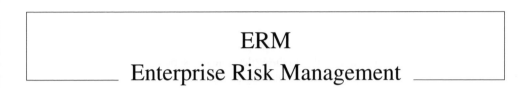

ERM
Enterprise Risk Management

For other titles in the Wiley Finance series
please see www.wiley.com/finance

ERM
Enterprise Risk Management

Issues and Cases

Jean-Paul Louisot
Christopher Ketcham

Registered office
John Wiley & Sons Ltd, The Atrium, Southern Gate, Chichester, West Sussex, PO19 8SQ,
United Kingdom

For details of our global editorial offices, for customer services and for information about how to apply for
permission to reuse the copyright material in this book please see our website at www.wiley.com.

Wiley publishes in a variety of print and electronic formats and by print-on-demand. Some material included with
standard print versions of this book may not be included in e-books or in print-on-demand. If this book refers to
media such as a CD or DVD that is not included in the version you purchased, you may download this material at
http://booksupport.wiley.com. For more information about Wiley products, visit www.wiley.com.

Designations used by companies to distinguish their products are often claimed as trademarks. All brand names and
product names used in this book are trade names, service marks, trademarks or registered trademarks of their
respective owners. The publisher is not associated with any product or vendor mentioned in this book.

Limit of Liability/Disclaimer of Warranty: While the publisher and author have used their best efforts in preparing
this book, they make no representations or warranties with the respect to the accuracy or completeness of the
contents of this book and specifically disclaim any implied warranties of merchantability or fitness for a particular
purpose. It is sold on the understanding that the publisher is not engaged in rendering professional services and
neither the publisher nor the author shall be liable for damages arising herefrom. If professional advice or other
expert assistance is required, the services of a competent professional should be sought.

Library of Congress Cataloging-in-Publication Data

ERM, enterprise risk management : issues and cases / [edited by] Jean-Paul Louisot, Christopher H. Ketcham.
    pages cm. – (The Wiley finance series)
    Includes bibliographical references and index.
  ISBN 978-1-118-53952-1 (hardback)
  1. Risk management.   I. Louisot, Jean-Paul.   II. Ketcham, Christopher.
    HD61.E74 2014
    658.15'5–dc23

                                                                                      2014005796

A catalogue record for this book is available from the British Library.

ISBN 978-1-118-53952-1 (hbk) ISBN 978-1-118-53951-4 (ebk)
ISBN 978-1-118-53949-1 (ebk) ISBN 978-1-118-89201-5 (ebk)

Cover images reproduced by permission of Shutterstock.com

Set in 10/12pt Times by Aptara Inc., New Delhi, India
Printed in Great Britain by CPI Group (UK) Ltd, Croydon, CR0 4YY

Contents

Contributor List

Franck Baron, private enterprise risk manager in the Republic of Singapore.

Laurent Condamin, Ph.D., is an independent consultant involved in risk modeling for industry and the financial sector specializing in: project risk quantification, business plan modeling, and operational risk quantification.

Richard Connelly, Ph.D., Chairman and Cofounder of Business Intelligence International, Wayne, Pennsylvania, USA.

Grace Crickette, SVP, Chief Risk and Compliance Officer, AAA NCNU, formerly Chief Risk Office for the University of California, USA.

Fiona Davidge, LLB., FIRM, MBCI, Enterprise Risk Manager for Wellcome Trust, London, United Kingdom.

Kenneth W. Felton, RN, MS, CPHRM, DFASHRM, Senior Vice President, National Healthcare Practice, Willis Group Holdings, Hartford, Connecticut, for introductions to key industry players.

Sophie Gaultier-Gaillard, Ph.D., is an associate professor at University Paris 1 Panthéon-Sorbonne (France) and director of the "Management in crisis situation" certificate; a French specialist of global risk assessment and crisis management in management sciences; and an executive member of the Society for Risk Analysis Europe. She is currently conducting research on reputational risk and crisis situations, studying the decision makers' perception.

Daniel A. Gaus, General Manager, Berkshire Hathaway International Insurance Ltd., Zurich Branch, Zurich Switzerland.

George-Yves Kervern (deceased), formerly Ancien Élève de l'Ecole Polytechnique; Founder of Cindynics.

Kevin W. Knight, AM, is the Chairman ISO Technical Committee 262 – Risk Management, and is a founding member of the Standards Australia/Standards New Zealand Joint Technical Committee OB/7 – Risk Management that produced the original AS/NZS 4360 Risk Management Standard in 1995 and its subsequent revisions in 1999 and 2004.

Duojia (Doug) Lu, Ph.D. Chairman, First Huida Risk Management, Beijing, China.

Christopher Mandel SVP, Strategic Solutions, Sedgwick, Inc., long-term senior risk management practitioner/leader.

Patrick Naim, ARM is a consultant involved in risk modeling and quantification for major banks, insurance companies and industries in France, UK and US. Patrick also co-authored several books in risk quantification, data mining, data modeling, and Bayesian networks.

Alain Ngolui, graduate student, Université Paris 1 Panthéon-Sorbonne, compiler of references for this text.

John R. Phelps, CPCU, ARM is the 2013 President and Director of the Risk and Insurance Managers' Society (RIMS).

Jenny Rayner, MIRM, Director, Abbey Consulting, UK.

Renee Reimer, J.D., Chief Risk & Legal Operations Officer, Memorial Hermann Health System, Houston, Texas, USA.

Marc Ronez, Chief Risk Strategist and Master Coach, Asia Risk Management Institute.

Robert L. Snyder, J.D. is a professional risk advisor and a member of the Texas Bar and has served as an adjunct lecturer in Insurance and Risk Management in the College of Business at the University of Houston – Downtown, Houston Texas, USA.

Samiha Viand, Directeur Gestion des Risques et Assurances, The OPAC du Rhône, France.

About the Editors

Christopher Ketcham, Ph.D., CPCU, CRM, CIC, CFP®, Formerly Visiting Assistant Professor, University of Houston Downtown, Houston, Texas; Garnet Valley, Pennsylvania

Pr. Jean-Paul Louisot, Formerly Université Paris 1 Panthéon-Sorbonne, Directeur Pédagogique du CARM Institute, Paris, France; Philadelphia, Pennsylvania

Acknowledgements

We would like to thank all of the contributors and others who helped make this book possible. The editors and authors also want to thank two anonymous reviewers who provided extensive and valuable feedback to the first draft of the text.

Introduction

"So, how are we doing?" is the question many in the board and C-suites are probably asking of their enterprise risk management team. The answers will likely vary from, "We are just getting started and it is too soon for results"; "While it isn't perfect, we are getting results"; or even, "I believe we have exceeded expectations." All three answers may also be appropriate for any given ERM implementation, for like any other strategic initiative operated by people, the take-up rate will vary from department to department. There is, of course, an answer in the other extreme: "It's gone off the rails … ".

As of yet there is no agreed upon definition for Enterprise Risk Management (ERM). The ISO 31000 and Guide 73 define risk management as "coordinated activities to direct and control an organization with regard to risk". Enterprise or enterprise-wide risk management has grown out of the need for financial and non-financial organizations to direct and control risks outside of the traditional operational hazards and events. Financial institutions (and some other enterprises) have, on the other hand, long been using risk management techniques of another sort to direct and control financial, credit, and market related risks. Enterprise-wide risk management has been expressed as a way to bring the direction and control of all categories of risks under one umbrella so that *all* critical risks to the organization are identified and directed and controlled. Towards this end, more and more organizations are locating their risk management (ERM) efforts at the senior levels of the organization and are linking risk management efforts towards critical risks that can impact the strategies and strategic goals of the organization. "Grafting risk management onto strategy" is a phrase that has been used to identify this change in focus. Unlike hazard risk where there is only the opportunity for loss, ERM also considers the possibilities of the positive effects of risks of outperforming strategies that may arise from unanticipated events, conditions, or opportunities. While traditional operational and financial risk management techniques are often retained in an ERM installation because they are effective, organizations are finding that other types of risks (some of these not anticipated) require unique risk management strategies that do not have traditional methods of treatment or control. Some of the cases in this book reflect the broadening horizon of risks that ERM has begun to identify and control.

This book has three purposes. The first purpose in the articles section is to address certain key issues of ERM implementations that may need greater explanation. The second is to provide a number of case studies of organizations in the midst of their strategic ERM implementations. Cases include mature implementations as well as organizations that are in the early stages of inculcating ERM into their organizations. No attempt was made to connect the articles section with the case studies section. Many of the topics addressed in the articles section are from issues raised in the broader risk management community or from discussions with individual risk managers who were not part of the case studies presented in this text. The third purpose of the text is to provide a more recent bibliography of resources for risk management professionals who are in the midst of, or are contemplating, ERM implementations.

The book was designed for the practicing risk professional and those who aspire to become risk professionals, including university students. The case studies in this book are appropriate for these readers as well as senior leadership in organizations in the midst of, or considering, adopting ERM. This said, there are other texts, white papers, and journal articles that will provide more extensive development and examination of sophisticated financial and other quantitative risk identification and analysis tools. Many of the sophisticated tools appropriate for quantitative risk identification and analysis have been used by risk management teams showcased in the case studies and are appropriate for certain of the processes and activities outlined in the articles. Risk managers have used these tools to identify the likelihood and probability of risk as well as its impact. However this text was written in response to one of the identified issues in ERM, and that is the need to provide accessible methods that all stakeholders in the organization can use to identify and assess the impact of critical risks. Risk managers have found that they can use sophisticated tools to quantify probability and impact, but it is crucial that all risk owners understand the "critical risks" and that they and the organization are engaged in the dialog necessary to begin the process of managing these risks. For this purpose, many are using "expert" methods to identify and assess the impact of critical risks. These "expert" methods require a combination of the analysis of quantitative data prepared by and from different sources as well as an ongoing dialog towards understanding the specific enterprise in context with its local and global ecology.

The other issue that risk managers are discovering is that they must prepare the organization to collect good and relevant data in sufficient quantities for these sophisticated tools to have any credibility. If critical risks are identified, this narrows the scope of data required to understand these risks. However, all are in agreement that ERM risk identification and quantification is a continual process, so over time, required data and the tools to analyse data will evolve. This is one of the distinct advantages of ERM because it continually develops the understanding of critical risks the organization is and will be facing.

Case Studies

There was no attempt to try to find a case study for every industry or in every part of the world. Case studies in the US include a hospital system, a health insurer, and a university system. There is a biomedical trust case from the UK, a public housing office agency in France, and an analysis of ERM implementations in various public sectors in China. Finally, there are observations from a veteran risk manager about negotiating the CRO job and establishing the scope both of the job and the ERM project in an organization. These case studies by no means represent a complete spectrum of the ERM environment today. However, we hope to show in this text the importance of collecting more case study data on more ERM installations simply because there are so many different approaches to the process. In addition it is likely that each organization that engages an ERM installation will have its own issues with change management and the actual environment of managing risks. The fact that no two ERM installations are likely to be the same is a reason why more case studies are required to broaden the available data on the issues that organizations can face in the ERM process.

Frankly, some organizations we approached declined to speak on the record because they have found that their ERM initiative has uncovered areas of improvement that at this point they would not want to make public. Others have been unwilling to explain how their ERM initiative went off the rails. While the cases in this text are limited in industry breadth and depth, and there is not more than one case for any one industry, there are some common threads in these cases that should be explored further.

One of the cornerstone requirements of ERM is strong management support. Case study participants agreed that this is important. However, many participants observed that management support will vary over time. There will be changes in leadership or priorities and like any initiative sometimes support can become stale. ERM is not like a project to develop a new product. Unlike most projects with end-stage goals, ERM does not have an end product – it is a process that never concludes. What risk managers must do is to find ways to keep the initiative on track even when the organization strays or priorities change.

The second observation gleaned from these case studies is that quite often the simpler the better. There is a time and place for sophisticated risk analysis using Monte Carlo and other tools but, by and large, the risk needs to be understood by managers, employees, and stakeholders. The case study participants provide a number of examples of how they have simplified processes, calculations, and explanations in a way that those who are not risk management professionals can understand and adopt specific practices in their departments and throughout the organization. What risk managers are finding is that if they have solid ERM practices in place that managers feel comfortable with, and it benefits them and their departments directly, they will continue to utilize these tools and techniques with little prodding. The goal, as risk managers explain it, is to have these practices become part of the everyday activity of the organization. This said, all of the quantitative and qualitative tools risk managers have traditionally used (and others are beginning to use) are available to the organization engaged in ERM. In fact, many of the successful ongoing operational risk management practices that mitigate workers' compensation, liability claims and the like are often retained in an ERM installation because they are already effective. However, ERM identifies broader areas of risk beyond the operational and with such categories as financial, strategic, and competitive risk. As a result, risk managers have had to learn new processes and procedures and find new tools to accomplish the task of ERM to manage risks to strategy.

A third observation is that there will be setbacks. Risk managers have had to first understand and then manage the risks of their ERM initiative. This means anticipating organizational, economic, and other changes that could derail an ERM initiative or make it more difficult to manage. This is codetermined with the first and second observations and it means that enterprise risk professionals must understand that management commitment will vary over time; keeping it simple helps to maintain the initiative even during periods when management attention is drawn to other areas.

The fourth observation is that the risk management job must be properly defined to meet the expectations of the risk manager and leadership but also should be designed so as to have the authority to do what is required to graft ERM onto the organization's strategy. This means having a seat at the highest leadership table. As ERM is a strategic initiative it should be at the same level as other strategic leaders in the organization.

While some of the risk management professionals who participated in the case studies have JDs and/or report up through the legal department, this may not be appropriate in all organizations. Where there are significant contractual obligations and litigation this may be proper. With other organizations that have heavy property and operational hazards, someone with considerable loss control experience might be a better fit. Suffice to say that the job must be structured to meet the requirements of the organization and the risk management team must draw its expertise from talented individuals both within and outside the organization. Specialty expertise can include legal, financial, credit, engineering, process improvement, actuarial, security, and other professionals where required. It may also make sense, as it has in some of the cases, to restructure the organization so that members from different but important departments such as legal, audit, and finance be aligned so that resources necessary to meet ERM expectations work together and through a single leader.

A fifth observation is data. Having good, available, and distributed data was deemed critical by participating risk managers. For some, building better and more robust data gathering techniques was the first task.

Each case study poses different challenges to the risk manager and to the organization. While operational risk management remains a mainstay in ERM implementations, case study participants quite often found that the operational risks that are important to the traditional risk manager may not be as critical to the organization as other risks. This is a good sign because discovering and managing risks from whatever source critical to the organization and its strategy is a key objective for any properly constituted ERM initiative.

Participating risk managers were also asked to speak about issues associated with research that needs to be done to make ERM a more robust process. Responses from risk managers included the need for additional research in: the analysis of decision making under uncertainty, the differences in risk appetite at different organizational levels, ways of improving empathy towards students in the collegiate setting, challenges facing ERM initiatives in China, and better business intelligence processes.

At the end of each case are "Questions for Students and Practitioners". These are intended for a university audience but can also be used by risk managers in their consultative and coaching role when the case is being used to help the risk management team or others in the organization better understand some of the issues that companies face in an ERM installation. There is sufficient diversity in these cases to provide most risk managers with a case study that can help exemplify an issue that their enterprises are confronting or will be confronted with.

The Articles

There have been many books and articles written about ERM. The articles in this book are intended to respond to issues being raised in the ERM community or as a result of discussions with individuals involved in ERM implementations. No attempt was made to correlate these articles with the issues raised in the cases although there are some issues such as group decision making, strategy, healthcare risks and risk uncertainty that were addressed in specific case studies found in this book.

> Particular attention has been paid to emphasizing that ERM is associated with managing risks to strategy – by Jean-Paul Louisot, Chris Ketcham, and Kevin W. Knight.
> There is also a need to understand how organizations and leaders and others make decisions under uncertainty. Towards this end, Daniel A. Gaus discusses some of the risk issues associated with group decision-making.
> In the US, recent healthcare legislation has altered the risk landscape for most companies, not just hospitals and health insurers. Robert L. Snyder reviews the emerging risks in the healthcare industry.

Jean-Paul Louisot brings to the fore ERM basics with separate discussions on GRC (Governance Risk and Compliance), communication, risk identification, risk quantification, and risk assessment.

Georges-Yves Kervern and Jean-Paul Louisot remind us through the science of Cindynics to be aware of the unknown risks and how to prepare for an uncertain future.

Richard Connelly and Jean-Paul Louisot provide an update on advances in business intelligence.

Sophie Gaultier Gaillard, Jean-Paul Louisot, and Jenny Rayner offer a rubric for assessing and managing risk to reputation, an asset that is not easily measured.

Managing the different levels of disturbance requires different strategies, which Jean-Paul Louisot explains.

Marc Ronez considers the ethical implications of ERM and risk management.

Sophie Gaultier Gaillard provides suggestions on how to structure and conduct questionnaires to gather data for risk identification and analysis.

The References

Many articles in this book have references associated with specific topics. We also provide a manageable list of ERM-related references from the past five years and others that have stood the test of time. This list is by no means exhaustive and we apologize if a favorite article or book of yours has been left off the list. Over time and as ERM matures we hope to expand this list into a more robust resource for practitioners and others.

ISO 31000 and Guide 73: 2009 Definitions

ISO 31000 provides risk professionals with an internationally recognized framework for enterprise risk management. Associated with this framework is a list of key risk management terms that have been carefully defined by the committees working on this project. As ERM evolves, the group working on ISO 31000 will have the opportunity to revise these definitions when the science of risk improves. Following this introduction is a list of some of the key terms that will be helpful to those who read this book. Unless a particular article or case otherwise defines a term in this list differently please consider the ISO 31000 and Guide 73: 2009 definition as your guide. Remember this is not a reproduction of the entire ISO 31000/Guide 73, only select terms that the editors considered to be especially relevant to the topics and cases explored in this text.

ISO 31000 and Guide 73: 2009 Select Terms and Their Definitions[1]

Guide 73 has additional notes for some definitions that are not included here. The definitions listed are select definitions chosen by the editors of this book and do not include all the key terms definitions in Guide 73.

Enterprise Risk Management: Not defined by the Guide 73

Event: Occurrence or change of a particular set of circumstances

Exposure: Extent to which an organization and/or stakeholder is subject to an event

Hazard: Source of potential harm

Resilience: Adaptive capacity of an organization in a complex and changing environment

Risk: Effect of uncertainty on objectives

Risk Appetite: Amount and type of risk that an organization is willing to pursue or retain

Risk Attitude: Organization's approach to assess and eventually pursue, retain, take or turn away from risk

Risk Management: Coordinated activities to direct and control an organization with regard to risk

Risk Management Framework: Set of components that provide the foundations and organizational arrangements for designing, implementing, monitoring, reviewing and continually improving risk management throughout the organization

Risk Management Plan: Scheme within the risk management framework specifying the approach, the management components and resources to be applied to the management of risk

Risk Management Process: Systematic application of management policies, procedures and practices to the activities of communicating, consulting, establishing the context, and identifying, analysing, evaluating, treating, monitoring and reviewing risk

Risk Owner: Person or entity with the accountability and authority to manage a risk

Risk Tolerance: The organization's or stakeholder's readiness to bear the risk after risk treatment in order to achieve its objectives

---

[1] The text taken from ISO Guide 73:2009 Risk management – Vocabulary, is reproduced with the permission of the International Organization for Standardization, ISO. This standard can be obtained from any ISO member and from the website of the ISO Secretariat at the following address: www.iso.org. Copyright remains with ISO.

Part I
ERM Articles

These articles are organized according to the major steps in the risk management process as expressed in the ISO 31000 framework. The steps are:

- Establishing the internal and external contexts
- Risk assessment (including identification, analysis, and evaluation)
- Select appropriate risk management techniques; Implement appropriate risk management techniques
- Monitor results and revise
- Communicate and consult with all internal and external stakeholders

1
Establishing the Internal and External Contexts

Establishing context includes understanding why the organization is engaged in ERM, the need and scope of the ERM program, and how the organization defines ERM. Defining strategy is often the first step for the organization because all risk management is associated with critical risks to strategy.

1.1 MANAGING RISKS TO ENABLE STRATEGY

Jean-Paul Louisot

Université Paris 1 Panthéon-Sorbonne, Directeur pédagogique du CARM_Institute, Paris, France

Christopher Mandel

SVP, Strategic Solutions, Sedgwick, Inc., long term senior risk management practitioner/leader

1.1.1 The Origin of Modern Risk Management

Spectacular events occurred during the final decades of the twentieth century that fed the "fear of the millennium". The first decade of the twenty-first century also fed fears, including alternating natural events or technological catastrophes, increasing terrorism, social upheavals like the "Arab Spring" that began in 2011, the Asian tsunami in 2004, and the typhoon in Japan in 2013. Traditional media, expanded by social media, did not miss an opportunity to blame the ravages of globalization, the brittleness of the world socio-economic system or to question its long-term sustainability. It is clear that the relationships between the different actors in the system are becoming more and more complex while their interdependencies are increasing. This is precisely the state of the system that might be explained by the tenets of chaos theory.

The last millennium came to a close with the resource-intensive campaign to prevent the anticipated damages of Y2K, the bug that was supposed to crash all computer activity on December 31, 1999. Apparently, to the general public at least, nothing serious occurred at midnight and some concluded, a little too quickly, that the threat was only a fabrication of IT consultants to ensure their business development for the previous three years. For risk management professionals Y2K was a vivid illustration of the fundamental paradox of the trade: the catastrophe was avoided thanks to heavy investments, and the success of the risk treatment avoided IT Armageddon! In France, it was ironic, however, that the Y2K crisis teams were activated when two exceptional storms, Martin and Luther, with winds close to 150 miles per hour hit the country right in the middle of the Christmas season in 1999. This is the main reason why the railway system, SNCF, and the electricity utility, EDF, were able to react promptly and save the day, and enhance their reputation.

The third millennium started with the fireworks of the September 11 terrorists attacks and ten days later by the AZF[1] complex explosion in Toulouse; a series of financial catastrophes, initiated as early as August 2001 with the Enron collapse; and natural events such as the tsunami in Southeast Asia at Christmas 2004, and more recently in the spring and summer of 2011 the tsunami in Japan and catastrophic floods in several countries. These events and others revealed dependencies, sometimes to unaware actors who suffered massive contingent business interruptions. The rise of aberrant situations brings about ruptures that leaders in the private as well as the public sectors must learn to address aggressively in order to avoid their degenerating into full-blown crises.

In such a context, it is all too clear that the traditional and static approach to managing risk, mainly organized around the purchase of insurance cover to protect physical assets, has become totally obsolete. We are well overdue in making room for a dynamic and global vision, integrating recently identified "black swan" type risks like the interconnected effects of global supply chain and terrorism. It is essential to encompass the world of threats and opportunities, not only from an inside out view formed at the board level, but enlightened by an outside in view reflecting the expectations and fears of all main stakeholders.

1.1.2   Strategic Risk Management?

The recently developed concept of strategic risk management can add value to the risk management process, provided it is interpreted as including the risk management disciplines of influencing, development and implementation of organization strategy, the ultimate responsibility for which rests with the board and the C-suite. The generic term used here, "organization", refers to all types of enterprises, private, for-profit enterprises as well as NGOs, healthcare providers, local authorities, etc. But nations themselves have to organize their internal (police and judicial system) as well as external (national defense) security in an ever more complex and fluid environment, not to speak of their reputation in the light of the fight against corruption and money laundering. Political leaders should therefore regularly review their approach and engage in an iterative risk assessment and management approach.

However, both academics and practitioners of risk management are aware that managing uncertainties is contained within a comprehensive package of concepts, principles, framework and process, well summarized in the ISO 31000:2009 standard. Risk management implementation in any given field requires a specific understanding of internal and external contexts, all the more complex when the system is open. No organization functions effectively today as an autocratic entity but, nevertheless, hospitals (in national healthcare countries), local authorities and nations have more authority to consider, and possibly a longer time frame to take into account, in their decision making processes in other than crisis situations.

All that said, the emergence of the term strategic risk management as a "new discipline" is probably unnecessary. This new term attempts to emphasize risks to strategy, a more than appropriate emphasis. However, this emphasis is one that should not have been necessary, had risk managers risen to the challenges posed by the original expansion of the discipline, i.e. enterprise risk management (ERM). ERM was always intended to capture the strategic emphasis now highlighted by SRM, but many failed attempts at ERM missed this opportunity.

---

[1] Explosion of an ammonium nitrate stock in a plant belonging to the Grande Paroisse Company (Total Group).

There are many reasons why ERM has failed in many venues, but that aside, we didn't need to add another moniker to enable what has always been assumed as central to ERM strategy. However, we can take this opportunity to leverage the new labeling as a de facto rebranding or risk management/enterprise risk management, often useful to initiatives that have failed to get the traction necessary for long-term acceptance and success.

1.1.3   Ethics, Sustainable Development, and Governance (ESG)

It is only in the last three decades, after the fall of the former USSR destroyed the communist alternative to the "free" economy model, that courses in ethics started to appear in the curriculum of MBA programs in leading universities. Business ethics became part of public speeches of leaders, both political and industrial, and took different forms: "sustainable development" when it comes to environment issues; "governance" or "compliance" in connection with societal issues and transparency.

But are these leaders' intentions followed by actions? Ethics cannot remain a nice concept only, it must become an integral part of the management toolkit; in commercial entities of course, but even more so in public entities where there is growing public demand for integrity and transparency. There is ethics only in ethical *behavior*; this is why a better phrase would be "ethics in action".

Obviously, if issues were black and white, most human beings would have a clear choice that would be obvious. But the set of values underlying an ethical behavior is in constant evolution, it changes through time and space. This notion of an active and progressive ethic implies that the decision makers must be ready at all times to question organizational objectives, and that managers and supervisors in the organization be willing to question themselves continuously in light of the set of fundamental values at issue.

In any decision process, ethics in action opposes the "could" and the "should". It questions the basic definition and meaning at the heart of the approach of many consultants specializing in human factors. These questions are dealt with in the next section.

1.1.4   Where Are We Heading? Why and For Whom? How?

Ethics in action also questions the validity of an old proverb: *NO, the end DOES NOT ALWAYS justify the means!* And it is becoming increasingly clear that the end (financial optimization) is not enough to justify any means (the negation of the universal human condition, the depletion of the planet's resources and contempt for the primitive rules and/or the fundamentals of collective life). Even at a time when most European governments are leaning to the right of the political spectrum (while the US leans to the political left while being troubled by the right e.g., The Tea Party), people are reacting more and more vociferously to the publication of record profits by leading economic entities who, at the same time, outsource jobs to "emerging" economies. Massive layoffs in profitable shops to enable hiring in *even more* profitable shops are viewed as morally unacceptable and the "license to operate" might well be revoked by public outcry or boycott before governments intervene. The challenge against greed and for social justice is especially vocal in European Union countries.

The fall of the Berlin Wall, signaling the end of the centralized economic alternative, has put free market economics at the forefront and since 1989 this free market has flourished in a world that seems more and more borderless. However, many do not understand the economic "reality". Wealth is mostly intangible, some would say even fictitious, and evermore excessive compared to real assets, not to speak of the average income level of the middle classes. This self-perpetuating system has grown beyond the grasp of human minds and has inflated bubbles in the stock exchanges of the world. Even after the series of financial collapses since July 2007 and the first sign of the imminent crisis with the "subprime mortgage meltdown", many economic players have resumed "business as usual" with collateral casualties: the working populations.

All this happened even as, before the start of the nagging economic crisis we are still going through, some states had taken measures to control some negative effects of globalization. The European Union produced its eighth directive on governance and France introduced the precautionary principle into its constitution. Clearly, survival under any circumstances requires a global and integrated approach to the management of the uncertainties. Felix Kloman championed the expression "holistic". Francophone academics prefer another Greek word, "Cindynics", or the "science of danger" based on a body of principles developed by Georges-Yves Kervern on the foundation of the systemic approach proposed by the Nobel laureate Herbert A. Simon.

What has come to light in the last ten years is that risk management is no longer the exclusive domain of a risk management professional at the headquarters of the organization. On the contrary, effective risk management requires all key stakeholders to be appropriately engaged in the process, within and outside the organization. This engagement is always important, but even more crucial for open systems, public space, and territories where all citizens are to be active participants. Therefore, the first challenge to meet is the risk illiteracy of the majority of stakeholders. This is nothing new, for in the eighteenth century, Benjamin Franklin envisioned a future for democracy only if the citizens were educated and learned to read, write and "understand risks". At a recent conference,[2] Professor Gerd Gigerenzer of the Kant Institute in Berlin denounced risk illiteracy as the root of broken communication and consultation with stakeholders who cannot understand the threat and opportunity challenges of our technological world. In reality, the issue at stake is an understanding of the benefits and limitations of statistics to avoid being manipulated by sorcerer apprentices (as Warren Buffet said, "beware of geeks bearing formulas") that arbitrage risks, threats and opportunities and which can lead corporate and other citizens to adopt solutions to their own selfish advantage, rather than the common good.

For example, commenting on the recent result of the election in France, a leader of a nationalist party mentioned the "tenfold result in his party's members of parliament". They went from zero to three, out of 572! From zero any increase is "infinite in percentage". In the world of finance, fat tails and mathematical models have deceived decision makers as to the level of risks at stake with derivatives, and induced the crisis of the second decade of the twenty-first century we continue to struggle with.

Ethics, sustainability and governance must rely on transparency and symmetry of information if all stakeholders will be efficiently involved in and make contributions to the decision-making processes. Therefore, understanding statistical concepts and limitations should be at the heart of any civic education, together with reading, writing and mathematics. For corporate and other citizens to make enlightened choices and decisions we must ask whether people understand how to question the validity of the figures that are put forward to them.

---

[2] Forum de l'IRM – Institute of Risk Management – Liverpool March 2011.

1.1.5   Fundamentals in Risk Management

ERM – Enterprise-wide Risk Management – relies on the fundamental assumption that all actors in the political, economic and social environments understand the risks generated within the perimeter of their responsibility, or the manifestation of a risk to the organization that first appears under their watch. Managing risk is at the heart of management's mission, but it is also a fundamental tool that can significantly influence and enable the achievement of optimal performance. It is therefore essential that each professional be equipped with an efficient and effective set of tools to manage risk. Since every organization has a risk culture, whether by design or default, it is essential that a more intentional effort be put forward to design an effective risk culture and integrate it into the desired corporate culture. In so doing the ideal result will be to enable every manager to be both a "risk owner" and risk manager. This is why the key to "effective risk management" is to integrate risk management competencies into the existing organizational culture, thereby improving the chances that the organization's mission will be accomplished.

Risk Management and Corporate Objectives

Risk management is one of the fundamental methods for managing organizations with the goal of optimizing performance while coping with uncertainties or risks; both threats and opportunities. All organizations are driven to achieve predefined objectives: profits, growth, public service, political goals, re-election, etc. But whatever the long-term goal or mission, there is the inescapable reality: ***Surviving any event or change of situation that may occur may result in losses, the threats . . . but there can also be situations where one can take advantage of those adverse events to open new possibilities and opportunities***.

The specific mission of the risk management professional, as part of the C-suite, is to propose a framework and a process for risk management and ensure that all managers (and risk owners) are equipped to act and optimize the impact of potential internal or external rupture points on the life of the enterprise, i.e. be accountable for curbing threats and enhancing opportunities: ***"Transmute disruptive ruptures into creative ruptures"***.[3]

As a process, risk management supposes to conduct an in depth analysis of the internal and external contexts of the organization to help refine sustainable objectives. A proper inclusion of uncertainties and adhesion to ethical values requires that risk management be integrated at all levels in the development of the strategy, to be in a position to systematically review and assess the scenarios on which it is based.

1.1.6   Risk Management Process

Once the corporate objectives are defined, the following three steps help increase the assurance of reaching an entity's strategic goals and by extension, its mission.

Step 1 – Risk Assessment: beginning with an inventory of all of the organization's exposures, i.e. all that could impact its fundamental objectives, define a risk profile, establish a risk matrix and develop a risk register with the following elements:

   Identification: the resources "at risk" and the uncertain events or change of circumstances that might impact their level (substantially);

---

[3] Bertrand Robert – Argillos.

Analysis: the impact and likelihood in light of the objectives and without any treatments (controls) in place *(gross or original risk);*

Evaluation: the impact and likelihood taking into account the existing treatment mechanisms *(residual risk).*

Step 2 – Risk Treatment: consists of all measures to mitigate risks.

As far as *risk reduction* is concerned, the whole range of mechanisms should be evaluated, spreading far beyond the traditional perimeter of insurance risk transfer, including risk avoidance. The array of possible actions covers all the major functions in the organization: marketing, production, procurement, legal, etc. The goal is to implement all instruments that will allow the reduction of impact and likelihood of threats to an acceptable level (risk tolerance). It is important to be clear that these threats and their treatments are related to the essential mission of management: continuity and optimization of operations.

As far as *risk financing* is concerned, the whole range of mechanisms should be evaluated to reinforce the finance strategy of the organization with an "exceptional financial resource plan", at the headquarters level.

The following process could be followed, for reduction of risk at the operational level, for financing at the C-suite level, and in all cases facilitated by the risk-management professional:

Identify all the instruments efficient to mitigate these exposures;

Outline and get concurrence from the person responsible and accountable for the exposures (the risk owners) the mitigation tactics best suited to achieve objectives *(at the operational level for risk reduction; executive level for risk financing)*;

Implement the agreed upon tactics by the person responsible and accountable for the management of these exposures *(risk owner).*

Step 3 – Monitor and Review: consists of the control of results to obtain assurance of proper implementation of the strategy and tactics as well as its efficiency and relevance. In this step the organization monitors and implicitly addresses the interests of the executives and the board in its desire for risk management program effectiveness.

Internal audit is the "natural" owner of risk management audit, but it works in cooperation with the risk management professional and audits the management of risk at the operational level. There is a growing trend for auditors to go beyond their natural role and absorb all the activities of risk management, including the mission of facilitator and consultant for the decision makers. As the number of seats at the table in the executive committee is limited, joining the universal corporate functions (audit, internal controls, quality, and risk management) may prove necessary but it is then essential that the officer in charge clearly defines the missions of each of the collaborators and their specific competencies.

To be specific, whereas rigor is the key attribute of an internal auditor, as far risk management is concerned, its implementation requires from the risk management professional a good dose of imagination at all stages of its development, especially to uncover the emerging risks.

A risk manager must always push for the mitigation of tomorrow's threats and opportunities, rather than the treatment of yesterday's catastrophic event! This is the price to pay to ensure continuity under all circumstances at the operational level *(risk reduction toolkit)* while ensuring sufficient cash and return at the level of the overall organizational financial strategy *(risk financing toolkit).*

Figure 1.1   The risk management process.

Finally the risk management process is in essence iterative and does not represent a vicious circle but on the contrary a virtuous circle, a permanently improving Deming wheel:[4] every turn aims at improving and refining the approach and updating the risk register by deleting obsolete exposures and introducing emerging ones in view of the evolution of the internal and external context of the organization, including its own mission, goals and objectives. The circle representing the ISO 31000:2009 risk management process (see Figure 1.1 above) illustrates the intimate interaction between strategy and risk management as well as the need to incorporate the expectations and needs of all major stakeholders in the process.

1.1.7   From Risk Management to Good Governance

As evidenced by all that is stated above, buying insurance is clearly now only a portion of a risk management strategy. It is a global and integrated management of risks that all organizations are expected to develop and implement, be it for compliance, or for governance issues. However, what has been learned through several centuries, financing and managing "insurable risks" should not be forgotten or discarded. In many organizations, the risk management learning process is initiated by request from insurance underwriters with the assistance of their expert teams visiting the insured locations. It is important to be candid and transparent with the insurer. Getting the best conditions from an insurer requires equipping it with precise and detailed information, reflecting a rigorous overall management and control system. Currently, this process is a necessary step towards timely and relevant information for all stakeholders in the communication and consultation processes.

The pressure from public opinion relayed in social media and the expectations of consumers and citizens does not leave any room for elected officials or executives to wiggle out of messy situations. A key mission of the public official is to develop a risk management policy that goes

---

[4] From W. Edwards Deming: Plan, Do, Check, Act.

beyond the protection of physical assets and liabilities to ensure the safety, security, and secure procurement for, all stakeholders, private and public, that are impacted by their decisions.

The rising importance of risk management during the first decade of the twenty-first century is translated at the organizational level by the evolution from a technical function embodied by a limited group of risk management professionals, to the extension of all managers' missions to effectively manage the risks they generate or identify. It is made possible only by the development of a body of concepts, methods and tools that have been created jointly by academics and practitioners. This risk management culture, defined by risk management competencies, must extend not only to all in charge, at the economic, political and social level, but also to all those who have a stake in the organization's success.

The widening of the scope and mission of risk management can only be successful if the risk management professional is better recognized inside and outside of the organization. The norm should be that a competent well-compensated risk manager should report to the CEO, board, most senior official or mayor (if a public entity). For this enlarged new risk management scope and mission to be successfully implemented within any organization, the risk management professional will need to be recognized by their leadership. This will require that the risk management professional gains a strategic vision and strong competencies.

The risk management profession has as its challenge the need to increase the level of competency that risk management professionals in organizations will require to manage twenty-first century risks. Whatever the title, CRO[5] or other, risk management professionals must earn the trust and confidence of leadership, the recognition of their peers, the support of the population at large and the organization's partners/stakeholders through the creation and management of sustainable risk-management policies. It will require patience and perseverance through advances and setbacks. But it will require from their leaders a continuous political will to keep the long-term course of the organization in focus.

Once all in charge have made the necessary efforts to enable a sound risk management policy, the ultimate result will be a more universal process that protects the security and safety of all consumers/voters whether for the next election, for social license, or the products they purchase. People will recognize that it is sound risk management, far beyond any compliance, that ensures *"Good Governance"* for the benefit of all.

This is not a new idea. In a position paper published in the daily *Le Monde* in Paris on May 27, 1981,[6] two weeks after the election in France of a socialist president, Jacques Ellul, sociologist, anarchist and theologian, took a position against the generally politically correct stance of the time when he wrote: *"Nothing essential in the fundamental trends of our society are going to be modified"* to further stress that to support the economic growth would be: *"complete foolishness"* as *"the quality of life is in utter contradiction with the growth of industrial production and the industrialization of agriculture"*.

A sound risk-management strategy, rigorously implemented at all levels of the organization is the perfect tool to enable effective communication and consultation with all stakeholders. It is the tool to demonstrate a real commitment to sustainability and the expectations and need of the populations in a proactive and structured approach to work better and more efficiently for the common good.

Hence, the assurance of resilience and the optimization of opportunity, the ultimate goals of risk management, are the keys to success in the economic, social and political arenas as it is accomplished by executing the tenets below.

---

[5] CRO – Chief Risk Officer.
[6] The Brundtland report on the environment of the United Nations was published in 1987.

It is essential to get ahead of, and gain some understanding of, emerging risks: While great debate continues about which "unknown" risks require an organization's attention, and even what a "black swan" event really represents, it is clear that senior leaders and boards (especially in the latter's oversight role) increasingly expect risk stakeholders to gather intelligence on far-off threats that could be company-ending events. This longer term, low probability view is not unlike how planners have long looked at the competitive landscape.

Assessing and aggregating all risk is essential: Individual exposure assessment is not enough anymore as it does not take into account correlations and more generally interactions within the set of exposures of a given organization, this is why it is necessary to implement a "portfolio approach" to the aggregation of risks.

Taking into account extreme, low probability events is required to inform a comprehensive strategy: A risk universe does not always follow the normal probability distribution and it is essential to take into account unexpectedly large deviation from the expected, i.e. fat tails or black swans that could produce catastrophic impacts.

Whereas quantifying tools are important, qualitative tools and sound judgment should not be neglected: Even if the kit of quantifying tools is quite comprehensive, it is imperative to keep in mind the limitations of mathematical models. They reflect past wisdom or experience more than they predict future behaviors as they rely on past data and implicit, as well as explicit, hypotheses that condition and limit their validity.

Risk appetite must be defined and understood: ERM is essentially strategic in nature; it must be able to balance costs and benefits with the acceptable level of risk necessary to achieve the organizational goals and objectives. It is the board's responsibility to define the risk appetite and risk tolerance level at which the organization can safely and efficiently operate but it must also provide key risk indicators that operational managers can monitor to remain within risk thresholds and be accountable for their results.

Risk culture must be rooted in the organization: While the board and executives must have the "reasonable assurance" that all risks the organization is exposed to are diagnosed and mitigated according to their guidance, it is totally unreasonable to think that senior executives will monitor all exposures included in the risk register. Therefore executives and the board must rely on upper, middle and lower management to manage operational and tactical risks so that only exposures with potential impacts on the strategy are brought to their attention.

In the United Kingdom, local authorities have been asked to develop a Long Term Sustainability Strategic Planning or SPP that aims at integrating in a holistic thinking process, or brainstorming, the economic, environmental and social issues in seven risk categories: environment and natural resources; finance and marketing; social license to operate; political, legal and regulations; services and production; and reputation. In the US the utility service of San Francisco (http://www.sfwater.org/) has established a team dedicated to ensure that all initiatives are coordinated and offers two recommendations to any entity that would follow the same route:

Identify all stakeholders and their expectations and needs to take them into account during all decision-making processes to ensure real sustainability;

Map on a matrix all exposures that could materially threaten the missions, goals and objectives at the heart of the organization in order to improve strategic action.

Global organizations are strongly linked to an open web of relationships with a number of stakeholders, some of whom they do not even recognize as such, and both corporate and societal resilience requires that all provide each other with the *"reasonable assurance"* that all threats are curbed and opportunities enhanced so that the world as a whole is a more secure place for the current as well as future generations. In the *"Orange Book"*,[7] the reference on risk management for British local authorities, it is stated that obtaining the "reasonable assurance" of sound risk management is an integral part of any public–private partnership. As such, this alignment between business and society is best exemplified through sustainability strategies that are by definition, joint efforts at resilience from threats and optimization of opportunities. This dual focus is the essence of what enterprise risk management (ERM) calls upon practitioners to adopt. And while we must always ensure that the downside is addressed as the management priority, the search for opportunities to exploit risk for gain enables risk managers to improve the chances of becoming more influential, respected and significant in the scheme of organizations and the strategies they employ to deliver their missions. The evidence for this possibility will be easy to spot as risk leaders get elevated in the hierarchy and are asked to contribute their opinions and expertise to not just the tactical but the strategic initiatives that most drive long-term success.

Julia Graham,[8] 2013–2014 President of FERMA[9] offers what we may view as an interim conclusion, (echoing the "Orange Book") that risk managers are the scouts of the future and that

> "In addition to all the current issues specific to risk management, the risk management community must stay on the alert to all the changes the world is going through at all times, and on the watch to anticipate and remain open minded to bring appropriate answers that the situations may dictate."

1.2 STRATEGY, CONSTRAINT, RISK MANAGEMENT AND THE VALUE CHAIN

Christopher Ketcham

Ph.D., CPCU, CRM, CIC, CFP®, Formerly Visiting Assistant Professor, University of Houston Downtown, Houston, Texas; Garnet Valley, Pennsylvania

Kevin W. Knight, AM

Chairman ISO Technical Committee 262 – Risk Management

1.2.1   Strategy and Constraint

Michael Porter contributed to the development of ERM by defining strategy. He said that, "A strategy is an internally consistent configuration of activities that distinguishes a firm from its rivals" (Porter, 1985, 1998, pp. 335, Kindle edition). Because strategy is that which produces a unique mix of values that customers will pay for, strategy is different for each firm. In addition, strategy is constraint, the reduction of degrees of freedom – we will do certain things, not others. In the end, strategy is what drives the organization and it is the risks to that strategy that ERM manages. Strategy narrows the scope of the business but at the same time creates vulnerabilities which are the risks to that unique set of values that customers will pay for.

---

[7] "Orange Book – Management of Risk – Principles & Concepts" – www.hm-treasury.gov.uk/d/orange_book.pdf.
[8] During her speech during AIRMIC 2012 Annual Conference in Liverpool June 1st.
[9] FERMA is the Federation of European Risk Management Associations and now includes 27 National Associations of risk managers, beyond the borders of the European Union (including Russia and Turkey).

Traditional risk management only looked at operational risks associated with the unique set of values customers pay for, ERM considers all critical risks.

Constraint eliminates or mitigates certain risks because the organization has committed to not doing the things that are not part of the strategy. At the same time constraints must be maintained because they are vulnerable to risks that can damage or eliminate the constraint. Therefore strategic risk management is all about maintaining the constraints that are part of the strategy.

The first prequel in risk management is to identify and define the right strategy for the organization. The second prequel in risk management is to identify the constraints associated with that strategy. When the constraints are identified the risk management process of identifying, analyzing, treating, and monitoring risks to strategic constraints can begin. It does not matter whether the organization subscribes to ISO 31000 or COSO or some other enterprise risk management framework; the need to develop a cohesive, workable, carefully defined value-oriented strategy and associated constraints is always the first task before any form of risk management can be implemented.

1.2.2   The Value Chain

If strategy is all about producing value then this is the first step in the process of strategic identification: identify value. In 1985 Michael Porter introduced the concept of the value chain. The value chain begins by identifying the activities or services of the organization that provide value to its customers. But it goes beyond customers: all stakeholders do business with the organization because it provides value to each of them in some form or another. To define value then is to define the value that customers, vendors, employees and others receive from doing business or working with the organization.

While customer value is paramount, the value-adds to stakeholders are part of that equation. If the organization can identify the competencies and activities that provide value to all stakeholders it can derive a clearer picture from what assets the value is derived in the organization. Says Porter, "Competitive advantage grows fundamentally out of value a firm is able to create for its buyers that exceeds the cost of creating it" (Porter, 1985, 1998, pp. 507–510, Kindle Edition). The assets that produce activities or services that provide value represent the assets that need to be risk managed.

The first of these activities or services are those that the organization provides today that provide such value. It isn't the activities or services that must be risk managed it is the assets behind them: the people, equipment, intellectual capital and other assets which are the subject of risk management.

Second, the value chain organization recognizes the evolution of value. In addition to maintaining the value proposition that exists today, the value chain organization is continually assessing what customers and stakeholders want and need. The first of these are those newly discovered activities or services that stakeholders have a demonstrated need for and are within the existing capabilities of the organization to perform. Second are activities or services that stakeholders have a demonstrated need for, which are outside of the current capabilities of the organization but for which it is conceivable that the organization may want to consider developing.

While the existing strategy must be carefully risk managed, any change in strategy must be carefully risk assessed before the value proposition can be valued. As a result, it is imperative that the risk management function be part of any discussions on strategy that will affect capabilities or assets that are valuable to customers. Engaging a risk assessment after the strategic change is announced poses two major problems. First, risk may be a very real cost that has not been assessed. The value proposition that is successful provides customer value but also an appropriate level of profit or cost offset for a not-for-profit entity. If risk or the cost to manage that risk adds more cost than is expected then the strategy may not be sustainable. Having risk management at the strategy analysis table will help mitigate such unsustainable strategic decisions. Second, strategic constraints are vulnerable the moment they are introduced. If the organization understands the risks associated with the strategic constraints before they are implemented then efforts to manage them can be incorporated into projects that will be required to facilitate the change in strategy.

Nor is the development of any strategy without risk itself. The first risk comes from identifying values that customers do not value and the converse, not identifying the values that customers do value. The second risk is underestimating the cost to produce those values. A third identifies the wrong customers for which the organization is equipped or could become equipped to provide value. There is, of course, the problem of not understanding the competition and their own ability to provide the same value proposition even at a lower cost.

Assume for a moment that the organization has analyzed and identified the key activities and services it provides that lead to value creation for its customers. This may, in fact, be a very small list. What the risk manager understands is that these outcomes are often part of a long list of activities, processes and supply chains, which if disrupted will corrupt the value proposition for the customer. However, if the organization has done its job to identify these value-creating activities and services then it is much more likely to be able to identify the critical risks associated with their generative process (value producing assets) than an organization that does not fully understand its value chain. This is not to say that it will be any easier to predict the fat tail events[10] or correlated risks that combine to produce worldwide changes in the marketplace. Risk management becomes the process of identifying risks associated with the assets that produce value to customers. In some respects the risk management task should become more efficient because instead of spending time analyzing all possible risks, the risk management function concentrates its efforts on the critical risks associated with value-creating activities and services.

The value chain focuses upon its stakeholders, and particularly its customers, to help drive the strategic direction of the organization. The strategy or constraint is not product- or service-focused but value-focused – the value to stakeholders. The value chain organization recognizes that risk is not being in tune with or being able to deliver the activities or services that customers and other stakeholders require today. The value chain organization builds a long-term strategy on identifying, building, and preserving those services and activities that customers and other stakeholders require. Value creation becomes the organization's long-term vision and strategy.

The strategy of value production is not decimated if the organization must retool, for example, from being a low-price to a high-quality service organization for this is an operational problem. If the change in strategy has been properly assessed, then the need for change is warranted and operations must conform. Certainly the retooling is expensive and introduces a whole new set of risks and challenges but the value of such a change is factored into the reorganization. The risk to strategy comes when the activities and services of the organization

---

[10] Think of a normal distribution – a bell curve. In a fat tail distribution the tails on either side of the bell never touch the x axis. This means that even at greater and greater standard deviations the risks of loss never quite disappear. In scenarios like floods, the thousand year flood probability of occurrence may actually be about the same as the hundred year flood probability.

do not align with the values of the customer and other stakeholders. The value chain organization can utilize short- and/or long-term goals and objectives as long as they align directly with customer values.

In many ways the value chain is a strategy of care, which means entering the world of the stakeholder and customer to find out what they need and what their values are. This is by no means an easy task. Customers can mislead on surveys and other methodologies used to identify values. Fads may disguise permanent long-term trends. The organization may not ask the right questions or have enough data to be able to make a good decision. Some decisions will be made in the presence of considerable uncertainty and as a result considerable anxiety, both internally and in the market and marketplace. Even if the narrowly defined critical services and activities that the organization provides can be identified, the risk associated with these may involve the entire supply chain. For example, if two-day delivery is what customers value most from the organization then maintaining that capability will require significant analysis of alternate supply routes, multiple delivery vendors, and even inventory build-up in anticipation of deleterious events or disasters.

The advantage to becoming a value chain organization is that it provides a cohesive strategic focus on customer and stakeholder values. It does not produce a product or service focus but a focus on developing a deep awareness of customer values and organizational competencies and process towards that end. The value chain organization is committed to maintaining its value proposition with its customers and stakeholders even as these values change over time. Strategy becomes care – caring about customer values and reciprocating with providing those values in a careful manner.

1.2.3 Risk Management and Strategy

Too many people still envision risk management as "something we do to cover our mistakes" or an attempt to offer a "risk-free work environment". However such a goal could be achieved only if the site was surrounded by a moat and did not need any human to work within the premises. Clearly, this goal is not reasonable and the best we can do is to "manage the risks" using a robust risk-management process.

However, the process must be completely embedded in the management process of the organization at all levels: strategic, tactical and operational, so that all decisions are made with the right level of risk awareness. This is required if the organization is to reach the objectives it sets itself to achieve. This is why risk management must be involved in the setting of achievable objectives through the strategic planning process, as well as in the implementation of the strategy to optimize the performance of the organization whatever the circumstances may be.

The importance of setting attainable and sustainable goals should not be underestimated. For instance a prison administration in Australia had set the following objective to prison managers: "Total eradication of all illegal substances within the prison". This proved to be unachievable as inmates' imagination is without limits and even fresh fruits can be brewed into alcoholic beverages with sufficient ingenuity.

Enhancing opportunities while curbing threats is at the core of any risk management exercise. Thus, identifying the uncertainties of the internal and external context of an organization may even make it, as events unfold, able to achieve a better goal than originally anticipated.

To be efficient, however, the management of risk must not be seen as a separate activity, but on the contrary woven intimately within the structure of the organization. The management of risk is not the realm of the specialists but an integral part of all management processes and frameworks.

Every risk must have an owner: orphan risks are not acceptable. Within that approach, the "RM practitioner" is there to service, coach, and educate the risk owners who must have the authority to make decisions, the resources needed to manage the risks within the limits of their "jurisdiction", and the capacity to assign the responsibility to carry out the decision to members of his/her staff that have the competences and talents so to do.

In spite of the existence of an accepted glossary, ISO GUIDE 73,[11] the ISO community does not speak one common language about risks in the standards and there remains work to do as the journey continues. However, something must be right about this standard, as a number of countries have adopted ISO 31000 as national standards, including the majority of the G8 and G20 countries as well as the BRIC nations.

All those entering the "risk management process" should be aware that the road to maturity can prove longer than anticipated and reasonable expectations should be set at the outset, and then met or even exceeded, as this is how RM value creation will be evidenced.

1.2.4   Towards Creating Strategy

There are a number of considerations required to begin developing a value-oriented strategy. Some might call these steps but they need to be considered concurrently. They include: defining the customer; defining the customer need for the organization's product or service; defining the customer value in the services the organization provides; and the determination of the company's existing competencies. The reason they need to be considered concurrently is that the deliberation towards defining each of these considerations may produce a different conception of the customer, value, or competency that the organization actually possesses. This process is part of the enterprise risk management step of identifying the internal and external context of the organization.

There are any number of ways to conduct this analysis. A SWOT analysis – strengths, weaknesses, opportunities and threats can be conducted within the organization. A team can be assembled to define the competencies that the organization possesses, not just in terms of products but in terms of capabilities. The capability of designing and producing precision toys likely indicates a competency towards precision machining which could broaden the product horizon for the company, even into military or other work. An inverse SWOT analysis can also be used to look at new opportunities. An inverse SWOT could look at weaknesses and threats to competition and customers in order to consider strengths and opportunities for the organization.

The analysis of capabilities may also produce the need for additional competencies that the organization does not possess. The issue associated with the development or the obtaining of additional competencies has major implications for the design of the strategy. The danger is conglomerate thinking – that more is better. Conglomerates have a spotty record of success simply because they often try to do too many things.

Another problem with competency identification is that management may try to stretch competencies too far and assign them to products or services that may not produce any value

---

[11] ISO 31000 Guide 73 is available for purchase at http://webstore.ansi.org/RecordDetail.aspx?sku=ISO+31000+%2F+ISO+Guide+73+%2F+ISO%2FIEC+31010+Risk+Management+Package#.UT3PeVfl_ko. For a brief summary of ISO 31000 and Guide 73 consult http://www.iso.org/iso/home/standards/iso31000.htm.

to the customer or differentiation in the marketplace. However, a missing competency can derail any strategy from being effective. If a sound strategy can be developed that will provide economic value to the organization and significant value to customers, then the strategy should be developed with existing competencies. If the organization determines that there are additional competencies that could expand the value to customer or increase the customer base these should be considered as part of the ongoing strategic evolutionary process, but what provides value today should be developed into an appropriate strategic plan. If no strategy will provide value without the development of additional competencies then the appropriate additional competencies will need to be developed or acquired. What the risk manager needs right now is a confirmed strategy and value chain that can be risk managed. As things change the risk manager can modify the enterprise risk management program to accommodate additional competencies.

Business intelligence associated with existing customers and potential customers can help identify who the existing customers are and even point the organization in the direction of identifying customer preferences. These customer preferences can be analyzed to determine what it is that customers value. Identifying the customer for the product or service is directly associated with value. For example, the customer base may be demographically very diverse. Serving a particular culture, age group, or geography may not be as important to the customer as two-day delivery. If two-day delivery is the value that the organization's customers need and want then the customer needs to be defined as someone who values two-day delivery. Two-day delivery also becomes the competency and the constraint that must be risk managed. The value chain of the organization becomes that which can guarantee two-day delivery.

It is likely that the analysis of each of these considerations will produce many additional questions and need for data. Some of this data may be readily available or can be obtained through surveys or similar customer analysis. Other data may not be readily available so there is an inherent risk in the strategic development process that the organization does not have all the information it requires to make a sound decision on strategic direction.

In recent years organizations have developed mission, vision, and value statements. Rather than being helpful starting points these can be seen as sacred cows that will impede the development of true value chain strategic plans. They can be vague and aspirational and so sweeping that any strategy that is developed will fit. For example, "We are the premier..." What does premier mean? "We are the premier...as stipulated by being number one in our industry." What does number one mean? "We are the premier...as stipulated by being number one in our industry, providing our customers with the highest value for their dollar." What value?

1.2.5   A Simple Strategy

Say the organization has determined that the person who purchases their product, for which there is any number of competitors, requires two-day delivery. Two-day delivery is the differentiator for their company compared to competitors. In this instance the organization does not have to produce a better product than the competitor, just deliver it to the customer sooner. This organization determines its strategy as "meeting the delivery expectations of customers" and has outlined its current strategic goals in two parts:

1. Deliver the product in two days or less to customers.
2. Meet quality expectations of customers who require two-day delivery.

Note that these strategic goal statements do not explain how the company will achieve the strategies. The company could use a balanced scorecard or similar approach to develop goals and objectives that will enable the strategies to be achieved. Nor do these strategic statements explain the value chain behind the values that the strategic statements espouse. The strategic statement only explains that the customer for this organization demands two-day delivery for a product that currently meets customer expectations. The strategy has competitive power because competitors have not been able to match two-day delivery within the same cost structure.

The risk management and business operational task once the strategy has been defined is to determine the value chain for each of the two elements. The value chain for two-day delivery will be different from the value chain that produces the product that meets customer expectations, though there likely will be some overlap. Once the value chain has been identified, the risk manager's job is to ensure that appropriate measures have been taken to mitigate the risk to the assets in the value chain from becoming corrupt or unable to fulfil the strategy. All of the risk management tools that are available today can be deployed in this endeavor.

The business side of the organization will likely develop metrics and objectives using a balanced scorecard or similar approach. Some of these may be associated with risk management; for example, the reduction of product liability claims associated with the product. The development of backup or duplicate shipping venues will also need to be explored in order to mitigate the risks from events such as strikes and weather-related risks.

Of course this simple strategy is subject to risks. Competitors may find ways of delivering in less than two days, or a change in customer demand for higher quality, or a product with additional features could derail the current strategy. The value chain organization continually identifies the value that its products generate for customers. If the values change, then the organization will need to determine how it will continue to differentiate itself from its competitors in its customers' minds, and in their purchasing activity.

1.2.6 Summary

Strategy must distinguish the organization from its rivals. This distinguishing feature becomes customer value. If the organization can deliver this value to the customers while offsetting the cost of producing the value while earning a reasonable profit (or covering costs for a not-for-profit) then this is a reasonable strategy. It may not be the "best" strategy in all cases but it serves as a starting point. The value that customers and stakeholders want is derived from services and activities of the enterprise including all of its stakeholders. The assets that drive value in the value chain are those that need to be risk managed. Critical risks to the assets in the value chain must be managed or the value could become impaired.

For risk management to be successful it must be embedded into strategy itself. However, the strategy and resulting goals must be attainable and sustainable. In the resulting structure every risk must have an owner; there must be no orphan risks.

Even before risk can be identified, strategy needs to be properly defined in terms of value. There are risks that the strategy will not be or has not been properly defined. If the strategy related to value is properly defined, then the risks to strategy associated with the value chain assets can be managed using any of the tools that risk managers have at their disposal. As the organization, competitors, and customers evolve, strategy will change. The risk manager needs to be at the table during strategic discussions in order to assess the risks associated with strategic change and to make appropriate changes in risk management activities that these changes require.

Reference

Porter, M. E. (1985, 1998). *Competitive Advantage* (Kindle edn.). New York: The Free Press.

1.3   THE RISK OF GROUP DECISION MAKING WITHIN ORGANIZATIONS: A SYNTHESIS

Daniel A. Gaus, MBA, MSc, ERM, AU, AIS

Berkshire Hathaway International Insurance Ltd., Zurich, Switzerland

1.3.1   Outline

Why do decision makers find it so inconvenient to come together in order to devise and decide on material action? Part of the answer is that there are many pressing individualized problems that must be dealt with on a day-to-day basis, which divert executive attention from the overall corporate context. The other part of the answer is that all important decisions are affected by uncertainty, an attribute that causes individuals anxiety and discomfort. The successful application of an integrated risk management initiative becomes less associated with the proper use of models and frameworks; it is seen in the governing perspectives and behaviors of decision makers and risk owners.

Group decision making is about negotiating and finding consensus, which are inherently challenging. Every individual has different views, personal (limited) experience and motivations which may influence collective decisions. To reduce anxiety, individuals actively search for certainty just by denying or ignoring uncertainty. The considerable literature on individual versus group decision making explains that there are different patterns of individual versus group behavior. Decision making is generally about taking risk, but risk perception remains a highly subjective and personal issue. One major misconception about risk is the common belief that well-established groups are more effective at identifying and handling risk than a single person. From history, there are myriad examples where such collective consensus did either not work or led to improper if not disastrous and fatal outcomes such as the space shuttle Challenger disaster in 1986 or the massive US subprime write-downs that investment banks and pension funds suffered in 2007 worldwide. Decision making in groups is not bad, but represents a challenging, often latent, strategic risk for any organization. This article will highlight the main aspects of this endogenous organizational risk of group decision making and discusses potential approaches to mitigate it.

1.3.2   Fundamentals – Setting the Frame

Risk is an inherent factor of virtually every human undertaking. Risk and opportunity are intrinsically intertwined and it is thus sensible to appreciate that one element cannot exist without the other (Bewley, 1989). As a whole, it is perhaps pretty accurate to consider risk as neither good nor bad; it is simply present. Of course such a bipolar situation leads to the fact that a "bad" risk for one person can be a "good" risk for another. Ultimately the question is how to address this continuum in order to avoid intolerable outcomes or losses respectively, a key feature of the traditional risk management domain.

When reading through the literature or professional journals one will find dozens of ways of defining risk and what it means to individuals, organizations or entire societies. The term "risk" can be further organized into multiple categories, depending on the person's vantage point. These different ways of looking at risk may be valid but it must be appreciated that there is no correct single or predominant philosophy of risk.

In the context of strategy formation multinational organizations tend to accept that there are various descriptive, prescriptive or combined approaches to remain successful (Mintzberg et al., 1998). However, it may take another few years for enterprise risk management (ERM) to become an important contributor to strategic management topics too. Nonetheless it is the human cognition process in particular, as well as the theory of risk perception evolved in areas of psychology, that may assist in the understanding of personal, organizational or societal risk attitude, risk appetite and respective decisions. Identifying a risk is one discipline, the "accurate" processing of it is another discipline, whereas both elements contain a significant level of individual or collective subjectivity. While modern financial theory started to import findings from the fields of psychology and sociology, summarized under the notion of behavioral finance, the perception of the risk-related decision-making process and any interrelated cognitive dissonance has not been fully utilized yet.

Each and every individual defines and perceives risk differently, although it all emanates from the individual's level of accepted uncertainty and anxiety. As the future cannot be foreseen, (human) life is exposed to uncertainty that in turn creates also feelings of anxiety. Conditions of uncertainty apply primarily where the outcome of an event is either unknown or cannot be accurately forecasted. "Anxiety has no object, and uncertainty has no probability attached to it. It is a situation in which anything can happen and one has no idea what" (Hofstede, 2001, p. 148). This circumstance gets even greater significance when focusing on cross-cultural differences in values or underlying risk perceptions. Based on extensive worldwide research Geert Hofstede proposed five categories that assist in appreciating such differences. Under the category of uncertainty avoidance he concludes that there are always approaches to express uncertainty as risk, but as soon as some degree of likely outcome is evaluated it is no longer regarded as simple feeling; it becomes an accepted routine. This distinction may seem meticulous but with floating boundaries. Nonetheless it becomes highly relevant in decision making at group level, notably in groups with rather low tolerance levels for uncertainty and ambiguity or vice versa.

1.3.3 Observed Limitations of Human Thinking

Introduction

The main challenge in decision making comes from the discovery that it is exposed to a number of systematic behavioral biases. In 1982 Howard Raiffa offered a useful distinction between three different approaches to analyzing behavior, i.e. normative, descriptive and prescriptive. When it comes to risk management or ERM, a considerable number of books have been written in the context of normative theories and the aspect of how people ought to behave. Such theories are based on rational choices, where "rational" means that individuals evaluate all possible alternatives using Bayesian reasoning.[12] The Western Hemisphere is full of laws, regulations, principles, frameworks and guidelines how organizations should manage risk and there are armies of consultants ready to assist in implementing such procedures. At the same time literature and journals provide numbers of diagnoses about poor decision making in

---

[12] Bayes' law prescribes consistent rules according to which people should incorporate new information in order to update their existing beliefs.

organizations in the aftermath of remarkable events or fatal incidents. Regardless of the effect, there was always an underlying significant risk component present that decision makers had either not identified, assessed, controlled or monitored. One prominent example is the space shuttle Challenger disaster on 28 January 1986, which killed seven astronauts and destroyed the USD 1.2bn vehicle. The accident was caused by the failure of a USD 900 synthetic rubber O-seal at a joint on one of the solid fuel rocket boosters. The delicate issue in this case was that the performance of the O-ring was known to be affected in low temperatures as was the case on that particular morning of launch. NASA decision makers were aware of these shortcomings but data remained hidden amongst a mass of other launch-monitoring data (McConnell, 1987). A specific risk is usually categorized with a likelihood and impact, but both of these variables can vary as a result of internal and external change. Inappropriate monitoring or reassessing the circumstances created a hidden, and in this case fatal, trap. Another example from the recent past is the massive subprime write-downs that caused banks, pension funds and finally the entire world economy, to suffer. The aftermath of this great financial crisis that unfolded in 2008 is still noticeable in some organizations and countries. Amongst many other financial institutes, the investment division of Union Bank of Switzerland (UBS) whose chairman aimed to form the world's number one investment bank, noticed a widening competitive gap between itself and its peers. A growth strategy and an internal reorganization should have immediately closed the gap between itself and other major investment banks such as Lehman Brothers, Morgan Stanley or Citigroup. Decision makers of UBS longed for success, at all costs. The pressure to report quick wins and growing revenues, which actually became the case during the first few quarters after the growth strategy decision had been made, created misleading positive signals and complacency. Risk management and credit accumulation control activities were completely overloaded as the new growth areas proved to be more complex than expected and required considerable effort across a range of logistics and control functions (UBS, 2008, p. 17). In other words it is fair to state that senior management and risk management had failed to control their investment bank division getting increasingly engaged in the overheated US real estate capital market. Besides the lack of oversight, the bank believed that their subprime positions were sufficiently hedged and the exposure was controllable. The outcome of the decision hit the bank severely, notably a financial loss over USD 40bn, heavy fluctuation within senior management and job cuts that affected more than 6,000 people worldwide. The share lost 70% of its value within a year (Baumgartner et al., 2008).

There have been and will be a myriad of situations where people notice (or have to admit) that a situation appears as "too complex". Insofar as this remains a true and valid statement, as can be seen from the principles of bounded rationality and behavioral decision making introduced later in this section, nevertheless, only limited qualitative and sufficiently longitudinal evaluation on how people really do decide within an organization is available yet. More descriptive insights would help to identify, understand or even close some gaps between theory and practice. Subsequent prescriptive theories would eventually offer advice on how organizations could move closer to the normative ideal, provided that the normative ideal is really the best option for a particular company. The current understanding of risk perception, particularly in groups, and respective decision making remains rudimentary. Economics provides theories that cover each of these areas, but until the last decade economists have rarely taken note of the theories and research of other social sciences and vice versa (Skipper et al., 2007). Recognizing the importance of the human cognitive process in decision making will provide a better understanding and acknowledgement of the limitations people subconsciously are confronted with. Research within the discipline of behavioral finance as a subset of modern financial theory gradually uncovered that decision making flaws among professionals are barely different from those of laypeople (e.g., Coval et al., 2001). In consequence, being a sophisticated well-educated and always informed expert, doctor, risk professional or senior manager does not guarantee immunity to biases (Gigerenzer, 2013).

1.3.4   Organizing and Processing Information – The Human Cognitive Process

Risk Perception

What can be learned from the prospect theory established by Daniel Kahneman and Amos Tversky during the late 1970s is that people make or are sometimes forced to make decisions in relation to perceived risks and rewards. Perception of risk varies from person to person and is also influenced by various social, political, cultural or psychological factors. It may seem comprehensible that an individual's risk perception might easily change during different stages of life and changes in risk behavior can even be observed during the course of a day (Thaler, 1981). Research in the field of psychology suggests that individuals are usually characterized as loss averse and when in doubt would play it safe.[13] In terms of the human cognitive process it is important to note that so-called "objective risks" do actually not exist but are perceptions derived from human-made appraisals (Skipper et al., 2007). This habit has developed significantly and became a powerful ability for efficient but subjective decision making. It is natural, if not pivotal, when considering how human beings are exposed to thousands of stimuli every day.

To appreciate human behavior in decision making it seems simultaneously important to appreciate the main concept of the human cognitive process. As soon as the human brain is presented with a stimulus, a certain amount of information (visual, aural or other) enters the brain and will attribute it with a schema. A schema can be defined as a cognitive structure that represents abstract knowledge about a concept such as an object, a person or an event (Fiske et al., 1991). Analogously a schema can be compared to a template to be filled with information in order to be matched to a specific situation. If the schema fits it will be used in further processing. To achieve this allocation a schema has to be applicable and available, i.e. an outside stimulus has to be recognized and recalled. Bearing in mind that individuals are faced with tons of stimuli every day, a second highly subjective step called "attention" assists to filter unnecessary information from decision-relevant information. Recognized information is then stored in the short-term memory, whereas some of this short-term memory will find its way to the brain's long-term memory. Although a memory is deficient due to limited storing capacity, each time a schema is actively remembered will strengthen the memory and increase the likelihood to recall it when required (Fischoff, 1975).

To come up with a timely decision, people automatically make use of cognitive shortcuts called heuristics, which are discussed below. The decision does not have to represent the best solution, but a satisfactory one considering the circumstances (McKenna, 2006). Therefore an individual can become overconfident in his/her abilities of sense making over time and tend to go for repetitive decisions even in the absence of sufficient or accurate information (Simon, 1979). In the context of risk perception this means that the probability of a rare event will usually be overestimated, because of the confirmatory bias of memory (Kahneman, 2011). Thinking about that event activates schemata and consequently a rare event will be

---

[13] Refer to prospect theory by Daniel Kahneman and Amos Tversky (1979).

overweighted as it attracts attention. Mass media use this approach in order to generate content and audience. Particular well-presented media-hyped dread risks like pandemics, airplane crashes or hurricanes lead people naturally to a biased risk perception (Gigerenzer, 2013). Hazardous risks to a human life like smoking, or writing text messages while driving a car, are perceived as known, controllable and underweighted.

Cause and Effect Thinking by Means of Schemata

Thinking is based on the implicit assumption of causality and this is one of the most fundamental structural features of human mind. It imposes on reality in order to make sense of it. Researchers in behavioral psychology like Daniel Kahneman and Amos Tversky propose that individuals make sense of the world by organizing and interpreting events in terms of cause and effect reasoning (Tversky et al., 1982). The causal schema feels natural and "logically" flows forward into consequences. However, causal thinking is caught in polarity which means that it can hardly process more complex, systemic relationships and is exposed to fallacies. For instance, there is not always objective evidence that cause and effect really do correlate let alone the fact that all causes can get captured and evaluated by one single person (see Kelly, 1994 or Caputi et al., 2006). Due to its simplicity and albeit highly superficial nature, people make or are made to believe causal statements all the time, which in turn can lead to common misconceptions and bias. Statements such as "bankers earn a lot of money" or "foreigners steal our jobs" or "smoking causes lung cancer" can probably be confirmed under some circumstances; they are not at all valid in every case. A high level of uncertainty, irrespective of whether it is imposed on an individual, a group or an organization triggers a search for a causal agent and by finding the causal agent, control over any situation is re-established (Weiner, 1985). Schemata eventually form a strong and illusory sense of logic. People are inclined with greater confidence to infer a consequence from a cause, than they would diagnose a cause for a consequence, even when the consequence and cause provide the same amount of information about each other (Tversky et al., 1980). Or in other words: completely independent cause and effects can be linked together by individuals, as long as it satisfies an easy explanation and "logical" coherence.

Heuristics[14] (Cognitive Shortcuts)

Heuristics in human judgments are a good example of how schemata influence causal thinking. Already in 1974 Tversky and Kahneman originally identified and investigated three heuristics, as briefly outlined below, that in consequence stimulated a vast number of follow-up researches:

1. **Availability heuristic** circumscribes the inclination to estimate the frequency of an event or the likelihood of its occurrence by the ease with which it comes to mind and by its salience. The flood of instant news available today accelerates this bias. After an airplane accident, people consider flying as more dangerous; a similar risk perception about use of nuclear power could be observed after the tragic incidents at Chernobyl in 1986 and Fukushima in 2011.

---

[14] For further background reading refer to 'Judgment under Uncertainty: Heuristics and Biases' by Tversky et al., 1974.

2. **Representativeness heuristic** means the inclination to overestimate the representativeness of a given sample on the basis of looking and associating similarities, beyond statistical considerations that would underpin these judgments. In practice this could end in biases like good companies produce good news or a stranger is more violent than a member of the family.
3. **Anchoring and adjustment** describes the tendency that people make estimations from an initial value and adjust therefrom. Once a value is communicated it sticks like an anchor in people's mind and can be used or misused very successfully. Tests indicated that it does not really matter whether experts or laypeople are asked for estimates on house prices (Northcraft et al., 1987). Anchoring is a powerful highly influential approach used for example in the form of sales promotion in every supermarket.

Hence, schemata provide a very efficient and amazing way of remembering something, as it would be too complex and inaccurate to remember everything. However, this naturally bears some risks and this could be observed when looking at the question of how people make decisions. A cognitive shortcut by means of rules of thumb or intuitive judgment is not bad. It is nonetheless worth considering that it also drives and influences people in organizations. Take sophisticated risk models of a bank for example, where such mentioned heuristics seem to apply in daily business. Financial mathematics provides a key indicator named value at risk that may assist in assessing exposures. Not discussing the usability of this factor here, it was supposed to provide a reasonable estimate of loss on investment bank portfolios during financial crises, such as in 2008. No financial institution was able to predict such value-destroying events when predominantly relying on past data (Gigerenzer, 2013). It is thus questionable whether institutionalized decision aids like risk models mitigate or foster the heuristics of their users.

Bounded Rationality and Risk Appetite

During the 1950s Herbert Simon came up with the model of bounded rationality. He proposed that instead of following a rational linear process, decision making is fragile. The constraint of human brainpower in combination with time pressure and limited available information makes people unable to solve problems optimally all the time (Simon, 1955). Most cognitive processes will be based on reasoning and therefore logical and rational outcomes are preferred to illogical and irrational ones. The decision maker within bounded rationality looks at all the possible actions and outcomes and separates the outcomes into acceptable and unacceptable, rejecting the latter. The relationship between possible actions and acceptable outcomes determines the action to take. Circumstances of individuals exposed to bounded rationality, particularly if it comes to decision making with highly uncertain outcomes, are explained by the prospect theory developed by the psychologists Kahneman and Tversky during the late 1970s. Their works clarified patterns of behavior that proponents of rational decision making such as the precedent utility theorem developed by John von Neumann and Oskar Morgenstern in the 1940s had ignored. The utility theory provides a basis for rational decisions under risk, according to which decision makers constantly attempt to improve their economic situation and select the one alternative that creates the greatest advantage (von Neumann et al., 1947). However, this is apparently not always the case. Kahneman and Tversky found that the homo œconomicus model[15] can seldom be applied in practice. One study (Kahneman et al., 1979) exemplified

---

[15] The model emanated from economics describing an individual who thinks and acts in an absolutely rational manner to choose the decision alternative that produces the highest expected benefit.

the asymmetry of decision making under uncertainty by means of framing the decision choice both in positive and negative terms. Subjects first could choose between (1) a gamble involving an 80 percent chance of winning USD 4,000 and a 20% chance of winning nothing, and (2) USD 3,000 with certainty. The USD 3,000 certain was chosen by 80 percent of their subjects and people behaved risk averse as the utility theory suggests. The choice was then restated into the negative and asked subjects to choose between (1) a gamble involving an 80 percent chance of losing USD 4,000 and a 20 percent chance of losing nothing and (2) a USD 3,000 loss with certainty. Risk aversion suggests that people should go for the USD 3,000 certain loss option but in fact 92 percent of the subjects opted for the gamble. They concluded that in an ideal environment a person's attitude towards risk generally considers risk-aversion as a rational characteristic whereas risk-prone behavior is regarded as rather abnormal. However, in the experiment people subconsciously became risk seekers and tried to avoid certain losses, even when compensated with much higher uncertainty. Following this logic it appears rational that a risk-seeking attitude is considered as negative to a certain extent whilst in practice emotions frequently superimpose or eliminate rational behavior. The difference apparently lies in how the choice is framed. People cannot recognize all the consequences of their actions and this plays a central role in comprehending the underlying behavior of decision makers (Bernstein, 1996). One good example is the decision strategy "satisficing". The aspiration level of the decision maker, which characterizes whether a choice alternative is acceptable or not, is thereby key (Simon, 1979). Simon's model suggest that individuals may commence looking for the best outcome but as they fail to find it (for whatever reasons) their aspirations are lowered and they accept second best. This can be exemplified by the familiar issue of job search. Simon's view would propose that the job search is concluded as soon as the expectations (e.g., function, location, salary, authority) are met. It is also possible that when exceptionally high expectations are not met or the job search runs unsuccessfully, the aspiration level is automatically lowered and previously unacceptable jobs could become desirable in the meantime.

Complexity and uncertainty are evidently a crucial aspect of the bounded rationality model and intuition is similarly often applied as rational behavior. Weston Agor analyzed and summarized the situations when managers might use intuition in decision making, being (Agor, 1986):

- Information is fairly limited.
- Uncertainty is high and there are few precedents.
- Mainly qualitative data available rather than quantitative.
- Available time to make decision is limited.
- Many equally attractive options.

In essence, decisions of individuals are always based within the perimeters of their (bounded) rationality, i.e. on past experience and currently available information. Nonetheless the bounded rationality model is not free of critique as, for example, satisficing could also be seen as an emotional response rather than a cognitive one (Kaufman, 1999). Others argue that the borderline between bounded rationality and more structured decision making models may be not as rigid as proposed, as decision makers tend to intrinsically combine strategies to solve decision problems (Behling et al., 1976).

Prediction Momentum

Evaluating the risk of making a decision uses knowledge of past events, and as a consequence assumes that acceptable outcomes from the past will continue to be acceptable in future, unless something interrupts the existing (bounded) rationale (Fischoff, 1975). This concept is known as prediction momentum and finds its analogy in physics where Newton's second law of motion states that any body will continue in its present state unless some other force acts upon it. If it comes to forecasting an end state, the decision maker notoriously infers what the future is like before the proposed action takes place and also infers what the future will be like after the action, known as hindsight bias. People are confident in their ability to predict a future event on hindsight, which means that they naturally seek information confirming the quality of their own predictions and tend to misremember their predictions (Fischoff, 1975). Consequently an individual will "recall" more correct predictions than actually made. This also addresses the notion that a decision is never wrong; the point in time may be. Learning requires accurate feedback on past experiences (Kolb, 1976). However, a predominance of biased recollections therefore precludes true learning from experience. In other words: how to learn from errors if not all the errors are remembered?

The future is by default uncertain. Decision makers may accept uncertainty even with the most careful predictions. Assumptions and inferences are likely to be wrong or inaccurate over time due to unexpected or unknown events. ERM or any other systemic forecasting framework will consequently serve as a useful approximation to reality for organizations and societies. However, it is important to also consider that the longer the timescale, the more difficult the predictions. As soon as a number of unknown variables come into the equation it will make every forecast fuzzy. Any prediction is in turn based on accurate and available data and organizations need to cope with economic as well as business intelligence (Louisot et al., 2010). The size of an organization eventually influences the (financial) resources that were attributed to such forecasting procedures. Fewer available resources may lead to less accurate predictions. However, such hypotheses could neither be accepted nor rejected for the time being.

Anomalies and Bias

As history shows individuals, groups, organizations or even entire nations are not immune to the limitations of the human cognitive process. By means of the prospect theory four most prominent cognitive shortcomings are explained below:

Decision Regret: People have a natural tendency to avoid losses at all cost (Loomes et al., 1982). Decision regret means that an individual would rather reject a right option than accept a wrong one or in other words, a "bad" choice hurts far more than a "smart" one, even if the latter turns out wrong. If a decision is enforced, people play safe and avoid being (publicly) exposed. This is one of the reasons why decisions are delayed or simply not made, because they could be painfully regretted (Loomes et al., 1987).

Sunk Cost Effect: Sunk costs are the costs that were incurred in the past and as a result cannot vary with respect to future output. The primary finding that people will throw good money after bad is well described by the prospect theory (Kahneman et al., 1979). Expenditure on product development or house building incurred in the past is a typical sunk cost and should have no bearing on whether to continue developing a product, finalizing the house respectively. The sunk cost effect is circumscribing the influence that historical, irrecoverable costs exert on the willingness to make future investments (Arkes et al., 1985). One of the classical mistakes is that people would invest money into existing venues, in the hope of one day being able to equalize or justify the amounts already spent.

Mental Accounting: The basic principle is that people tend to "book" the payments connected with a decision into different mental accounts (Tversky et al., 1981). Separating a whole into individual components instead of looking at the big picture and making related decisions could create an enormous imbalance within an overall risk portfolio. ERM could be considered, for example, as one important factor to overcome mental accounting in respect of risk management decisions that are usually made on departmental levels, which presumably focus on hazardous and insurable risks only. Whilst a risk management professional would immediately recognize the necessity of a reasonable risk management strategy with allocated (financial) resources to achieve the objectives, senior management and particularly the financial department will primarily recognize this as a cost driver. The longer no material incidents occur, the greater the discussion as to whether the underlying (sunk) costs are justified at all.

Endowment effect: The endowment effect (Thaler, 1980) stresses that most people demand a significantly higher sale price for something they possess than they would be willing to pay for it if they did not own it. Although findings of such effects are related to numerous investment decisions, this shall not be confused with greed alone. Although it is comprehensible that possessed items carry automatically a higher value and a consequent resale should be realized as a gain, the spread between appropriate and requested value appears often very significant. In the context of ERM such a phenomenon could likely occur during the determination or re-evaluation of buildings and material in a property insurance program. If such values are owned, risk professionals maybe inclined to ascertain higher values than economically justified.

It becomes obvious that all decisions are somehow exposed to personal or group biases that misinterpret data or observations because of individual perceptions or outcome preferences. Psychology uses the theory of cognitive dissonance originating from the 1950s work of psychologist Leon Festinger. The theory in brief states that people have misgivings about their decisions as the alternative chosen has positive and negative characteristics and so does the rejected alternative. Based on individual cognitions such as available information, beliefs, values and elements of knowledge each attempts to eliminate inconsistencies in perception (Festinger, 1957). One of the preconditions for the existence of dissonance is an emotional tie with the decision that has been made, labeled as "commitment". Research evidenced that there is a functional relationship between level of commitment and dissonance aroused when the underlying decision does not turn out as imagined (Brehm et al., 1962). The degree of commitment and the intensity of the resulting dissonance depend on five factors being freedom of choice, responsibility, material costs, psychological costs and deviation from the norm. Research also uncovered that groups who made an initial collective decision that proved unsuccessful, have allocated significantly more funds to escalating the commitment to the decision than groups who inherited the initial decision (Bazerman et al., 1974).

Asymmetric or Non-Existent Information

Apart from the personal or organizational schemata subconsciously in use, another important aspect worth considering is the level of accurate and relevant data and information available at the time of decision making (Agor, 1986). Based on economics and the recognized market imperfections, everyone can agree or has personally experienced that in practice buyers or sellers often lack sufficient information to make a fully informed decision. The same principle applies in any decision making process, including classic risk transfer of insurance where negotiations between insured and insurers take place. Hence the problem of asymmetric information has to be factored in at every decision to be made. Imbalanced degrees of information can be classified in various ways but eventually lead to the fact that at least one of the parties may only disclose information that is ultimately required or requested. In-depth research or investigations of the counterparty can uncover important additional facts and assist in assessing and evaluating the risk of making a decision. However, a so-called residual risk always remains and trade-offs are inevitable. This means that either the cost of eliminating (instead of reducing) a risk is too high or eliminating the risk is impossible to achieve. There is a functional relationship between the cost of reducing a risk and the extent to which the reduction is achieved (Skipper et al., 2007). The functionality will reach a point where it becomes extremely expensive or uneconomic to make any further reduction in risk particularly when searching for information prior to any decision. Additionally there is also a level of non-existent information, mainly associated with macroeconomic factors (political, economic, social, technological, ecological or legal development) that increase the level of uncertainty for all decision makers and many risky decisions could also impose costs on others (externalities), which is an important factor to watch within the discipline of societal risk management (Skipper et al., 2007).

1.3.5 Summary

As with any other generic and path-breaking theories that emanated from economics or psychology during the last 50 years, it is important to note that the majority of experiments are contrived and may not reflect real-world conditions. It would also be inappropriate equally comparing utility theory with prospect theory, as the utility theory features a more numeric (positivist) approach whereas the prospect theory contains a mostly linguistic (phenomenological) methodology. It is important that decision makers and risk owners know and appreciate the limitations of human thinking and consider this at best possible terms when evaluating a choice. The risk of flaws and blunders during the decision making process will, however, gain significance when such aspects are ignored or glossed over. Particularly, decisions made in groups tend to be prone to divergence and dissonance as discussed in the following section.

1.3.6 Behavioral Decision Making in Groups – Power of the Crowd

Introduction

Today, many businesses utilize committees, project teams or other group activities to discuss matters in great detail and arrive at generally safe and risk optimized decisions, provided a group is able and willing to make a firm decision. This is in fact a pretty incomplete opinion. Insights from the field of cultural anthropologists (Skipper et al., 2007) enhance the context with their conviction that risk perception stems from a social process. Literature (for example Dake, 1992 or Hofstede, 1995) suggests that individuals act differently when part of a (peer) group, as the sense of group is primarily stronger and promotes solidarity and interdependence. Consequently the group impacts on and strengthens individuality with a tendency that such individual is prepared to make more risky decisions than he/she would make alone. This increased risk-seeking level of a group member echoes and reflects on the group as the collective outcome tends to approximate the average of individual outcomes.

There are two primary reasons for this behavior. First, people become anonymous in a group and the level of decision regrets is decreasing. Then in a group environment it becomes less obvious who initiated or proposed decisions with poor outcomes. Second, individuals being part of a group tend to revalidate personal choices and avoid difficult and stressful decision dilemmas (Janis, 1989). Depending on their role within the group, people generally incline to be seen as risk-seeking rather than risk averse as this attitude may be considered as brave, bold and in some cultures more attractive (Hofstede, 2001). This forms the breeding ground for overconfidence or over-reliance on routines.

Communication Difficulties as Main Challenge of Group Work

Stimulated by the familiar notion "one who reckons does not really know", Jerry Harvey's story about the Abilene paradox remains memorable (Harvey, 1974). He characterizes a family scene in a house on a Sunday afternoon in Coleman, Texas. The temperature is hot at 104° and the wind is blowing fine-grained topsoil. It is just one of those relaxing Sunday afternoons only tolerable with a cooling fan and a fresh drink on a porch. Suddenly, Jerry's father-in-law says, "Let's drive to Abilene and have dinner at the cafeteria." Jerry thinks, "Why go to Abilene? Fifty-three miles in a dust storm and with this heat, in a non-air-conditioned Buick." But his wife says, "Sounds like a great idea, let's do it. How about you, Jerry?" Jerry replies, "Sounds like a great idea, I just hope your mother-in-law wants to go too." "Of course I want to go," she says. "I haven't been to Abilene in a long time." So, the family went to Abilene in the heat, dust and a fine layer of perspiration, where they finally eat a terrible meal. On completing the long round trip, each of the family members argues that they would not have gone if the others had not wanted to go. Even the father-in-law claims, "I never wanted to go. I just thought you might be bored. I would have preferred to play dominoes, but you visit so seldom that I wanted to make sure you enjoyed the time with us."

Jerry Harvey concludes that the Abilene paradox is similar to many organizational situations, i.e. choices are validated even though all individuals involved have their reservations – they simply are not voiced. "The key issue is the lack of honesty in communicating thoughts and feelings" (van der Heijden et al., 2002, p. 71). In groups, homogeneity, cohesion and shared experience keep traditions alive and lead to hidden routine processes that are guides to thinking and acting (Bazerman et al., 1974). In extreme cases, attitudes of smaller teams or peer groups can even negatively divert from corporate thinking, which may end in very polar perceptions. Development of sentience or a misplaced sense of identity between professions or specializations could create a material endogenous risk on overall strategy of an organization. It seems all too human that a group of military leaders having studied and trained for war for a substantial time of their life are inclined to go to war. Similar tendency may apply for any other expert group such as salespeople, engineers, firemen, consultants, etc. In essence they subconsciously all want to sense and exercise their "vocation". Particularly if it comes to group dynamics and commitment there are various reasons why risks might be taken just for the sake of taking them or alternatively the group does not consider risks but only sees opportunities. Such reasons include but are not limited to groupthink, bravado and desperation (Russo et al., 1989). Considerations that are not communicated could result in a difficult situation, both for the group as well as for the individual. Many decision makers see a direction as a solution because they do not know what they want until they see what they can get (Wildavsky, 1979). While having a ready-made idea may generally appear as convenient, there is a risk that options worthy of consideration will be prematurely eliminated. The likeliness of similar thinking in any kind of peer group appears given. To illustrate this, take the recruitment process of an organization as a simple example. Today recruitment decisions are usually made in groups of at least two people. Apart from working for the same company the interviewers may share a number of common views and values and therefore feel very comfortable when jointly making the decision to employ a candidate. However, it is not usual practice to monitor what happened to the candidates who were rejected. Unless accurate feedback is gained, decision makers do not really know whether their decisions were sound, which forms a dilemma. Individuals and groups seek confirming evidence that supports their favored thinking. There is an underlying iterative danger of self-fulfiling prophecy and increasing confidence to make the right judgments (van der Heijden et al., 2002). Groups with a high level of uniformity are exposed to biased and uniform decisions, also known as groupthink (Nutt, 2002).

Groupthink

People with homogenous backgrounds or obvious similarities often constitute formal or even informal, random groups with high commitment and motivation. In her works during the 1960s anthropologist Mary Douglas illustrated the power of common moral, beliefs and political or religious order, which triggered considerable follow-up research in this area.

Today, groups or teams process much of the work, particularly in large organizations. When it comes to efficient decision making and managing risk, groups or teams may have a drawback called groupthink. Groupthink is the collective social suppression of ideas to maintain harmony and the tendency to concur with the prevailing positions and views of the group (Janis, 1989). Groups with high cohesion and commitment create shared stereotypes, beliefs and self-censorship among team members, where dissenting voices fall silent. Powerful group cohesion can lead to an intolerance of any dissenters such as people with alternative points of view or ideas (Bazerman et al., 1974). Taking into consideration the discussion about schemata in the previous section, groupthink is exposed to filter incoming information to portray only good results and nobody dares to criticize the present decision making processes or its leadership. This is likely to result in incomplete survey of alternative courses of action (March, 1988) and may even lead to incorrect risk assessment and consequent handling. Thus implications of groupthink for analyzing risk and developing alternatives within the perimeters of organizational risk appetite are very significant. The phenomenon has a very powerful track record of groups that incorrectly identified, evaluated or handled risks. Interested readers can learn more about decision debacles in, for example, the book *Why Decisions Fail* by Paul Nutt, who cross-sectionally researched and documented over 400 strategic decisions around the world during the last three decades.

Inertia of Groups

Decision making in groups is exposed to two extreme forms, either overreaction or no action at all. "When teams work well, they elevate the performance of ordinary individuals to extraordinary heights. When teams malfunction, they erode the potential contributions of the most talented members" (Boleman et al., 2003, p. 95). The same applies for decision making in groups when individuals are compiled in looser or non-hierarchical forms or tighter strongly controlled structures (Russo et al., 1989). No group is immune to having flaws or generating biases in collective thinking, though routine and overconfidence may increase the likelihood of framing issues poorly (Nutt, 2002). When focusing on risk-related decision making it seems appropriate to simultaneously consider the extensive literature available on innovation. As a general observation it seems fair to state that "company leaders privately acknowledge the need for new ideas but shy away from introduction arrangements and approaches that can stimulate creativity in management initiatives, such as decision making" (Nutt, 2002, p. 147). Business economics suggests that decision makers should determine opportunities and identify risks and how they can be managed (Mintzberg et al., 1998). In corporate environments a fresh idea has naturally a long and steep way to go. Ideas have to be formulated in great detail and coherence evaluated, i.e. the more complex the internal organizational structure, the less likely the discovery of a path-breaking idea. Groups generally gravitate to consensus or in doubt prefer the status quo (Simon, 1979). It is difficult to think about or solve risk/benefits conflicts; it would require the disregard of own personal motivations to the benefit of the group or organization respectively. Even with the best intentions, groups are most often confronted with the dilemma of achieving a degree of consensus that initiates action or that navigates around delicate exhausting subjects, both of which aggravate the risk of ignoring signals of unexpected change (van der Heijden et al., 2002). Depending on the group's size and the assigned underlying tasks, group work could become clumsy and its individual members lethargic. As long as performance or any circumstance is perceived to be satisfactory, routine or business-as-usual is key and management (or even public attention) remains rather low (Janis, 1989). Decades of research into innovation reveal that incubation should occur before innovative ideas surface, but this is hardly achievable in a safe, funneled comfort zone with well-versed procedures and formalized hierarchical structures (see Christensen, 2006 or Drucker, 1985). Risk is as important as opportunity and the significance of a given risk can vary in relation to circumstances. However, the most significant risk may be those that have not been identified or wrongly interpreted. Furthermore, it seems unforgivable to abandon or detach evolving pre-mature cognitive ideas or clues, both in terms of innovation or risk management.

Situation and Context – The Level of Available Information

During the 1970s, Edward J. Russo demonstrated from marketing research that choices are strongly influenced by the way in which information is presented. In the context of a supermarket he noted that customers' information processing is influenced by the sequence in which they walk through the racks and come across the brands. Russo arranged a list with unit price information for a range of similar products to be displayed at the end of the aisle, ordered with the most expensive at the top and the cheapest at the bottom. In his study he found that shoppers chose the cheaper brands in those situations where a well-ordered price list was available. In reality, supermarket owners would hardly provide such a price list due to revenue considerations. More generally, however, Russo could evidence that choice can be influenced and changed by changing the way in which information for the decision is obtained (Russo, 1977). Observations of other research confirmed that choice is contingent on the decision situation or context (Kahneman et al., 1982), which means that decision makers frame the context in situations with a single dimension of cost and several dimensions of benefits differently. Considering a complex issue with various options being discussed under a level of uncertainty within a group could lead to the situation that people try to simplify the decision making process whenever possible and become inclined to use either intuition or other non-compensatory[16] decision strategies within causal thinking. This is all comprehensible, particularly when bearing in mind the reservations of bounded rationality and heuristics mentioned earlier. Such in-depth knowledge of natural human limitations has even been commercialized, as the marketing discipline has successfully demonstrated such suggestive practice for decades. This know-how is also used to form and influence chain of arguments or to sway the outcome of a decision in one or the other way. Without going too much into detail of influencing people, it is worthwhile to mention at least one example known as intransitive preference. There is a possibility where a set of choices is contradictory, usually because the choice between different pairs of alternatives causes the decision maker to focus on different attributes (Belton et al., 2007). Imagine you go shopping and in respect of a specific product the following decision strategy should be applied: "If the price difference between brands is less than 50 cents choose the higher quality product, otherwise choose the cheaper brand". The following choice alternatives are available:

Brand	Price	Quality
A	USD 3.00	Low
B	USD 3.30	Average
C	USD 3.60	High
D	USD 3.50	Medium

If the choice were between brands A or B, then brand B would be favored. If the choice were between brand B and C, brand C would be chosen. If the choice were between brand A and C, brand A would be selected. It follows that using what appears to be a sensible decision strategy results in B being preferred to A and C being preferred to B. This would imply that C is preferred to A, but in fact, A is preferred to C. Depending on the criteria, the set of choices become contradictory and a selection which first seemed reasonable suddenly gets irrational. Similar observations can be made if it comes to consensus decision featuring multiple criteria as well as different parties with differing objectives (Belton et al., 2007). Some argue that voting eliminates the power of any individual and it enables the weight of opinion to sway the decision. However, voting is as subject to manipulation as any other decision technique, although less recognizable. Voting procedures can lead to similar intransitive paradoxes described above. This should be borne in mind by the team member who is frequently part of a consensus voting team.

Summary

Every group evolves a structure, though the formal design may not be coherent with the underlying hierarchy (Boleman et al., 2003). These informal dynamics have a remarkable influence on when and how group decisions are made. Biases in individual thinking may rise and expand in a group context, which will impact collectively made decisions. There is some psychological evidence to suggest that groups form and frame possible solutions in much the same way as individuals do (Janis, 1989). The group seems to act as a kind of "collective brain" that represents the sum output of each of the individuals who are represented in the

---

[16] A non-compensatory choice strategy is where poor performance on one attribute is not compensated for by good performance on other attributes (Belton et al., 2007, p. 19).

group. Other observations suggest that the riskiest solutions are arrived at by groups acting as advisors or counselors to an overall leader. The group generates more risky solutions than most of the individual members would have done, but the final choice is made by one single leader, who in turn exhibits an individual risk temper based on the collective group response (Nutt, 2002). This type of situation is typical for material decisions that have to be made quickly and within a high-risk environment based on limited information (Belton et al., 2007). In any event, when visualizing the story about Abilene it seems clear that even in simple non-critical and low context situations, group behavior and bad assumptions could dominate group dynamics (for years).

1.3.7   How Organizations Deal With Decisions – Will ERM Assist?

Without risk there is no reward and risk eventually breeds innovation (Rogers, 2003). In consequence, risk is therefore to be encouraged within an organization as long as it is carefully managed. There are various types of risk management approaches in use, whereof ERM methods eventually provide a holistic and systemic approach in order to deal with strategic, organizational, change and unforeseeable risks (and opportunities). The concepts are by far not new but they are gradually getting more normative attention and character, also by legislators and authorities. Everyone agrees that risks are everywhere and every crucial decision should be the result of a careful risk diagnosis (Bewley, 1989). However, most risk assessment is intuitive and should be practical, realistic, compliant with (internal and external) standards and above all remain cost efficient (Louisot et al. 2010). Protecting the economic value of an organization remains the overall objective (Skipper et al., 2007). The enhancement from an existing risk management practice to ERM may break up habits and scrutinize the corporate risk approach from various perspectives. However, as experienced in quality management systems, risk management approaches can soon become extremely complex, labor-intensive and costly (Skipper et al., 2007). The previous sections about the limitations of human thinking and group decision making will in the short-term not encourage senior managers to follow too advanced methods. Nonetheless it is not all that arbitrary. There are rudiments that close procedural gaps and mitigate subjectivity, although there are no standardized recipes available. Ultimately it all reflects back on good leadership.

   One major topic to be remembered is that organizations should consider endogenous (behavioral) risks as they would consider material risk from the environment. Irrespective of the decision maker's job level, individuals will follow cognitive habits in their thought processes and behavior (Caputi et al., 2006). Some of those practiced habits seem quite handy as it leads to increased efficiency. When it comes to significant decisions facing major strategic stress, it seems utterly important to choose the right decision strategy. Apart from the skills which individuals and managers may possess, leadership style and company culture exert a significant impact on the ability of the organization to make decisions and undertake change. Organizations vary substantially in their approaches to leadership, which is the subject of significant management psychology research. Some organizations lay stress on a hierarchical structure and adopt a rather top down if not dictatorial approach to decision making (Boleman et al., 2003). Others attempt to be democratic, making efforts to involve employees at all levels in the management process by adopting such policies as "open door" and management by walking about (Mintzberg et al., 1998). In some instances it may appear obvious that the management style is not consistent with planned strategic changes and this is another way that decisions could get biased or even manipulated (Nutt, 2002).

Management literature provides a number of approaches to formally assist in achieving an "objective" decision such as decision trees, multi-criteria decision analysis, sensitivity analysis, cost-benefits assessments, risk modeling etc. where alternatives are scored and weighted or probabilities and impact are assessed (Belton et al., 2007). Irrespective of the approach applied, all tools create certainty with mathematical precision and in turn offer the best (available) solution. At times the most sophisticated systems fail and that could be a reason that at first glance the holistic ERM process still lacks prominent adherents and extensive corporate support so far. A system or a process is not a substitute to making own decisions. It is a technologized compilation of human behavior (March, 1988). People like to be able to rely on a consistent system of opinions, beliefs and knowledge as it creates stability, which results in certainty. Even after decisions are made, people could theoretically ask themselves whether they made the right choice. In practice, presumably they discretely do so, but within an organization it is easier to adapt the perception of the situation to conform to the decision made (van der Heijden et al., 2002).

As Geert Hofstede observed in his research on uncertainty avoidance, or Daniel Kahneman and Amos Tversky developed under the prospect theory, it seems fair to assume that people make a subjective evaluation of risk, subconsciously driven by underlying uncertainty about future events (see Hofstede, 2001 or Kahneman et al., 1992). Organizations will always carry a residual risk of not identifying, poorly assessing or failing to monitor or control circumstances that lead to a loss of economic value. The poor framing of issues may solve the wrong problems (March, 1988); just as wrong information provided would lead to wrong conclusions. People tend to stick to their patterns and habits while talking to the same group of people who see the world similarly (Janis, 1989). Group consensus is laudable, but often not achieved through an iterative process of discussing conflicting arguments or circumstances. In the context of day-to-day management, where operational decisions need to be made, non-compensatory decision strategies are probably rather positive and acceptable. However, the accurate decision strategy in the scope of strategic or unforeseeable risks or uncertainties is essential and the discovery of unseen or undervalued linkages within the business context eventually key. ERM may provide a way for less causal and more systemic thinking, provided that honesty in communicating thoughts and feelings is not hindered or censored by group dynamics. In other words, schemata and causal thinking are a good natural starting point but should not form the end state when high-level decisions in a group become necessary. To clear and reset existing habits of a group, it seems inevitable that each individual member including the chairman (if any) evaluate and accept his/her predominant attitude to uncertainty and risk. People who embrace and appreciate uncertainty by allowing imagination and vision are able to transcend inherent bounded rationality for a certain time. This may only be achieved when leaving pressing operational issues outside any meeting room, wipe off existing fashions and entirely focus on the applicable subject. James March suggested five aspects to help individuals and organizations to leave existing habits and pave the way for new thinking (March, 1988):

1. **Treat goals as hypotheses.** It is human to doubt, but the likelihood of doubting one's own objectives is rather low. March argues that goals should be seen as a hypothesis that intrinsically leads to seeking alternatives.
2. **Treat intuition as real.** According to March, intuition is presumably just an inexplicable way of consulting that part of intelligence not organized in the way standard theories or models could cope with. Intuition is rather a partner to think about actions outside the usual (rational) behavior.

3. **Treat hypocrisy as a transition.** Hypocrisy is described as inconsistency between expressed values and behavior. People usually reject inconsistency, though mankind at least mentally experiments with non-ethical shady considerations too. March suggests that such process is fair within the merits of controllable experimentation and should not be hindered.

4. **Treat memory as enemy.** As learned from the scope of the human cognitive process, good memories ideally make good choices. However, exercising the ability to memorize will evoke the ability to overlook or forget things at the same time.

5. **Treat experience as a theory.** March sees learning as series of conclusions based on concepts of action and consequences. Experience can be changed retrospectively, as evidenced in the studies of hindsight bias. He proposes to frequently affirm the ability of "self-deception" in experience and acknowledge that experience is an interpretation subject to conscious revision.

To consult an experienced individual from outside the organization who acts as impartial facilitator during crucial decision making sessions seems not to be a bad idea. Otherwise the probability to fall back into the usual roles and patterns of the group is rather high. Particularly, group activities such as strategy development, expectation approach or scenario planning seem to be ideal areas in which to introduce a facilitator, ready to assist the collection of and, more importantly, to devise, various differing perspectives, opinions and drivers.

With regard to behavioral decision making within groups, below is a brief summary of factors to watch and suggestions to try:

Information Processing: Economic and business intelligence that is easily available for one should be made available for others. Proper information is a crucial feature for accurate decisions. Latent schemata of individuals will bias the way data and information is collected. Therefore it is advisable not to rely on a single source only. Furthermore, continuously repeated news in different media does not make a situation more desirable or more risky. It is simply more often reported, regardless whether justified or not. If it comes to scenarios or general forecasts of any experts, prudence is key even though individuals are often hooked on something due to pattern recognition and attention, i.e. their information filters are biased or influenced.

Timing: Difficult decisions made in a hurry seldom turn out well, and due to hindsight bias this is anyway difficult to validate. Moreover, under time pressure people may use non-compensatory defensive decision strategies such as satisficing and thereby consequently increase the likelihood of failing to consider all options, i.e. all available attributes or any alternative solutions. Taking time to make a more complex decision is not a weakness as long as a decision will be finally made.

Dissonance: Devotion and commitment influence many decisions. Everybody is exposed to cognitive dissonance. In groups with high homogeneity, overconfidence and complacency flourish. In order to elaborate a decision in a group, unless there is a particular incident to be examined, it is better not to focus on past events but to provide new food for thought (stimuli). Trying to refocus the approach towards avoiding losses (as per Kahneman and Tversky's experiments) may potentially reveal surprising risk-seeking behavior. Another approach could reveal escalating (emotional) commitment and illustrate how subjective topics could get.

Routines and Habits: The notion "believe it in order to achieve it" is pretty powerful, as an individual's convictions cannot be changed overnight. Maybe they should not be changed at all. However, it is advisable to occasionally take individuals out of their comfort area and impose a change in habit. Putting people in a fresh cognitive condition gets them into a mental state in which they are more apt to find creative ideas (Nutt, 2002). Consider a meeting where all attendees have to stand around instead of sitting comfortably in a chair drinking coffee and eating a cookie for example, may produce significantly different outcomes. Also the time of day is influencing the activity level of a group (Brehm et al., 1962). Overheated discussions with no expectable solutions should be interrupted. De-emotionalizing the venue and rewinding or even sleeping over it could effect miracles. If not, it will at least save time and energy and may ultimately lead to a vigorous clear approach the following day.

It is obvious that every organization has its own procedures, risk attitude, behaviors and culture. What works for one may not work for the other, but there are similarities and common issues that affect entire industries or even societies. A lot of information and context has been provided throughout this article. However, the most important finding about group decision making in organizations is to cherish an open learning environment. It may all start with observing one's own (decision making) behavior, to keep watching and not get stuck in routine patterns. Major progress is only achievable when individuals, including staff, appreciate the importance of a frank and honest dialogue. Vocalizing concerns or providing critical reflection without being characterized by any (group) bias is therefore one crucial element. The courage to face anxiety and accept responsibility is another. No doubt there are many subconscious obstacles in an organizational or cultural environment that hinder or misguide proper learning and abandon creativity (Christensen, 2006). However, flaws, errors or unpleasant negative decisions should primarily not be a question of guilt and punishment, but eventually an indicator of a too-strict normative and causal thinking. There are approaches like ERM that exploit new ways of corporate thinking. The only major challenge is to rediscover one's own personal curiosity and eagerness to continuously learn and competently develop within a team, group or organization. Ultimately, it could result in achieving unforeseen competitive advantage, personally and corporately.

Bibliography

For readers wishing to further expand their understanding of decision making and the issues raised in this article, the following shortlist of recommended reading may be considered:

On Prospect Theory and Decision Making

Janis, I. (1989) *Crucial Decisions*, New York, NY: The Free Press.
Kahneman, D. and Tversky, A. (1992) Advances in prospect theory: cumulative representation of uncertainty. *Journal of Risk and Uncertainty*, Vol. 5, pp. 297–324.

On Decision Flaws

Gigerenzer, G. (2013) *Risk Savvy. How to Make Good Decisions*. New York, NY: Viking Adult.
Nutt, P.C. (2002) *Why Decisions Fail*. San Francisco, CA: Berrett-Koehler Publishers.
Russo, E.J. and Schoemaker, P.J.H. (1989) *Decision Traps. Ten barriers to brilliant decision-making and how to overcome them*. New York: Doubleday.

On Organizational Behavior and Learning

McKenna, E.F. (2006) *Business Psychology and Organizational Behavior*. 4th edn. New York: Psychology Press.

Van der Heijden, K., Bradfield, R., Burt, G., Cairns, G. and Wright, G. (2002) *The Sixth Sense: Accelerating Organizational Learning with Scenarios*. Chichester: John Wiley & Sons.

On Strategy

Mintzberg, H., Ahlstrand, B. and Lampel, J. (1998) *Strategy Safari: A Guided Tour Through the Wilds of Strategic Management*. New York: Free Press.

On Risk Management

Skipper, H.D. and Kwon, W.J. (2007) *Risk Management and Insurance: Perspectives in a global economy*. Oxford: Wiley-Blackwell.

References

Agor, W.H. (1986) How top executives use their intuition to make important decisions. *Business Horizons*, Vol. 29, pp. 49–53.

Akelof, G.A. (2006) The market for lemons: qualitative uncertainty and the market mechanism. *Quarterly Journal of Economics*, Vol. 84, pp. 488–500.

Arkes, H.R. and Blumer, C. (1985) The psychology of sunk cost. *Organizational Behavior and Human Decision Process*, Vol. 35, pp. 124–140.

Baumgartner, M., Gaus, D. Hawaldar, S., Meury, P., Al-Otaiba, H. and Tanner, D. (2008) UBS subprime write-downs in the U.S. Working Paper, University of Strathclyde Business School, Glasgow, UK.

Bazerman, M.H., Giuliano, T. and Appelman, A. (1974) Escalation in Individual and Group Decision Making. *Organizational Behavior and Human Decision Performance Journal*, Vol. 33, pp. 141–152.

Belton, V. and Wright, G. (2007) *Making Decisions*. University of Strathclyde Business School, Glasgow (UK).

Behling, O. and Schriesheim, C. (1976) *Organizational Behavior: Theory, Research and Application*. Boston, MA: Allyn and Bacon.

Bernstein, P.L. (1996) *Against the Gods: The Remarkable Story of Risk*. New York, NY: John Wiley and Sons.

Bewley, T. F. (1989) Market innovation and entrepreneurship. A Knightian View, Cowles Discussion Paper, no. 905, New Haven, CT.

Boleman, L.G. and Deal, T.E. (2003) *Reframing Organizations: Artistry, Choice and Leadership*, San Francisco, CA: Jossey-Bass.

Brehm, J.W. and Cohen, A.R. (1962) *Explorations in Cognitive Dissonance*. New York, NY: John Wiley and Sons.

Caputi, P., Foster, H. and Viney, L.L. (2006) *Personal Construct Psychology: New Ideas*. Chichester: John Wiley and Sons.

Christensen, C.M. (2006) *The Innovator's Dilemma*. New York, NY: First Collins Business Essentials.

Coval, J. and Shumway, T. (2001) Do behavioral biases affect prices? Working Paper, University of Michigan, MI.

Dake, K. (1992) Myths of nature: culture and the social construction of risk. *Journal of Social Issues*, Vol. 48(4).

Douglas, M. (1966) *Purity and Danger: An Analysis of Concepts of Pollution and Taboo*. London: Taylor.

Drucker, P.F. (1985) *Innovation and Entrepreneurship. Practice and Principles*. Oxford: Harper & Row.

Festinger, L. (1957) *A Theory of Cognitive Dissonance*. Stanford, CA: Standford University Press.

Fischoff, B. (1975) Hindsight ≠ Foresight: the effect of outcome knowledge on judgment under uncertainty. *Journal of Experimental Psychology: Human Perception and Performance*, Vol. 1, pp. 288–299.

Fiske, S.T. and Taylor, S.E. (1991) *Social Cognition*. New York, NY: McGraw-Hill Humanities/Social Sciences/Languages.

Gigerenzer, G. (2013) *Risk Savvy. How to Make Good Decisions*. New York, NY: Viking Adult.

Harvey, J.B. (1974) The Abilene paradox: the management of agreement. *Organizational Dynamics*.

Hofstede, G. (1995) Insurance as a Product of National Values. *The Geneva Papers on Risk and Insurance*, Vol. 20 (77), pp. 423–429.

Hofstede, G. (2001) *Culture's Consequences*. 2nd edn. Thousand Oaks, CA: Sage Publications.

Janis, I. (1989) *Crucial Decisions*, New York, NY: Free Press.

Kahneman, D. (2011) *Thinking Fast and Slow*. New York, NY: Farrar, Straus and Giroux.

Kahneman, D. and Tversky, A. (1979) Prospect theory: an analysis of decision under risk. *Econometrica*, 47, pp. 263–291.

Kahneman, D. and Tversky, A. (1982) The Psychology of Preferences. *Scientific American*, Vol. 39, pp. 136–142.

Kahneman, D. and Tversky, A. (1992) Advances in prospect theory: cumulative representation of uncertainty. *Journal of Risk and Uncertainty*, Vol. 5, pp. 297–324.

Kaufman, B.E. (1999) Emotional arousal as a source of bounded rationality. *Journal of Economic Behavior and Organization*, Vol. 38, pp. 135–144.

Kelly, G.A. (1994) *The Psychology of Personal Constructs*, 2nd edn. London: Routledge.

Kolb, D.A. (1976) *Organizational Behavior: An experiential approach*. 7th edn. pp. 270–286. New Jersey: Prentice Hall.

Loomes, G. and Sudgen, R. (1982) Regret theory: an alternative theory of rational choice under uncertainty. *Economic Journal*, Vol. 92, pp. 805–824.

Loomes, G. and Sudgen, R. (1987) Testing for regret and disappointment in choice under uncertainty. *Economic Journal*, Vol. 97, pp. 118–129.

Louisot, J-P. and Ketcham, C. (2010) *Enterprise-Wide Risk Management: Developing and Implementing*. Malvern, PA: The Institutes.

March, J.G. (1988) *Decisions and Organizations*. Chapter 12 'The Technology of Foolishness', pp. 253–265. Oxford: Wiley-Blackwell.

McConnell, M. (1987) *Challenger: A Major Malfunction*. New York, NY: Doubleday.

McKenna, E.F. (2006) *Business Psychology and Organizational Behavior*. 4th edn. New York: Psychology Press.

Mintzberg, H., Ahlstrand, B. and Lampel, J. (1998) *Strategy Safari: A Guided Tour Through the Wilds of Strategic Management*. New York, NY: Free Press.

Northcraft, G.B. and Neale, M.A. (1987) Experts, amateurs, and real estate: an anchoring-and-adjustment perspective on property pricing decisions. *Organizational Behavior and Human Decision Processes* 39, pp. 84–97.

Nutt, P.C. (2002) *Why Decisions Fail*. San Francisco, CA: Berrett-Koehler Publishers.

Raiffa, H. (1982) *The Art and Science of Negotiation*. Cambridge, MA: Harvard University Press.

Rogers, E.M. (2003) *Diffusion and Innovations*. 5th edn. New York, NY: Free Press.

Russo, E.J. (1977) The value of unit price information. *Journal of Marketing Research*, Vol. 14, pp. 193–201.

Russo, E.J. and Shoemaker, P.J.H. (1989) *Decision Traps. Ten barriers to brilliant decision-making and how to overcome them*. New York, NY: Fireside.

Simon, H.A. (1955) A behavioural model of rational choice. *Quarterly Journal of Economics*, Vol. 69, pp. 99–118.

Simon, H.A. (1979) Rational decision making in business organizations. *American Economic Review*, Vol. 69, pp. 493–513.

Skipper, H.D. and Kwon, W.J. (2007) *Risk Management and Insurance: Perspectives in a global economy*. Oxford: Wiley-Blackwell.

Thaler, R.H. (1980) Toward a positive theory of consumer choice. *Journal of Economic Behavior and Organization*, Vol. 1, pp. 39–60.

Thaler, R.H. (1981) Some empirical evidence on dynamic inconsistency. *Economic Letters*, 8, pp. 201–207.

Tversky, A. and Kahneman, D. (1974) *Judgment Under Uncertainty: Heuristics and Biases*, pp. 1124–1131. Cambridge: Cambridge University Press.

Tversky, A. and Kahneman, D. (1980) Causal Schemas in Judgments under Uncertainty. Published in *Progress in Social Psychology,* Fishbein, M. (Ed.), Hillsdale, NJ.

Tversky, A. and Kahneman, D. (1981) The framing of decisions and the psychology of choice. *Science*, Vol. 22, pp. 453–458.

Tversky, A., Kahneman, D. and Slovic, P. (1982) *Causal Schemes in Judgments Under Uncertainty: Heuristics and Biases*. Cambridge: Cambridge University Press.

UBS (2008) *Shareholder Report on UBS's Write-Downs*. Zurich: UBS AG.

Van der Heijden, K., Bradfield, R., Burt, G., Cairns G. and Wright, G. (2002) *The Sixth Sense: Accelerating Organizational Learning with Scenarios*. Chichester: John Wiley & Sons.

Von Neumann, J. and Morgenstern, O. (1947) *Theory of Games and Economic Behavior*. 2nd edn. New Jersey: Princeton University Press.

Weiner, B. (1985) "Spontaneous" causal thinking. *Psychological Bulletin*, 97, pp. 74–84.

Wildavsky, A. (1979) *Speaking Truth to Power*. Boston, MA: Little Brown & Company.

2

Risk Assessment

In the risk assessment step the enterprise identifies the critical risks to strategy, it analyses and evaluates these critical risks and it prioritizes the critical risks. Risk assessment has been the traditional focus of many risk managers for decades. However, in ERM critical risks include *all* risks whether operational, competitive, financial, regulatory or from other sources. Finally both positive and negative risks are considered in the context of their criticality as it could affect the strategy.

2.1 RISK QUANTIFICATION: CORNERSTONE FOR RATIONAL RISK MANAGEMENT

Jean-Paul Louisot

Formerly Université Paris 1 Panthéon-Sorbonne, Directeur pédagogique du CARM Institute, Paris, France

Laurent Condamin, Ph.D

Consultant and Partner ELSEWARE

Patrick Naim

Consultant and CEO ELSEWARE[1]

Enterprise-wide risk management (ERM) is a key issue for boards of directors worldwide. Its proper implementation ensures transparent governance with all stakeholders' interests integrated into the strategic equation. Furthermore, risk quantification is the cornerstone of effective risk management, at the strategic, tactical, and operational level, covering finance as well as ethics considerations. Both downside and upside risks (threats and opportunities) must be assessed to select the most efficient risk control measures and to set up efficient risk financing mechanisms. Only thus will an optimum return on capital and a reliable protection against bankruptcy be ensured, i.e. long-term sustainable development.

Within the ERM framework, each individual operational entity is called upon to control its own risks, within the guidelines set up by the board of directors, whereas the risk financing strategy is developed and implemented at the corporate level to optimize the balance between threats and opportunities, systematic and non-systematic risks, pre- and post-loss financing and finally retention and transfer.

However, those risk reduction measures, including risk avoidance, that entail substantial investments and financial impacts may have to be decided at the top management level for approval within the global financial strategy.

However daunting the task, each board member, each executive and each field manager must be equipped with the toolbox enabling them to quantify the risks within his/her jurisdiction

---

[1] For further details and implementation refer to Laurent Condamin, Jean-Paul Louisot, Patrick Naïm; *Risk Quantification – Management, Diagnosis and Hedging*, John Wiley & Sons, Chichester, 2006.

to the fullest possible extent and thus make sound, rational and justifiable decisions, while recognizing the limits of the exercise. Beyond traditional probability analysis, used by the insurance community since the 18th century, the toolbox offers insight into new developments like Bayesian expert networks, Monte Carlo simulation, etc., with practical illustrations on how to implement them within the three steps of risk management: diagnostic, treatment and audit.

Recent progress in risk management shows that the risk-management process needs to be implemented in a strategic, enterprise-wide manner, and therefore, account for conflicting objectives and trade-offs. This means that risk can no longer be limited to the downside effect; the upside effect must also be taken into account. The central objective of global risk management is to enhance opportunities while curbing threats, i.e. driving up stockholders' value, while upholding other stakeholders' expectations. Therefore, risk quantification has become the cornerstone of effective strategic and enterprise-wide risk management.

2.1.1   Why Is Risk Quantification Needed?

The volatile context within which organizations must operate today calls for a dynamic and proactive vision aimed at achieving the organization's mission, goals and objectives under any stress or surprise. It requires a new expanded definition of "risks". The "new" risk manager must think and look beyond the organization's frontiers, more specifically to include all the economic partners and indeed all the stakeholders of the organization. Special attention must be devoted to the supply chain, or procurement cloud, and the interdependences of all parties.

The ISO 31000:2009 standard provides a very broad definition of risk as the impact of uncertainties on the organization's objectives. It provides a road map to effective ERM (enterprise-wide risk management) rather than a compliance reference; this is why the principles and framework provide a track to explore.

But whatever the preferred itinerary, all managers will need to develop a risk register and quantify the possible or probable consequences of risks to make rational decisions that can be disclosed to the authorities and the public. In many circumstances the data available are not reliable and complete enough to open the gates for traditional probability and trend analysis, other toolboxes may be required to develop satisfactory quantification models to help decision makers include a proper evaluation of uncertainty in any strategic or operational decision.

As a reminder, we believe that the cornerstone of risk management is the risk management process completed by a clear definition of what is a risk or exposure:

- The definition of an exposure: resource at risk, peril, and consequences.
- The 3-step risk management process: diagnostic of exposures (risk assessment), risk treatment, and audit (monitor and review), the risk treatment step being further broken down into design, development, and implementation phases of the risk management program.

Therefore, quantification is the key element for strategic – or holistic – risk management, as only a proper evaluation of uncertainties allows for rational decision-making. Only a robust perspective on risk could support the design of a risk management program, both at tactical and strategic levels, for implementation at the operational level. One of the key tasks of the risk manager is to design a risk management program and have it approved.

2.1.2   Causal Structure of Risk

Risks are situations where damaging events may occur but are not fully predictable. Recognizing some degree of unpredictability in these situations means that events must be considered as random. But randomness does not mean that these events can't be analyzed and quantified!

Most of the risks that will be considered throughout this book are partially driven by a series of factors, or drivers. These drivers are conditions or causes that would make the occurrence of the risk more probable, or more severe.

From a scientific viewpoint, causation is the foundation of determinism: identifying *all* the causes of a given phenomenon would allow prediction of the occurrence and unfolding of this event. Similarly, the probability theory is the mathematical perspective on uncertainty. Even in situations where an event is totally unpredictable, the laws of probability can help to envision and quantify the possible futures. *Knowledge is the reduction of uncertainty – when we gain a better and better understanding of a phenomenon, the random part of the outcome decreases compared to the deterministic part.*

Some authors introduce a subtle distinction between *uncertainty* and *volatility*, the latter being an intrinsic randomness of a phenomenon that cannot be reduced. In the framework of deterministic physics, there is no such thing as variability, and apparent randomness is only the result of incomplete knowledge. Invoking Heisenberg's "uncertainty principle" in a discussion on risk quantification seems disproportionate. But should we do it, we understand the principle as stating that the ultimate knowledge is not reachable, rather than that events are random by nature:

> "In the sharp formulation of the law of causality (if we know the present exactly, we can calculate the future) it is not the conclusion that is wrong but the premise." (W. Heisenberg, 1969)

Risk management is maturing into a fully-fledged branch of managerial sciences dealing with the handling of uncertainty with which any organization is confronted, due to more or less predictable changes in the internal and external context in which they operate, as well as evolutions in their ownership and stakeholders that may modify their objectives.

Judgment can be applied to decision making in risk-related issues, but rational and transparent processes called for by good governance practices require that risks be quantified to the fullest extent possible. When data are insufficient, unavailable or irrelevant, expertise must be called upon to quantify impacts as well as likelihoods. This is precisely what this chapter is about. It will guide the reader through the quantification tools appropriate at all three steps of the risk management process: diagnostic to set priority; loss control and loss financing to select the most efficient methods with one major goal – long-term value to stakeholders – in mind; and audit to validate the results and improve the future.

2.1.3   Increasing Awareness of Exposures and Stakes

The analysis of recent major catastrophes outlines three important features of risk assessment. First, major catastrophes always hit where and when no one expects them. Second, it is often inaccurate to consider they were fully unexpected, but rather that they were consciously not considered. Third, the general tendency to fight against risks that have already materialized leaves us unprepared for major catastrophes.

A sound risk assessment process should not neglect any of these points. What has already happened could strike again; and it is essential to remain vigilant. What has never happened may happen in the future, and therefore we must analyze potential scenarios with all available knowledge.

The Bayesian approach to probabilities can bring an interesting contribution to this problem. The major contribution of Thomas Bayes to scientific rationality was to clearly express that *uncertainty is conditioned to available information*. In other words, risk perception is conditioned by someone's knowledge.

Using the Bayesian approach, a probability (i.e. a quantification of uncertainty) cannot be defined outside an information context. Roughly speaking, "what can happen" is meaningless. I can only assess what I believe is possible. And what I believe possible is conditioned by what I know. This view is perfectly in line with an open approach of risk management. The future is "what I believe is possible". And "what I know" is not only what has already happened but also all available knowledge about organizations and their risk exposure. Risk management starts by knowledge management.

2.1.4   Risk Quantification for Risk Control

Reducing the risks is the ultimate objective of risk management, or should we say reducing *some* risks. Because risks cannot be totally suppressed – as a consequence of the intrinsic incompleteness of human knowledge – risk reduction is a trade-off.

Furthermore, even when knowledge is not the issue, it may not be "worth it" for an organization to attempt a loss reduction exercise, at least not beyond the point when the marginal costs and the marginal benefits are equal. Beyond that point it becomes uneconomical to invest in loss control. Then two questions will have to be addressed:

- At the microeconomic level: how to handle the residual risk, including the treatments through risk financing.
- At the macroeconomic level: or should we say at the societal level, in the situation left as is by the individual organization, are there any externalities, risks or cost to society not borne in the private transaction? In such a case the authorities may want to step in through legislation or regulation to "internalize" the costs so that the organization is forced to reconsider its initial position. A clear illustration is the environment issue: many governments and some international conventions have imposed drastic measures to clean the environment that have forced many private organizations to reconsider their pollution and waste risks.

Beyond the macro-micro distinction, there are individual variations on the perception of risk by each member of a given group; each group and the final decisions may rest heavily on the perception of risk by those in charge of the final arbitration. This should be kept in mind throughout the implementation of the risk management process. Why do people build in natural disaster prone areas without really taking all the loss reduction measures available, while at the same time failing to understand why the insurer will refuse to offer them the cover they want or at a premium they are willing to pay?

Every individual builds his own representation that dictates his perception of risks and the structural invariants in his memory help in understanding the decision he reached. His reasoning is based on prototypes or schemes that will influence the decision he reaches. In many instances, decisions are made on a thinking process based on analogies: they try to recall previous situations analogous to the one they are confronted with. Therefore, organizing systematic feedback at the unit level and conducting local debriefing should lead to a better grasp of the local risks and a treatment more closely adapted to the reality of the risks to which people are exposed.

This method should partially solve the paradox we have briefly described above, as the gradual construction of a reasonable perception of risk in all should lead to more rational decisions.[2]

There remains to take into account the pre-crisis situation when the deciders are under pressure and where the time element is a key to understanding sometimes disastrous decisions. Preparing everyone to operate under stress will therefore prove key to the resilience of any organization.

From a quantitative point of view, the implementation of any risk control measure will:

- Change the distribution of some risk driver, either at the exposure, occurrence, or impact level;
- Have a direct cost, related to the implementation itself; and
- Have an indirect or opportunity cost, related to the potential impact on the business.

Therefore, the cost of risks is the sum of three elements: accident losses, loss control cost, and opportunity cost.[3] These elements are of course interrelated. Reaching the best configuration of acceptable risks is therefore an optimization problem, under budget and other constraints. From a mathematical point of view, this is a well-defined problem.

Of course, since loss reduction actions have an intrinsic cost, there is no way to reduce the cost of risks to zero. Sometimes, the loss control action is simply not worth implementing. The opportunity cost is also essential: ignoring this dimension of the loss control would often result in a very simple optimal solution – reducing the exposure to zero, or in other words, stopping the activity at risk! This loss control method is called avoidance, and will be discussed further.

As we will see, the quantitative approach to risks is a very helpful tool for selecting the appropriate loss control actions. But here we must be very careful as four categories of drivers can be identified:

- *Controllable drivers* can be influenced by a decision.
- *Predictable drivers* cannot really be influenced by a decision, but their evolution can be predicted to some extent.
- *Observable drivers* cannot be influenced, nor predicted. They can only be observed after the facts, a posteriori. Observable drivers should not normally be included in a causal risk model, since they cannot be used as levers to reduce impacts. On the other hand, they are helpful to gain a better understanding of risk and as some of these drivers are measurable they assist in piloting the risk.
- *Hidden drivers* cannot be measured directly, not even a posteriori, but may be controlled to some extent.

When a first set of risk models is created during the risk assessment phase, the use of observable and hidden drivers would generally be limited to the initial risk assessment, simply because they cannot assist in the evaluation of the impact of proposed loss reduction measures.

For instance, when dealing with terrorist risks, the hostility of potential terrorists cannot be measured. When dealing with operational risks, the training level and the workload of the

---

[2] Further comments chapter 1 – S. Gaultier Gaillard & J.-P. Louisot – *Le diagnostic des risques* – AFNOR Paris 2004.

[3] Risk transfer costs should be included, but are ignored at this stage.

employees certainly impact the probability of a mistake. However, this dependency is very difficult to assess. But should these drivers be ignored in risk reduction? Should a state ignore the potential impact of a sound diplomacy or communication to reduce terrorist exposure? Should a bank neglect to train its employees when striving to improve the quality of service and reduce the probability of errors?

Simply said, we must recognize that causal models of risks are partial. And, although using this type of models is a significant improvement when dealing with risk assessment, they should only be considered as a contribution when dealing with risk reduction.

2.1.5   Risk Quantification for Risk Financing

Risk financing is part of the overall medium- and long-term financing of any organization. Therefore, its main goal is derived from the goals of the finance department, i.e. maximizing return while avoiding bankruptcy, in terms of obtaining the maximum return on investments for the level of risk acceptable to the directors and stockholders. In economic terms, that means riding on the efficient frontier.

To reach this goal the organization can use a set of tools aimed at spreading through time and space the impact of the losses it may incur, and more generally taking care of the cash flows at risk. However, deciding whether it can retain or must transfer the financial impact of its risks cannot be based merely on a qualitative assessment of risks. A quantitative evaluation of risks is necessary to support the selection of the appropriate risk financing instruments, to negotiate a deal with an insurer or understand the cost of a complex financing process.

The question is to identify the benefits of building a model which quantifies the global cost of risks, thus providing the risk manager with a tool that allows him to test several financing scenarios: the benefits of quantification to enhance the process of selection of a risk financing solution. Financing is the third leg of risk management based on the initial diagnostic and after all reasonable efforts at reducing the risks have been selected. Risk financing, even more than risk diagnostic or reduction, requires an accurate knowledge of your risks. "How much will you transfer?" and "How much will you retain?" are questions about quantities, the answers to which obviously require fairly precise figures.

Insurance premiums are set on the basis of quantitative models developed by the actuaries of insurance and reinsurance companies. Thus, insurance companies presumably have an accurate evaluation of the cost of your (insurable) risks. The problem is to ensure a balanced approach at the negotiation table. It is not conceivable to have a strong position when negotiating your insurance premiums equipped with only a qualitative knowledge of your risks. You may try, but it will be difficult for you to convince an insurer.

A complex financing program is usually expensive to set up, and sometimes to maintain; therefore the organization must make sure that the risks to be transferred are worth the effort. As part of their governance duties, the board of directors will expect from the finance director a convincing justification of the proposed program both in terms of results and efforts.

Any decision concerning the evaluation or the selection of a financing tool must be based on a quantified knowledge of your risks. Defining the appropriate layers of risk to be retained, transferred, or shared involves a clear understanding of the distribution of potential losses. Deciding whether you are able to retain a €10 million loss requires that you at least know the probability of occurrence of such a loss.

Before developing any risk financing programs, the first decision concerns what risks must be financed. This issue should be addressed during the diagnostic step. Diagnostic has been extensively developed in a previous article. This step provides a model for each loss exposure and sometimes a global risk model. This model quantifies:

(i) The probability of occurrence of a given peril;

(ii) The distribution of losses should the peril occur; and

(iii) The distribution of the cumulated losses over a given period.

Developing and implementing a risk financing solution involves being able, at least, to measure beforehand the cost of retention and the cost of transfer and this is possible only by combining the risk model and a mathematical formalization of the financing tool cost.

2.1.6 Conclusion

Risk quantification is essential for risk diagnostic, risk control and risk financing. All steps of the risk management process involve indeed an accurate knowledge of the risks an organization has to face and of the levers it could use to control risks, and finally what remains to be financed.

However, under certain circumstances, an organization could still rely on qualitative assessment to identify and control its risks. For risk financing, qualitative assessment is definitely not adequate to deal with evaluating premiums, losses volatility, etc. An accurate quantification of risks is necessary for a rational risk financing.

Several motivations lead the risk manager to address the quantification of risks:

- **Financial strategy:** Any organization should know if its financing program is well suited for the threats it has to face, and the opportunities it may want to seize. Financing program features must be linked to the distribution of potential losses that have to be covered, and of the potential needs to finance new unexpected projects. Answers to these two questions cannot be based on qualitative assessment of risks. Quantitative risk models are the basic tools to run an efficient analysis of this issue.

- **Insurance purchasing:** When an organization has to negotiate with insurers or insurance brokers, it has to be aware of the risks it wants to transfer and more precisely of the distribution of the potential losses that could be transferred. If the insurers rely on internal quantitative models generally based on actuarial studies or on expert knowledge (especially for disaster scenarios), the organization should have a more accurate knowledge of its own risks, at least for exceptional events which would not be represented in insurance companies' databases. Therefore both insurers and organizations must share their knowledge to build an accurate model of risks.

- **Program optimization:** The optimization of an existing financing program or the design and selection of a new one require building quantitative models. In the first case, the quantitative model will help to identify the key financing features required to improve the organization coverage. In the second case, plugging the different financing alternatives with the risk model will give the organization a clear view of the risks it would have to retain and transfer.

However, modeling the risks may prove insufficient if we want to address the three challenges listed above. We also have to model the financing program. A general framework can be developed where any financing program can be considered as a set of elementary financing blocks and then used as a base model for the present financing program. This model should suffice for many of the classical financing tools – self-insurance and informal retention, first line insurance, excess insurance, retro-tariff insurance, captive insurer, cat bonds – but it should be adapted to take into account a complex financing set up.

But even if an organization did its best and built an accurate model of risks and financing tools and even if it is able to evaluate the theoretical premium it should pay, the market will decide the actual price the organization should pay to transfer its risks. This market may be unbalanced for some special risks. When the insurance offer is tight, actual premiums could differ from theoretical primes calculated by models. This does not invalidate the need for accurate quantification as, even if the final cost of transfer depends on the insurance market, the organization should be aware of that fact and assess the difference. Also, the liquidity of the insurance markets is likely to increase as they become connected with the capital markets. The efficiency of these markets leads us to expect that the price to be paid for risk transfer will tend to be the "right" one.

Reference

W. Heisenberg (1969), *Der Teil und das Ganze*. Munich: Piper. English: *Physics and Beyond: Encounters and Conversations*. A.J. Pomerans, trans. (New York: Harper & Row).

2.2 BRIEF OVERVIEW OF CINDYNICS

Georges-Yves Kervern

Formerly Ancien Élève de l'Ecole Polytechnique, and founder of Cindynics

Jean-Paul Louisot

Formerly Université Paris 1 Panthéon-Sorbonne, Directeur pédagogique du CARM Institute, Paris, France

One of the major difficulties for a risk manager is not only to identify and quantify the emerging risks, the known-unknowns, but also to imagine those that are not yet emerging, the unknown-unknowns. For that brainstorming exercise there is no relying on past events, on data bank and mathematical models that have no basis to be developed. Even systems safety approaches fall short of a total vision as they incorporate human elements as components of the system with their own rate of failure, but fail to really take account of what is now known as the "human factor". The human element is part of the system, but he acts also to modify it for his benefit. Understanding everyone's motivation and point of view is essential to foresee what may contribute to future risks, opportunities and threats.

It is with this objective in view that some French scientists and executives, led by Georges-Yves Kervern, developed a new approach to foreseeing, rather than forecasting, future developments when they imagined the "hyperspace of danger" and founded what they called Cindynics.

Since the early 1990s, a group of practitioners gathered around Jean-Luc Wybo, a professor at the École Nationale Supérieure des Mines de Paris, to develop practical examples of using Cindynics to understand past complex events and project their findings for future action and decision making. Their application included "Explosion", for example, the explosion at the

AZF factory on September 22, 2001 in France; "Pollution", like that on the beaches of Brittany, "Social Unrest" events, as occurred in the suburbs in France, to name but a few.

Some trace the first step in Cindynics[4] to the earthquake in Lisbon. Science starts where beliefs fade. The earthquake in Lisbon in 1755 was the source of one of the most famous polemic battles between Voltaire and Jean-Jacques Rousseau. The main result was the affirmation that mankind was to refuse fate. This is reflected in Bernstein's[5] comment "Risk is not a fate but a choice."

In a way, the Lisbon episode may well be the first public manifestation of what is essential in managing risks: a clear refusal of passively accepting "fate", a definite will to actively forge the future through domesticating probabilities, thus reducing the field of uncertainty.

However, since the financial crisis of 2008, black swans or fat tails represent a major challenge to all professionals in charge of the management of organization. Clearly, the traditional approaches to identifying and quantifying uncertainties based on probability or trend analysis are at a loss in a world that changes fast and may be subject to unexpected, and sometimes unsuspected ruptures.

As a matter of fact, these "dangerous or hazardous" situations can develop into opportunities or threats depending on how the leadership can anticipate them and exploit them for the benefit of their organization, and its growth in a resilient society.

Human factors are a key factor in the anticipation and development of such situations. Although it is essential that decision-makers learn to make decisions under uncertainty, it is far from sufficient to prepare for the black swans. Furthermore, system safety approaches that consider the human component as a physical element fall short of taking into account the fact that humans are part of a complex system that they influence and try to change to their benefit; and the system can be affected and modified even through a simple act of observation.

In such a volatile situation, the concepts developed as early as the late 1980s could prove very valuable if properly used and translated into practical tools, even though they may appear at first to be too conceptual for practical application. As a matter of fact the concepts of "Cindynic situation" and "hyperspace of danger" allow for the identification of divergences between groups of stakeholders in a given situation and thus allow for the anticipation of "major uncertainties" and to be able to work on them to reduce their likelihood and/or their negative consequences (threats) while enhancing the positive consequences (opportunities).

This scientific approach to perils and hazards was initiated in December 1987 when a conference was called at the UNESCO Palace. The name "Cindynics" was coined from the Greek word "kindunos", meaning hazard. Many industrial sectors were in a state of shock after major catastrophes like Chernobyl, Bhopal, and Challenger. They offered an open field for experience and feedback looping. Since then, Cindynics continues to grow through teaching in many universities in France and abroad. The focal point is a conference organized every other year. Many efforts have been concentrated on axiology and attempts at objective measures. Before his death in December 2008, Professor Georges-Yves Kervern reviewed the presentation that follows (see bibliography) in the light of the most recent developments in Cindynics through the various Conferences, until September 2008.

---

[4] Cindynics, from the Greek Word Kindunos, is the science of danger.
[5] *Against the Gods: The Remarkable Story of Risk*, Peter L. Bernstein, John Wiley & Sons, New York 1996.

2.2.1   Basic Concepts

The first concept, **situation** requires a formal definition. This in turn can be understood only in the light of what constitutes a peril and hazards study. According to the modern theory of description, a *hazardous* **situation** (*Cindynic situation*) can be defined only if:

The field of "hazards study" is clearly identified by
- Limits in time (life span).
- Limits in space (boundaries).
- Limits of the actors' networks involved.

The perspective of the observer studying the system. At this stage of the development of the sciences of hazards, the perspective can follow five main dimensions.
- **First dimension:** Memory, history – **Statistics** (the space of statistics)

  This consists of all the information contained in the data banks of the large institutions, feedback from experience (Electricity of France power plants, Air France flights incidents, forest fires monitored by the Sophia Antipolis Centre of the École des Mines de Paris, claims data gathered by insurers and reinsurers).
- **Second dimension:** Representations and models drawn from facts – **Epistemic** (the space of models)

  This is the scientific body of knowledge that allows for the computation of possible effects using physical and chemical principles, material resistance, propagation, contagion, explosion and geo-Cindynic principles (inundation, volcanic eruptions, earthquake, landslide, tornadoes and hurricane, for example).
- **Third dimension:** Goals and objectives – **Teleological** (the space of goals)

  This requires a precise definition by all the actors, and networks involved in the Cindynic situation of their reasons for living, acting and working.

  In truth, it is an arduous and tiresome task to express clearly why we act as we act, what motivates us. However, it is only too easy to identify an organization that "went overboard" only because it lacked a clearly defined target. For example, there are two common objectives for risk management "survival" and "continuity of customer (public) service". These two objectives lead to a fundamentally different Cindynic attitude. The organization, or its environment, will have to harmonize these two conflicting goals. It is what we call "social transaction", which is hopefully democratically solved.
- **Fourth dimension:** Norms, laws, rules, standards, deontology, compulsory or voluntary, controls, etc. – **Deontological** (the space of rules)

  This includes all the normative sets of rules that make life possible in a given society. For example, the need for a highway code was felt as soon as there were too many automobiles to make it possible to rely on courtesy of each individual driver: the code is compulsory and makes driving on the road reasonably safe and predictable. The rules for behaving in society, like how to use a knife or a fork when eating, are aimed at reducing the risk of injuring one's neighbor as well as a way to identify social origins.

  On the other hand, there are situations in which the codification is not yet clarified. For example, skiers on the same track may be of widely different expertise thus endangering each other. In addition some use equipment not necessarily compatible with the safety of others (cross country skis and snowboards, etc.). How to conduct a serious analysis of accidents on skiing domains? Should experience-drawn codes be enforced? How can rules

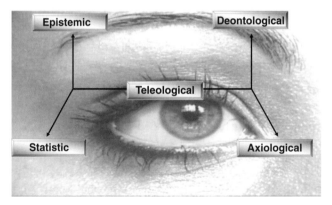

Figure 2.1   Hyperspace of Danger – the result of the look.

be defined if objectives are not clearly defined beforehand? Should we promote personal safety or freedom of experimentation?

- **Fifth dimension:** Value systems – **Axiological** (the space of values)

    It is the set of fundamental objectives and values shared by a group of individuals or other collective actors involved in a Cindynic situation.

    As an illustration, when the forefathers declared that "the motherland is in danger", the word motherland, or "patria" (hence the word patriot), meant the shared heritage that, after scrutiny, can be best summarized in the fundamental values shared. The integrity of this set of values may lead the population to accept heavy sacrifices. When the media use the word apocalyptic or catastrophic, they often mean a situation in which our value system is at stake.

These five dimensions, or spaces, can be represented on a five-axis diagram and Figure 2.1 is a representation of the "hyperspace of danger".

In combining these five dimensions in a different way – these five spaces – one can identify some traditional fields of study and research.

Combining facts (statistics) and models gives the feedback loop so crucial to most large corporations' risk managers.

Combining objectives, norms and values leads to practical ethics. Social workers have identified authority functions in this domain. These functions are funded on values that frame the objectives and define norms that they enforce hereafter. If there is no source of authority to enforce the norms, daily minor breaches will soon lead to major breaches and soon the land will dissolve into a primitive jungle.

This new extended framework provides a broader picture that allows visualizing the limitations of the actions too often conducted with a narrow scope. Any hazard study can be efficient only if complete, i.e. extended to all the actors and networks involved in the situation. Then, the analysis must cover all of the five dimensions identified above.

2.2.2   Dysfunctions

The first stage of a diagnostic to be established as described above consists in identifying the networks and their state in the five dimensions or spaces of the Cindynic model. The next step will be to recognize the incoherencies, or dissonances, between two or several networks of actors involved in a given situation.

These dissonances must be analyzed from the point of view of each of the actors. It is therefore necessary to analyze dissonances in each dimension and between the dimensions. In this framework, the risk control instrument we call prevention is aimed at reducing the level of hazard in any situation. In a social environment, for example, some actors may feel that an "explosion is bound to occur". This is what is called the Cindynic potential. The potential increases with the dissonances existing between the various networks on the five spaces.

A prevention campaign will apply to the dissonances: an attempt at reducing them without trying to homogenize all five dimensions for all the actors. A less ambitious goal will be to attempt to develop for each dimension a "minimum platform" shared by all the actors' networks thus ensuring a common set of values as a starting point. In other words, it is essential to find:

- **Figures, facts or data,** accepted by the various actors as a statistical truth.
- Some **models**, as a common body of knowledge.
- **Objectives**, that can be shared by the various actors.
- **Norms**, rules or deontological principles that all may agree to abide by.
- **Values**, to which all may adhere, like solidarity, no exclusion, transparency and truthfulness.

The minimum foundation is to establish a list of points of agreement and points of disagreement. Developing a common list of points of disagreement is essential.

The definition of these minimum platforms is the result of:

- Lengthy negotiations between the various actors' networks; and, more often
- One particular network that acts as a catalyst or mediator. It is the coordinator of the prevention campaign for the entire situation.

The "defiance" between two networks, face to face, has been defined as a function of the dissonances between these two networks following the five dimensions. Establishing confidence, a trusting relationship, will require the reduction of the dissonances through negotiations, which will be the task of the prevention campaign. This process can be illustrated by three examples.

Family systematic therapy: Dr. Catherine Guitton[6] focused her approach on dissonances between networks:

- The family requesting therapeutic help.
- The family reunited with the addition of two therapists.

When healing is reached on the patient pointed to by the family, the result was obtained thanks to work on the dissonances rather than a direct process on the patients themselves.

Adolescents and violence: Dr. M. Monroy's[7] research demonstrates that violence typically found in the 15–24 age group is related to a tear, a disparity along the five dimensions. This system can be divided into two sub-systems between which a tremendous tension builds up.

- The traditional family with its set of facts, models, goals, norms and values.
- An antagonistic unit conceived by the adolescent, opposed, often diametrically and violently, to the "family tradition".

---

[6] Doctor Catherine Guitton, Psychiatrist, Hôpital Psychiatrique Paul Guiraud, Villejuif (France).
[7] Doctor Michel Monroy, La société défensive (French Edition), PUF, Paris (Feb 15, 2003).

These dissonances can lead the adolescent to a process of negotiation and aggression with violent phases in which he will play his trump card, his own life. From this may stem aggressions, accidents and even, sometimes, fatal solutions of this process of scission, specific to adolescence.

The case of the religious sects: It is during this process of scission that the success of some sects in attracting an adolescent following may be found. Their ability to conceal from the adolescents their potential dangers comes from the fact they sell them a ready-made "turn-key" hyperspace. The kit, involving all five dimensions, is provided when the adolescent is ripe. As a social dissident, any adolescent needs to develop his own set of references in each of the five dimensions.

Violence in the sects stems from the fact that the kit thus provided is sacred. The sacredness prevents any questioning of the kit. Any escape is a threat to the sacredness of the kit. Therefore, it must be repressed through violence, including brainwashing and/or physical abuse or destruction, as befits any totalitarian regimes that have become masters in large-scale violence.

In a recent book on the major psychological risk (see Bibliography) where the danger genesis in family is analyzed according to the Cindynic framework, Dr. M. Monroy tries to grasp all the issues by numbering all the actors involved in most of these situations.

Network I	Family
Network II	Friends and peers
Network III	Schooling and professional environment
Network IV	Other risk takers or stakeholders (*bike riders, drug users, delinquents*)
Network V	Other networks embodying political and civilian society (*Sources of norms, rules and values*)
Network VI	Social workers and therapists

This list of standard networks allows spotting the dissonances between them that build the Cindynic potential of the situation.

In the case of exposures confronting an organization, an analysis of the actors' networks according to the five dimensions facilitates the identification of the "deficits" specific to the situation. For example, the distances between what is and what should be provides an insight of what changes a prevention campaign should bring about. These deficits should be identified through a systemic approach of hazardous situations. It can be:

- Total absence of a dimension or even several (*no data available*).
- Inadequate content of a dimension (*an objective such as "let us have fun"*).
- Degeneration, most often a disorder, of a dimension (*Mafia model in Russia*).
- Blockade in a plan combining two dimensions:
  - Blockade of feedback from experience (dimensions statistics and models).
  - Ethical blockade of authority functions insuring that rules are respected in the social game (dimensions norms and values).
- Disarticulated hyperspace in the five dimensions creating isolation, lack of cohesiveness between the dimensions. (*Fiefdoms splitting a corporation*).

These deficits always appear in reports by commissions established to inquire on catastrophes. It is striking to realize how all these reports' conclusions narrow down to a few recurring explanations.

How do these situations change? Situations with their dissonances and their deficits "explode" naturally unless they change slowly under the leadership of a prevention campaign manager.

In the first case, non-intentional actors of change are involved. The catastrophic events taking place bring about a violent and sudden revision of the content of the five dimensions among the networks involved in the "accident". Usually all five dimensions are modified: revised facts, new models, new goals, implicit or explicit, new rules, and new values.

In the second case, that all organizations should prefer, the transformer chooses to act as such. He is the coordinator of the negotiation process that involves all the various actors in the situation. Deficits and dissonances are reduced through "negotiation" and "mediation". The Cindynic potential is diminished so that it is lower than the trigger point (critical point) inherent to the situation.

2.2.3   General principles and axioms

Exchanges between different industrial sectors, Cindynic conferences and the research on complexity by Professor Le Moigne[8] (University of Aix en Provence, derived from the work of Nobel Prize winner, Herbert A. Simon[9]) have developed some general principles. The Cindynic axioms explain the emergence of dissonances and deficits.

1. CYNDYNIC AXIOM 1 – RELATIVITY: The perception of danger varies according to each actor's situation. Therefore, there is no "objective" measure of danger. This principle is the basis for the concept of situation.
2. CINDYNIC AXIOM 2 – CONVENTION: The measures of risk (traditionally measured by the vector Frequency – Severity) depend on convention between actors.
3. CINDYNIC AXIOM 3 – GOALS DEPENDENCY: Goals are directly impacting the assessment of risks. The actors in the networks may have conflicting perceived objectives. It is essential to try to define and prioritize the goals of the various actors involved in the situation (insufficient clarification of goals is a current pitfall in complex systems).
4. CINDYNIC AXIOM 4 – AMBIGUITY: This states that there is always a lack of clarity in the five dimensions. It is a major task of prevention to reduce these ambiguities.
5. CINDYNIC AXIOM 5 – AMBIGUITY REDUCTION: Accidents and catastrophes are accompanied by brutal transformations in the five dimensions. The reduction of the ambiguity (or contradictions) of the content of the five dimensions will happen when they are excessive. This reduction can be involuntary and brutal, resulting in an accident, or voluntary and progressive achieved through a prevention process.

   The theories by Lorenz on chaos and Prigogine on bifurcations offer an essential contribution at this stage. It should be noted that this principle is in agreement with a broad definition of the field of risk management. It applies to any event generated or accompanied by a rupture in parameters and constraints essential to the management of the organization.

---

[8] **Jean-Louis Le Moigne** is a French specialist of systemic and constructivist epistemology.

[9] **Herbert Alexander Simon** (June 15, 1916 – February 9, 2001) was among the founding fathers of several of today's important scientific domains, including artificial intelligence, information processing, decision-making, problem-solving, attention economics, organization theory, complex systems, and computer simulation of scientific discovery. He coined the terms bounded rationality and satisficing, and was the first to analyze the architecture of complexity and to propose a preferential attachment mechanism to explain power law distributions, http://en.wikipedia.org/wiki/Wikipedia:Text_of_Creative_Commons_Attribution-ShareAlike_3.0_Unported_License, http://en.wikipedia.org/wiki/Herbert_Alexander_Simon.

6. CINDYNIC AXIOM 6 – CRISIS: This states that a crisis results from a tear in the social fabric. This means a dysfunction in the networks of actors involved in a given situation. Crisis management exists in an emergency reconstitution of the networks. It should be noted that this principle is in agreement with the definition of a crisis as included here above and the principle of crisis management stated.

7. CINDYNIC AXIOM 7 – AGO-ANTAGONISTIC CONFLICT: Any therapy is inherently dangerous. Human actions, medications are accompanied with inherent dangers. There is always a curing aspect, reducing danger (cindynolitic), and an aggravating factor, creating new danger (cindynogenetic).

The main benefit of the use of these principles is to reduce the time lost in fruitless unending discussions on:

The accuracy of the quantitative evaluations of catastrophes – Quantitative measures result from conventions, scales or unit of measures (axiom 2);
Negative effects of proposed prevention measures – In any action positive and negative impacts are intertwined (axiom 7).

2.2.4   Perspectives

In a Cindynic approach, hazard can be characterized by:

• Various **actors' networks** facing hazardous situations.
• The **way they approach** the whole situation.
• The structuring of these approaches following the **5 dimensions** (Statistics, models, objectives, norms and values).
• The identification of **"dissonances"** between the various actors' networks.
• The **deficits** that impact the dimensions.

Dissonances and deficits follow a limited number of "Cindynic principles" that can be broadly applied. They also offer fruitful insights to measures to control exposures that impact the roots of the situation rather than, as is too often the case, reduce only the superficial effects.

For more than a decade now, the approach has been applied with success to technical hazards, acts of God and more recently on psychological hazards in the family and in the city. It can surely be successfully extended to situations of violence (workplace, schools, neighborhoods, etc.). In some cases, it will be necessary to revisit the 7 principles to facilitate their use in some specific situations.

The objective is clear: Situations that could generate violence should be detected as early as possible, they should then be analyzed thoroughly, their criticality reduced and, if possible, eliminated.

Cindynics offer a scientific approach to anticipate risks, act and improve the management of risks. Thus, they offer a new perspective to the risk management professional, they dramatically enlarge the scope of his/her action in line with the trend towards holistic or strategic risk management while providing an enriched set of tools for a rational action at the roots of danger.

Bibliography

Kervern, G-Y. (1993) *La Culture Réseau (Ethique et Ecologie de l'entreprise)*, Paris: Editions ESKA.
Kervern, G-Y. (1994) Latest Advances in Cindynics. *Economica.*

Kervern, G-Y. (1995) Éléments fondamentaux des cindyniques. *Economica.*

Kervern, G-Y. and Rubise, P. (1991) L'archipel du danger. Introduction aux cindyniques. *Economica.*

Kervern, G-Y. and Boulenger, P. (2008) CINDYNIQUES Concepts et mode d'emploi. *Economica.*

Kervern, G-Y. *The Evil Genius in Front of the Risk Science: The Cindynics.* Risque et génie civil. Colloque, Paris, France (08/11/2000).

Wybo, J-L. et al., *Introduction aux Cindyniques.* Paris (France): ESKA, 1998.

2.3   RISK ASSESSMENT OR EXPOSURE DIAGNOSTIC

Jean-Paul Louisot

Formerly Université Paris 1 Panthéon-Sorbonne, Directeur pédagogique du CARM Institute, Paris, France

2.3.1   Foreword

The purpose of this article is to zoom in on a subject not really addressed in the RM Standards published worldwide, including ISO 31000; it proposes a practical tool for identifying, analysing and prioritizing the portfolio of exposures, and opportunities, as well as threats that confront any organization that envisions its future.

The "space of exposure" will prove a powerful tool for all embarking in the ERM (Enterprise-wide journey) to help "lift the fog of uncertainties in decision making and implementing" to paraphrase a recurring theme in Felix Kloman's[10] conferences and presentations.

2.3.2   Threats and Opportunities: How to deal with uncertainty in a changing world?

The future is never known with certainty, "Who knows what tomorrow will bring?" but managing organizations means making decisions, enlightened by information drawn from different methods that shed light on the future.

For a long time, men have tried to improve tomorrow by influencing the forces that guide the future, or by offering sacrifices to the gods. It was only at the end of the seventeenth century, that Pascal and Fermat and their successors, including Bernoulli, started developing ways to open the gates to the future by drawing from past and present experiences. Probability and trend analysis were the first approaches to see through the "cloud of unknowing".[11]

During the last decade of the twentieth century, the development of risk management, resting on more elaborate forecasting models, seems to have focused on only the downside aspect of risk, the threats, and has slowly put aside the upside, usually called "opportunities". Confronted with the uncertainties of the future, organizations are rediscovering that "threats" and "opportunities" – the yin and the yang of risk – represent two sides of the same coin.

It has never been more important that directors and officers, as well as investors, remember the basics of economic and financial theories. Risk is inherent to the undertaking of any human endeavor. Indeed, it is the acceptance of a significant level of risk that provides the type of return on investment that is expected by investors. The theory of finance defines the expected rate of return as the sum of two components:

> Basic return, of the risk less investment (usually measured by the US treasury bond rate of similar maturity); and

---

[10] Felix Kloman IRM Annual Conference 2005.

[11] The cloud of unknowing is a theological essay written in England in the fourteenth century, by an author whose attempts to discover his identity have so far failed.

The risk premium, i.e. an additional return that the investor deserves for having accepted a higher volatility of profit, to enhance some societal goal, like improved technology, a new drug, etc.

Of course, all volatilities are not "equal". Traditionally, scientific authors distinguish between probabilistic future (risk) and non-probabilistic future (hazard).

Most of the time, deciders are in the first situation (risk) when they have enough reliable data to compute law of probability or draw a trend line for future events and can define confidence intervals, i.e. limits between the likely and the unlikely future. For example, in analysing past economic conditions, it should be possible to have a reasonable idea of the numbers of cars to be sold in the EU, in the US or in Australia. The booming and recent Chinese market may not lend itself easily to this type of reliable trending. While an automobile company can predict with a fair degree of precision its mature market, forecasts are far more volatile in emerging markets. Therefore, there is a higher risk to market cars in emerging markets, but the reward may be much higher in case of success.

On the other hand, when launching a new model, especially if some defects are revealed in the first year of sales, it is much more difficult to justify the investments if reliable forecasts can prove the existing models will be profitable. Banks have experienced a similar situation when they embarked on the management of operational risks to comply with the new Basel II[12] requirements. When no data bank is at hand, experts' opinions will have to be formalized using a Bayesians network[13] approach and scenarios.

As a matter of fact the above examples might be considered as incorrect for looking only at the negative side of risks. However, operational risks are also a significant opportunity for competitive advantage for the banks that invest more than others in this endeavor. Not only are banks likely to "save" on internal funds, they may even gain expertise that could benefit their clients in the longer term.

A current trend in risk-management is to minimize risk silos in order to reach a real global optimization of the management of risk, taking into account for each unit, each process, each project both threats and opportunities. The organization is analysed as a portfolio of risks with an upside and downside that must be optimized, much as an investor would optimize a personal portfolio of shares.

---

[12] **Basel II** is a document summarizing the recommendations on financial regulation developed by the Basel Committee on Banking Supervision.

Basel II, published in June 2004, was intended to create an international reference for control agency to verify the adequacy of capital banks can provide to face their financial and operational risks. One of the objectives is to ensure sufficient international consistency to avoid a competition to the lowest common denominator. Clearly Basel II was unable to prevent the debacle of 2008 mostly because it was not really fully implemented at that time mostly due to political difficulty.

Now that it is more generally implemented it has not been brought to the test but while Basel III was negotiated the crisis was in the head of the negotiators and it seems that more stringent regulation may become acceptable as is evidenced by the legislation passed in the USA.

[13] **Bayesian network:** "A Bayesian network, or belief network, is a probabilistic graphical model (a type of statistical model) that represents a set of random variables and their conditional dependencies via a directed acyclic graph (DAG). For example, a Bayesian network could represent the probabilistic relationships between diseases and symptoms. Given symptoms, the network can be used to compute the probabilities of the presence of various diseases.

Formally, Bayesian networks are graphs on which the nodes represent random variables in the Bayesian sense: they may be observable quantities, latent variables, unknown parameters or hypotheses. Links between nodes represent conditional dependencies; nodes which are not connected represent variables which are conditionally independent of each other. Each node is associated with a probability function that takes as input a particular set of values for the node's parent variables and gives the probability of the variable represented by the node. For example, if the parents are m Boolean variables then the probability function could be represented by a table of 2^m entries, one entry for each of the 2^m possible combinations of its parents being true or false. Similar ideas may be applied to undirected, and possibly cyclic, graphs; such are called Markov networks.

Efficient algorithms exist that perform inference and learning in Bayesian networks. Bayesian networks that model sequences of variables (*e.g.* speech signals or protein sequences) are called dynamic Bayesian networks. Generalizations of Bayesian networks that can represent and solve decision problems under uncertainty are called influence diagrams." Bayesian Network: http://en.wikipedia.org/wiki/Wikipedia:Text_of_Creative_Commons_Attribution-ShareAlike_3.0_Unported_License, http://en.wikipedia.org/wiki/Bayesian _network, Accessed 11/13/13.

In practice, this integration of all risks is achieved more easily for the financial consequences at the risk financing level. More and more economic actors consider their risk financing exercise as part of their overall long-term financial strategy. However, it is possible to integrate risk assessment and loss control provided all in charge (at whatever level) are included in the risk management process. This integrated approach is now called ERM and within ERM the managers become "risk owners". The globalization of risk management is ensured through the principle of subsidiarity: the directors and officers should deal only with the exposures that have impact on the strategy, assured that the risk management process implemented throughout the organization will take care of "minor" threats and seize "tactical" opportunities. That should sound familiar to many in Australia, as this is a fundamental tenet of management guidelines in the Australian/New Zealand Framework (companion to AS/NZ 4360 used in various versions since 1995 and finally replaced since 2009 by the adoption of ISO 31000 under the name AS/NZ 31000:2009).

What Do We Mean by Risk?

Risk management, risk mitigation and risk financing – indeed the word "risk" is used by all risk management professionals as well as by many others in their daily life. But do we really know what we mean by risk? The Australian RM standard states, ". . . the chance of something happening that will have an impact on objectives", whereas ISO 31000 proposes an even wider definition: "the effect of uncertainties on objectives". But this is not the final word because there are other common understandings of the word risk.

Risk (pure, speculative, hybrid)

This definition is most commonly used by specialists, which is compatible with the definition of risk in the ISO 31000:2009 standard, depending on the nature of the consequences involved.

Systematic and Unsystematic Risk

Systematic risk (*i.e. non diversifiable*) is the result of non-hazardous causes that may happen simultaneously. That means that it does not lend itself to diversification. As an example, all economic actors can be affected by a downturn in the economy or a rise in interest rates.

Unsystematic risk (*i.e. diversifiable*) is the result of hazardous causes and lends itself to probabilistic approaches. They are specific to each individual economic entity and offer the possibility to build a "balanced portfolio" of risk sharing. Therefore, insurance cover might be designed to cover them.

Insurable Risk

This is a more restrictive definition as it refers to an event for which there is an insurance market. Furthermore the work "risk" is used commonly by insurance specialists to refer to the entity at risk, the peril covered, the quality of the entity risk management practices (level of risk), and the overall assessment of a site ("good risk for its category").

One must be cautious because this commonly used word may have totally different meanings for different individuals. This requires all involved to be aware of that diversity when communicating and consulting in the boardroom or with different stakeholders.

This reality must be kept in mind when communicating about risks, whatever the media or audience. Any "risk management" professional should be always aware of one of the main challenges and hazards of risk awareness and understanding: how risk is perceived by stakeholders and decision makers is more important than any "scientific" assessment of risk. Recommendation: Whenever possible avoid using such an uncertain word; another, less common, should be substituted: exposure, threat, opportunity, peril, impact, etc., are acceptable alternatives but there is a caveat here as well – the use of any term depends on which facet of "risk" is the subject of the discussion! Sometimes, a specifically crafted professional word needing some explanation may prove safer than a commonly used word that may be understood differently within a group. A common taxonomy of terms is vital not only for understanding but also in developing consistent data across the organization.

What is an Exposure?

The word "risk" has several meanings and can be misleading when used in a professional context, especially in the case of an organization communicating on risks with a broader audience. Therefore, practitioners and academics in risk management need to define a more precise concept. This is what George Head, who developed the Associate in Risk Management designation, attempted with the word "exposure" as early as 1975. However Head's definition considered only the downside of risks. A new definition more appropriate for today's global approach is required:

> An exposure is characterized by the consequences on its objectives resulting from the occurrence of an unexpected (random) event that modify the resources of an organization.

This definition allows for an exposure to be clearly identified with three factors:

Risk Object: The resource "at risk" that the organization needs to reach its goals and missions. We have defined 5 classes of resources: Human, Technical, Information, Partners and Finance as well as the expression "Free" for those taken from the environment without a payment (externalities)(these classes are reviewed below).

Random Event (Peril): It is "what" may happen that would modify permanently or temporarily the level of the organizational resources resulting either in an opportunity (sudden increase in the level or quality of the resource) or a threat (sudden decrease in the level or quality of the resource). The likelihood of the event will lead to a measure of the "frequency".

Potential Impact (Severity): Most organizations strive to quantify the financial impact of the exposure identified through the resources "at risk" and random events. However, the goals and objectives of a given organization are not all necessarily translatable in financial terms. For example: ethics and corporate social responsibilities must be also taken into account. However, one should keep in mind that the "severity" is nearly always measured in financial terms.

However, it should be noted that not all consequences touch only the organization under study; therefore, especially for the downside risk, it is essential to distinguish:

Primary & Secondary damages: i.e. the impact on the organization itself and its resources through a loss of assets or potential loss of revenues.

Tertiary damages: i.e. the impacts on all third parties and the environment. Special attention should be given to impacts on the organization's partners (both downstream, customers or clients, upstream, suppliers or subcontractors, and temporary for special projects). The analysis should extend to all consequences and not be limited to liabilities, as long-term consequences with no immediate legal implication can prove costly, specifically for reputation. On the other hand "tertiary damages" involving contractual, tort or penal liabilities will impact the organization's resources through its executives, employees, finances and even its "social licence to operate".

"Quaternary" damages: those long-term impacts on the trust and confidence of "stake-holders" that may eventually taint or destroy the organization's reputation, and its "social licence to operate".

In a complete analysis, the upside risk should be included, as the threats to one organization may well create an opportunity for another organization!

Once the concept of "exposure" is clearly mastered, it provides a model to develop a systematic approach to managing risks. As a result, any organization will be seen as a portfolio of exposures, with a special attention to those that represent challenges to the optimal implementation of a strategy. The risk register suggested by the Australian standards appears as a list of "risk assets". Therefore, the decision tools developed in finance for the management of investment portfolios – the portfolio theory – are pertinent towards implementing a rational decision making process in risk management that will ultimately lead to sound governance.

Once again, the concept of exposure constitutes a step towards the integration of risk management in an organization's strategic process by leveraging opportunities and mitigating threats, not only as they are anticipated at the development stage but also as they materialize along the path of the implementation towards achieving strategic goals.

What are the Resources at Risk?

Any organization can be defined as a dynamic combination of resources pulled together to reach its goals and objectives. Therefore, developing and communicating these objectives is at the heart of any risk management, indeed any management, exercise. This is the reason why, for risk management purposes, we have defined an organization as a portfolio of exposures, both threats and opportunities, to be managed in the most efficient manner to reach these goals and objectives under any circumstances. Within the context of a competitive economy, efficiency means either to reach the most ambitious objectives with the available resources or reach the assigned goals with as little resource as possible.

While many would agree on this simple approach, it must be determined how many classes of resources should be considered. The model proposed here is limited to a small number of classes, five, that will take into account practically all the resources involved in the management of an organization, which can be used to list the resources in a specific organization. This will permit a systematic and global identification because the classes of exposures will be directly linked to the classes of resources. Each of these classes calls for specific forms of loss control measures. Thus, the five classes of resources are as follows:

H = Human: This includes all personnel linked to the organization through a labor or an executive contract. Their specific experiences and competencies are an asset for the organization although they are not always assessed and valued in the accounts. For this resource, elements like age, gender, and marital status that may have an impact on the actual capacities should be carefully monitored. In other words, the exposure associated with the human resources should be investigated both as key persons, and labor costs, or social liability (pensions and employee benefits). The main element to risk management is linked with what is now usually known under the term "knowledge management" and sometimes talent management. Therefore, it does not refer only to technical skills but also to social skills and attitude that are essential to embedding risk management throughout an organization.

T = Technical: These are buildings, equipment and tools, i.e. all physical assets under the direct control of the organization. The legal status of those assets is of secondary importance; the organization may own, lease, rent them or simply keep them for a third party. What is essential is that the organization has complete responsibility for those items. Even if there are contractual terms over how to manage them, the organization is completely in charge of the management of risks to them and from them.

I = Information: All the information that flows throughout the organization, in whatever form (electronic, paper, and human brains). This may cover information concerning the organization itself, information regarding others (medical files for patients in a hospital) but also what others may want to try to know, and what the organization wants to know about others (economic intelligence of different forms). Also included are intangibles like goodwill, credit score, rating agency evaluation, and other financial or cross-discipline metrics.

Furthermore, the ability to do business depends on the trust established with others: the perception that all the stakeholders have of the organization is an essential "asset", the risks to reputation have become an important item in boards' risk agendas.

P = Partners (upstream and downstream): They are all the economic partners that the organization is intertwined with (and recognized by the World Economic Forum) and specifically upstream (suppliers, service providers and sub-contractors), and downstream (customers and distribution channels). Of those some are key, those without which the organization could not continue to operate, or operate efficiently, and they must be identified clearly if the dependencies on the supply chain are to be treated appropriately. It is an essential source of exposure in an economy where outsourcing has become so important. In some organizations they include volunteers contributing their time and talent, sometimes money, to the organization.

F = Financial: This comprises all the financial streams that flow in and out of the organization, short-term (cash, liquid assets, short-term liabilities) and medium or long-term (capital and reserve, long-term debt, project financing, etc.). In other words, all the risks linked with the financial strategy of the organization and the balance between return and solvency.

Free Resources = However, the analysis would fall short if the organization did not take into account its non-contractual exchanges with the environment, i.e. those resources that the organization does not pay directly for and yet that could prevent it from operating smoothly. In other terms, these "free resources" that do not appear in the organization accounting books and yet are essential: air quality, access to sites, social licence to operate, etc. Further investigation of those would be warranted.

2.3.3   How to Manage the Risks Derived From Partners' Resources?

Market globalization has generated ever more complex webs that link many organizations worldwide through the externalization process. The large conglomerate has become more and more focused on conception, marketing and assembling parts from all over the world. Many smaller or medium size organizations are only one cog in a very complex supply network.

In most situations, we are confronted with a network of partners rather than a chain, indeed a cloud when the frontiers are not completely defined. This is the reason why procurement risk management has become the backbone of most organizations producing goods and services, while their production relies on an ever-expanding number of outsourced tasks.

Therefore, what "partners' resources" encompass are raw materials, parts, equipment and services as well as distribution networks on which organizations depend on a daily basis for their own operations. These resources can be grouped in three distinct categories:

Upstream resources: These are purchased by suppliers, service providers and sub-contractors, and delivered to production sites by transporters.

Lateral resources: These are goods and services provided to clients and that are integrated in complex systems, projects and products, of which your own contribution is part. You may not know them and yet there is a de facto solidarity that links you together. As an illustration you may produce tires that match a given sort of wheel and when the manufacturer goes bankrupt, your client does not need your tires anymore.

Downstream resources: These are customers or intermediaries, including distribution networks and the transporters that deliver the goods, and financial institutions that guarantee the successful conclusion of transactions.

It is essential to clearly identify all the elements of this class of resources while conducting a risk management assessment as the same principles apply but with a major difference that the three categories have in common: the organization is dependent for its own security on the actions and attitudes that it cannot monitor daily as is the case for the resources under its direct command. In other words, consciously or unconsciously, the organization has "transferred" to a third party an essential part of its risk management activity. Therefore, the crucial question in procurement risk management is to find ways to ensure the organization's overall resilience should one of the "partners' resources" fail to be delivered, in time and to the quality desired.

The basic rule of thumb is not to be too dependent on one given partner, be it a supplier or a customer. Basic common sense applies here: "Don't put all your eggs in the same basket." Most recommend having at least two or three sources at all time. However, this is not always possible, especially when there is a very advanced technology, patents, or some very specific know-how that can only be obtained from one source. Furthermore, the multiple sources must be balanced against the cost of maintaining several suppliers, with the advantage of them entering a competition to retain the organization's business. Finally, there is increased risk of information leaks if the relationship involves sharing trade secrets of any sort.

Beyond, this basic principle, the same rule applies upstream and downstream, which could be called the **"3 Cs"** rule.

Choose – You must choose carefully the partners you want to do business with. First, you must evaluate if the products or services offered meet your needs in quality, quantity and timely delivery. Then you must investigate their financial strength, because a partner that would fail rapidly would be of no use. Furthermore, it is essential to assess their "ethical compatibility" with your own values, specifically those you stress when exchanges with stakeholders take place (one must remember that a major sports good manufacturer went through a difficult period in 1998 during the Football World Cup when it was revealed in the media that a supplier of a supplier was using underpaid, underage children to produce the balls).

Contract – The quality of risk management throughout the partner's operations must be contractually sealed. It is even more imperative because there is no universally accepted standard so far, contrary to quality. It must provide for your access to site and documentation to ensure that proper risk management is designed and implemented. Also, the contract should resolve ahead of their occurrence any potential conflicts so that the partnership can remain harmonious even through difficult times. For many organizations, too much time is devoted by lawyers to defining the products or services involved in a contract, too little to solving conflicts ahead of time.

Control – It is essential that staff regularly meet with the organization's partners and be kept informed of developments to make sure they remain the reliable sources its leaders wish to deal with. You must be aware of major changes in their leadership, their ownership, their environment and their strategy.

As far as lateral resources are concerned, unless you are a project leader, which is rarely the case for small or medium size organizations, they are typically partners you have not chosen and you may have no contract with whereas each of them has a contract with the leader. Therefore, the only way to ensure the quality of the risk management is through your common partner, project leader, large firm, etc. In your dealings with the team leader, you should have access to the list of all those involved in the project you share.

Finally, remember that when you transfer risks, you are still socially responsible for the well-being of those who are stakeholders in the overall process. If a member of the team betrays their trust, all the members of the team will suffer. In other terms, risks to reputation are never transferred!

2.3.4   Are There Any "Free" Resources? Taking into Account Externalities

In our global economy, who would dare to claim that there are resources that we do not pay for? Clearly any organization needs both internal and external resources that have been detailed in a previous question. By external we mean those exchanged with the economic partners both up and down stream. These resources are paid for. However, there are also non-transactional exchanges with the environment that are essential for the organization's development, even its survival. These resources received from the environment without direct financial compensation are labeled "free resources" insofar as they do not appear on the organization's accounting documents. However, the term environment is too broad and in each situation should be investigated:

Physical environment: Comprising air, water and earth.

Political, legal and social environment: This requires looking at all of the aspects of life conditions and society organization, including cultural differences.

Competitive environment: This entails looking at all aspects of the current competition, technological breakthrough, and shift in consumers' tastes, but also substitutes for the organization's products and services. Furthermore, one should always analyse the reason for the appeal of our offering; the notion of "magnet site" allows for the investigation of the circumstances outside of our management sphere that are key to our success.

These exchanges represent what economists call "externalities" that are not part of any contractual transaction with economic partners. Remember that these externalities can be positive (society receives a benefit from a private transaction, which is additional to the private transaction), or negative (society incurs a cost additional to the private transaction). It should be noted that the domain of these externalities may vary from country to country; in terms of pollution, the development of codes to protect the environment has forced the "internalization" of the costs of cleaning sites or restricting contaminant releases as private producers have seen some "social costs" transferred to their operation.

It is crucial for any organization planning to diversify or enter new markets in any locale to be aware of its needs for "free resources" as they may not be available in the prospective locations and/or countries involved. More precisely, a very successful SME might well be unaware of the specific circumstances that led to success in its original location that may not be found in the proposed sites, or lost in the case of fusion or acquisition.

The concept can be illustrated with some specific situations keeping in mind that these are only common cases and that each individual organization must conduct a systematic analysis of its circumstances:

• There are industrial processes that use substantial amounts of "cooling water"; the water is released downstream with no chemical or biological pollution, but at a higher temperature than the intake upstream. Have we imagined extreme winters (the river is frozen), summers (a temperature that is too high does not allow for a correct biological exchange or fish cannot survive at the release temperature for lack of oxygen)? In a new proposed location, is there upstream a chemical plant that could release toxics with potential damage to our installation, or a production interruption?

• Throughout the plant, the air must be of a quality compatible with human life and even satisfying local ordinances regarding "workplace conditions". Is there a neighboring plant that could release a toxic cloud? On the other hand some production processes require the atmosphere to be totally cleaned of any dust. Is it possible that very fine particles would slip through our filters polluting our products (like optical lenses or medical devices)?

• A single historic bridge is the only direct route to a factory. After a minor earthquake, concerns are raised as to its long-term robustness. Local authorities decide to limit its access to trucks of less than 5 metric tonnes. It may be that the new route from a key supplier to the factory is so much longer that delays and costs increases make the plant "uneconomical" with no easy remedy.

• Production in a new country, with substantial gains on wages and salary costs: but is the country politically sound? Is there any threat of nationalization should an opposition party seize power? Will the "social and political" climate remain favorable to foreign investment?

• The precaution principle[14] is now incorporated into the French constitution. It is not yet clear what the consequences will be for the corporation whose domicile or activities are in France. Could it be that innovative products sold in France will in the future come from foreign companies?

• Local cultures may have an impact on the way business is conducted, be it only working hours. When entering a new country, a new province, has the organization questioned its commercial and human resources practices to align them with local customs, even beyond mere compliance to local legislation?

• Do customers come to us because of the superior quality of our products or services or merely for convenience? A retailer in the commercial centre where a national brand hypermarket

---

[14] The Precaution Principle aims at framing and guiding decision making, through a compulsory global assessment of risk for all stakeholders of an organization.

draws customers should ask himself such a question. But it could be also the case for a restaurant close to an industrial zone from which he draws most of his clientele; what would happen if the industrials chose to establish a restaurant for their workforce?

2.3.5 What Do We Mean by Peril or Hazard?

An organization has been defined as a portfolio of risks or exposures, i.e. threats and opportunities. Each exposure is defined by three dimensions – resource at risk, peril or hazard and impact. Thus the peril is the second of these parameters.

Some define a peril as that which gives rise to a loss whereas a hazard would be that which influences the operation of the peril, i.e. fire would be a peril, a house that could burn a hazard. For others the peril is commonly defined as the cause of loss, whereas the hazard is commonly defined as a condition that creates or increases the chance that a peril will occur.

Here for management purposes, a "peril" is an event that may or may not happen, the occurrence of which would change in a drastic manner the level of one of the organization's resources: for the downside, the resource would be destroyed partially or totally, permanently or temporarily, for the upside a sudden increase of the resource would become available. In most organizations, for risk management purposes, only the downside impact would be assessed.

The two dimension vector, resource/peril, identifies the exposure, and is the foundation for the analysis phase that investigates the impact, quantifying the financial or other consequences, without any consideration for reduction methods.

"Known" perils are qualified with a probability measured through experimental probability drawn from historical data and/or mathematical models. In other cases, the "known unknown", only a qualitative approach will be possible for lack of reliable data as in the case of emerging risks and even more so for the "unknown unknown" fat tails or a black swan event. Under such circumstances a qualitative scale (exceptional, rare, infrequent, or frequent) could prove useful, provided the group in charge of evaluating the probabilities has a common definition for these terms (once a decade, once a year, twice a year, once a month, etc.).

Many phenomena follow normal distributions (bell-shaped curves) which are completely defined by two parameters:

- Mean or "average", e.g. hurricanes will hit Florida 4 times a year on average.
- Standard deviation, which allows to define a confidence interval (i.e. the lower and higher level of a given phenomenon, if the standard deviation is 1, the confidence interval at 68% is that there will be between 3 and 5 hurricanes hitting Florida next year, 95% between 2 and 6, and more than 99% between 1 and 7).

For instance, from historical evidence, it is "practically" certain that Florida will be hit by at least one hurricane every year and no more than seven.

For phenomena more easily controlled than natural events, for example, the number of accidents per year in a given large fleet of vehicles, or the number of fires in plants of large multinational firms with over 2,000 sites worldwide, the occurrence of a number of events significantly outside of the confidence interval is valuable information for a long-term number of losses forecast. Depending on the sign of the deviation, improvement or deterioration, the situation will call for an explanation of this evaluation; a check on the deep-root causes.

When the peril lends itself to a quantitative probability distribution, the uncertain future is deemed "probabilistic"; in other cases it is called "non-probabilistic". This distinction is essential as the tools available to make decisions for an uncertain future rely heavily on the quality and the risk diagnostic is aimed at improving information to make "sound" decisions.

In any case, the probability distribution of occurrence coupled with the probability distribution of impact or severity is the key to rational decision making as it allows for justifying the investments or recurring costs of proposed loss control measures as well as the premium quote by insurers.

It should be stressed that for extremely infrequent events, the average number of occurrences "in the long run" (law of large numbers), has not much meaning for the decider. In these situations, the decision will be based mostly on the impact level, the severity, and consists in reducing the probability of occurrence below a level that will be deemed acceptable by the major stakeholders. For example, when the officers in an organization managing nuclear power plants make a decision on "nuclear risks" they will assess the likelihood of a major accident occurring "tomorrow" rather than on the average cost in the long run, meaning 1 or 10 million years! They must take into account the level of probability above which the population would no longer be prepared to live close to one of their plants.

The nature of the peril will dictate the type of loss control measures that could be implemented. For instance, in the case of a vehicle fleet, if the peril is "drivers' skills", the remedy will call for training the drivers to modify their attitude behind the wheel – i.e. defensive driving.

2.3.6 Is It Possible to Develop an Efficient Classification for Perils and Hazards?

There are many ways to classify the events that may occur to alter the state of affairs on which an organization formed its strategic decisions. Some would look at the causes, others at the consequences. An analogy that is useful to consider here is the knot of the bow tie rather than the two wings. The classification proposed has no scientific pretension; rather it focuses on providing the risk management professional with a first approach to what loss control instruments might prove appropriate to mitigate the exposure at hand. Perils and hazards are classified under two criteria:

Where the hazard or peril originates
>   **Endogenous:** The origin is found within the organization itself, i.e. within the perimeter it controls (be it physical or procedural). For example, it can be a fire in the premises or an employee going around procedure to wire money to an offshore account. The solution must be found within the organization, and prevention will be often the best approach.
>   **Exogenous:** The origin is found outside of the organization, i.e. outside the perimeter it controls (be it physical or procedural). For example: a strike in a nearby facility, with employees occupying the premises thus preventing access of own employees to the building; a long haul drivers' strike; water pollution due to a chemical spill preventing a brewery from continuing its production. The solution must be initiated by third parties if the probability is to be reduced. Internally, "Plan B" will be the key to loss control, from business continuity planning to disaster recovery and including strategic redeployment planning in the worst-case scenario.

1 THE NATURE OF THE HAZARD OR PERIL
>   **Economical:** The event would be a dramatic change in an economic parameter in the organization's environment creating an unexpected opportunity or a substantial threat. It could be the bankruptcy of a major global competitor opening new markets, a change

in the currency exchange rate affecting long-term prospects, a change in consumers' tastes ... to name but a few. Clearly, forecasts and attentive global economy monitoring are keys to efficient reaction.

Natural: It would typically take what some insurance policies call an "act of God", for example, a hurricane, earthquake, flood or tsunami, not to speak of global warming: too vague a term to be split into its different consequences to be treated. Clearly, prevention is not an option as there is no way to "prevent" a volcano from erupting or a hurricane from forming. That does not mean that a study of data and some scientific evidence would not help in choosing more suited sites and better prepare for what might happen someday. Therefore, pre-event and post-event loss reduction measures are going to be the appropriate mitigation routes. One reminder with natural disaster: the key to choosing the proper investment can be found in a phrase that summarizes the sequence TAI or "Threat, Alert, Impact". The longer the time elapse between the elevation of the degree of probability (Threat) and the actual strike (Impact) the easier it will be to prepare when the event becomes very likely, which means that investment on loss reduction measures can be channelled to high velocity risks where action prior to any development is essential (compare an earthquake with a flood near the mouth of a river).

Industrial: These are all the events that result from the overall human economic activity, without the direct implication of human elements in the actual scenario. It could be fire, water damages (other than flood), machinery breakdown, etc. In other terms those are typically non-systematic risks for which the insurance industry is well equipped, both in terms of financial risk sharing and in loss control. Insurance companies have developed a robust experience in dealing with insurable risks like fire and explosion, machinery breakdown, etc. as they did it to protect their own interests as well as those of the insured in their portfolio. Therefore, insurers and reinsurers have developed elaborate competencies in this realm. They are also sometimes referred to as "accidental risks".

Human: These are the most common in frequency; it is rare when there is not a human element in the scenario leading to an accident, for example, like a fire in the premises where welding was conducted.

However, the human origin is not enough to understand the root cause of the phenomenon. It must be further differentiated:

The involuntary human peril results mainly from an error, an omission or negligence. It can induce the event immediately (a lighted cigarette thrown out on flammable material) or much later (the basement of a house in a flood area not being properly protected by a complete insulation). Finding the person responsible, pointing a finger to the "culprit" will not help. If important damages result from an "involuntary human act", it is the system that must be reviewed and the procedures: human errors will occur and their consequences should be controlled. This is the obvious common responsibility of quality and risk management.

The voluntary human peril results exclusively from a conscious and deliberate act from an individual or a team of individuals. However, all conscious acts are not aimed at doing harm to others; therefore we further contrast:

(i)   **The voluntary human peril:** The "wise guy", which is the unintended consequence of a legitimate action by some actors in a system. They embark on modifications aimed at improving performances and/or facilitating work. However, they do not document their modifications and the rest of the team, unaware of them, can create problems. An example provided by many organizations is the nightly inspiration of a computer specialist "improving" software but warning nobody of the changes. The cure for that resides clearly in procedures to channel the individuals' imagination and transmute it into useful opportunities. (*A word of caution for those contemplating operations in France, French employees are particularly prone to the "wise guy" syndrome!*).

(ii)   **The voluntary human peril:** "Malicious acts" occur when an individual or a group of individuals embark on a mission to appropriate third parties' belongings or assets, be they tangible or intangible. Therefore, they are usually illegal acts, punishable in most countries where they would be performed, for instance, industrial spying, arson, forgery, assault, etc.

It is further essential to qualify the acts as to whether the individuals try to get wealthy (*lucrative malice*) or to further a political, religious, or ideological agenda (*non-lucrative malice*).

In the first case we are dealing with an enterprise, illegal but still governed by profit seeking. Therefore, these individuals make their decisions like legitimate entrepreneurs and they can be deterred by lowering the "return" on their investment (time, effort, and/or money). Strategies such as the following could work: increase the costs (prison terms, security efforts, etc.) or reduce the value (lower inventories, published information and know-how made public).

In the second case we are dealing with individuals who work for a cause (from vandals scratching cars in the wealthy section of the town to outright terrorism) and their motivations transcend economical issues. Their reasoning is much harder to crack, punish or "bring heaven to earth". The tragic events in the USA on 9/11/2001 and also Madrid (2004) and London (2005) are all reminders of how difficult it is to fight terrorism within the framework of a democratic society.

In any case, "voluntary human perils" are always the most elusive to fight. It is important to recognize that we are confronting an intelligent mind that can and will adapt to whatever new form of loss control measure we will imagine and wait patiently to strike when our guard is lowered. One illustration would be information systems: new worms and viruses are created every day and firewalls and other protections are to be updated all the time. Furthermore, employees may become complacent if not always reminded of the uphill battle to be fought every day.

2   THE CONSEQUENCES OF THE HAZARD OR PERIL

The third dimension of an exposure is its impact or consequences on the organization's objectives and these consequences can be good, creating an opportunity, or bad, generating a threat. In principle, an unexpected high level of a resource would create an opportunity, and a sudden depletion a threat, but unexpected constraints could provide a path to higher efficiency whereas a sudden affluence of resources could be squandered without careful prior planning.

Therefore, the "impact" can be positive or negative and be seen at three levels as defined earlier:

- **Primary and Secondary impact:** These cover the change in the level of assets and of capacity of earning of the organization in the short term (up to 18–24 months).

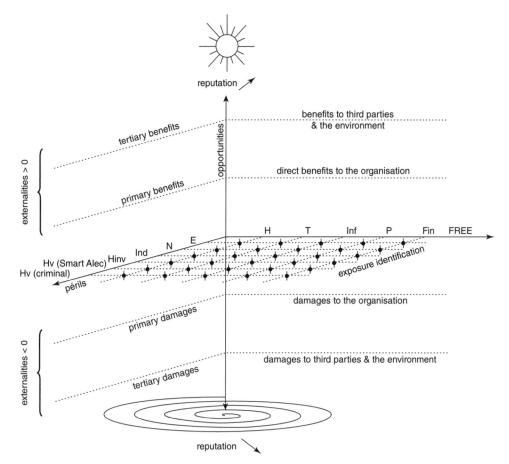

Figure 2.2   Space of Exposures.

- **Tertiary impact:** This covers the impact on third parties, including economic partners and other stakeholders, society and other impacts on the environment.

    When they are negative, they may engage the contractual, professional or other civil as well as penal bodies. If they are not involved in a transaction they represent an externality in the sense of economy and can be positive or negative.

- **"Quaternary" impact:** This covers the long-term effect when the trust and confidence of stakeholders is enhanced (opportunity) or tainted (threats). Thus the impact can have a long-term impact on the social licence to operate of the organization, in other words, its reputation.

Figure 2.2 summarizes the elements that are included in the exposure diagnostic, or risk assessment, to retain the expression used in the ISO 31000:2009 standard. The risk identification step means marking the first two dimensions that define any exposure (resource and event) whereas the third (impact quantification) will constitute the risk analysis step. The risk evaluation step consists in comparing the quantified impact under current circumstances to the risk criteria defined as acceptable by the leadership (risk appetite or risk tolerance).

2.3.7   VoR or Velocity of Risk?[15]

Understand the probability of loss, adjusted for the severity of its impact, and you have a sure-fire method for measuring risk.

Sounds familiar and seems on point; but is it? This actuarial construct is useful and adds to our understanding of many types of risk. But if we had these estimates down pat, then how do we explain the financial crisis and its devastating results? The consequences of this failure have been overwhelming.

However, a new concept has developed to describe how quickly risks create loss events. "Velocity of risk" provides an additional insight into the concept of risk through an evaluation of "time to impact" that implies proactively assessing when the chain of events will actually strike. While it is still relatively new and not yet widely used, it is gaining momentum in professional circles, as it is a valuable concept to understand and more so to apply.

Whereas it is necessary to know how likely it is that a risk will manifest itself into a loss or a gain, and the impact of the manifestation, it is not enough to make the most of the opportunity, or limit the loss. Therefore a better way to generate a more comprehensive assessment of risk is to estimate how much time will be available to prepare a response or make some other risk treatment decision about an exposure when its occurrence becomes imminent. This allows you to prioritize more appropriately between exposures; those that require immediate preventive action and those that can be treated when the event is becoming imminent. An efficient allocation of limited resources is the key to robust risk management.

As a matter of fact, expending limited resources on identification and assessment really doesn't buy much more than awareness; and awareness, from a legal perspective and governance perspective, creates an additional risk, that could prove quite costly if reasonable action is not taken to reduce them in a timely manner. Not every exposure will result in this incremental risk, but a surprising number do.

Even five years into the crisis, there's a substantial number of actors in the financial services sector who wish they'd understood risk velocity and taken some form of prudent action that could have perhaps altered the course of loss events that triggered the situation in which the developed world has since been engulfed.

To better understand the velocity of risk there are several avenues to follow:

- **At the operational level:** Investigate how the circumstances of concern are impacting others who may have the same or similar exposure. Talk to risk owners who've already been affected and get insight and intelligence about how the event evolved for them. When did they first see evidence of its appearance? What horizon scanning methods did they use to see it coming?
- **At the legal level:** Consider where attorneys seem to be directing their attention and resources. Consult subject matter experts in your company who understand developments in the fields of technology, advertising or research. Find out what they're concerned about and understand why. These efforts, while typically limited in scope and rigor, can reveal much about the potential for new risks and the speed at which they may emerge, influenced heavily by product development goals and pressures.
- **At the intermediate management level:** A group of managers who have some accountability for strategy and tactics should be interviewed to get their inputs on where they're going and what factors are driving their plans.

---

[15] Chris Mandel, former president of RIMS.

Collectively, these efforts can provide a few of the many data points that can help in piecing together a picture of emerging risks and give some context around the speed with which they could develop and cause loss.

The more of these elements can be assessed, the more opportunity will be offered to develop and implement loss prevention plans that could lead to the avoidance of the loss altogether. Between efforts at prevention and protection, it may prove possible to avoid or mitigate the next crisis, an experience any organization would be better off not going through.

2.3.8   What About Business Impact Analysis?

There is a growing trend to consider BIA (Business Impact Analysis) as a new discipline that consultants promote heavily in the wake of the huge contingent loss of profit experienced by many organizations as a consequence of the various natural disasters that hit Asia in 2011.

However, if we refer to ISO 31000, clearly a growing reference worldwide, the risk assessment part of the risk management process calls for a longer view of the impact of a given event or change in situation. It would be a very poor practice to envision only the immediate consequences at the site of the event. Furthermore, risk should be reassessed as soon as there are significant changes in the organization, its internal and external context, and/or its missions or strategic goals. I trust that encompasses the entire scope of the BIA, which appears only as a tool in the risk assessment process and a reminder to look beyond the immediate and local effect.

Back quickly on the assessment/impact issue: personally I prefer the word "diagnostic" and the analysis/evaluation stage of this process clearly must encompass all of the potential impacts: primary damages, secondary damages (loss of profit), tertiary damages (to third party and society), and "quaternary", i.e. impact on reputation or "social license to operate".

It seems to me that the "invention" of impact analysis is linked to insufficient attention to a thorough risk analysis (unless it provides a consultant with a competitive advantage and the actuaries a legitimacy to invade the RM field!).

2.3.9   Why Must Risk-Management Objectives Be Clearly Defined?

Within the ERM framework, as per the ISO 31000:2009 standard, risk management objectives can only be derived from the organization's strategic objectives that they are meant to serve with a major focus on pulling through difficult situations.

Clearly, the mission is to plan for all the resources that will be needed to achieve the organization's goals whatever the circumstances may be, more specifically when it is hit by a severe event. Among the resources vital to the organization are the cash flows needed to compensate for the losses whatever their origin may be. This will be the role of risk financing that will remain a corporate function, part of the overall finance strategy, no matter how decentralized risk management may be to the operational risk owners.

Even when approached from both the perspective of threats and opportunities, the essence of risk management is to plan for situations of high volatility; otherwise it would interfere directly with the cost control mission of any manager. The essential volatility of risk management performance has driven the professionals to contrast clearly two sets of objectives that some call "pre-loss" and "post-loss" objectives. However in a global approach, it would be better to call them "pre-" and "post-" event, thus not pre-judging the nature of the impact of the event, which also could be positive.

It is necessary therefore to set the objectives prior to any unexpected event but with a clear understanding of the different timing with regards to major events occurring.

Post-Event Objectives (continuity of operations)

In any case, the first objective is the organization's survival, which could be achieved if there is enough cash at hand when the demands from the event are due. But there is a continuum of objectives depending on how resilient the organization should be. If we look at it from the perspective of the resources at risk:

(a) **Technical, information and partners**

Continuity of operation is the key. However, the question is rarely that of an absolute continuity but rather how long an interruption the organization and its partners can pull through and continue to strive. The longer the acceptable downtime can be, the lesser the investment necessary in "continuity measures" to mitigate the threat. However, when public service is at stake, the acceptable may be very limited: birth and death certificates must be issued daily; schools should open every day to educate children, not to mention the utility in a hospital where surgery theatre and intensive care units need electricity without a break.

(b) **Financial**

Even when there is enough cash to survive, that may not prove enough for the investors' community, which may require proof of the executives' foresight whatever the circumstances:

• "Maintain a profitable situation" even in the year when a disaster occurs.
• "Maintain the expected level of profit" (the median over the past three years for example).
• "Maintain the growth rate" (of earnings per share).

Financial markets do not take lightly to a publicly traded company showing erratic results. In such a case the share price may sink, providing takeover specialists with a tempting target, which is a risk for the independence of the organization and the security of the "executive team"!

(c) **Human and social**

This is the social responsibility of the firm. The question is how to limit the impact on its environment, employees, up and down stream economic partners, and the society at large, both now and in the future: in other words the impact on the "social licence to operate" and its reputation.

Pre-Event Objectives

These are the objectives that, like any other department in any organization, risk management is expected to be efficient and deliver service to the organization while consuming as little resource as feasible, i.e. contain ongoing costs as much as possible. However, the level of desirable post-event objectives will govern the level of resources to be allocated to risk management.

Other Possible Secondary Objectives

Contain uncertainty: i.e. the volatility of the organization's financial result, to a level acceptable to the executive (risk appetite).

Compliance with legal and regulatory requirements: It may seem self-evident but when an organization operates globally then the question may become: what legal framework (?), where (?), should it state its own standards beyond local legal requirements (?), etc.

Society's expectations: In fact the alignment of the organization's goals and objectives with citizens' expectations should be ensured through the:

1. *Laws enacted in the land* that the legislative branch should vote in accordance with their popular mandate.
2. *Ethical behaviors* that should guide any executive and he should therefore act for the common good in the interests of all stakeholders.

2.3.10   Managing Risks or Containing the Cost of Risk, Is It the Same Objective?

The core mission of risk management in any organization is to maintain some degree of activity through any type of turbulence in order to allow it to reach its strategic objectives, no matter what happens. The risk manager's core job is to make sure that the vital resources needed to achieve this will be available to reach the level of post-event objectives set by the board.

However, this mission must also be fulfiled with as little resource as possible. To reach the optimal level of economic efficiency, the risk-management operations must be measured against some objective yardstick. Minimizing the long-term cost of risk represents such a standard. However, what is the "cost of risk" in a given organization?

Traditionally, the cost of risk has been broken into these four components:

Administration costs: These are the expenses directly linked with the implementation of the risk management process throughout the organization. They include the salaries, office expenses, and travel and communication expenses for the personnel in the risk management office as well as the costs of outsourced services for risk assessment or other purposes. These costs are relatively easy to track. However, it is essential to include the additional costs of the time and efforts devoted to risk management in the operational units and other executive branches, and these are far less easy to evaluate properly and objectively.

Loss control costs: Including not only the annual depreciation of loss control investments but also recurring costs linked to risk mitigation efforts. For instance, when dealing with automatic systems for detecting and extinguishing fire (sprinkler) the initial investment is substantial but the system must be maintained regularly and receive major overhauls over the twenty years of its lifetime. For individual protection, there may be the cost of purchasing the adequate equipment, and replacing it regularly, but sometimes "control" is achieved through modifying processes that may increase the production times, and hence costs. These are not always easy to identify and measure precisely.

Transfer risk financing costs: For the most part these represent the insurance premiums paid to insurers or reinsurers (through a captive company). These costs are quite easy to track and consolidate, as they should appear as such in the accounting documents. However, with the new ART (Alternative Risk Transfer) instruments, some of which are implemented through financial markets or banks, the organization should be careful to include every element of the cost of transfer, especially in a large global conglomerate. Furthermore, the cost of risk contractual transfer for risk financing to non-insurance partners is extremely difficult to "price" as it is part of an overall deal.

Retention risk financing costs: These represent all the claims and fractions of losses that remain in the books of the organizations. Clearly that includes those that are not insured or not insurable but also the deductible, self-insured retention, and/or the portion above policy limits, especially in the liability area. For the losses outside the realm of insurance, retention risk financing costs will be reported only if the RM accounting practices provide for their tracking.

However this breakdown of the "cost of risk" concentrates on the downside, the threats, and does not take into account the upside of risk, the opportunities. A "fifth" component should be added:

The cost of investments deemed "too risky", made possible thanks to a robust risk management process: It is extremely difficult to assess the potential opportunities that are passed up. However, this impact should always be kept in mind when running any investment analysis.

In all organizations, executives are always tempted to benchmark, with competitors as well as partners. A typical question would be "Is our cost of risk in line with the competition?" This is a very difficult game to play as no two organizations have the same risk profile (each has its own specific portfolio of exposures) and no two executives' teams have the same risk appetite.

Once again it should be stressed that if the organization excludes the high frequency losses that should be treated as quality failures, in the short run, an organization with no risk management in place might seem more efficient as it incurs little "cost of risk". This will last until a catastrophic event happens that kills it off, for it has no means to rebound. Therefore the cost of risk should always be assessed taking into consideration the company's resilience.

2.3.11   Why Is the Concept of Resilience Becoming So Popular With Board Members?

The underlying objective of any risk management program is the survival of the organization under whatever stress level, but it has to include within its scope the very important concept of sustainable development, not only in terms of preserving the natural resources for future generations but also as a way to provide the investors with a reasonable long-term return on investment. This may call for measures far beyond available sources of cash to pay for the damages that would ensure survival in the aftermath of a major claim.

However, even this minimum objective may prove elusive should some extraordinary circumstance take place; of course this may be the case essentially for liability and environment exposures, e.g., the cost of Exxon Valdez and the BP Gulf oil rig disaster which for smaller firms would have threatened their survival. For extremely catastrophic events, it may be necessary to engage with the stakeholders to find an acceptable compromise where the perception of risk is not excessive, in order to grant the organization its "licence to operate" in view of the positive societal advantages: the opportunities it brings to all.

On the other hand, this "survival" approach to risk management may fall short of stakeholders' expectations especially in the "moderate risk class", i.e. those scenarios that are due to happen with a good degree of certainty over a 5–10 year horizon, but whose annual impact may fluctuate significantly. The objective of survival would not treat situations that take the financial results of a company through a true rollercoaster that would not please the investor community. Furthermore, employees and managers, as well as customers and suppliers, might question the long-term viability of the organization and seek employment and/or partnership elsewhere to protect their own interests. In the same way, the government, the local authorities and the citizen consumers might well be impatient when confronted with what they would perceive at best as short-sighted management.

It is under these circumstances, and with the capital "reputation" in mind, that both the directors and the executives might well consider a higher level of post-event objectives to assign to the risk management operations in the organization, like limiting service or production interruptions to a level compatible with the partners' interests, or imposing a minimum level of profits and/or growth even in the case of unexpectedly large losses. Clearly, they will expect the organization to rebound faster and higher than mere survival would allow, even after a serious loss.

Without undue developments, it is all too clear that these higher post-event objectives are going to require investing more resources, financial in particular, into the risk management process than "absolutely" necessary. This "additional investment" is in conflict with the pre-event objectives of economic efficiency, which call for containing the cost of risk.

Once again, risk management efficiency has to be assessed in the long term. However, long term must be defined. For a CEO whose tenure is going to be anything from three to six years, this is long term; for a government it should be the well-being of this and at least the next generation of human beings (and not the next election); for an environment specialist is a millennium enough (think nuclear waste)? Pension funds that are such an important player in the financial market should look at 20–40 years' horizon for the benefit of their "investors", not just the next three quarters, which may represent the best interest of their funds managers.

Therefore, if purely financial returns do not provide a clear view on the long-term sustainability of the firm, a new concept, a new measure, is needed to provide a comparison tool. Resilience for an organization was forged as a social concept by analogy with the quality of a metal that regains its quality after a stress. It is often used in modern risk management literature, not always with a clear understanding of its underlying meaning. It was used for the first time in an audit context by the Canadian Auditors Association, too happy to find a word that is the same in English and in French. The definition can be summarized as follows: "The capacity of an organization to rebound even after the most severe stress and still maintain its strategic objectives in the interest of its main stakeholders."

Therefore the resilience must be assessed by each stakeholder in view of the preservation of its stakes or interests in the organization. As an illustration, the expectations of the organization from the points of view of different groups are:

- Society: Fulfil its obligation.
- Employees: Maintain employment.
- Partners: Insure security of orders/delivery.
- Stockholders: Provide long-term dividends.

2.3.12   How to Conduct an Exposure Diagnostic?

Establishing a diagnostic of the exposures for a given organization is the first step in the risk management process. It can be split into three different phases: identification, analysis and assessment.

One of the problems of the emerging risk management science is that, in spite of the definitions offered in the ISO Guide 73 vocabulary for risk management, so many concepts remain ill defined. Let us therefore state that here we mean by "*identification*" the recognition that some undesirable event may occur; "*analysis*" means quantifying the consequences for the organization and hence also its stakeholders, without any consideration of the control measures in place; while "*evaluation*" takes into account the best possible outcome if all current control measures operate at full capacity, i.e. an analogy with the insurance concepts of MPL (maximum possible loss) and ERL (expected reasonable loss). It should be noted that what we call exposures diagnostic is also referred to in ISO 31000 as "risk assessment".

It is obvious that the good risk manager envisions the probability of the event occurring, the frequency, the importance of the impacts, and the severity of potential losses. However, this would fall short of an understanding of the phenomenon without giving due consideration to a measure of the uncertainty of the consequences, i.e. the dispersion of the consequences. At the end of the day, what the risk management professional should be concerned with are the *consequences on the ability of the organization to achieve its goals and missions*, no matter what, i.e. what we have called its *level of resilience*.

The diagnosis is the cornerstone of the risk management process: our decisions are only as good as the information we base them on; if a risk is not identified, the opportunity will be missed or the threat will not be curbed. On the other hand, when a risk is identified and properly quantified, the risk management treatment may just pop out for the experienced risk manager. Later in the book we will come back to how the diagnosis is transformed in an ongoing process of risk mapping through the feedback loop.

A single event may impact a number of organizations. For example, a used tire facility burns in the vicinity of a populated town. Toxic fumes from the fire are blown by the wind in the direction of a nearby industrial and commercial park. The impact of this event must be analysed from different perspectives, but first of all from the company who owns the inventory and manages the site. The analysis will cover property and equipment damages, loss of personnel, and loss of net revenues. Of course the consequences for all economic partners should be assessed, if only to analyse the potential contractual liability losses. However, each of the partners should also conduct their own evaluation of the consequences. If the context has been defined accurately, then the eventuality of this exogenous event should be included in the exposure diagnosis of each of them as an "external" hazard. Finally, for the tire owner the impact on reputation and image should not be forgotten as economic partners may also suffer. Nevertheless, the impacted organizations may also experience reputation loss even if "innocent", especially if they cannot demonstrate a proper preparedness for such a "foreseeable" event!

But this analysis in a semi-open system, i.e. a system that is not totally self-sufficient, is not enough as many other stakeholders, some of whom the organization has no contractual ties with may be impacted, e.g. the neighbors, the city and surrounding communities, as well as regional and national authorities, and even other private entities. Therefore, an investigation on the potential impacts on all stakeholders will have to be conducted at the organization level to further assess tort and criminal liabilities that the fire might induce. This is after all an endogenous hazard that may have consequences on an extended environment.

Furthermore, the risk manager of a healthcare organization located within a mile radius should have identified the "tire inventory operation" as a potential hazard as part of its community wellness program, especially in the context of its pulmonary patients, children, and other at-risk persons.

To summarize, the exposure diagnosis consists of a recurring exercise to keep an updated register of the exposures confronting the organization, as exhaustive and current as possible.

The second phase develops a quantified evaluation of the impacts on the organization's resources and objectives, as far as possible. This can be achieved through the use of probability and trend analysis for the "frequency risks" for which there is a data bank. Other quantification methods such as expert advice and Bayesian networks can be used for the median risk category, and scenario analysis is appropriate for "catastrophic" events, especially when many stakeholders could be impacted.

It is a "no brainer" that the more open the system, the more delicate the diagnosis process. Such is the case of malls, healthcare establishments and local authorities where most of the stakeholders have no direct subordination or contractual links with the organization. It is clearly easier to manage risk within the limit of a manufacturing plant where most actors can be trained and educated to recognize risks and act responsibly to limit their consequences.

Finally, there is the case of managing the risks in a project. Projects usually involve different partners that may have not necessarily entirely convergent goals and objectives, indeed even sometimes divergent interests. Project risk management in such a case will require a common approach to managing the risks in the most efficient way while satisfying the needs of all participants.

2.3.13   How to Analyze and Evaluate Risks?

The realm of possibilities that may arise in a situation of uncertainty for a given organization is practically without borders. And even if risk management tends to look principally at downside risk when referring to risk diagnostic, it is essential to have a broad perspective on their potential impact, if only to prioritize risk control efforts.

Too often the risk impact evaluation is limited to the two traditional variables used by the insurance industry to calculate an expected value of the claims:

- The probability, also called frequency, as claims do occur even in a well-balanced portfolio (law of large numbers).
- The severity, or the financial impact, usually measured within the scope of the insurance cover granted to the insured in the contract.

As a matter of fact, if the portfolio is large enough and underwritten cautiously, the multiplication of the frequency by the severity, or expected value, is indeed what the insurer can expect to pay in claims on his portfolio in the long run.

However, when applied to a single organization, large as it may be, the formula will not give insight into the adverse conditions that it may be faced with, except for the very limited and frequent claims like physical damages to a fleet of vehicles. A major variable is missing, that could be summarized in the volatility of the annual losses and the negative cash flows that stem from the realization of the hazardous events. An example drawn from the nuclear industry will illustrate. If any nuclear power plant has a probability of 1 in 10,000 million of suffering a major catastrophe with a $2,000 billion loss, then the long-term annual "cost of risk" for Electricité de France (EDF) that operates less than 100 sites is less than $20,000 a year. That is a quite acceptable burden for EDF; however, does this answer the question for the public: "Is the nuclear industry in France safe enough to ensure both permanent supply of electricity and safety for those living close to one of the power plants?" Who cares if the annual long-term cost over 10 million years is negligible? At the end of the day the question is linked with sustainable development, not expected value of cost. In other words, any exposure assessment will have to take into account the dispersion of the force of the impact, be it in financial terms or in human or environmental evaluation.

For the high frequency risk, the "non risk" exposures in terms of financial implications like health cover for a large population or vehicle fleets, the historical data will provide a good start to forecast the future losses provided trend variables are properly inserted in the model.

Furthermore, the "expected value" of annual cost may even prove a reasonable base for a budget exercise, as it will be relatively non-volatile.

For exceptional exposures on the other hand, it is more the severity and the spread of consequences that will guide in the decisions of risk treatment, even to the ultimate option of discontinuing or not engaging an activity deemed too risky. In those situations, what is essential is to determine the stakeholders' appetite for risk. To summarize, the parameters should not be multiplied; it is the three dimensions vector (F, S, and σ)[16] that must be assessed: "At a given level of confidence, are the consequences socially and economically acceptable?"

Some authors have recently advocated looking at the worst case scenario and defined for financial institutions the "value at risk" and for non-financial the "cash flow at risk" as a measure of the stress that the system, the organization, can endure without permanent damage or impairment. Now, recent authors place it in the QBRM (quantile-based risk measures) and argue that it is fundamentally flawed and does not represent a coherent risk measure. It is not within the scope of this book to fully address the debate, which will be left to the FRM (financial risk management) specialist and the actuaries. Suffice to know that it is a fast developing field that the risk management professionals must be aware of.

In any event, assessing severity requires developing an "extreme scenario" according to Murphy's Law (everything that can go wrong, will go wrong). Clearly, from the organization's point of view, recognizing all the negative (and positive?) impact is essential. The worst-case scenario will have to address the question of the stakeholders' confidence and the loss of reputation.

Finally, when dealing with risk assessment, one must exercise caution as some consequences are not readily measurable in monetary terms (long-term impact on the environment) and cannot always be positioned in the financial model of the firm even with the long-term view of value creation for the stockholders. Other objectives have to be taken into account such as whether they are true missions or merely constraints; it is for each board of directors to answer, but they include sustainable development, assistance to distressed persons, etc. It is probably necessary to broaden the assessment tools to include other variables than the three mentioned here.

One final piece of advice: as all is not quantifiable in monetary terms, all that can be must be, with utter care and application, be it only to limit the residual uncertainty!

2.3.14   Risk Centres and How to Use Them for Risk Assessment

The "risk centre" method for assessing risks, exposure diagnostic, is founded on the model that describes an organization as a dynamic combination of five classes of resources (**H**uman, **T**echnical, **I**nformation, **P**artners, and **F**inancial).

The crux of the method is to split the organization defined as a "complex system", i.e. a system of systems surrounded by environments, into as many sub-systems as needed to make the smaller entities "user-friendly". Then the sub-system is analyzed as a combination of the same resources.

This identification of sub-systems within an organization is totally compatible within the system safety approach. It must stop when the level of "elementary sub-system" or "micro firm" is reached. It is still a living cell with a manager aware of the missions he/she is to fulfil with the help of the necessary resources in the five classes. It is then possible to identify,

---

[16] F = Frequency, S = Severity, and σ is the standard deviation expression the volatility.

analyze and mitigate the risk at the risk centre level, which is a "micro-organization" that can be defined as a set of resources, combining to reach an identified sub-goal, contributing to the organization's overall goals and missions.

The boundaries of the risk centre and the forces of its environment should be apprehensible by the risk centre manager who should have the initiative to manage this "micro enterprise" and navigate at best within the threats and opportunities identified. This is precisely the "risk owner" often referred to in all ERM (Enterprise-wide Risk Management) presentations.

We have already listed and explained the seven risk identification tools; however, once the risk centres have been identified, the main tool to use is the questionnaire, or preferably, the interview of the identified risk-owners. The information gathered during the interview will be the material used for the workshop organized henceforth with the management team to appropriate the risks and agree on priorities and actions.

The interview should be conducted according to the main points listed in the box below:

OBJECTIVES
1. What are the missions of your department, service, business unit, or profit centre?

RESOURCES
2. How are you organized?
3. Who are your staff, what are your buildings/workspace, your equipment and material?
4. Where do you source your products, your raw materials, and your information?
5. Where do your products, your information go?
6. What are your communication channels?

STRATEGIC QUESTIONS
7. Assuming your building/office is destroyed by fire tonight, with all its contents, with no injuries to your personnel, how would you be operational tomorrow if your personnel are ready to work?
8. Assuming, on the other hand that you have suffered no damage, but your personnel are not present (strike, pandemic, access closed), how can you still manage to be operational?

HOW ARE YOU EQUIPPED TO MITIGATE THESE RISKS?
9. Immediately (pre-event mitigation):
   – Prevention/protection.
   – Contractual risk sharing.
10. When the hazard strikes (post-event mitigation):
   – "Business continuity planning."
   – "Crisis management & redeployment planning."

Question 1: Aims at understanding the activity of the risk centre and testing the manager's grasp of his missions and position within the organization.

Questions 2 to 6: Aim at identifying the resources currently used by the centre, including the "free resources" and the interaction with other actors, within and outside the organization.

Questions 7 & 8: Aim at questioning the manager's comfort so that he/she can accept that potential destabilizing events may occur and envision how he/she would cope in an emergency. Through the absence of staff, on the one hand, and the loss of all equipment on the other, the manager is led to consider which among his/her resources are really "vital" for the continuation of the operation. Furthermore, through the wish list of what to do now, and what to do in the case of a disruption, the manager initiates the process of scenario identification that will help the staff workshop to lead to a robust mitigation plan at his/her level, i.e. to the definition of BCP, the quantification of the need for "exceptional financial resources" to implement it, and the "sentinel event" that should prompt top management attention.

Questions 9 & 10: Aim at developing a preliminary BCP, the conditions for its successful implementation as well as early detection of the development that may lead to a crisis through media attention and public implication in the consequences of the "undesirable event". Those situations might develop into crises that are likely to require headquarters input and assistance. Early warning may make all the difference between an aborted crisis and full-blown havoc!

2.3.15   Risk Map or Risk Matrix: What for?

The desired output of the diagnosis exercise is a list of exposures, as exhaustive as possible and a classification by order of priority. It is customary to assess a priority on the basis of the "long-term economic impact" measured by the two variables: *frequency and severity*.

The risk matrix, that some consultants still insist on calling a "risk-map", is a two-axis table: on one axis the probability of the event taking place (or frequency) and on the other the potential impact (usually in monetary terms). This matrix does not have the permanency of a physical geography map: it is merely transitory help to decision makers, whose decisions will immediately alter the risk profile of the organization, not to mention the evolution in the external and internal context. However, this function as an information tool for managers and executives must provide them with some insight into the risk; therefore the classes of risks thus described must be in measures that make sense to them in the light of the decision to be made:

- On the probability axis, for example: once a week, once a month, once a year, once a decade, possibly once a century, once a millennium; and
- On the impact axis: for low or middle severities, a reference to the annual profit should be enlightening (less than 1 per mil, 1 percent, 10 percent, etc.); and for catastrophic risks a reference to the company's net worth may prove more appropriate (20%, 50%, and possibly 1000%, or ten times, etc.).

Combining frequency and severity provides the long-term weight of the risk, but judgment must be exercised, especially where improbable catastrophic events are concerned. At this stage the traditional green, yellow and red zones depending on the acceptability of risk level dictated by the deciders' or stakeholders' risk appetite. If an event whose potential impact is 1 per mil of the profit would only happen once a year, it can be ignored. If the same event could occur once a week, the situation will call for treatment. On the other hand, a millenary flood, even potentially catastrophic, may be left untreated.

Clearly the key to efficient risk management is an in-depth understanding of all the exposures to which an organization is confronted, their characteristics and root causes to infer their potential economic impact. The risk matrix clearly provides an appropriate tool for classifying the risks.

Risk Matrix, a Permanent Process

However, more than the transitory output, the risk matrix, essential in the diagnosis exercise, is the permanent process that facilitates the appropriation of their risks by each risk owner in the organization. The approach that we describe here is a mirror of any project management exercise and will engage all operational managers (be they local risk owners or chief risk officer). It is a three-stage process:

- *Collecting data* – All the elements pertinent to the management of risks must be collected and analysed in the light of their potential impact on the organization's strategic objectives. Therefore, constituting and keeping updated the risk data bank is at the heart of the risk management culture and the tool for it is the RMIS (Risk Management Information System). The data bank is also enhanced through direct interview of the risk centre's manager to uncover local potential threats and opportunities that could not be seen from documents.
- *Self-evaluation workshop* – On the basis of the elements in the RMIS and the subsequent interview of the manager, this is a meeting of the team in charge of the risk centre (operational unit). Each member is asked to provide an assessment for each of the exposures. The difficulty in this type of exercise is to really obtain a consensus with each team member initially expressing his/her own opinion, notwithstanding the hierarchy. This is where "voting pads" become handy. Each member is equipped with one and a computer program will provide a consolidated visualization of all the answers. The graph is intended to provide a starting point for a discussion where both assessment and possible treatment can be openly discussed to reach a fruitful consensus.
- *Feedback loop* – At the end of the self-evaluation workshop all exposures that are deemed strategic, i.e. those that impact the timely achievement of the organization's strategic goals and missions, must be taken into account in the "business continuity plans" developed by the group. However, they may require to be passed on to a higher level in the hierarchy to have a broader perspective on their global impact on the organization, including external stakeholders. It is at this stage in the assessment process that a Cindynic analysis may prove indispensable to extend the root cause analysis beyond mechanical failure and focus on the social, cultural and human components of the system. Defining the situation at risk in terms of space, actor, networks, and time will require a good understanding of the ins and outs of the organization as well as an outsider's "eye" to avoid too much a "business as usual" approach. The final report to be consolidated in a bottom-up movement will be only the starting point of the next iteration when the executive team and/or the risk committee of the board has reviewed the results and made the necessary arbitrage to initiate the iterative improvement program.

2.3.16   Why Does It Make Sense to Invest in a System to Gather and Transform Information?

During the course of the last decade, risk management has clearly become a system to gather, process and communicate information as is clearly illustrated by the developments of analytics and "big data". At each step of the process, from the diagnosis or risk assessment to the audit of the program, there is a constant need of communication (to obtain the necessary information) to manage information (gather and explain), and communicate again (to present the results and draw practical consequences). This is precisely why installing a risk management information system (RMIS), i.e. a set of hardware and software to gather and treat all relevant data for making and implementing decisions, is an essential tool to manage efficiently risks in any organization. Its main attributes are:

Assistance to Decision Making

The decisions made with and all along the risk management process are based on systems that efficiently link data and people. The following are illustrations of what can yield a RMIS:

- Exposures identification, analysis and assessment: Collecting data on production sites, properties and equipment, loss histories, values and localization of assets, etc.
- Investigation of the risk treatment options: Looking at past claims, including values and cash-flows at risk to integrate trends in the investigation of the potential impacts of control and financial measures under consideration to mitigate risks, etc.
- Development and approval of the risk management programs: Using investigation tools and models to quantify the measures matrix and thus select those bringing the maximum expected value (enhancing opportunities and/or curbing threats).
- Implementation of the risk management programs: Bringing risk-owners up to speed with their targets and ways to reach them, whatever happens. Providing insurance underwriters with quality information to come up with best cover conditions, and provide data needed for an efficient management of retention programs.
- Audit of the risk management programs: Producing timely and accurate reports for top management to monitor organization-wide risk management efforts (activity standards) and achievements (results standards), thus enabling them to decide on necessary corrections if and when needed.

Reducing Uncertainties

One of the most difficult challenges for any risk management professional is to narrow down the range of possible outcomes in any decision-making circumstance, i.e. limit the uncertainties at a level that the "stakeholders can live with". However, there remains the daunting question of defining and measuring uncertainty. One definition could be: "The doubt concerning the capacity to forecast future events." In financial terms, most models take the standard deviation of the probability distribution of potential outcomes as a measure of the risk/uncertainty. Clearly improving the quality of information is transferred in a reduced standard deviation; avenues of possible futures are drawn through "the cloud of the unknown." Enhancing the decision processes within the organization is probably the main contribution of an efficient RMIS.

Improving Management Efficiency

In addition to improving the decision process, the RMIS impacts other aspects of risk management. Among others, it improves productivity and plays a key role in the swift and efficient implementation of the risk treatment programs in the following:

- Collecting data on individual large claims or a series of smaller claims, on exposures and insurance covers enables a swift and equitable compensation, especially in the case of multiple or basket coverage.

- Selecting appropriate information to help management with a clear picture of risk financing solutions, specifically insurance cover, and ensuring that proper insurance certificates are issued.
- Keeping track of the transactions processes and settlements reached in the case of retention programs, printing relevant letters and reassessing reserve levels.
- Documenting proper information for future reference, like notes on claims history and historical covers, including trial-proof evidence, should it be needed.
- Keeping a written track of important events; planning "flags" to make sure of the progression of a file, close claim files in due course, etc.

Enhancing Communication

Analysis and reporting functions can be used to inform both staff and management on the progress of risk management within the organization, the major trends and individual department contribution to risk management. The RMIS system should be linked to the information system capabilities of the organization to facilitate interaction and edit clear and synthetic documentation to illustrate the impact of risk management on all the activities of the organization.

As an illustration, let us consider intranet and internal email capabilities that is more and more common for organizations, even of middle size, to have developed to inform their entire staff. It is an excellent vehicle to keep supervisors and field managers informed on the evolution of their loss history in a timely fashion so that they can swiftly respond if a situation is deteriorating, like in the case of workers' compensation or fleet accidents where information can be updated in less than 48 hours.

The visibility of risk management is greatly improved where operations receive accurate information on risks together with other information on management. This puts risk management on an equal footing with other sources of controllable costs within the organization, and managers can take it as seriously as other disciplines.

At the foundation of Enterprise-wide Risk Management, the RMIS plays a key role to instil a risk-management culture throughout the organization and with its main partners.

As an illustration, let us consider a decentralized structure, in which each entity may have developed through time its own ways of managing risks and tending to claims from third parties. In some cases, it may be warranted because of differences in local and industrial cultural differences; in most cases, it will project an image of incoherent and uncoordinated management, an overall lack of professionalism reflecting badly on the corporate image and reputation.

Implementing a RMIS where all claims information is collected and processed will provide a tool to ensure proper and coordinated claims management policies, especially those involving third parties. Furthermore, the global picture thus produced will allow headquarters to make policy decisions and measure the anticipated impact of its decision on future claims costs.

Beyond RMIS, the BIS

In reality, nowadays the question of a separate system for managing information regarding risks is superseded by the need for top management to be able to have a complete view of the information flows within and outside the organization breaking the silos of specific applications for individual functions or departments. This overall strategic information system is often referred to as the Business Information System involving the collection of information throughout the organization and includes intelligence gathered, so that both the inside-out and the outside-in perspective are available to make or revise strategic, tactical and operational decisions in a coherent "risk intelligence".

2.4 MANAGING THE COLLECTION OF RELEVANT DATA FOR AN ERM PROGRAM: THE IMPORTANCE OF EFFICIENT AND NEUTRAL QUESTIONNAIRES

Sophie Gaultier-Gaillard

Assistant Professor, Université Paris 1 Panthéon-Sorbonne, Paris

An ERM program's path to maturity rests heavily on the adhesion of both internal and external stakeholders that some call "instilling a risk management culture". Furthermore, the ISO 31000:2009 standard recognizes the importance of stakeholders' trust and confidence by stressing in its proposed risk-management process the "communication and consultation with stakeholders".

On the other hand, if we agree with Felix Kloman's view of risk management as "lifting somewhat the fog of uncertainties about the future" to enhance the decision process at all stages, collecting relevant data and transforming it into information is key to any risk management program.

Behind the development of efficient data banks, many different tools can be used to evaluate the stakeholders' perception of risk and measure their trust and confidence in the organization to optimize risk-taking by enhancing opportunities and curbing threats.

However, in many situations, building and administering questionnaires will prove to be the only efficient way to gather or develop these data, both to assess the current situation, and model possible outcomes depending on the course of action chosen, taking into account the potential evolution of the internal and external context in which the organization operates. There is a systematic approach to developing and implementing questionnaires that will help ensure optimal data gathering. Creating an efficient questionnaire is not as simple as it may appear. Many designers were disappointed by the results of their enquiries, only because they did not devote enough time and energy to a preliminary thought process.

A questionnaire developing process is split into four stages: conception, construction, administration and analysis. However, the two first stages should represent two-thirds of the time devoted to the whole process. Administration and treatment require rigor essentially, but should not prove very time consuming, somewhat less than a third of the total duration of the study.

2.4.1 Conception Stage

Before writing any question it is essential to define the study/project objectives and the issue on which the survey is to shed light. This stage will allow the development of questions that will lead to answers that will effectively address the study's scope and produce the types of results desired, which is the key to a successful questionnaire administration.

While there are many ways to survey people, and many will be touched upon in the analysis, this paper will explore the in-person interview in more depth as a way of gathering data from stakeholders in a risk management context. Interviewees can be employees, management, the board, key shareholders, customers, regulators and others. The nature of the interview and the persons interviewed are directly related to the goals and objectives of the survey.

Initial Thought

This first step, like for any IT program, is essential for success as the questionnaire will provide information as good as the specifications that have been developed:

Survey Objectives

One way to define clear survey objectives is to conduct a feasibility study to **explore, describe, explain and predict** what is being pursued. The feasibility study aims at understanding the context of the situation without attempting to validate the results. The current lack of hard evidence or data is the reason that the survey is to be conducted in order to produce enough information for the decision makers to make qualified decisions. A feasibility study helps to better define the information required for the survey to gather. In the three other situations (describing, explaining and predicting) it is possible to refine the questions and answers format to obtain a more granular analysis.

Questionnaire Issue(s)

To better formalize the issues the questionnaire will address write down **4 or 5 questions** that the survey should answer, in no more than 4 or 5 sentences.

Targeting Interviewees

All survey participants have to be carefully chosen according to criteria that depend on the aim of the survey. They have to be targeted to specific characteristics studied by the questionnaire. The main socio-economic characteristics of the target interviewees (*organization, position in the organization, seniority in the position, geographic location, age, education level, etc.*) should be calibrated to provide exploitable answers for the survey objectives. This means that the participants must represent a credible sample of the targeted population so that the results are not biased. This specific targeting will help to match participants' profiles to the objectives and ultimately the results of the questionnaire.

Nature of Data/Information to be Collected

Information to be collected may be **qualitative** or **quantitative**. This initial choice is essential as these categories require significantly different statistical treatments and question format. Most often we use verbal data. It has to be thought about how the data will be analyzed at the time that the questions are being formulated. There are several methods that can be used depending on the level of directivity sought in the administering of these questionnaires.

- A non-directive interview will use **open questions**, meaning that it allows an infinite number of possible responses, providing the interviewee with an opportunity to respond without any interruption by the interviewer, once the scope of the survey has been clearly explained, such as asking people what they think about a specific brand reputation. The range of possible answers is not suggested in the question and the interviewee can respond with his own words. The upside of this approach is that it can possibly provide new ways of thinking or insight on the topic of the survey. The downside is the risk that the interviewee might provide superficial answers, or provide information, outside of the scope, resulting in unusable answers, because he might have misunderstood the scope of the survey or reinterpreted it. A lexical analysis is required to obtain satisfactory information. It analyses the frequency of the main concept in the responses and provides statistical results from verbal data. However, if the interviewer is skilled and understands the subject matter of the interview, the interviewer may be able to overcome superficiality with more detailed questions that drill down to more valuable answers.
- A directive interview implies that the questionnaire contains only **closed questions**, which can be, for example, answered by "yes" or "no", or by giving a precise number such as age, or the number of activities done in a month, and calling anyway for short answers.
- A **semi-directive interview** is a balanced approach tapping on the two preceding methods and is based on **semi-closed** (*or semi-open*) **questions**, most often **pre-coded questions**, meaning that it allows a finite number of possible answers. A semi-directive interview is particularly suited for studies on individual perceptions and/or representations.

Level of Details Expected in the Answers of Closed and Semi-Closed Questions

Depending on the level of precision expected for the results, question formats may differ. For exploratory studies, it is recommended to adopt a binary format (yes/no). The type of results expected is then "for or against" the survey subject. If more detailed information is needed then more answers should be offered through the use of a multi-level scale. It can be a **numeric scale** (i.e. boxes marked 1 to 4, in increasing preference order), or a **qualitative scale** (i.e. four boxes like "never", " rarely", "sometimes", "often"). The scale may be comprised of "2" to "10" graduations or boxes, "2" is the minimum to allow comparing, "10" the maximum number of items that an individual can order mentally. Between these two limits, the choice will be dictated by the level of detail expected from the answers:

- A **"2 points"** scale allows only a binary approach, and therefore only a very general appreciation on the study subject.
- A **"4 points"** scale will provide more precision like "rather in favor" or "rather against" the study subject, but does not allow for more precision to be able to explain the considered individual choice.
- A **"5 points"** scale represents an odd number of choices and like any odd scale it allows for a median position, used when a large number of interviewees is likely to have no opinion. These individuals, that can be tempted not to answer the questionnaire, can choose a median position. The advantage of this intermediate box is to collect an answer for the specified question, as any not fully filled questionnaire should not be considered in the statistical results.
- A **"6, 7 points"** scale opens the door to inferential statistical analysis, like "probit" or "tobit", econometric tools, to be able to determine a specific profile of the individual for each studied topic. The "7 points" scale, developed by the psychologist Rensis Lickert, is

the most commonly used as it allows for a satisfactory level of detail giving the interviewee a more nuanced level of answers.

- All the questions of a given questionnaire must be identically formatted so that the interviewee mental framework is not disrupted. The questions should have the same scale, in the same increasing or decreasing order, and should all be written in a positive or negative approach. This simple point would help the interviewee to better answer the questions as he/she doesn't have to reevaluate the levels of the scale with each new question.

Pragmatism

A major flaw in survey technique is impatience. Those who want data want it now and sloppy question writing is often the result, leading to misleading or even unusable data and frustration at all levels. For example, if interviewees are asking, "why are you asking ME this" you know there is a disconnection between the interviewee and the content of the survey.

Type of Treatment Envisioned

Treatment is dictated by the way the interview is conducted and how the questions are formatted. If the interviewer, or his/her statistical team, has limited statistical competency, it is advisable to limit the format to 3 to 4 points scale relying only on descriptive statistics. If the interviewer, or his/her statistical team, is more statistics-savvy then more extended scales can be used.

Type of Collection Envisioned

It is quite essential that the individuals selected to conduct the interviews (when the questionnaire is administered by direct interviews) be quite aware of the importance of their mission, i.e. that the quality of the conclusions drawn from the process relies heavily on their accomplishing their mission with integrity and professionalism. Questionnaire protocol must spell out specifically what the interviewer can and cannot do. For example: absolutely refrain from faking interviews and filling out the questionnaires themselves. They must understand the importance of providing adequate time so that the interviewees can structure their answers. In most instances, some training will be needed to make interviewers aware of their responsibilities and of the ultimate importance of the quality of data collection.

The conceptual stage of the questionnaire process will allow the study manager to ensure that all interviewers will collect all the necessary data for the successful completion of the study through appropriate implementation and treatment.

2.4.2   Construction Stage

Reassure the Interviewee

At the beginning of the questionnaire the interviewee must be confident that the sponsoring group is only interested in his/her opinion. It will require explaining to the interviewee that this is not a test, and interviewers must be trained to build trust in the interviewee. A sentence specifying that there are no good or bad answers may prove useful in all cases. All interviewees should be offered the opportunity to review a summary of the survey's results. These two measures will help to put the interviewee at ease and should enable the interviewee to provide more thoughtful answers.

The Context

The person in charge of writing the questionnaire is confronted with an alternative as he/she has the option of:

- **Explaining in detail the scope of the study**, which can induce an anchoring or framing bias, that would tend to overestimate systematically the risk being tested. The decision process of the interviewee is influenced by the context of the questions or by specific words contained in it. For example, if you ask students how much they are going to earn after their degree, you'll get a quite different answer if you explain, before asking them this specific question, that their colleagues from the past year earned around three thousand per month. Even explaining that the scope of the study has to do with income potential after college could introduce some bias as students may have a preconceived idea about what the media has had to say about what students can expect to earn after college. The alternative is keeping the scope of the study secret.
- **Keeping secret the scope of the study**, while eliminating the bias described above, this second choice can increase the volatility of the answers. The scope of the results is going to be wider. As the respondent does not know the risk involved he/she can imagine a situation far different from the one being tested. This will require analyzing the answers as a variation from an initial benchmark, corresponding to the initial choice of the individual. The respondent just has to analyze if he's going to have a gain or a loss comparing to that benchmark, then decides how to act.

If the interviewer is experienced in developing questionnaires, and if he/she is convinced that through the conduct of the questions he/she can guide the interviewee to answer the question being asked, then he/she can afford not to describe the context at the beginning. Otherwise, if the context is presented to the interviewee, it should be kept in mind that the value of the results is overestimated. In fact, in such a case, the interviewee has become aware of a risk that might have been ignored, and this awareness usually makes him/her more afraid of that risk, and this explains the overestimation of the results.

The Questions

Several points have to be considered when it comes to managing the questions. It is advisable to:

- **Couple systematically semi-closed questions with one open question like:** "What other…", "Could you be more specific?" or even "Can you comment?" This approach will give the interviewee an opportunity to expand his/her answer so that responses are clearer and more specific which will allow the interview to capture strategic information that could have been lost otherwise. However, the interviewer skill will be essential in limiting the scope of the answer. It must answer the appropriate question or the subject matter at hand.
- **Preserve a balance between the number of questions and the number of interviewees**. Should the number of questions be too large compared to the number of individuals being tested, the information collected is likely to be so diverse that the study results will be less satisfactory and weak. If a statistical analysis is to be performed, the recommendation is that the number of individuals be three times larger than the number of questions. For example, if the questionnaire contains twenty questions, sixty individuals, at least, should be interviewed.

- **Limit the number of questions so as not to reach the exhaustion level of the interviewee** and thus a lowering of the quality of the answers. The rule of thumb is not to exceed 4 pages, if possible, and never go beyond 6 pages, which represents approximately around eight to ten questions per page. The attention of the interviewee could soon wear out if the questionnaire is too long. The maximum recommended time for administering a questionnaire is 20 minutes. Only open question questionnaires can override this rule. Even then it may be advisable to pre-test open question surveys to determine whether interviewee fatigue sets in. If an open question survey proves too long it should be redesigned, some open questions could be changed into closed questions where appropriate for the sake of timing.
- **Ask simple questions, understandable by all target audience**, that are unambiguous, meaning that everyone understands it the same way. This point can only be verified through a pre-testing with volunteers. A small group (3 to 5 individuals) should be selected to test the quality of the questionnaire; this includes asking questions when they feel they encounter ambiguous phrasing, and provide comment to improve the questionnaire. However, these volunteers will be excluded from the final panel.
- **Avoid to the extent it is feasible, any anchoring or framing bias** in the questions. If a negatively constructed question is asked the individual will tend to provide a pessimistic answer, and the reverse is true for a positively constructed question. The connotation of some terms influences individuals considerably. Negative questions influence people to answer in a pessimistic way. Positive questions influence people to answer in an optimistic way. All questions, in the survey, have to be constructed to be either all positive or all negative, depending on the chosen context, either positive questions to obtain more optimistic answers, or negative questions to obtain pessimistic answers. Every single word in the question must be selected carefully so that it does not induce a specific answer or an answer biased because of the way the question is constructed. The ordering of the questions must be given full attention too. A previous question shouldn't influence the following one. However, it would be illusory to believe all biases can be eliminated. The person writing the questions should have a solid understanding of behavioral science, and has to weigh each word carefully. Experience and scientific honesty are recommended. A few years of psychometric or behavioral studies is recommended, otherwise it might be better to outsource the writing of the survey to professionals in order to minimize all possible biases.
- **Insert socio-demographic questions at the beginning of the** questionnaire, such as male/female, job, and experience in the job . . . but locate personal questions, such as income for instance, at the end of the questionnaire so that they do not block the individual. Also a solid understanding of the interviewees' perception is necessary to position these questions most effectively. The writer has to get information of the targeted population, of their social environment, in order to use appropriate vocabulary to be better understood.

2.4.3 Administration Stage

Whatever the technique chosen to administer the questionnaire, the administrator must provide the interviewee with a brief presentation of himself/herself and the organization, in order to demonstrate his/her legitimate right to conduct the survey. The interviewer should try to engage the interviewee to explain that he/she should take the time to provide answers. It must always be kept in mind that the interviewee may have been asked many times to participate in surveys and must prioritize attention and time. This is especially true when surveying executives or individuals in positions of power who are a frequent target for surveys. A letter or a short presentation limited to a few minutes may capture the attention of the selected target respondents and raise their trust level which will help improve the quality of the result. Emphasizing the importance of the survey may also assist in getting the attention of busy executives and employees.

Individual or Face-to-Face Interview

Individual interviews may take place at the workplace of the interviewee, in the risk manager's office, or consultant's offices or even on the street. In any case, the key to the validity of the findings is to ensure the professional integrity and the reliability of the interviewer who must vouch for compliance with the rules for administering the questionnaire. This can be both a strength, as the interviewer is in a position to help individuals better understand the questionnaire, and a weakness as the interviewer might influence their answers.

Focus Group

The facilitator that took part in the development of the questionnaire must conduct the group interviews so that he/she can lead the discussion in the right direction to fulfil the objectives of the study. Typically the groups will gather a minimum of 10 participants. The leader may need to focus the interviewees on the subject at hand and not hesitate to add open questions if the group gets off track or provides inadequate information. In most instances group interviews will be recorded and this needs to be explained to the group up front. Group answers may prove difficult to analyze as they tend to be more extreme, and sometimes emotional, than individual interviewee answers; participants may be more optimistic, or more pessimistic depending on the presence in their midst of a leader, or not. The upside to focus groups is that they can open debates and exchanges where very different points of view are confronted. The downside is that the results tend to be multiple and complex and require careful analysis. The interviewer may also need to address directly to individuals that are shy in the group, especially when there are some dominant participants that might monopolize the conversation. The leader of the focus group should, in this specific case, interrupt the dominating voice and give the right to answer to the other members of the group.

Mail in Questionnaire

This method is often used in the case of panels to be followed over several months. Its use is rare as they are expensive (costs of sending and returning the questionnaire by mail) and response rate tends to be low. The upside is that each individual has ample time to answer the questions. The downside is that the respondent may not answer the questions in the order they appear on the questionnaire, and this may influence answers to questions answered out of the intended order. The participant may also review the questionnaire later in the day or the day after to finish up, or even days later if it has not been sent yet or a reminder is sent.

Mailing/Internet

This technique is gaining momentum, as the cost is very low once the proper names database has been built. The upside is a swift collection of data; an easy exploitation of data. Sending reminders is facilitated when potential interviewees have not responded. The downside is that the increase of such solicitations tends to lower the rate of answers by individuals who feel harassed. Also many organizations may filter these out as spam. Other organizations may have strict guidelines about whether employees can provide answers to such questionnaires whether related to the organization or not.

Telephone Survey

This technique allows for contact with individuals who may be geographically dispersed. However it supposes that the questionnaires are simple and short as the time that respondents are ready to invest to answer telephone questionnaires is much more limited than in the case of individual meetings. In the United States the "Do Not Call" statute prohibits solicitation by for-profit entities (including surveys) if the phone number has been entered into the Do Not Call database.

2.4.4   Analysis Stage

Data treatment must take into account the competencies of the developers and consultants involved in the study.

Caveat

This section provides only a brief overview of some of the categories of analytic tools available to the researcher. In most cases, proper statistical analytic techniques may require professional competencies to apply the appropriate technique to produce quality results. It may also be necessary to hire such talent during the preliminary stages of questionnaire development and delivery to test subjects to facilitate discovering and fixing early in the process potential problems that might lead to problematic or even invalid results.

Descriptive Statistics

Whatever the level of detail sought in the study, this step is essential as it provides a precise description of what has been studied. It will therefore improve the understanding of the results further derived from most questionnaires. Descriptive statistics lends itself to graphic presentations such as histograms, sectorial diagrams, or pie charts.

Data Analysis

This step allows for the sorting of data and the cleaning of data that may be vague, inadequate, or misleading. The proper use of data analysis techniques is important at this stage. Data analysis techniques consider each answer as a potential explanatory variable. If there are "n" answers there will be "n" spaces, but an individual is not able to think in more than a three-dimensional space. For that reason, the technique consists in representing these "n" spaces in a two-dimensional space, to make them more readable, and allow for comparing. Then, after this spatial projection, each space corresponds to an axis, also called vector, more or less explanatory of the subject studied. The developer may then choose the quantity of information he wishes to see explained by the variable retained and thus determines the number of explanatory variables to be used in the follow-up analyses.

Inferential Statistics and/or Econometric Analysis

Thanks to the econometric analysis and depending on the data selected before, the developer may determine which type of individual (age, sex, occupation, income level, etc.) is more likely, for example in a risk-taking survey, to take risks related to the subject of the study, or uncover which variables influence risk taking. Inferential statistics lead to testing the significance on series determined before, or test cohesiveness or homogeneity. This step is to be done by a statistician.

When these first four stages of the process have been completed, the final step consists in developing and writing the results in a language and tone that the target audience will understand (board of directors, management, staff, economic partners, and any other internal or external stakeholders when dealing with risks). Graphic presentations may help visualize statistical results. It is often essential that interviewees themselves be forwarded the results, maybe in the form of an "executive summary", especially if they wished to be informed and might need to be interviewed for further studies. This is particularly true in studies concerning an organization's risk management practices as all interviewees are likely to be stakeholders and monitoring their perception through time is essential to manage the risk management efforts, let alone in terms of risk to reputation. (However there are situations where the organization may not want to disseminate results too widely because they could help competitors and create a competitive disadvantage; also the media may make an inadequate use of the information for the organization's sake.)

Appendix A: Questionnaire on Corporate Reputation

Implementation of the Process in the Case of Risks to Reputation

The model to manage risk to reputation (see Section 3.1 on risk to reputation in this book), stresses the importance of consulting stakeholders to define a reputation index that can be monitored. As an illustration of the process a risk to reputation questionnaire has been developed. To better illustrate the process we have selected one specific driver and one specific stakeholder, chosen among the list provided in the previous article. This questionnaire presents a common model for a study, in the pole "action", of the perception of risks to reputation of the staff (stakeholder) through a "leadership/governance" approach (driver). It might be written the following way:

The Questionnaire Model

This questionnaire is aimed at collecting staff's views based on recent studies (the interviewer has to precisely frame the references of the studies in brackets in order to give scientific references and increase the confidence of the interviewee). It is directed at a selected group of senior executives in New York Insurers and Reinsurers and is not intended to reflect any aggregate or industry-wide opinion on the matter. Furthermore, it is not engineered towards practices in the companies involved but rather their opinion on the practicability of the previous listed studies. There's no right or wrong answer, but your personal opinion on corporate reputation in your firm. Your answers will be used anonymously for providing statistical results to the insurance and reinsurance industry. We will send you the final report and thank you for being involved in this study.

In Your Opinion:

1. **Is reputation a key factor in reaching your company's strategic objectives?**

Essential	Very important	Moderately important	No impact

2. **Have you formalized any metrics to measure your company's reputation?**

YES	
NO	
DON'T KNOW	

3. **How do you measure your company's reputation?**

a. Specific field evaluation	
b. Informal observation	
c. Financial results	
d. Media coverage	
e. Published ranking	
f. Others	

4. **What are the key drivers for your company's reputation?** (*check/tick the "key" for you*)

DRIVERS	KEY (?)
a. Ability to attract and retain best talents	
b. Quality of management	
c. Corporate social responsibility (community)	
d. Sustainable development (environment and future generations)	
e. Innovation	
f. Cover extensions and quality	
g. Claims handling and insured satisfaction	
h. Efficient use of corporate assets	
i. Financial soundness	
j. Long-term investment value	
k. Effectiveness in doing business globally	

5. **Could you rank from 1 to 11 (1 – key to 11 – little or no impact) the same "key drivers"**

DRIVERS	RANK
a. Ability to attract and retain best talents	
b. Quality of management	
c. Corporate social responsibility (community)	
d. Sustainable development (environment and future generations)	
e. Innovation	
f. Cover extensions and quality	
g. Claims handling and insured satisfaction	
h. Efficient use of corporate assets	
i. Financial soundness	
j. Long-term investment value	
k. Effectiveness in doing business globally	

6. **What impact level do the following factors have on your company's reputation?**

Factor	Essential	Very important	Moderately important	No impact
Clients				
Employees				
CEO's reputation				
Stockholders				
Public Officials				
Media – press				
Media – Radio & TV				
Media – social media				
Financial Analyst				
Activity Analyst				
Trade Union				
Internet				
Plaintiff Attorneys				

7. **When selecting the present CEO's successor, how important will his/her potential impact on the company's reputation be?**

Essential	Very important	Moderately important	No impact

8. **How important is Internet for your company's reputation, through . . . ?**

Question	Essential	Very important	Moderately important	No impact
Internet strategy management				
Control negative information on Internet				
Internet monitoring (blog and forum)				

9. **What would be your definition of corporate reputation?**

10. **Finally, do you have any further comment on your perspective on corporate reputation in the insurance and reinsurance industry (including the pertinence of the questions above)?**

PLEASE RETURN COMPLETED QUESTIONNAIRE BY EMAIL, MAIL or FAX

BY *precise deadline*

2.5 ENTERPRISE RISK ANALYTICS SYSTEMS

Richard Connelly, Ph.D.
Founder and Director, Business Intelligence International

Jean-Paul Louisot
Formerly Université Paris 1 Panthéon-Sorbonne, Directeur pédagogique du CARM Institute, Paris, France

"Risk doesn't mean danger – it just means not knowing what the future holds." (Peter L. Bernstein)

This quote is at the heart of what risk management should be for any organization, whether when managing the potential downside of an investment or putting a value on the option of waiting when making irreversible decisions. The ISO 31000:2009 RM standard points to the needs for applying sound enterprise business intelligence analysis to risk management programs through the alignment of the GRC – Governance/Risk Management/Compliance Triangle.

Long before "analytics" came to be known as the reference for the compilation of decision information within and outside an organization, Howard Dresner in 1989 proposed a definition of "business intelligence" as an umbrella term to describe "concepts and methods to improve business decision making by using fact-based support systems" (Dresner, 2009).

Enterprise-wide risk management maturity means auditors' assertions can state that decision making is based on reliable data management processes that comply with governance requirements and legal matters management controls. This can be achieved only through maintaining documented assurance that international standards for evaluating performance accountability, reporting transparency and audit integrity are embedded in the roots of organizational culture.

The value of an investment in enterprise risk management information, as requested in the ISO 31000 standard, may be assessed by the depth of risk factors disclosure information reported to stakeholders and credit analysts. Credit agencies need "reasonable assurance" that the risk assessment data is reliable and consistent throughout the organization. Technical advances in enterprise information technology provide the means to connect management's performance guidance statements to predictive analytics that correlate financial results with asset–liability reserves and risk mitigation response plans. These are the key elements that investors, underwriters and regulators are assessing when stress testing economic forecasts and applying valuation models to capital liquidity analysis.

2.5.1 Enterprise Risk Management Analysis Information Orchestration

ERM – Enterprise wide risk management – is a global and integrated approach to risk management program implementation:

- **Global** means that ERM programs take into account all risks, upside as well as downside, across all legal entities and work functions to ensure optimum risk taking through proper management of risks, i.e. curbing threats and enhancing opportunities. An organization can confirm whether its risk management decision-making process is effectively orchestrated by documenting how the transaction data in its information assets is connected to key decision makers, who have IT access privileges into relevant risk monitoring information systems.

- **Integrated** means that all the organizations' functions and processes are involved, as risk owners who are responsible for the risks they control and accountable for their proper management. It supposes that a risk management culture is grafted on the existing organizational culture. It applies audit practices that monitor how specific workflow controls are applied to risk management documentation that impacts upside and downside results.

Enterprise risk management and loss control programs are efficient only if they are based on consistent, complete and reliable risk management documentation. This is why every organization can improve risk management decision making at all levels, from strategic to tactical, by applying business intelligence analytics to generate risk exposure insights from their information system assets.

Enterprise risk analytics (ERA) systems integrate enterprise-wide data flows for management reporting, business planning, internal controls testing, and credit evaluation. The evidence of ERA systems use helps to fulfil regulatory oversight needs for transparent reporting. Data management logs that show IT Governance practices are orchestrated across risk management collaboration groups support enterprise corporate governance objectives for performance reporting accountability, regulatory compliance fulfilment, and audit assertions integrity.

Enterprise Risk Analytics Systems

Enterprise risk analytics systems are IT applications that use business intelligence functionality to maintain master data management integrity controls when applying complex calculations to transactional and external data sources.

The processing capacity of enterprise information architecture has expanded to accommodate "big data" transaction file sizes and "in memory processing" of complex calculations. The business intelligence technical reference to ETL (extraction, transformation and loading into functional data marts) has been supplanted by the computational capability to do direct analytic calculations against transaction files. This reduces storage requirements, processing time and applies risk detection to more immediate notifications across a broad monitoring array of operational and financial system mappings.

Enterprise business intelligence analytics systems ensure that there are consistent definitions and calculations in the data management foundations of business reporting and analysis. These are the primary business intelligence functions that apply to documenting enterprise-wide risk management decision analysis practices:

- **Performance management scorecards** show risk evaluation in change monitoring metrics.
- **Organization reports** profile job role performance responsibilities and accountability management metrics.
- **Data mining programs** are applied to operational processes for data quality assurance, detective controls and risk mitigation role responsibilities.
- **Data security administration logs** show IT Governance oversight is applied to risk management collaboration networks and role-based access to key documentation.
- **Risk notification logs** show risk alerts communicated to risk management collaboration group members.
- **Master data management** practices documentation fulfils IT governance auditing standards for audit test design benchmarking.

Risk management culture auditing is reflected in assessing how information that passes IT governance standards is used by directors and officers to confirm there is enterprise-wide oversight of risk management performance roles delegation. The chief executive officer (CEO) and chief financial officer (CFO) of public corporations have fiduciary oversight responsibility to certify the integrity of internal risk controls. The application of enterprise risk analytics information to specific ISO quality standards illustrates to stakeholders that risk management culture principles originate at the top of the business's hierarchy. ISO implementation status reviews set the "tone at the top" that reinforces the organization's commitment to managing risk enterprise-wide through each person's job activities.

The consolidated documentation of how enterprise analytics systems, IT governance and risk monitoring outputs are orchestrated by senior management forms the basis of enterprise risk factor case reviews; these confirm organization roles' decision-making accountability for achieving risk management culture goals.

Management agendas for enterprise risk analytics reviews are set by prioritizing specific risk factors that may rise to the strategic impact level. The ERA review process covers all issues that may have a material impact on financial results. Each risk factor is associated with programs or projects where managers are assigned to assess upside opportunities and downside loss exposures.

The ERA agenda always includes core topics such as Cyber Risk Exposures, Stage 1 Disaster Recovery Plans, Business Continuity Risk Mitigation Plans and Systemic Investment Market Risk Exposure Response Plans. The chief risk officer (CRO) also puts significant Insurance Coverage/Catastrophic Loss potential/Risk Retention decisions on the agenda for active discussion of financial and operational risk treatment plans.

Enterprise risk analytics systems' information can solve the problem of connecting risk management program plan objectives across organization departmental silos and external supplier/vendor networks. Outcomes from enterprise risk analytics reviews provide assurance that risk management plans fulfil fiduciary oversight of six key risk management orchestration factors:

Financial and Credit Reporting
- *Risk factor disclosure information* is linked to the correct legal entities, financial statements and general ledger financial account balances.
- Financial statement accuracy is validated by systematic tests of GAAP, IFRS and statutory accounting standards reconciliation.
- Risk exposure analysis detail reports fulfil disclosure information frameworks proscribed by credit rating agencies, banking relationships and insurance underwriters.

Legal Matter Management
- Insurance coverage analysis is assessed for enterprise coordination of coverage across insurance policies with primary, excess and reinsurance underwriters.
- Supplier/vendor and customer contracts are analyzed for ISO Standards alignment and risk factor exposures impact.
- Legal case status analysis calculations are aligned with loss development forecast reports and financial reserve account balance statement updates.

Audit Programs Synchronization
- Tax liability analysis preparation reconciles with federal, state and local authorities' reporting schedules and accounting reconciliation programs.

- Regulatory reporting analysis confirms the systems of record and workflow controls for aligning compliance standards documentation.
- Regulatory compliance metrics are benchmarked to synchronize audit test plans and examination processes.

IT Governance
- Risk management documentation access privileges are aligned with risk management collaboration group members' roles.
- Data security administration practices fulfil professional standards for privacy management controls over financial and operational information.

Risk Exposure Analytics
- Claims experience trends are monitored systematically.
- Risk root-cause event analysis identifies the physical locations of potential losses.
- Risk management program leaders are able to assess the factors that impact loss development forecasts.

Risk Management Programs
- Loss controls planning documentation is updated systematically to reflect changes in loss experience and risk mitigation success.
- Risk treatment plans are associated with insurance coverage and risk retention analysis.
- Risk management skills training is provided to key roles participating in risk management programs.

Chief risk officers and other staff members who prepare enterprise risk analysis cases for senior management reviews maintain enterprise-wide oversight of the organization decision making roles that contribute to evaluating resource time and expense budget line items. These oversight steps are critical to confirm risk management programs are operationally viable.

Risk management program implementation plans include ongoing assessment of enterprise risk management indices. The index includes **inherent risk assessments** of potential maximum loss severity events that address catastrophic risk planning. The **residual risk assessment** will show how COSO (Committee for Sponsoring Organizations) standards for mitigation controls maturity are applied to calculating loss frequency and severity probabilities. The active use of enterprise risk analytics distinguishes legal entities that are able to link risk management program decision owners to the specific risk assessments and risk mitigation plans for his/her areas of job role responsibilities.

2.5.2 Making the Case for Enterprise Analytics Systems to the Board

Insurance, reinsurance companies and banks have regulatory guidelines in place to frame ERM programs goals for managing business process risks in the wake of Solvency 2 and Basel banking standards enforcement. Responsible board members in all companies need to understand how the use of enterprise risk analytics systems relate to assessing decisions that strengthen management capabilities to predict opportunities for growth and prevent potential losses.

ERM or enterprise-wide risk management topics are now high on the boardroom agendas of financial committees, human resources/compensation committees, and risk committees. Whatever board committee structure is in place, board consensus on both upside opportunities, and downside threats, are clearly the cornerstone of directors' fiduciary monitoring responsibility for the GRC triangle's principles that connect governance, risk and compliance oversight standards.

Managing risk uncertainty is essential to develop and execute enterprise performance strategies that can adapt to the unexpected – and still deliver company value expectations to all stakeholders. The main driver is to target the application of enterprise risk analytics systems from directors' understanding of the complexities in enterprise risk case prioritization decisions, whether the subject may be maintaining desired credit rating documentation or applying risk analysis information to business continuity contingency planning.

Directors and officers recognize that each entity must develop its own risk management program plans. They must assess whether internal resources that do not have access to risk analysis systems have adequate capacity to maintain reporting programs accountability and their risk mitigation treatment plan responsibilities. As risk information reporting requests from regulators and business contract counterparties expands, the need increases to monitor fulfilment of risk management-related reporting responsibilities for the organization's goals and strategic performance management missions.

Regulatory changes in global financial risk information reporting from "systemically important financial institutions" provide test cases for all directors and officers to assess how they are adjusting banking and insurance information exchange practices with "SIFIs" that may be "too big to fail."

US regulators are linking the systemically important financial institutions' (SIFIs) capital adequacy calculations with bankruptcy stress testing analysis reports. SIFIs are required to file corporate living wills (CLWs) documentation that shows how their simulations of global asset value meltdowns are linked to risk mitigations plans and ultimately to bankruptcy trustee filings. SIFIs' CLW reports provide inputs for all company treasurers to assess how their bank's and investor's stress test scenarios affect Treasury management contingency plans.

Intraday credit monitoring regulatory changes are now in place to reduce the threats of how asset liquidity meltdowns can freeze global banking relationships. Over-the-counter derivative instruments now require three-way settlement reconciliation with clearing banks to assure adequate margins are on deposit to match derivatives transactions. Investor cash balance adequacy assurance now requires the enterprise total collateral valuation reports support financial guarantees. Portfolio securities price value aging must be disclosed to investors. Companies that are near credit cap requirements must prioritize daily securities trades in advance of a common (US East Coast) afternoon settlement time. Maintaining securities settlement fiduciary documentation simply requires risk analytics mastery to exchange information and risk notifications with investment counterparties.

The case for enterprise analytics systems starts at the top of the organization with assessment of the largest risk exposures. The following box provides a partial explanation of enterprise risk analytics systems benefits that are relevant across all organization levels.

Enterprise Risk Analytics Systems Benefits

- Achieve consensus on ERM program priorities at the top of the enterprise across the legal entities and key work functions that report to the CEO and the Board.
- Connect the board of directors' risk committee reporting package to drill down on the fiduciary oversight accountability for strategic goals review.

- Apply ISO standards review to enterprise risk analytics systems' frameworks and accounting templates, which highlight where global best practices are connected to ERM programs implementation.
- Promote visibility into risk root-cause issues that cut across traditional financial and operational systems reports.
- Assess risk information gaps that can affect loss reserve forecasting accuracy and higher loss adjustment services expenses for risk response plan implementation and legal case documentation needs.
- Strengthen AUDITS that use enterprise risk analysis information to provide systemic validation of management reporting TRANSPARENCY and confirmation that the appropriately ACCOUNTABLE risk management network roles are connected via IT networks to make timely decisions. (This is invaluable analysis for preparing stakeholders' risk disclosure reports and structuring regulatory compliance testing programs.)

All US 10 KQ filing companies are on an XBRL detailed reporting implementation timetable to apply disclosure analytics to financial statement account line balances and footnotes. The filings are used by investors and regulators for industry peer group performance analysis.

Table 2.1 Enterprise risk analysis case issues

Risk Management Programs	Case Review Issues	Functional Leadership
Cyber Risk Treatment Plans	• Cyber Attacks • Intellectual Property Targets • Fraud Detection	• IT • Legal • Risk Management
Property – Environment Treatment Plans	• Environmental Forecasts • Business Interruption Estimates • Disaster Recovery Resources • Property Replacement Value	• Property management • Operations • Finance
Accident and Safety Treatment Plans	• OSHA Standards • Accident Rates • Workers Compensation Experience	• Risk Management • Human Resources • Regulatory
Health & Wellness Treatment Plans	• Health Insurance Premiums • Wellness Program Participation Rates	• Human Resources • Regulatory
Pension & Savings Programs Treatment Plans	• Investment Asset Types Value • Funded Liabilities • Qualified Plan Standards	• Finance • Investments • Regulatory
Investment Market Risk Plans	• Investment Asset Types Value • Collateral Requirements • Securities Clearance Cycles • Market Risk Notifications • Corporate Action Events	• Finance • Investments • IT • Legal
Country Risk Recovery	• Global Business Risks • Supply Chain Exposures • Employee – Contractor Risks • Asset Recovery Exposures	• Risk Management • Procurement • Operations • Human Resources • Finance

(*XBRL is a global data tagging standard for exchanging information through accounting tax-onomyschemas and linked databases that are tested for financial reporting validation checks.*) The XBRL Analytics tagging framework has also been extended to cover all investment securities' corporate actions events that relate to changes in the valuation of capital and equity.

Should your company not have had the ERM discussion in the boardroom yet, it will happen soon. Obtaining the board's support is necessary but not sufficient for successful ERM program implementation.

Table 2.1 shows a set of enterprise risk analysis cases that have risen to the strategic review level in many companies. Case review issues and functional leadership highlight topics covered and organization participants who are typically involved in risk management analysis and risk treatment program planning. All companies will add a priority rating and risk readiness evaluation to the specific issues that apply to their legal entities.

Risk treatment plan leaders use risk analysis metrics dashboards to plan and control risk management programs. Table 2.2 shows examples of organizational job roles that maintain key information that goes into risk analysis decisions and implementation activities for specific programs.

Table 2.2   Risk analysis metrics dashboard

Enterprise Risk Analysis Metrics	Metric Type	Risk Management Collaboration Group Roles
Inherent Risk Financial Impact	Currency Value	• Chief Risk Officer • Chief Financial Officer
Risk Factors Impact – Stakeholder Reporting Footnotes	Count #	• Chief Risk Officer • General Counsel • Chief Financial Officer
Relevant Insurance Coverage Policies/Premiums – Financial Guaranty Contracts/Amount	Count # Currency Value	• Chief Risk Officer
Claims Pending/Paid/Reserves	Count # Currency Value	• Chief Risk Officer • General Counsel
Loss Adjustment Services Providers/Expense	Count # Currency Value	• Chief Risk Officer • Procurement Officer • Controller
Related Legal Matter Documents/ Legal Matter Expense	Count # Currency Value	• Chief Risk Officer • General Counsel
Residual Risk Control Tests/Audit Documents/Business Process Maturity (COSO) Assessments	Count # Assessment Score	• Chief Audit Officer • Chief Risk Officer
Regulatory Authority Filings/ Regulatory Filing Documents/ Regulatory Penalties	Count # Currency Value	• Chief Compliance Officer
Risk Management Collaboration Group Members	Count #	• Chief Information Officer • Data Security Manager
Risk Documents Access Privileges	Count #	• Chief Risk Officer • Documentation Administration Manager

Risk management action plan preparedness metrics provide the keys to assessing the difference between paper-based programs and executable action that reduce ultimate losses. Experience shows that success is correlated with how risk owners are empowered and trained for their enterprise risk analysis roles in ERM programs (Table 2.3).

Table 2.3   Risk management action plan

Enterprise Risk Analysis Metrics	Metric Type	Risk Management Collaboration Group Roles
Risk Response Resources	Full Time Equivalent Staff (FTE) Commitment	• Chief Risk Officer • Chief Financial Officer
Risk Response First Stage Recovery Budget Expense Estimate	Currency Value	• Chief Risk Officer • Controller
Risk Treatment Plan Workshops	Count #	• Chief Risk Officer • Training Director
Risk Treatment Plan Workshop Participants	Count #	• Chief Risk Officer • Training Director • Operations Managers

Higher analytics system user percentages of all company managers leads to measureable success in loss experience ratings that lower the cost of risk and increase performance goal forecasting accuracy. The information in the Enterprise Risk Analysis Case Issues and the Enterprise Risk Analysis Metrics Dashboard examples provide baselines to evaluate how well current IT Assets support risk management planning and control. Understanding Risk Information Cycle Management "gaps" between current risk decision information reliability and desired risk analytics mastery targets is the foundation of risk management planning leadership.

Reference

Dresner, H. (2009) *Profiles in Performance: Business Intelligence Journeys and the Roadmap for Change.* New York: John Wiley & Sons.

2.6   EMERGING ENTERPRISE RISKS FACING THE US HEALTHCARE INDUSTRY

Robert L. Snyder, BA, JD, ARM

Professional risk advisor and a member of the Texas Bar. and has served as Adjunct Lecturer in the College of Business at the University of Houston – Downtown

Healthcare delivery is one of the most complex industries in modern American society. Taken as an "enterprise", healthcare is comprised of a diverse set of service providers and stakeholders, ranging from direct healthcare providers represented by physicians, nurses, therapists and an array of other clinicians and allied health professionals. There are institutional care facilities such as hospitals, long-term care facilities (e.g. nursing homes, assisted living facilities, senior living communities), rehabilitation centers, ambulatory surgery centers, diagnostic imaging centers, and other facilities. On the supply side there are pharmaceutical and medical device manufacturers, and medical research facilities. On the business end there are private and institutional investors and shareholders in many of these businesses. Finally, there are the payers for services, including governmental programs, such as Medicare and Medicaid, health insurance companies and self-insured employers.

Healthcare is an enterprise that touches every individual throughout life in material and profound ways that other industries do not. There are many products and services one might elect to purchase or not purchase in the course of a lifetime (a house, an automobile, a personal computer, a vacation, a college education – all "elective" purchasing decisions). However, it is virtually 100% certain every person will need healthcare within the delivery structure that exists for providing it at a given point in time during his or her life.

The business, technological, political and societal influences on healthcare are also complex and interrelated. "Healthcare reform" efforts undertaken in the United States in the late twentieth and early twenty-first centuries (to be addressed further below) have revealed many challenges in identifying and addressing "risks" associated with healthcare.

Enterprise level risks, broadly stated, apply within the healthcare industry as they do in a host of other settings, along the following lines:

- Financial risks.
- Hazard risks.
- Operational risks.
- Strategic risks.

Financial risks can be generally defined as risks affecting profitability, and/or economic efficiency in the case of not-for-profit institutions. Financial risks include those that impact the enterprise's cash position, access to capital or favorable financial ratings, business relationships with other parties, such as suppliers, and the timing of recognition of revenues and expenses.

With respect to healthcare, while the "system" overall is comprised of an amalgamation of both for-profit and not-for-profit sectors, "profitability" applies to both. In for-profit endeavors, it is easy enough to understand that investors seek a return on their capital that is at risk in the enterprise. Although much healthcare is provided through not-for-profit institutions, these entities likewise must normally earn a financial margin (a surplus that is akin to profit) to be sustainable. For instance, a common motto among faith-based, not-for-profit healthcare organizations is, "no margin, no mission."

The government at various levels has a major and increasing role in delivering and managing healthcare. Arguably the government does not seek to, and need not be concerned about, operating at a "profit." However, if entities under governmental control accumulate large deficits over time, the burden falls on the taxpayers, which has significant political consequences, including the continuation (or not) of certain programs.

Hazard Risks, generally speaking, are risks resulting in loss or damage to physical assets of the business, or injury or property damage to other parties, including customers, patients, employees, business trading partners or other third parties, arising from the actions or alleged negligence of the business. Hazard risks are sometimes thought of as "insurable risks," in that they are comprised of the types of damage or injury for which most businesses can readily purchase insurance. Examples in the healthcare setting include medical malpractice and product liability lawsuits, and natural disasters (e.g. hurricanes, tornadoes, floods) causing damage to facilities such as hospitals or nursing homes.

Operational Risks refer to risks to the ongoing conduct of the business that result from changes in business practices, allocation of entity resources, effects of external regulations or requirements, inadequate or failed internal processes, people or systems. Operational risk is sometimes referred to as the risk associated with "doing the (strategic) thing right."

Strategic Risks are risks that impact the organization's ability to achieve its broader goals and objectives, such as risks to market position or reputation, or the risk that a business plan to which major resources and effort are committed will ultimately not be successful due to lack of acceptance in the marketplace. Strategic risk is sometimes referred to as the risk associated with "doing the right thing."

In fact, it is important to understand *strategic risk management*, in particular as a critical component ultimately driving "enterprise" risk management. "Strategic risk" is associated with adopting or not adopting the correct strategy for the organization in the first place, or, once adopted, not *adapting* the chosen strategy in response to competition or other forces. Strategic risk management contemplates the integration of strategic planning, the setting of organizational objectives and the identification of "risk" with the organization's enterprise risk management program.

Enterprise risk management addresses risks *to* strategy at its core. ERM significantly looks for critical risks (and, as noted below, opportunities) associated with the defined strategy. In the context of healthcare reform (to be discussed further), for instance, an important strategic shift for both providers and payers is the realignment from "fee for service" medicine (i.e. the more services and procedures provided the more revenue generated) to "global" type payments that will generate rewards, presumably for all parties, including patients, through wellness and quality metrics associated with managing the health of certain defined populations, especially including population groups characterized by common chronic conditions, such as hypertension, obesity and diabetes.

It is further important to note that "risk" does not merely denote the likelihood of failure. Risk also represents opportunity, and in fact, from a business perspective in healthcare, or other industries, any opportunity worth pursuing is likely to entail risk. A chairman of Lloyd's of London phrased it this way:

> But risk management is not simply about preparing for the worst. It's also about realizing your full potential. With a clear understanding of the risks they face, businesses can maximize their performance and drive forward their competitive advantage.[17]

Further, it will be obvious that while the "four quadrants" represent a convenient manner for broadly categorizing risks, risks within each quadrant do not exist in isolation from the risks in other quadrants. There is significant overlap, and an area of convergence, where particular risks may be regarded concurrently as financial, strategic, operational or hazard risks in various combinations. "Enterprise-wide" risk management essentially focuses on the overlapping risks. These risks might be thought of by the managers or leaders of the enterprise in the form of the question, "What keeps you up at night?"

To illustrate within a specific segment of healthcare, consider for a moment the risks associated with a Managed Care Organization (MCO). The MCO is typically a third-party payer for medical or other healthcare services, such as a health insurance company or Healthcare Maintenance Organization (HMO). These are licensed, regulated entities, business enterprises generally subject to a specific set of laws and regulations promulgated on a state-by-state basis. Within the context of "managed care," not only do these entities negotiate contracts to pay healthcare providers, typically on behalf of employer-funded health insurance programs, they

---

[17] Levene, Lord. Risk management is essential to every business. *Financial Times*, October 17, 2006.

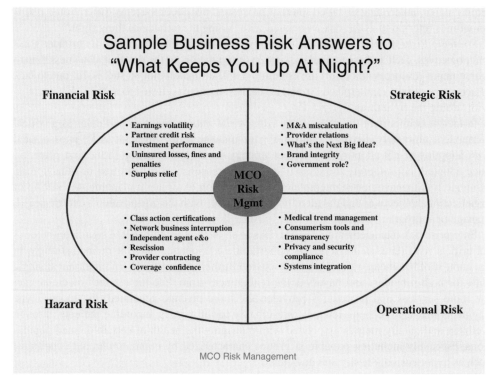

Figure 2.3   "What keeps you up at night?"

establish the parameters for coverage, such as which tests and procedures will be covered, what treatments will be accepted, based on a particular diagnosis, and what preventive services will be offered.

Examples of risks within each of the "quadrants" appear within Figure 2.3. For many MCOs these risks (or some subset thereof) have been the focus of attention for quite a long time. In the current environment, where new or significantly modified risks will arise under recently enacted federal and state laws, consider how the illustrated risks might change.

Similar matrices can be created for other business sectors, which collectively represent the sweep of entities comprising the healthcare industry.

One overriding factor impacting enterprise risk in the healthcare industry has been the evolving healthcare reform. During the past generation the first serious reform at the federal level was the effort actively promoted during the first term of the Clinton administration in the early 1990s. "Reform" objectives had long been debated both in society and in Congress. Generally, these objectives related to proposed measures for increasing access to healthcare by a large and growing segment of the population lacking health insurance, coupled with measures designed to control costs and improve outcomes for those receiving healthcare. For many years, influenced by many factors, medical cost inflation had outstripped inflation in the general economy. At the same time, despite an ever-growing proportion of the United States' gross domestic product consumed by the cost of healthcare, the country actually began to lag behind other developed economies in a number of quality indicators.

Ultimately, the healthcare reform effort of the 1990s did not succeed, but the nation's attention was focused on the issue in a way that it had not been in many years. Coming into the 21st century, the effort was rekindled after the election of Barack Obama as president in 2008. Although there was great political and public debate, in 2010 Congress passed the Patient Protection and Affordable Care Act (PPACA), the most sweeping set of reform measures relating to healthcare in many years. The new law was challenged in federal court, ultimately leading to the 2012 decision by the U.S. Supreme Court[18] upholding the major provisions of the law.

The Supreme Court decision, coupled with the re-election of President Obama to a second term in November, 2012, have made it clear healthcare reform is here to stay for the foreseeable future. Profound implications are created at the enterprise level for entities and providers involved in the delivery of healthcare.

Thus, enterprise risk management stands to be a topic of increasing importance in healthcare. It remains to be seen exactly what risks will emerge and how they will be managed, but the following are suggested as major risk drivers, which will impact different sectors of healthcare:

Accountable Care Organizations (ACOs)   PPACA provides for the formation and licensing at the federal level of "umbrella" entities within geographic areas that will contract with health-care providers and manage the delivery of care to designated population groups participating in governmentally funded programs, particularly Medicare (primarily focused on the elderly) and Medicaid (primarily focused on the poor). ACOs will be financially incentivized by the government to contain costs and improved quality through a shared savings program and a set of metrics relating to health outcomes of the population served. ACOs are required to be independent legal entities and may be not-for-profit or investor owned. Health systems, for instance, will be being challenged to determine whether there is a particular competitive advantage (or disadvantage) to them in ACO development or participation.

Health Insurance Exchanges   PPACA also directs the creation of state run health insurance "exchanges," which will serve to provide insurance to segments of the population that might otherwise be unable to obtain it. States are incentivized within the law to participate in the exchange program on an optional basis through enhanced funding from the federal government to support the Medicaid program, which has long been administered at the state level. For states that reject the option and refuse to establish exchanges, the federal government is authorized to set up the exchanges.

Population Health Management   An important aspect of healthcare transformation will be the management of care within specific "populations" in ways not previously utilized. This might include, for instance new collaborations among providers targeting specific chronic diseases, such as high blood pressure or diabetes, affecting a certain population segment. Care will require coordination among specialists, which may or may not be formalized by specific contractual agreements allocating legal and financial liabilities. Revenue sharing among collaborating providers will have to be agreed. Population health management is likely to transcend medical care and also involve "quality of life" assistance from home aides, for instance, running errands or assisting with household needs.

---

[18] *National Federation of Independent Business v. Sebellius*, 132 S. Ct. 2566. The case was heard together with *Florida v. Department of Health and Human Services.*

Decreases in Reimbursements to Providers   Over a period of years the federal government will substantially decrease the level of reimbursements for many healthcare services provided primarily by physicians and hospitals. Presumably, the providers will have access to a larger insured population and thus the reduced reimbursements will be offset by greater volume generating additional revenue for the providers, as opposed to them having to "write off" a certain proportion of uncompensated care provided to an indigent population.

Physician Employment and Contracting   The complexities associated with complying with the new law, and the need to be part of provider networks, are likely to have the practical effect of forcing many physicians out of their traditional independent practitioner roles and into either direct employment by hospitals or health systems, or into various contractual relationships that will result in a high degree of control over their practices. This trend is well underway in many parts of the country. The acquisition of physician practices and the negotiation of physician employment contracts are both complex undertakings.

Electronic Medical Records and Patient Privacy Considerations   Going beyond the 1996 HIPAA act, the new law effectively mandates that healthcare providers adopt and implement systems for electronic medical records, in order to facilitate the timely and accurate exchange of patient information among an array of providers, such as primary care physicians, specialists and hospitals. The federal government has allocated "stimulus" funds available to providers to encourage their adoption of EMR systems. At the same time, providers are subject to strict constraints and penalties under a prior federal law, the Health Insurance Portability and Accountability Act of 1996 (HIPAA), for security breaches resulting in the intentional or unintentional disclosure of "personal health information."

Implications for Medical Technology Companies   Both pharmaceutical companies and medical device manufacturers stand to be impacted by material changes in the healthcare business environment. Pharmaceutical companies will be under pressure to document the effectiveness of medications in producing positive clinical outcomes at acceptable cost for various populations under medical management. Insurers may refuse to include medications falling outside certain parameters on their approved formularies. Funding for development of new therapies may become more difficult to generate. With respect to device manufacturers, they are impacted by a new 2.3% excise tax called for by the Accountable Care Act as of January 1, 2013. Small start-ups, in particular, which represent a material proportion of all medical device development may be disproportionately impacted and placed at a competitive disadvantage.

Industry Consolidation   As the impact of many aspects of the healthcare reform law at the federal level, and various counterparts at the state level, takes hold the financial viability of many healthcare entities will become tenuous. In a competitive environment inevitably there will be consolidation and contraction in various forms, such as through mergers and acquisitions. This activity logically will increase the probability that investors, such as shareholders, and other stakeholders will find themselves financially disadvantaged and will seek legal redress.

   All of these risks, as well as others undefined, can be seen as emerging "enterprise" risks for healthcare organizations. Enterprise risk management, therefore, stands to serve a major role in development of business strategies for the healthcare industry in the years to come.

3

Select and Implement the Appropriate Risk Management Technique

Risk treatment occurs after risks have been identified, evaluated and assessed. Treatment can include avoidance, acceptance, mitigation, transfer (for example, insurance), separate, and optimize and exploit. ERM often produces novel risks that require novel treatment. What organizations are beginning to understand is that proper treatment can be used not just to reduce the cost of loss but also increase the bottom line. Examples of exploitation include venturing into niche markets where others have been unable to control loss, or using risk control techniques to increase reputation and by doing so increase revenue and the acquisition of more profitable business.

3.1 RISK TO REPUTATION

Sophie Gaultier-Gaillard
Associate Professor at Paris 1 Panthéon-Sorbonne University, Paris

Jean-Paul Louisot
Formerly Université Paris 1 Panthéon-Sorbonne, Directeur pédagogique du CARM Institute, Paris, France

Jenny Rayner
Director of consulting firm Abbey Consulting

Warren Buffett (Chairman and CEO, Berkshire Hathaway) once said: "It takes 20 years to build a reputation and five minutes to ruin it. If you think about that you'll do things differently." The teachings to draw from this quote are manifold. Firstly, it demonstrates that risk is a social construct (Douglas and Wildawsky, 1982). Secondly, it shows that people tend to perceive it as a threat and totally miss the dual aspect of risk, i.e. the potential opportunities. Thirdly, it implies that people should react and learn from past errors and improve their behavior.

But is this what happens in real life? At the start of the twenty-first century managing reputational risk has become a major preoccupation for businesses in the private, public and not-for-profit sectors. A survey conducted by Aon in 2007[1] rated damage to reputation as the number one global business risk, although half of the survey's respondents said they were not prepared for it.

In the aftermath of the Enron, WorldCom, Parmalat and other corporate catastrophes, more stringent corporate governance and regulatory compliance requirements, strengthened regulator powers, the growing influence of pressure groups and rising stakeholder expectations have sharpened the focus on business reputation. Added to this, the advent of real-time global

---

[1] Aon's Global Risk Management Survey 2007 was based on responses from 320 organizations in 29 countries.

telecommunications and 24/7 media scrutiny and social media can result in an apparently minor incident in a far-flung part of a company's operations hitting the international headlines and provoking a major crisis.

Enjoying a good reputation yields many rewards: not least the continuing trust and confidence of customers, investors, suppliers, regulators, employees and other stakeholders, the ability to differentiate the business and create competitive advantage. A bad reputation, conversely, can result in a loss of customers, unmotivated employees, shareholder dissatisfaction and ultimately the demise of the business itself.

The challenge of managing reputation and its associated risks is well illustrated by the Warren Buffett quote at the start of this article. Hard-earned reputations can be surprisingly fragile and can be tarnished or irrevocably damaged as a result of a moment's lapse of judgment or an inadvertent remark. That is why it is so vital to manage risks to reputation as rigorously as more tangible and quantifiable risks to the business.

3.1.1 What is Reputation?

This question is worth asking because there is still some confusion between brand and reputation. Here we reserve the word "reputation" to cover all aspects of the stakeholders' perception of an organization, whereas the name "brand" applies more to a specific product or service. Therefore, a company's reputation may incorporate several brands and be influenced by them. It is therefore of interest to the "reputation scholar" to study brand building and maintaining. A recent study[2] shed an interesting light on a five-stage process stressing for brands attributes similar to those described here for reputation:

Differentiation: How to stand out from competition?

Positioning: Why do consumers and employees need this new product in their lives?

Personality: How is the message communicated to employees and consumers? Are they involved in a dialogue through a consultation process?

Vision: How do we convince consumers and employees of the high-minded values embedded in the brand?

Added value: What do the consumers and the employees get, that they could not with another product (competition/substitution)?

According to the *Compact Oxford English Dictionary*, reputation is "the beliefs or opinions that are generally held about someone or something". Depending on the field studied, reputation may have different meanings (Gaultier-Gaillard and Louisot, 2006) but always constitutes an intangible asset. The main question should then be to determine what makes a good reputation. The theory is simple: an organization enjoys a good reputation when it consistently meets or exceeds the expectations of its stakeholders. A bad reputation results when the organization's words or deeds fall short of stakeholder expectations. This concept is expressed in the reputation equation in Figure 3.1 below.

Reputation = experience − expectations

Oonagh Mary Harpur

Figure 3.1   The Reputation Equation[3]

---

[2] Leslie de Chernatony, Towards the Holy Grail of Defining Brand, *Marketing Theory, vol. 9*, n° 1 – May 2009.

[3] Harpur, Oonagh Mary, in *Corporate Social Responsibility Monitor* (2002). London: Gee Publishing, Chapter B4.

Stakeholder expectations are shaped by their beliefs about what a business is and what it does. These beliefs are influenced by what the business says about itself and by what others say about it. Stakeholders then measure their actual experience of how the business acts against their expectations.

A good reputation is achieved when there is congruence between a business's purpose, its goals and values (what it professes to be), its conduct and actions (what it does in practice) and the experience and expectations of its stakeholders. Maintaining a good reputation therefore requires continuing identification and management of emerging gaps between experience and expectations and between claims and reality using a risk-oriented approach.

3.1.2   Why is Reputation Valuable?

A business's reputation is valuable on two counts: first, its intrinsic current value as an intangible asset and secondly, its ability to create – or destroy – future value.

Reputation will not appear as a separate item on a business's balance sheet but generally represents a significant proportion of the difference between market value and book value (minus any quantifiable intangibles such as trademarks and licences). As total intangibles now often account for some 75% or more of market value, reputation is, for many businesses, their single greatest asset.

A good reputation not only underpins a business's continuing licence to operate, but provides it with a licence to expand and generate new partnerships and income streams, for example, by helping to secure preferred partner status on future projects or by enabling premium pricing for products and services. Reputation is often not only a business's single greatest current asset but also a potential source of competitive advantage and a key determinant of future business success (see Figure 3.2).

Reputation is also a critical business differentiator. As Alan Greenspan, former US Federal Reserve Chairman, has observed: "In today's world, where ideas are increasingly displacing the physical in the production of economic value, competition for reputation becomes a significant driving force propelling our economy forward. Manufactured goods often can be evaluated before the completion of a transaction. Service providers, on the other hand, usually can offer

---

Reputation may impact:

- Stockholders' decisions to hold onto their shares.
- Customers' desire to buy products and services.
- Suppliers' desire to establish partnerships.
- Competitors' eagerness to enter the market.
- Media coverage.
- Pressure groups/NGO activity.
- Control and regulatory authority attitudes.
- Cost of capital.
- Recruitment of high potential individuals.
- Motivation of current workforce.
- Inclination of stakeholders to grant the benefit of the doubt when a crisis emerges.

Figure 3.2   Reputation impact on stakeholders' behavior

only their reputations."[4] This is particularly true of service industries where the end product is invisible, as the present crisis illustrates clearly and gives an ironical twist to Greenspan's assertion. Insurers, for example, are in the business of promising to pay out on a claim at an unspecified date in the future. The policyholder cannot assess the insurer's willingness and ability to fulfil the promise at the time of purchase and may have insufficient grasp of the fine detail of a complex policy. Their purchase decision can therefore only be made based on the business's reputation and the level of trust and confidence it engenders. If the business's reputation is eroded, and stakeholder trust and confidence diminish as a result, the insurer may find that policyholders rush to surrender their policies.

The queues of customers desperate to withdraw savings outside Northern Rock's branches in August 2007, jammed telephone lines and a website crash are a graphic example of how quickly stakeholder trust can evaporate and a corporate reputation can crumble amidst rumors of financial difficulties. British Government assurances did little to restore public confidence and this first run on a British bank since Victorian times led ultimately to the temporary nationalization of Northern Rock and attacks on the reputations of the Bank of England and the Financial Services Authority, the company's regulator.

Perhaps the greatest benefit of a "good" reputation is its capacity to provide a reserve of goodwill (often called "reputational capital" or "reputational equity") that can help the business withstand future shocks and crises. Such reputational capital, which underpins stakeholder trust and confidence, can act as a buffer at times of crisis and persuade stakeholders to give a business the benefit of the doubt and a second chance. In the case of Northern Rock, the shock was too severe, should have been predicted and had too immediate an effect on customers for the bank to weather the storm.

3.1.3   The Stakeholder Perspective: Who Counts?

As the key to a good reputation is meeting stakeholder expectations, it is vital to establish who your most significant stakeholders are, what expectations they have of you and how they currently perceive you. Only then can you pinpoint any gaps and start to correct them. You might start by listing and then prioritizing your business's stakeholders – both internal (employers) and external (shareholders, investors, suppliers, customers, regulators, analysts, insurers, government, etc.). The relative importance of stakeholders will vary between sectors. For example, in heavily regulated sectors such as financial services the regulator is likely to be a key stakeholder. It also is vital to consider a sufficiently broad range of stakeholders to ensure that no major interest group is neglected, as the sole omission may prove to be the source of an unidentified killer risk. Their expectations depend on the sum of their perceptions and their representations. As reputational risk is a social construct, their expectations on reputational risk are also a social construct (see Figure 3.3).

Once you have identified the main characteristics of the context where your stakeholders are, your prime focus should be on key players: those critical stakeholders with whom it is vital to maintain an active two-way dialogue so you can continuously track what they are thinking and saying about your business and what they expect of you, both now and in the future. Only in this way can a business truly identify not only its vulnerabilities but also opportunities to create competitive advantage.

---

[4] Remarks by Chairman Alan Greenspan, Commencement Address, Harvard University, Cambridge, Massachusetts, June 10, 1999, avail: http://www.federalreserve.gov/boarddocs/speeches/1999/199906102.htm

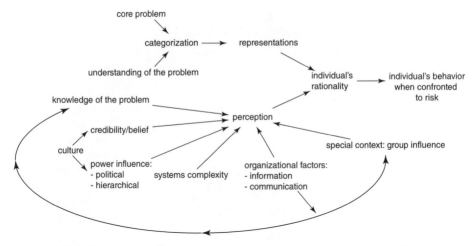

Figure 3.3   Risks and perception[5].

3.1.4   Reputational Risk: Risk or Impact? Threat or Opportunity?

There is no such thing as reputational risk – only risks to reputation. The term "reputational risk" is a convenient catchall for all those risks, from whichever source, that can *impact* reputation. The source could be legal non-compliance, a data security lapse, an unexpected profit warning or unethical behavior in the boardroom.

This broad interpretation of reputational risk has a growing following compared with the school of thought that classifies reputational risk as a discrete class of risk in itself that should be isolated and managed. It requires a business to assess *all* risks for potential reputational impact and ensures that risks to reputation are fully integrated into the core business risk management framework, are reported alongside other business risks and receive attention from the right person at the right level. Reputational risks are not simply parcelled up and handed to the public relations department for action, although PR can play an important supporting role.

When discussing reputational risk, many organizations consider only the downside threats that could damage corporate reputation. However, uncertainty can also have positive outcomes and can present business opportunities, which, if exploited, can create competitive advantage and added value for a business. Climate change is a potential business threat but many firms have spotted and exploited the flip-side opportunity to create a competitive edge by developing green technologies and promoting themselves as environmental leaders in their sector.

Reputational risk can be defined as:

> *Any action, event or situation that could adversely or beneficially impact an organization's reputation.*

3.1.5   Key Sources of Reputational Risk

The most crucial step in managing reputational risk is the initial identification of those factors that could impact reputation, either positively or negatively. But there remains the question of finding a starting point. You may wish to consider the key drivers of reputation as defined

[5]Gaultier-Daillard, S. (1997) Ph.D. Dissertation, *Précis et Logiques de Décision*; ENS Cachan (France).

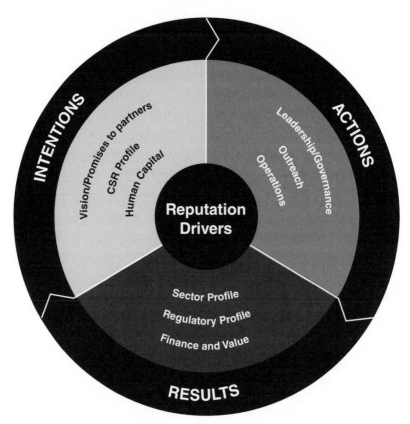

Figure 3.4   Reputation drivers and source of risk. Reproduced with permission. Rayner, J. (2003). *Managing Reputational Risk: Curbing threats, leveraging opportunities.* Chichester: Wiley.

by several well-respected reputation surveys around the world[6] as they are likely to be the most fertile sources of reputational risk. These are distilled into nine drivers of reputation and sources of reputational risk in Figure 3.4.

A useful question to tease out risks to reputation is: What newspaper headline would you least like to see about your business? And what event or situation could trigger it?

With increasingly complex supply chains and partnership arrangements and a wide range of customers in different sectors and territories, today's businesses need to consider *all* risks within the extended enterprise. Risks to reputation cannot be outsourced and should be borne and managed actively by the business itself. If a supplier's sub-contractor is found to be using child labor or a toll manufacturer slips a cheap toxic ingredient into a supposedly "green" product formulation the reputation of the company marketing the product will be tarnished, as companies including Nike and Mattel have learned to their cost.

A good starting point is to consider each of the nine drivers of reputation in the light of the stakeholder group(s) that have an interest in it. This can be mapped on a reputation risk

---

[6] These include: *Fortune* magazine's annual *Most Admired Companies* survey; the *Financial Times, World's Most Respected Companies survey*; and the Reputation Institute's Global Pulse study on the World's Most Respected Companies. No French companies were ranked as "Excellent/Top tier" (required score above 80/100) in the 2008 Global Pulse Survey. L'Oreal achieved the top score in France (75.68), with Société Générale scoring the lowest (37.82).

	Vision and Promise	CSR profile	Human capital	Leadership and governance	Outreach	Operations	Sector profile	Regulatory profile	Finance and value
Employees									
Customers									
Suppliers									
Community									
Pressure Groups/NGOs									
Investors									
Supervisory bodies									
Government									
Media-actors									
Partners									

Figure 3.5   Stakeholders/reputation drivers. Reproduced with permission. Rayner, J. (2003) *Managing Reputational Risk: Curbing threats, leveraging opportunities.* Chichester: Wiley.

driver/stakeholder matrix (illustrated by Figure 3.5) to produce a "heat map" highlighting potential reputational hot spots that warrant further attention.

Each of the nine drivers of reputation must be examined in more detail, so as to understand better the interactions between them and to identify potential dissonances (see the article in this text on the Cindynic approach).

3.1.6   Implementing Risk Management for the Risks to Reputation

As the Cindynic framework indicates[7] and the cases illustrate[8] the risk management for risks to reputation is based on a few simple principles and trust of others is at the heart of any strategy. However, if the strategy seems relatively easy to develop, risk management for reputation is above all an art of execution and therefore some key elements to ensure success, or at least avoid abysmal failure can be summarized here.

3.1.7   Evaluating and Prioritizing Reputational Risks

"While reputation is 'intangible', damage to an institution's reputation (and the resulting loss of consumer trust and confidence) can have very tangible consequences – a stock price decline, a run on the bank, a ratings downgrade, an evaporation of available credit, regulatory investigations, shareholder litigation etc."[9]

---

[7] Louisot, J-P. *Trois 'etudes de Jean-Paul Louisot: Managing reputational risk – A cindynic approach; Managing reputational risk – Case studies; Managing reputational risk – From theory to practice*, pp. 115–178.

[8] Alex Hindson, Jean-Paul Louisot, *Managing Reputational Risk – Case Studies*. In Klewes, J.P., Wreschniok R. (Eds) *Reputation Capital*, Spinger.com (2010).

[9] Stansfield, G. *Some thoughts on reputation and challenges for global financial institutions*, The Geneva Papers (2006) 31 (470–149).

What makes risks to reputation particularly difficult to evaluate is the random nature of its occurrence. Often, an issue deemed minor by a business can cause severe reputational damage, whereas an apparently major issue can pass without comment. Geography can also play a part. A minor event at a distant manufacturing site in a developing country may attract little or no media or stakeholder interest, whereas that same event in the business's heartland can provoke a reputational storm.

An assessment of reputational impact also needs to take into account the resilience of corporate reputation. This will depend on the amount of "reputational capital" built with stakeholders and the nature and extent of the issue or risk. Was this a predictable and preventable incident, such as anti-competitive activity, bribery condoned by senior management or an accident resulting from blatant disregard for human safety? If so, stakeholders are unlikely to be forgiving. Or was it an unforeseeable occurrence, which could not have been avoided, such as 9/11 or natural disaster where stakeholders will be sympathetic? Even after such catastrophic events stakeholders expect businesses to learn and adapt. So, post 9/11 and Hurricane Katrina, investors, regulators and customers now require businesses to have risk management systems and business continuity plans in place to counter the effect of such risks.

Another challenge in assessing impacts on reputation is that the initial impact of a risk crystallizing may be relatively small, perhaps a fine resulting from a minor breach of regulations. However, this may chip away insidiously at stakeholder trust. A series of minor bad news stories can have a cumulative effect whereby a "tipping point" is reached, after which stakeholders suddenly lose confidence, the business's share price plummets and current and all past misdemeanors are raked over in the ensuing media frenzy making it very difficult to recover.

Oil and gas company, BP, enjoyed a formidable reputation with investors and other stakeholders under the leadership of its much-admired former CEO Lord John Browne. Its hard-won reputation allowed it to withstand a number of crises in the early 2000s. However, the death of 15 workers and injury of 500 others when overfilled storage tanks exploded at BP's Texas City refinery in the US resulted in a massive loss of confidence in the company, a top-management shake-out and a new strategic approach.

Understanding precisely how stakeholders perceive your business at any point in time can help you judge whether you are approaching your reputational tipping point, where just one more bad news story could push you over the brink, and to evaluate reputational impact and respond accordingly.

It may be possible to place a monetary value on reputational risk, for example, via loss of future contracts/income; cost of loss of licence to operate; impact on Net Present Value (NPV); impact on share price; or impact on brand value. However, these cannot be applied to all reputational risks. Many businesses therefore use a qualitative approach to initially assess reputational impact (see Table 3.1, which uses a four-level scale), alongside financial and other relevant impact criteria. Both the short-term and longer-term impacts of a risk on the business's reputation should be considered, including the effect on stakeholder behavior and hence on the future value of the business.

3.1.8 Developing Risk Responses

The appropriate response to a risk impacting reputation will depend on its source (safety, project management, acquisition, IT security, and supply chain labor practices), whether it

Table 3.1   Assessing impact on reputation

Low	Moderate	High	Very High
Local complaint/ recognition	Local media coverage	National media coverage	International media coverage
Minimal change in stakeholders' confidence	Moderate change in stakeholder confidence	Significant change in stakeholder confidence	Dramatic change in stakeholder confidence
• Impact lasting less than one month	• Impact lasting between one and three months	• Impact lasting more than three months	• Impact lasting more than 12 months/ irrecoverable
		• Attracts regulators' attention/comment	• Public censure/ accolade by regulators

is a threat or an opportunity, its expected impact, the exposure relative to the business's risk appetite, whether the risk is treatable and the cost of treatment. The right response may be a zero tolerance accident regime, recruitment of a professional project manager, more rigorous due diligence covering ethical standards and commercial practices, enhanced security standards or independent third party audits of suppliers and sub-contractors. Suppliers and contractors themselves are now often required to abide by a business's code of conduct and core standards as part of their contractual relationship so they do not bring it into disrepute.

Risk responses should be designed to bridge gaps between reality and perception, between experience and expectations. They may therefore also include improving communications to certain stakeholder groups or helping to shape stakeholder expectations so they are more closely aligned with what the business can realistically deliver.

However good a business's risk management systems, there will always be an unforeseen crisis or risk that cannot be mitigated. Having an "off the shelf" generic crisis plan, which is proven, well rehearsed and can be quickly adapted and invoked to suit specific circumstances is an essential contingency measure to minimize reputational damage. The nature of the risk event needs to be carefully considered when mounting a response; a huge damage limitation exercise in the case of a self-inflicted wound such as loss of data due to poor internal security will be ineffective.

3.1.9   Monitoring and Reporting

Once risks to reputation have been identified and responses designed and implemented, the risk should be regularly monitored by management to ensure they are having the desired effect. The trick with risks to reputation is to build in early warning indicators that will provide advance warning of an impending crisis while there is still time to take corrective action. Systematic review of complaint trends may point to a product performance weakness, which can be dealt with long before disgruntled customers resort to litigation. Data on safety near misses, if collected and analysed with the right mindset, may provide vital insights into an impending fatal accident.

In so many reputational disasters the early signs were missed, sidelined or ignored. If spotted early enough and dealt with promptly by involving relevant specialist personnel (legal department, safety advisers or public relations) at an early stage, a crisis can be averted or even turned to reputational advantage.

Risk information needs to reach the right people (both internally and externally) at the right time if it is to have the desired effect. Timely and accurate reporting of reputational risks is an important, and often neglected, aspect of the reputation risk management process.

3.1.10   Roles and Responsibilities

Who should be the custodian of a business's reputation? Ultimately the CEO supported by the board of directors, but everyone working for an organization bears some responsibility for safeguarding and enhancing the business's reputation. This includes suppliers, contractors and other partners. All need to be made aware of the value of the business's reputation – and of the risks facing it – so each can play their part as reputational ambassadors.

The CEO and Board should set an appropriate tone through a corporate vision, values and clearly articulated risk appetite, which inform decision making and prescribe behaviors throughout the business and its supply chain. If awareness of reputational and other risks can be raised sufficiently the warning signs are more likely to be spotted and corrective action taken before a crisis strikes.

External non-executive and independent directors can play a particularly crucial role by using their broad experience to constructively challenge the business's risk profile. Have the right risks been identified? Have key stakeholders been consulted? Is anything missing? Has reputational impact been correctly assessed or is the business deluding itself?

Management's role is to continuously scan their area of operation for threats and opportunities that could impact business reputation; record and assess them; design, put in place and operate appropriate responses; monitor their effectiveness and hence the changing status of risks; and report to senior management and the board.

Risk management personnel can ensure that the risk management system is functioning well and that the data within it is updated regularly so timely and accurate reports can be generated to inform decision making.

An internal audit function can assist by providing independent assurance to the Board and management on the effectiveness of the risk management system and on whether individual key risks are being managed appropriately within the risk appetite set by the Board.

Public relations and communication staff can also play a critical role by monitoring and evaluating stakeholder perceptions and expectations to inform the risk management process, particularly in the evaluation of reputational impact and design of appropriate responses to mitigate threats and leverage opportunities. PR can help to design stakeholder engagement processes that not only help the business to keep in tune with the changing stakeholder mood, but also provide the opportunity to shape stakeholder opinion and minimize any perception/expectation gaps. The PR department should be involved sufficiently early in the process to make a difference; summoning PR at the eleventh hour when a crisis is about to erupt is not good risk management!

As suppliers and logistics personnel are often in the front line interacting daily with customers and communities, they too, if properly harnessed can become effective ambassadors for the business by working to enhance its reputation.

3.1.11   Overcoming the Barriers to Effective Reputation Risk Management

So why, when risk to reputation is rated the number one risk to business today, do so many organizations struggle to manage it effectively? A full 62% of companies in the Economist Intelligence Unit *Risk of Risks*[10] survey maintain that reputational risk is harder to manage than other types of risk.

There are several reasons for this:
- Low awareness of the true value of reputation as a key intangible asset and driver of business success and the need to safeguard and enhance it.
- Lack of awareness of potential sources of reputational risks so they can be identified and managed actively.
- Lack of clarity on ownership and consequently regarding reputational risk as a category of risk in itself, which is the preserve of the PR department. Defining reputational risk as anything that could impact reputation, either positively or negatively, can help to ensure that risks affecting reputation are mainstreamed, actioned at source and attract attention at the right level.
- Underestimating the impact of risks to reputation by focusing exclusively on short-term financial impact. Thinking that if you can't quantify the impact precisely it's not worth managing. A guesstimate of reputational impact, involving the right people and based on sound management judgment can make a big difference.
- Having a defensive, downside focus on threats; neglecting the positive upsides of reputational risk and failing to capture and exploit opportunities to boost reputation.

3.1.12   Building Resilience Through Sustainable Reputation: The Way Forward

"You can't build a reputation on what you're going to do" (Henry Ford)

Reputations are ever shifting and potentially transient; they need to be painstakingly built and carefully nurtured. Businesses must be constantly vigilant, not only thinking about reputation when things go wrong, but actively managing risks to reputation all the time. Reputation risk management is both an "inside out" and an "outside in" challenge.

The starting point is setting out your stall "inside out" by defining a clear vision and values, backed up by policies and procedures which will guide behaviors and inform decision making throughout the business and its supply chain. This will also enable your stakeholders to know what you stand for, what your goals are and how you plan to achieve it so they know what to expect.

The second part of the challenge is "outside in": keeping in close touch with major stakeholders and systematically tracking their evolving perceptions and expectations so gaps are minimized, emerging trends are spotted early and opportunities to offer new products and services in new ways in new markets are exploited.

Stakeholder expectations of businesses and their reputations have never been so high; being authentic, being "the real thing" has never been so important. The concept is far from new, but the way it's handled by businesses is quite new. The corporate responsibility (CR) and sustainable development (SD) agendas have clearly modified the traditional economic role of firms and added aims to their strategies. Nowadays businesses must integrate all their

---

[10] Ibid.

stakeholders, not only shareholders. In this way, they try to create competitive advantage and improve their reputation by the addition of an ethics element. Reputation must always be adapted to the context if it is to be resilient and sustainable. It is all the more crucial that perceived reputation is taken into account, for perception *is* reality in the minds of stakeholders. It is not enough to be sure of one's actions but the organization must also monitor carefully the image perceived by its stakeholders, even if it is subjective. This bias may be the source of many dissonances between the value put into reputation and the perceived value, which is the only "real" value at the end of the day.

3.1.13   Reputational Risk Management – A Vital Element of an ERM Program

The International experts gathered in Davos in January 2009 for the World Economic Forum seem to have developed a new concept: *"The Financial Crisis has demonstrated that risk management is not enough; it is imperative now to develop risk governance."* And John Drzik, the CEO of Oliver Wyman even adds: *"For Risk Management to be efficient it must be approached in a strategic prospective, not a mere compliance exercise."* The need for such a stance clearly shows the damages caused by the rush to compliance, be it called Sarbanes-Oxley, COSO 2 or by any other name. Any time brainstorming is replaced by box ticking there is a minefield ahead!

These high profile individuals, among whom many serve in several boards worldwide, and may even sit in risk and audit committees, have even produced the solution: *"Risk governance is about asking the right questions to the right persons so that it can be assured that the risks taken are within the boundaries of the organization's risk appetite."* Sounds familiar? The Davos delegates had to take the measure of the economic turmoil of the world to reinvent in 2009 the global and integrated management of risks that the professionals have developed for over a decade and ERM; no doubt they will need many more years to reinvent business intelligence systems to provide the *"reasonable assurance"* that the information received, transformed and released to all parties is of the highest quality. As a matter of fact "risk management" did not make it in Davos in 2010 or 2011, but the risk review for 2012 and 2013 risks to reputation is to be high on boards' agendas.

It is very important development as it is likely that non-executive board members will feel the need to gain the competencies to do a good job at monitoring risk management activities in their organizations all the more with the transposition of the European directive[11] 4, 7 and 8 in national laws, as was done in France in 2008; the responsibility for managing risks really rests on the board and the executives. At their level the issue is long-term sustainable growth and the key asset is reputation.

To be successful and sustainable, i.e., to achieve a sound level of resilience, any business needs to enjoy the trust and confidence of all its stakeholders and that can be achieved only when its actions are in harmony with its words. In practice, that requires integrating into the overall strategy the key elements of trust building: corporate governance, risk management, corporate social responsibility and reputation management.

Although stakeholder trust is important for all industries, it is vital for financial institutions, food industry, water supply, pharmaceutical, hospitals, to name but a few at a time when there is:

---

[11] These European Directives coordinate member states legislation on specific subjects. The eighth Directive deals with corporate governance.

- Public anger: backcloth of public spending cuts, rising unemployment, food safety compromised, etc.
- Criticism of government policy and sanction voting in several developed countries.
- Increased government, regulators, scrutiny.
- Creation of independent commissions to supervise industries in the public eye.
- Threat of increased regulation/structural form (financial sector, food and drug, etc.).
- The exploding influence of social media.
- Growing investors/rating agency interest in sound risk management (ERM).
- Mandatory disclosure of "principal risks and uncertainties" in listed company annual reports, and regulator wielding of reputational sanctions.

Through their own analysis of the context in which their organization operates or pressured by new legislations, like the 8th directive on governance in the European Union, practitioners, directors and officers have become aware of the need for a global corporate risk management strategy. However, there seems to be a mushrooming of new "silos" in risk management such as sustainable development risk management, procurement risk management, marketing risk management, etc. In view of the social demand and the development of the CSR (corporate social responsibility) an integrated approach to risk management is not an option but a necessity. Trust can be gained, preserved, and enhanced only through transparency and ethical behavior. This is why, in any organization, and even more for publicly traded companies, reputation risk management has become the cornerstone to the desired integration, provided executives and board members are aware that a reputation must be built both "inside out" and "outside in."

Furthermore, a corporate reputation serves as a reservoir of goodwill to draw upon when challenges and difficulties arise. More than ever in this time of crisis, triggered by a justified drop of confidence in the financial sector, executives must strive to build an authentic business:

> "A defining feature of an authentic business is that its profound and positive purpose shines through every aspect of what it does, whether paying invoices (claims), parting with a member of staff, or presenting at a conference" (Crofts, 2005).

Ethical conduct is the core ingredient of trust, hence of reputation. As several situations illustrated individual lapses are always possible but they may uncover systemic risks. Such situations can be drawn from events that took place from the beginning of the century:

- In 2001, the ENRON debacle brought the demise of Arthur Anderson, shaking the entire audit community resulting in the Sarbanes-Oxley[12] legislation in the USA.
- In 2007/2009, the financial crisis generating an economic crisis put the banking system on the spotlight.
- In 2011 several drug scandals shook the pharmaceutical industry.
- In 2013, when the mad cow disease had become history, a scandal on the horse meat mixed in all-beef prepared food evidenced that even top brands products were produced in the same factories as store brands and that may prove to have a long-term effect on "top brand reputations".

As the financial industry has experienced since the summer of 2007, and more recently the food and pharmaceutical industries, individual lapses are always possible, but they may uncover systemic risks. Therefore, we must stress how important it is for any organization to

---

[12] Public Company Accounting Reform and Investor Protection Act – enacted July 30, 2002.

prepare for a disaster, should it strike. In a recently published book on corporate integrity the authors stress that:

> "As we found with Hurricane Katrina, being unprepared can cause a disaster that is far greater than the damage caused by the underlying event. The ethical disaster risks facing organizations today are significant and the reputational damage caused can be far greater for those companies that find themselves unprepared for an Ethical Misconduct Disaster. Although we can't predict an ethical disaster, we can and must prepare for one."[13]

However, as important as ethics are, we have seen there are many drivers to reputation and many stakeholders whose confidence has to be nurtured and simple common sense would not allow to make sound decisions in such a complex network of intertwined relationships. This is the reason why a model to pilot efficient reputation was needed. Left to their own devices, decision makers would typically *"tend to avoid the problem [of interacting criteria] by constructing independent (or supposed to be so) criteria"*.[14] The same expert points out that:

> "the distinguishing feature of a fuzzy integral is that it is able to represent a certain kind of interactions between criteria, ranging from redundancy (negative interaction) to synergy (positive interaction)."

The model for managing risk to reputation is based on nine drivers described earlier. The model is complemented by a kit which can:

- Provide an objective assessment of the nine drivers and an evaluation for the global reputation index, synthesis without loss of information (in this case, it even provides additional insight), and produce analysis tools resulting in an efficient handle on the drivers identified as having the optimal impact on the global reputation index, hence optimizing resilience for a given budget of resources allocated.
- Produce analysis tools resulting in an efficient handle on the drivers identified as having the optimal impact on the global reputation index, hence optimizing resilience for a given budget of resources allocated.

Furthermore the process of data collection is greatly enhanced by using a semantic engine best designed to capture even *low noises* in the evolution of stakeholders' perception hence all aspects of the reputation, even beyond the *e-reputation*. It is worth stressing that each driver need be assessed only once before any aggregation, i.e. at level 3 in the model.

This model will equip the board of directors, or governing body, with the tool box that will allow them to best utilize their talent for the benefit of the organization as the optimal solution provided will rely heavily on their own competencies and insight. However, this will require an ongoing effort on the part of the organization. The reputation index at a given point in time provides less information than its evolution through time and this is precisely why it provides a tool to monitor reputation investments at the strategic decision level. Therefore there is no doubt that this index monitoring process will represent an ongoing cost if the optimal return on the initial investment is sought.

---

[13] Lynn Brewer, Robert Chandler, O.C. Ferrell, Managing Risks for Corporate Integrity: *How to survive an Ethical Misconduct Disaster*, p. 3. Cengage Learning: Connecticut, USA.

[14] M. Grabisch (1996) The application of fuzzy integrals in multi-criteria decision making? *European Operational Research*, Vol. 89(3).

Some may question the complexity of the model and it is true that it relies on "expert opinions" but initially only for each branch and in some cases for each organization. However, individual board members need not grasp the complex relationship between the different drivers as it is the model itself that will generate them. This is precisely why it provides additional information through the aggregation processes, contrary to what would happen with a weighted arithmetic mean that would destroy information. Thus, the expertise of the board will be enhanced by the model rather than replaced by its use.

The final word we borrow from Madeleine Albright, former Secretary of State of the US, while addressing the subject of risks of war, terrorism and deadly pandemics and reflecting on her work during the Clinton administration. At a Marsh breakfast during the RIMS convention in Honolulu on April 25, 2006, she gave this essential piece of advice to risk management and business leaders regarding crisis, which are in the end the times of trial for reputation:

> "Decisions are only as good as the information you have... Although the crisis for which you prepare may never happen, one will happen... Being prepared for a crisis is never a waste of time."

References and Further Reading

Crofts, N. (2005) *How To Create and Run Your Perfect Business*. Oxford: Capstone Publishing.

Douglas, M. and Wildavsky, A. (1982) *Risk and culture: an essay on the selection of technical and environmental dangers*. Berkeley: University of California Press.

Fischhoff, B., Gonzalez, R. M., Small, D. A., and Lerner, J. S. (2003) Judged terror risk and proximity to the World Trade Center. *Journal of Risk and Uncertainty, 26*(2–3), pp. 137–151.

Gaultier-Gaillard, S. and Louisot, J.-P. (2006) Risks to reputation: A global approach, *The Geneva Papers*, The International Association for the Study of Insurance Economics.

3.2 DISTURBANCE MANAGEMENT

Jean-Paul Louisot

Formerly Université Paris 1 Panthéon-Sorbonne, Directeur pédagogique du CARM Institute, Paris, France

There are many definitions of risk management because organizations deal differently with how they cope with uncertainty, enhance opportunities and curb threats. However, the core mission of risk management is to ensure the organization's long-term resilience. Therefore, knowing how to manage situations that differ substantially for the expected, exceptional situations is a key competency for a risk management professional. Too often, the whole toolbox is summarized in one term: crisis management.

However, not all disturbances that may touch an organization are of such amplitude that they could trigger a crisis. Therefore any organization must develop a taxonomy of the situations it may be confronted with that may require prior thinking and/or preparation to be handled with optimal efficiency. These situations may present the organization with a threat to curb, or an opportunity to enhance.

The basic concept used here is derived from an article published in the Harvard Business Review.[15] In this article the authors outline a framework for decision making in complex

---

[15] A Leader's Framework for Decision Making by David J. Snowden and Mary E. Boone HBR Nov 2007 – Harvard Business School Publication Corp.

systems they call Cynefin. The Cynefin framework is a scale of disturbance levels from low to high: simple or nominal; complicated; complex, chaos. The Cynefin framework can be extended to disturbance management in the context of ERM.

Level 1 – Simple or Nominal State

This is the state for which the system has been developed and set up and based on "best practices" for optimal efficiency. It is characterized by stable and clearly identified causal relationships, slow evolution, order and accomplishment. The main pitfall would be to become complacent if nothing happens.

Level 2 – Complicated State

This is the state, within the confidence interval, where expertise and good practices prevail where multiple answers are possible and several solutions must be analyzed. It is the time when non-conventional wisdom may prove essential. The main pitfall would be to delay decision making until the best is identified.

Level 3 – Complex State

This is the state where new and innovative solutions may have to be tested. Feedback from the experience will provide the learning curve necessary to understand causal relationships. The key is to be ready to embrace creativity and innovation and adopt new management models. The pitfall would be to attempt a straight return to prior situation without analyzing the new context.

Level 4 – Chaos State

This is the state where ruptures may evolve into crisis, while offering real opportunities if top management proves able to make swift decisions. The situations are evolving quickly and it is impossible to discern stable causal relationships; no manageable schemes are identifiable. It is the time for transparent and genuine communication, but based on schemata developed with stakeholders prior to the event, as there is no time to engage at this stage. The time may prove ideal to implement a new business model as deep uncertainty facilitates change management. The main pitfall would be to charge ahead without prior restoration of some order by returning the system to a level three.

As mentioned above the level of disturbance identified will dictate the optimal course of action for management. The adequate reaction from the local or top management will depend on the level identified and can be described as follows:

Level 1 – Simple or Nominal State

This state represents the equilibrium of the system but it is basically an unstable equilibrium around which the system oscillates constantly.

Level 2 – Complicated State

This is a state that any organization may experience regularly that remains within the expected interval. This is why it is important that operational managers, field managers, be responsible for managing daily variations by implementing "good practices" rather than the nominal best practices. This supposes that managers are granted the authority to make the necessary changes and have the expertise to understand what to do in any given situation.

Level 3 – Complex State

This is a state where managing the "accidental" system oscillations, or disturbances, is beyond the daily routine of field managers. Ensuring continuity is the key mission of the operational managers but it requires the preparation and rehearsal of a business continuity plan.

Level 4 – Chaos State

When the required level of "continuity" cannot be achieved at the operational level, it falls on top management to act because the rupture may threaten to develop into a full-blown crisis. The directors' responsibility is to maintain the organization's RESILIENCE through strategic redeployment planning.

In the case of scenarios or exposures that might generate disturbances at level three or four, the preparation of the business units consists of the following steps:

1. Elaborate the scheme that will insure continuous operations for all the departments, whatever may happen to current facilities (business continuity planning). Develop alternative strategies where necessary that may preserve the essential of the organization's strategic goals and objectives when continuity cannot be preserved ("survival planning").
2. Identify the critical resources vital to the daily operations of departments, define concrete prevention measures to preserve them, evaluate costs (investment, maintenance and operational) and implement. The critical resources are those that condition the survival of the organization.
3. Search for temporary relocation or alternate sourcing for all critical processes, departments, and/or facilities and define procedures to monitor evolution (regular updating) and evaluate costs involved.
4. Define temporary equipment and communication devices required in case of an emergency, where to get them and the costs associated.

These solutions must be approved by top management, developed in a crisis manual provided to all managers involved in the implementation, but also explained and rehearsed with all involved in their implementation should the need arise. Detail is essential as to practical measures to be implemented; communication channels with the crisis management team must be clearly identified and open at all times.

During the course of this process, risk control measures vital for the continuity of operations will be elaborated at the same time that the exposures are identified, analyzed, and evaluated. The final risk control program will have to take into account the cost/benefit analysis to be approved by the finance department.

This process may seem to depart from the traditional risk management process as defined in most textbooks. However, it is totally in line with the ERM concept that calls for a portfolio approach at the operational level where all risk owners must provide simultaneous answers to two fundamental questions for the risk management professional:

- *What risk am I exposed to?* This is answered by developing a risk assessment and a risk matrix to rank the exposures.
- *How can I secure the objectives?* This is the object of the disturbance management (business continuity planning).

But risk professionals and the crisis management team must always keep in mind that the CEO is the ultimate risk manager of any organization, especially in the case of level four disturbances and disturbances with level four potential. This is the reason why the risk management professional must be positioned as an internal consultant to the executive committee. In such a set-up, the CRO (chief risk officer) is but the "threat shadow" of the "opportunity" chief executive officer: the ultimate risk owner who can make sure all risks are turned into opportunities wherever possible within the risk appetite defined by the board.

Both continuity and survival planning must be coherent plans including prevention measures, temporary alternatives, sub-contracting and purchasing, redundancies and robust and available sources of funds that will enable the organization to survive and reach its goals under most circumstances. This new framework takes into account the level of disturbance; and crisis management is the ultimate tool when the situation is verging on chaos to ensure resilience and continued sustainable growth.

To summarize, the complicated state requires the organization to provide enough leeway to operational managers to navigate daily variations, whereas "emergency situations" (complex states) call for the implementation of business continuity planning. In a rupture situation (chaos state) the event(s) may develop into full bloom crisis and call for strategic redeployment planning.

3.2.1   Business Continuity Planning

The guidelines provided here are sufficient to develop an "in house version" of business continuity planning (BCP) catering to the specific needs of the organization. Depending on the level of disruption, starting up production is the key mission, but a host of questions remain to be answered, e.g., Where? How? When?

There are international and national standards to help organizations develop proper BCP operations, some of which are certifiable, like the ISO 22301 for which several vendors are available. Many organizations have appointed "continuity officers" within their RM department.

The traditional BCP process is split into two phases with the first one aimed at stabilizing the situation, and the second at restarting the operations as soon as possible, if needed, on a temporary basis. The two stages are:

- Emergency stage.
- Restart stage.

The following provides information of how to develop the two stages.

Stage 1 "Emergency"

As soon as the event is threatening, or striking, emergency measures must be activated. These emergency measures aim at:

Protecting people:
- Call and guide public emergency services (firefighters, etc.).
- Verify all safety equipment.
- Warning to neighbors (if necessary).

Protecting reputation:
- Crisis communication with all parties involved:
  - Public authorities.
  - The general public.
  - Economic partners (customers, suppliers and sub-contractors).
  - Stockholders (and financial analysts).
  - Media.

Protecting physical assets:
- Guard the site.
- Organize salvage operations.

Stage 2 "Restart Production"

Production must resume but how it resumes will depend upon the marketing plan. There remain some important points to cover:

Site: Are there other facilities available?
- Plant and equipment? (the same, identical, new technology?)
- Machinery (performances, delivery time).
- Equipment (replacement, rebuild).

Supply chain:
- Origin.
- Quality.
- Costs.

Logistic:
- Transportation and routes.
- Packaging and shipment of production.

It is essential to evaluate the maximum downtime acceptable for any "vital resource" as the cost of restoration likely will be high with a goal of short downtime. In many cases approaching "start-up" as a project may prove to be efficient especially with a PERT (Project Evaluation and Review Technique).

Business Continuity Planning is developed and implemented by the operational managers and risk owners but should follow the process and objectives provided by the risk management office, and be audited regularly. However, local situations and context must be taken into account to develop BCP for each of the local "killer" scenarios, i.e. the situation that could result in an unacceptable downtime from the overall organization's perspective.

3.2.2   Strategic Redeployment Planning (SRP)

Strategic Redeployment Planning is a process that must be conducted by top management, C-suite and/or board when the situation leads to a rupture – chaotic state. The key to success in the SRP implementation phase is to equip the leaders with the competencies to make decisions under stress and duress.

The leaders must concentrate their attention on:

The evaluation of the situation of the organization
- Can persons and assets be secured?
- Can production continuity be insured?
- Is our reputation at stake?
- The organization resilience (based on the available information) i.e. could the organization survival be in jeopardy in the medium or long run although it might limp along in the short term?

Can the existing "business model" survive?
- Should a "new" business model be developed and implemented?
- Investigate all the options open to the company.
- Place sentries and scouts to capture "low noises" as the risk owners on the field may be able to see early signs that the context is changing, and gathered at the headquarters level, they may provide crucial information dictating to revise the strategy before any generalized disturbance appears.
- Create a team spirit to survive even the worst tempest.

When the situation reaches the "chaos" disturbance level, returning to a pre-event status is generally not feasible. Therefore, top management will be called upon to define a new course of action based on the information gathered in the proper receptacle. An organization experiencing a chaos disturbance will add two phases to the BCP: strategic review and communication.

Phase 1 "Strategic Review"

Evaluate impact on reputation and/or market share of temporary withdrawal for the market?
- Customer loyalty?
- Suppliers and sub-contractors loyalty?
- Window of opportunity for old or new competitors?

New Marketing Strategy (needed or not needed?)
NOT NEEDED:
- The organization to stick to its traditional products and markets.
- Set priorities (managing limited output).

What lines of business, products (or services)?
What customer segments?
- For low priority products, evaluate:
  - When there is temporary halt of production: conditions for re-entry on the market.
  - When halt of production is final: commercial impact (synergies?)
  - Financial impact.
  - Compensation for loss of revenues (new products, new clients, new countries?)

NEEDED:
- The organization redeploys its resources to cater to new markets and customer needs.
  - (Evaluate competencies and develop a new strategy).
    - How, substitution?
    - Commercial action.
    - How to restore profit growth?

Phase 2 "Communication"

Beyond crisis communication, which is a part of the emergency procedures in Phase 1, maintaining or restoring the long-term reputation is a necessity that requires attention beyond the crisis itself:

- Maintain permanent link with "news media".
- Keep in touch with local authorities and professional associations.
- Keep all employees and sales force updated on progress and development.
- Treat all suppliers and sub-contractors as partners in good and bad times alike.
- Use all means possible to build and consolidate *customers* loyalty (including speedy delivery of orders even in difficult times).
- Keep stockholders informed.

This will require special efforts in the case of a strategic redeployment decided in Phase 2.

3.2.3 Specific Elements Common to BCP and SRP

Two elements are common to the two levels of planning: crisis communication and emergency fund.

Crisis Communication

The preceding remarks on crisis development clearly point to the fact that in post-event redeployment planning, the impact on the environments with which the organization interacts is a determining factor in pulling through the crisis. It is essential to differentiate between planned post-event survival and crisis management. According to French specialists, the term "crisis" should be used only in a situation where all the organization's processes and milestones are destroyed, leaving an empty field where no forward planning provides answer to the exceptional circumstances encountered.

In situations like those involving Union Carbide in Bhopal and Perrier (when the bottles were allegedly contaminated with pollution and had to be recalled in the USA, depriving the company permanently of its exclusivity in the top market for sparkling waters), the entire organization is put in jeopardy. Reputation or brand name can be permanently compromised. Therefore, under such circumstances, nothing short of a company-wide mobilization with the help of economic partners is necessary to preserve and even boost reputation.

In any situation where reputation is at stake, it must be remembered that reputation ultimately rests in the continuing trust and confidence of the stakeholders. Therefore, some rules must be adhered to in communication with all: *credibility* and *transparency* (speak the truth) are the key to success:

- **Credibility,** like trust, takes a long time to earn and a short time to lose. However, crisis communication success is based on long established trust relationships with the news media, involving years of hard work.
- **Transparency** can only result from a long learning process by top executives so that they can feel at ease with (sometimes tough) questioning journalists. Executives appointed to communicate with the media must know how to give quick direct answers to direct questions. Not everyone has the competencies and talent to confront the media. Specifically, the CEO may not be the right person. Who will be in charge of communication with the media and other stakeholders must be determined before any crisis.

An important reminder: time is of the essence in any crisis situation. The chain of events that cause and develop with the crisis is always rooted in the quick pace of alterations of some key factors. Time is particularly important in the degradation of the information: a delay in media confrontation may pave the way to rumors that may continue spreading, especially through social media, even after they have been dispelled with data and better information, especially with the impact of social media. The media carry an "emotional way" to get public attention. And also remember that bad news sells more than good news for commercial media.

But any amount of advance planning is never enough. Prepared and informed executives will have to improvise as the crisis develops; but sound improvisation is the result of much advance preparation and executives must be well trained in making decisions under uncertainty and stress. Sound risk control measures explained ahead of time to employees, economic partners and news media would build credibility, a "good citizen", "sound management" image that will be rewarded in time of a crisis. Also, through a "crisis scenario" drill the members of the "crisis management team" will be trained in reacting positively and to be efficient leaders under stress.

However, the CEO may view such activities as costly and fail to see the value creation. The "next door syndrome" is also common: dire events happen only to the "others" because they did not have proper R&D, proper marketing, proper quality management or proper safety and environment management. The risk manager must develop enough understanding of the decision makers' psychology to assess how they will take to crisis preparation activities and have a sound plan on how to respond to negative reactions.

And it is true, nobody wants to live through a crisis and it may well be in many cases an investment without an obvious return. It may require the auditors to come up with a method to measure the added resilience gained by the organization in order to evaluate a return on investment. However, the requirement for corporate governance may, and compliances may prove to be, the best way to justify efforts and resources deployed to develop sound crisis management.

It is not always easy to define what would be the best attitude towards crisis management. Bertrand Robert and Daniel Verpeaux (FRANCOM group) in an unpublished manuscript titled "Crisis Communication", define several attitudes using different "caricatures" that may reflect different organizational cultures:

- **The wellness doctor:** a global approach is aimed at patient health without waiting for any symptom of illnesses. In time of a crisis, there is no time to build confidence in dealings with the public and the media; it is the time to harvest the fruit of patient prior efforts.

- **The lawyer:** a essential quality is to listen and understand the victims' point of view in order to build an efficient defense strategy in line with the legal environment.
- **The preacher:** a faith strong enough to remove the mountains of taboos and superstition, and facilitate team sharing and efforts.
- **The marine officer:** is on the battlefield with his/her troops and takes part in all the combat drilling.
- **The gardener:** knows that plants need time to grow ("leave time to time", the late French president, François Mitterrand, was fond of saying). He/she cultivates his/her media network to build a strong image in the time of peace to capitalize on when the time of duress comes.

In a matter of reputation, image, or loyalty, one must remember that proper and timely communication is essential. However, the subjective reality (emotions, feelings) is often more important than the objective reality (hard facts). This is the reason why the perception of hazards by the community in which an entity is established is a crucial element of any communication strategy about hazards and perils. The extent to which hazards and perils are perceived and evaluated in a crisis can be summed up in Figure 3.6.

That means that the risk assessment must address these questions of risk perception as well. The exposures cannot be viewed in a closed system (the entity) but must do so from the point of view of and in context with the organization's stakeholders (including economic partners, stakeholders, and the society at large).

Therefore, the risk manager professional must be able to develop a matrix similar to Figure 3.6 for any "sensitive issues", that are significant for the public, pressure groups or the elected officials. Understanding stakeholders' perception and sensitivity is a necessary step in the development of an effective preventive communication strategy with the proper priority (message content, target groups, media, etc.).

One of the key ingredients to any good communication is a feedback loop. A crisis is not a time when "authority" can dictate a "truth" that will be automatically accepted by a passive public. The public wants to be an active partner and feedback channels must be established to allow the authority to reconsider their position to reflect public expectations. At all times, security measures must take this into account and diffuse public anxiety, remembering that the level of anxiety reflects the perceived risk and not scientific evidence to measure risk "objectively".

Risk control measures that the stakeholders do not adhere to may prove inefficient, even if these measures are recommended by scientific experts or are in compliance with legal and regulatory requirements. The public must adhere to the project that the organization is promoting, adopt the entity and live in osmosis with it: the public is the main partner and it is for the public to decide if an appropriate level of safety is reached.

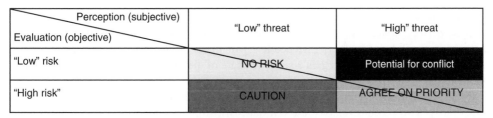

Evaluation (objective) / Perception (subjective)	"Low" threat	"High" threat
"Low" risk	NO RISK	Potential for conflict
"High risk"	CAUTION	AGREE ON PRIORITY

Figure 3.6   Perception and evaluation of hazards and perils.

It is the level at which the public trust and confidence is preserved that will ensure the organization's resilience. This opens the new field of business ethics where one must always ask the question "should I do this" rather than the more mundane question of the past "could I do it", i.e. what I do may be "legal" but if it is perceived as unethical by the stakeholders, the organization's reputation will be at stake.

Emergency Funds

Post-event redeployment planning, like any industrial or commercial project, must translate into budget and cash flows forecasts. The cash flow elements are crucial because in difficult time new sources of funds are not easily acquired unless they have been secured ahead of time. The aftermath of a large incident may last from 6 to 24 months or longer; therefore sources and uses of funds forecast should be established on a monthly basis for up to two years (or more) following a "crisis". The net deficit is precisely the amount of funds, month by month, that has to be secured through these new sources of funds from lenders, insurers, and others. But this is precisely the core mission of risk financing.

3.2.4 Summary

While preparing for a crisis is key to any organization's long-term survival, not all disturbances are at a level that would require implementing a crisis plan. Reacting appropriately to match the disturbance level is essential so that operational managers and risk owners have the responsibility to manage the risks within their area of command. They must also have the authority to implement temporary measures to respond to daily deviations from the optimal situation, and develop a business continuity plan in order to navigate through complex situations and limit the consequences for the organization and its main partners.

The presentation on level of disturbance can be used to "coach" risk owners in how to engage and apply appropriate risk management techniques and BCP processes. More than "compliance issues", they constitute a toolkit that helps them cope with situations and optimize their performance in cases outside of their comfort zone (complex state).

However, there are chaotic situations that require top management attention and sound preparation to make appropriate and effective decisions under stress with only limited information. The framework developed as a strategic exercise before any event is called the strategic redeployment plan and it should be designed to prepare for alternate courses to protect the goals and objectives, or mission of the organization to the extent possible in the new context created by the event.

In all situations, responding to the public's perceived risks through open and straightforward two-way communication is essential. Building trust and confidence with media, and social media, will prove essential in times of tumult and upheaval.

Two situations may illustrate this fact. When Perrier was confronted with traces of benzene in their "perfect" water, a swift reaction to recall all bottles in the channels of distribution was a costly proposal; however Perrier needed to regain market share of high-end mineral waters. Swift reaction helped Perrier regain a sizeable share of the market because public confidence was restored.

By the same token, companies that have failed to answer the public have suffered, if only temporarily. Two recent examples are relevant: British Petroleum after the Gulf of Mexico explosion; and Toyota after repeated brake failures. In the long run, however, both changed their strategic response and were able to build on their otherwise strong image and rebound both in the public opinion and in the stock exchange.

However, there is a word of caution about disturbance management from Paul Coehlo in a forthcoming work where he summarizes the key to resilience for any organization: "Discipline is important but it needs to leave open doors and windows to intuition and the unexpected."[16]

---

[16] Paul Coehlo, Manuscript from ACCRA, p. 178 – Knopf, New York, 2013.

4

Monitor Results and Revise

Things change; organizations change; the environment changes; leadership changes; the economy changes. Risks themselves change. As a result the organization must periodically evaluate the efficacy of the risk treatment techniques it is utilizing with critical risks. Are they still working or must they be revised? Secondly, new risks can become important and risks that were previously considered to be non-critical may be critical. Critical risks on the priority list may rise and fall in importance and impact over time. Assurance, audit, review of data, and periodic reassessment of the risks to strategy are steps that cannot be overlooked. The strategy itself must be reconsidered when necessary.

4.1 BUSINESS ETHICS AND RISK MANAGEMENT

Marc Ronez

Chief Risk Strategist and Master Coach, Asia Risk Management Institute

"It's only when the tide goes out that you learn who's been swimming naked." (Warren Buffett, Berkshire Hathaway)

A string of economic crises (the Asian financial crisis, dot-com bubble and the subprime collapse) as well as major corporate collapses (Enron, WorldCom and many others) have put the issue of business ethics under the spotlight and made it top item on the "To Do" list of boards of directors all around the world. The reason for this increased scrutiny is simple: At the root cause of most corporate collapses and economic crises, you will find an ethical issue that had not been properly addressed.

For example, many corporate scandals of the 1990s and 2000s were the result of companies trying to evade regulatory rules to either hide problems (creative accounting to take losses out of the balance sheet, e.g. Barings (1995), Enron (2001)) or to do something they were not supposed to do (bribery, abuse of power, e.g. Marsh (2004), BAE systems (2010)).

And each time, regulators around the world reacted in a typical fashion by enacting new laws with the aim to prevent such behavior from repeating itself. Unfortunately more rules and controls like the ones enforced by Basel II or SOX have proven to be little help to resolve the problem. On the contrary, it appears that smart people in organizations found different even more creative unethical ways of dealing with regulatory constraints as in the case of the subprime market bubble and subsequent collapse.

Hence in today's global and uncertain world, where the collapse of major corporate players and/or the next financial bubble might lead to a systemic collapse of our financial system and world economy, the apparent lack of ethics in the business world is a crucial issue that needs to be addressed effectively.

4.1.1 Defining What Business Ethics Is

Ethics refers to the moral philosophy, values and norms of behavior that explain and guide an individual's behavior in society. Ethics as a system forms a moral code of conduct, a sort of compass that helps people in differentiating what is right or wrong, what is good or bad.

To be considered of good character, i.e. displaying good ethical behavior, it is generally understood that you need to take into account and live up to a set of moral principles such as:

- Dignity: refers to treating each individual with respect.
- Equity: is just being fair and even-handed in decisions.
- Prudence: think and prepare carefully before you do something.
- Honesty: is being straightforward and truthful.
- Transparency: is about not concealing that which should be revealed.
- Goodwill: concern for others, kindness and tolerance.
- Integrity: when we say we do something, we will do it.
- Spirit of excellence: always trying to do our best.

This list is by no mean exhaustive and just highlights some of the key moral principles that should be used as a guide when making decisions.

Business ethics refers specifically to those moral principles and rules of conduct that are governing the business world and activities. To support effective compliance, many of these principles and rules have over time been formalized into legal rules embedded in various regulatory frameworks. As a matter of fact the rule of the law is a key force unifying and controlling corporate behavior within society and the entire body of rules is based explicitly or implicitly on ethical principles. The purpose of the law when it comes to ethics is to enforce certain minimum standards of ethical business practices in the business world. This is also the limitation as, most of the time, regulatory rules merely specify the lowest common denominator of what can be accepted by all the parties involved, as illustrated by the intense negotiation and lobbying that surrounded the development of the Basel III accords. This means that typically, legal requirements will lag behind moral expectations of what would be considered as an unethical behavior as illustrated in Figure 4.1. For example, in many industries, it has been common advertising practice to make exaggerated claims about the quality and effectiveness of the products and services offered. While those practices may be unethical, as long as there are no laws against them, they are legal. Furthermore, it is a continuously evolving situation as new laws are enacted all the time and what is legal today may not be legal tomorrow.

This time-lag problem cannot be resolved as the continuous development of new technologies and products as well as the ever-changing expectations of stakeholders will give rise to new ethical issues and questionable practices that will not have yet been addressed by the

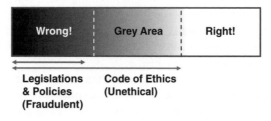

Figure 4.1 Illegal vs. Unethical.

current body of legislation. It must also be noted that the same practices may be legal in one country but illegal in another where the laws have expanded faster to cover the issue. This adds another level of complexity in managing compliance and ethical risk issues.

Hence it is clear that ensuring ethics cannot be achieved by merely complying with the law. Organizations must look beyond and seek to understand how the ever-changing moral expectations of their stakeholders may affect an organization's ability to create value.

4.1.2   Business Ethics: "Good to Have" or Business Imperative?

In today's world, business leaders talk a lot about "ethics" and "values". When speaking publicly about their organizations, they will usually stress the important role of corporate values in the success of their business. To be fair, a lot of visible efforts have been undertaken to develop "values statements" as well as embed moral principles and rules into codes of conduct supposed to guide the behavior of the employees in organizations. Hence it is extremely ironical to observe that despite all the talking and actions, we can generally observe that very few organizations have made any real improvements in their actual ethical practices. It actually seems that the more business leaders talk about ethics, the less they practice it. In other words, the business ethics efforts are more about form than substance. Abraham Lincoln, 16th USA President highlighted this gap when he famously declared:

> "Character is like a tree and reputation like its shadow. The shadow is what we think of it, the tree is the real thing."

It seems that business leaders care more about the "shadow" appearing to be good than about the "tree" to really be good. So while most people will pay lip service to the importance of ethical principles, the reality is that, unfortunately, ethics is often considered as a "good to have", something of a "luxury" in the fast-paced turmoil of today's volatile business environment. Modern organizations are indeed operating in an environment characterized by multiple pressures: a constant pace of change, continuous pressures on both revenues and earnings, where the share price is "king" and where the average life expectancy of a CEO is continuously reducing. Hence it may not be so surprising that in some companies, the top management can lose sight of the right course of actions by focusing on short-term opportunities at the expense of longer-term impacts and needs. In this context, business ethics will be obviously perceived as an impediment to doing business. Of course, the subprime crisis and the many corporate collapses making headline news are strong reminders of the fundamental need for stronger ethics, risk management and regulatory compliance practices. As usual, after those events, regulators around the world have responded once again, with landmark legislation with the aim to raise the standards of business ethics in the industries considered.

Benefits of Business Ethics and Cost and the Lack of It

Ethics is not important merely because the law says so. It is not just a question of legal compliance and you do need to care about the rest. In fact, letting stakeholders develop the perception that ethical behavior is not important to an organization will be incredibly damaging to its reputation and business prospects. More than just a public relation talk, a breach of ethics when exposed will result in wide range of negative direct and indirect consequences for an organization such as negative media coverage, regulator investigation, customer boycotts, reduced share price, drop in revenue and profitability, loss of key staff, even possibly criminal investigation and imprisonment for the executives involved. This, of course, applies equally for individuals, and there are plenty of cases of highly talented and successful individuals who were castigated because they violated ethical and legal requirements.

Conversely, good ethics is also good business. Treating stakeholders ethically will have direct impact on organizational performance by providing the following benefits:

- Build a solid reputation providing a differentiator edge in competitive markets.
- Attract consumers and have them buy products/services at a premium price.
- Attract investors and secure capital at a lower cost.
- Recruit and retain high-quality employees.
- Be recommended as a good partner.
- Nurture a positive relationship with regulators and the media.
- Provide protection against crisis by receiving the benefit of the doubt from loyal customers.

Anita Roddick, the founder of Body Shop is often cited (*The New York Times*, 2007), as an example of how doing good things is good for business. She has built a business model around developing quality beauty products that did not involve testing on animals and was the first to introduce "Fair Trade" to the cosmetic industry. By this strong ethical stance, she won the support of a growing number of more ethically and socially conscious customers.

The Emergence of the CSR Agenda: A New Moral Code of Conduct for Doing Business?

This leads us to another reason why business ethics is essential for business: the emergence of corporate social responsibility (CSR). CSR is about seriously considering the impact of an organization's activities on society. It requires organizations and their staff to consider the impact of their actions in terms of a whole natural and social system, and holds them responsible for the effects of their actions anywhere in that system. It could also be the impact on the natural environment or the communities living there.

In recent years business has been viewed increasingly as a major cause of social, environmental and economic problems. Organizations, especially commercial companies, are widely perceived to seek short-term profits for themselves at the expense of the broader community and future generations. It seems that in their pursuit of short-term profits, too many companies overlook the well-being of their customers, the depletion of natural resources vital to their businesses, the viability of key suppliers, or the economic distress of the communities in which they produce and sell.

CSR proponents advocate that this narrow view of value creation prevailing in many companies seeking to optimize short-term financial performance while essentially ignoring the broader influences that determine their longer-term success is not sustainable. It will ultimately lead to the collapse of the companies following that model and tremendous cost to society as a whole.

Furthermore as the standards for ethical behavior continue to evolve and increase, your company's key stakeholders – shareholders, clients, employees and others, will increasingly expect you to meet or exceed those standards. This is true to various degrees in most industries today. While the value creation objective of organization is well understood and accepted, it cannot be achieved by ignoring basic ethical norms, values and standards of business practices. Companies get their "official" license to operate from the regulators, but also get an "unofficial" license to operate from their other stakeholders and the wider public. Therefore it is important for organizations to meet public expectations through proactive compliance with ethics codes, industry practices, and developing CSR-based business models.

4.1.3 ERM: A Rules or a Values-Based Approach?

Enterprise Risk Management (ERM) has emerged over the past 15 years as a "new paradigm" for managing holistically the portfolio of risks that organizations face in today's global and uncertain environment. Riding on the wake of numerous crises and corporate collapses, ERM concepts, tools and practices have gradually invaded both private and public organizations including governments all over the world. Evidence for this development can be found in the number of articles, books, and guidelines published on the subject (COSO, ISO 31000) as well as in policy and regulatory development over the past 10 years (Basel II, III, Sarbanes-Oxley, and many other regulations). The rise of risk management has been so spectacular, that Michael Power, in his book *The Risk Management of Everything* (2004) describes it as an "explosion of new risk control practices resulting from emerging social and political pressures aiming to manage everything" that could potentially go wrong. It is quite natural to understand that economic crises and corporate scandals have typically resulted in the creation of more rules in an attempt to prevent such behaviors repeating themselves in the future. It is to be expected that industry players and policy makers will continue to focus more and more on mechanisms to improve corporate governance, ethics and risk management.

But is it the right approach? There is a danger with continuously adding new layers of rules and controls. The problem is that it will drive to a defensive risk management approach in organization. To be controllable and manageable, risks must be made measurable, auditable and governable. Hence, many risks have been operationalized as organizational processes of control. Such systems translate primary or real risks into systems risks with focus on rules, compliance and warning mechanisms. Ironically, this approach will ultimately be detrimental to ethics and risk management as people will find a way to hide behind the system to avoid being responsible and accountable as was exemplified during the subprime crisis where the poor quality of the primary risks, i.e. the NINA (no income, no assets mortgage loans) were ignored because the risks had been repackaged and securitized, hiding their true nature behind clever packaging and the inherent human greed and blindness to risk. Solely adding controls does not deal the real issue, which is the importance of the human factor.

To make it short, the effectiveness of enterprise risk management cannot rise above the integrity and level of ethical values of the people who create, administer, and monitor an organization activity. Ethical values are by definition, essential elements of an organization's internal environment, affecting the design, administration, and monitoring of other enterprise risk management components. No matter how well designed and "strong" a risk management system may be, smart people will always find loopholes, a way to cut corners or go around it. It is just a question of time. Therefore to support good and effective risk management practices and achieve core objectives, an organization corporate culture must have integrated important key ethical values. If it has not done so, while the organization may appear in the short run to be successful, poor performance and ultimately failure is inevitable.

Beyond the diversity of values in organizational cultures, ERM is based on and promotes a values system that will require people to:

- Think in terms of shared value and sustainability.
- Act with integrity and discipline.

- Be responsible and accountable for what they do.
- Be honest and transparent about how they do things.
- Share information and knowledge proactively.

This is not an exhaustive list but the above values are some of the most important moral principles on which a strong and effective ERM system can be built. Reading the above list also explains why it is difficult to implement ERM effectively as those values are in contradiction with many management practices in today's modern organizations. Nevertheless, in the wake of the recent financial crisis and corporate collapses, ERM is a rapidly evolving discipline that places ethical values at the heart of good governance, risk management and compliance.

4.1.4 Building Ethical Risk Management in Organizations

To address the legal, ethical, social responsibility and environmental risks they face, organizations should design and implement business ethics risk management programs. This is not just about the system, it is actually primarily about the people and the culture of the organization considered. An organization's objectives, strategy and the way they are implemented are based on preferences, values, judgments and management styles. Management's integrity and commitment to ethical values influence these preferences and judgments, which are translated into standards of behavior. Leaders and managers of well-run organizations increasingly understand that ethical behavior is good business. If so why do unethical behaviors still seem to be so prevalent in many organizations? Organizations should create an environment both in terms of culture and system where ethical behavior is encouraged while unethical behavior is prevented and punished. To do so it is necessary to understand first what constitutes unethical behavior and how it can happen in organizations.

How Unethical Behavior Can Happen in Organizations

Every day, managers are confronted with risks in any activities they undertake. And every day, they may have to make decisions about what they are going to do about those risks. Some of those decisions are simple while others can be particularly difficult to make. In the pursuit of short-term profits to achieve their bonus targets or for many other reasons, managers can sometime lose sight of what is right or wrong. Business ethics problems can involve any of the following issues (this list is not exhaustive):

- Bribery in the private and public sector of contracting officer.
- Money laundering.
- Improper sales and marketing practices (misleading or exaggerated advertising).
- False financial accounting.
- Environmental irresponsibility.
- Breach of privacy.
- Insider trading.
- Use of child labor.
- Tax evasion.
- Improper competition practices.
- Unfair labor practices.
- Counterfeit goods.
- Breach of copyright.
- Industrial espionage.

Facing and Resolving Dilemmas

At the core of many difficult decisions about personal or business issues, there is some sort of dilemma. A dilemma can be defined as a difficult choice with no simple easy solution. For example you might have received two job offers. The first one is exactly the kind of senior marketing position you were vying for and comes with a great salary but it is with a tobacco company and selling a product that slowly kills people is against your principles. The second offer is from a small company and the job scope is fine but the compensation package is very unattractive for you. You have been looking for a job for more than a year now and those are the only two offers available and due to financial constraints, you cannot afford to wait any longer. You are in situation requiring you to make a choice between equally undesirable or unfavorable options. Which one will you take?

A dilemma will put managers in an exposed position, as whatever the decision they take there will be an unacceptable downside, a negative consequence for somebody. Hence it is difficult to determine what course of action to pursue. Another example, imagine that you are negotiating a large, very lucrative deal for your organization. The problem is that you are aware of a potential downside that had not been properly evaluated using the current company assessment process. On the plus side, closing this deal will guarantee a fat bonus for your entire team. And you know that other teams within your organization have closed similar types of deals with similar risk profiles. Will you close one eye and secure that deal? It means leaving your organization exposed to significant liabilities if the deal goes wrong.

The basis of dilemma is often a contradiction between good and bad. Doing the right thing might lead to bad results and vice versa. Imagine for example that in order to buy a large amount of product from your company, a potential client requires receiving an "under table" commission. If you do not close this deal, you will miss your quarterly revenue target for the third time and most likely get fired. Will you seal that deal? Moral dilemmas arise when the division between what is ethically right and wrong gets blurred.

Dilemmas make managers very stressed as there are no easy ways out and there will often be severe short-term and/or long-term, tangible and intangible costs associated with any decision taken. Dilemmas cause what psychologists call a cognitive dissonance. This is what happens when there is a conflict between values and when somebody acts in a way that is inconsistent with his or her prior belief. This dissonance is a very disturbing and unpleasant experience, usually leading to strong negative emotions such as fear, anger and frustration. The individual experiencing the dissonance will feel the intense need to restore harmony by reducing the dissonance. Managers engaging in unethical and even fraudulent behavior when facing dilemmas will usually be subjected to a strong cognitive dissonance. The factors that help explain why managers will engage in unethical and even fraudulent behavior and how they may be able to reduce the cognitive dissonance and resolve the dilemma can be categorized as follows:

- Ethical Relativism.
- Pressures / Incentives.
- Opportunities / Risks.

Ethical Relativism

People do have principles they believe in but when they practice them, they will also have many exceptions to those principles. For example people may believe in honesty and the importance of always telling the truth. Yet in many cases the same people will not hesitate to lie and by doing so, go against the very principles they profess to follow. We could say that people are morally flexible. It means that practically what is good or bad depends on the context and consequences. To decide, it is necessary to analyze and carefully weigh the options when facing a dilemma. The goal is primarily to avoid negative consequences (especially the one that may affect personally the individual making the decision) by developing creative options.

Hence from that perspective, everything is relative and it is more and more commonly accepted that there are different ways to define truth and exhibit moral behavior. The rationale is that different people may hold different views and follow different principles or interpret those principles differently because of different cultural backgrounds, experiences or personalities. Who is right, who is wrong when everything is relative?

With that in mind it will not be too difficult for managers to rationalize their behavior and reduce the cognitive dissonance even if it violates important values and principles using the following types of arguments:

- **"I have been unfairly treated."** The employee has been passed over for a promotion, given a very small bonus despite great results or has just been bullied by the boss. This might lead the employee to feel that taking home company assets is his or her right that he is just restoring the balance of what should have been done.
- **"Everybody else is doing it."** Illusion of morality can set in when everybody in the same group is engaging in the unethical or fraudulent behavior. For example, using the corporate credit card for non-business related expenses. The fact that everybody is doing it may give each employee an incorrect sense that it is fine after all.
- **"It is not me, it is my Boss."** In some cases, employees will engage in unethical or fraudulent behaviors because their boss told them to do it and they felt they cannot disobey their boss even if the order is unethical, or worse, fraudulent. It is a case of submission to authority, and the employee will rationalize himself as just a tool without free will and responsibility.
- **"I'm not stealing, I'm just borrowing the money."** The employee sometimes does have the best of intentions to return the stolen funds. However, there's a snowball effect. The longer the employee gets away with the fraud, the more casual he becomes about the situation. The fraud usually escalates to the point where the employee is unable to pay back the stolen money.
- **"I have no choice."** The employee believes he'll lose everything dear to him, including his job, home and family, unless he steals the money or commits the unethical act.
- **"I will use it for doing good."** This "the end justifies the means" kind of justification is where the employee can rationalize his or her unethical and even fraudulent behavior because the end result is supposed to be good.
- **"If I don't do it, somebody else will."** The inevitability justification: The idea that you cannot go against the flow because then you are missing opportunities or worse you could even get drowned. In 2007, Chuck Prince, former CEO of Citibank Group, to justify his blind pursuit of short-term profit during the subprime bubble, infamously said, "*As long as the music is playing, we have to keep on dancing!*" (*Business Times*, 2007).

Pressures / Incentives

It is about the pressure or "need" felt by the individual, which will lead him to commit the fraud. It might be real financial problems coming from personal problems such as unhealthy personal money-sucking addictions/vices (gambling, drugs, alcohol, mistress), or family needs (sick spouse, children), combined with insufficient capital, high debt level and credit difficulties. In most cases, the individual does not want his spouse, child, or parent to know about the problem. He will resort to self-help rather than risk being shamed by admitting that his debt is out of control. It could also come from work-related factors such as being overworked, underpaid and not promoted. There could be the case of too high a level of management pressure to achieve financial results coupled with inappropriate compensation systems that encourage excessive risk taking or a need to cover up someone's poor performance and hide losses. Finally, it could simply be pure greed, such as when a person has a strong desire for material gratifications and will stop at nothing to get what he or she wants. This includes the selfish pursuit of short-term financial gains generated at the expense of other key stakeholders, as Mr. Smith, a former vice president at Goldman Sachs puts it, referring to what he called the toxic culture of his organization in his resignation opinion published in the *New York Times* (2012, March 14), when he declared that *"Not one single minute is spent asking questions about how we can help clients, it's purely about how we can make the most possible money off of them."*

Opportunities / Risks

Regardless of the strength of the pressure or incentive that an individual has, unethical acts can take place only if the opportunity is present. The opportunity for unethical acts or frauds can result from:

- **Weak internal controls:** Strong internal controls are a business's first line of defense.
- **No separation of duties:** This occurs when one employee handles many different related tasks. For example, the same employee opens the mail, logs in payments, and prepares and takes the deposit to the bank.
- **Indifferent management:** Sometimes management doesn't enforce the internal controls set in place.
- **Ineffective monitoring of management:** This takes place when the company is small and has few managers.
- **Collusion among employees** can circumvent even the strongest of internal controls.

As a French proverb states, *"The opportunity makes the thief"* – as soon as there are opportunities you will find people who will take advantage of them. The limitation is that the violator must feel that he/she can take advantage of the situation without getting caught and punished for it.

In conclusion, we need to be aware that when making decisions, pressures and rationalization from conflicts of interests and psychological biases are often underestimated, and will compromise our professional and moral judgment.

Establishing a System and a Culture of Risk Awareness and Ethics

For organizations to manage ethical risk issues effectively it is necessary to stop thinking like mechanics (hard controls) and to start acting like gardeners (soft controls). More and more, management control models emphasize the importance of soft controls and require the development of a pervasive ethical culture to support the control systems and processes in place. It is further recognized that effective compliance is an outcome of ethical behavior.

Hence managing ethics and compliance risk holistically is key to fostering and sustaining a strong ethical corporate culture, to support ethical behavior in an organization. As the old adage says, *"An organization is only as good as its people."* This is especially true in ethics and legal compliance, where successful management depends as much on how leadership and culture influences employee behavior as on the strength of controls and processes in place. From an understanding of the key factors that explain how unethical behavior can happen in organizations, we can define the key objectives of an effective ethical risk management system as follows:

1. Reduce and monitor pressures/incentives factors on employees to engage in unethical acts or even commit fraud.
2. Reduce an employee's ability to do the wrong thing and remain undetected for long periods.
3. Promote a strong risk aware ethical culture to make rationalization difficult.

Reduce and Monitor Pressures / Incentives Level

It is possible to reduce the pressures created by the stress of work by setting challenging yet realistic performance targets, ensure that pay systems can be perceived as fair by the employees and linking performance reward to real KPIs, i.e. drivers of value not financial results indicators. It also necessary to monitor "red flags" that may indicate that an employee is subjected to personal problems creating financial strain.

Reduce Opportunities, Increase Risks

It is essential to design and implement a solid system of internal management controls combined with effective management oversight of what is going on at every level in the organization. Checks and monitoring employees must be an ongoing process. Finally it is also important to keep people moving through job rotation and promotion so that they cannot build their own "black box" in their department.

Deal with Ethical Relativism and Make Rationalization Difficult

It is important never to underestimate the ability of the human mind to rationalize anything. Thanks to ethical relativism, with little efforts, people can actually rationalize a crime as being a benefit to society. Then the question is how to prevent inappropriate rationalization. The answer can be found in the nurturing of a strong ethical culture supported by adequate control systems. To reiterate, a corporate culture to support good and effective ethical risk management practices must have integrated at least the following values/principles:

- Think in terms of shared value and sustainability.
- Act with integrity and discipline.
- Be responsible and accountable for what they do.
- Be open and transparent about how they do things.
- Share information and knowledge proactively.

If it has not, unethical behaviors are inevitable and will ultimately lead to corporate failures. To create that kind of positive and ethical workplace environment and culture, it would be helpful the follow the steps highlighted in Figure 4.2.

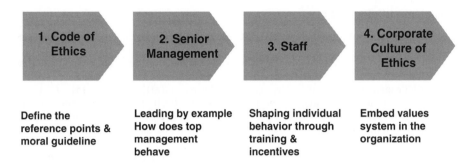

Figure 4.2   The four steps to ethical behavior.

First, the organization should develop a written code of ethics. The purpose of the code is to deter wrongdoing and to promote honest and ethical conduct that supports the business model of the organization and ensures compliance with applicable governmental laws, rules and regulations. The code of ethics should highlight the key principles and values that are supposed to guide decision making and describe what would constitute unethical or fraudulent behavior. It should also include a process for internal or external reporting of violations of the code to an appropriate person or persons identified in the code. Finally, it should define the accountability for adherence to the code and the sanctions to be imposed on those who breach it.

Second, it is also essential that the board and the senior management team take the lead in establishing the "tone at the top" by "walking the talk" as employees will naturally tend to follow the behavior of their leaders. Hence it is critical for the leaders to lead by example in setting professional standards and corporate values that promote integrity for themselves and other employees throughout the organization.

Third, shaping of employees' behavior can be achieved through the leading example of the senior management team supported by appropriate communication and regular training about the code of conduct and other important ethical issues. It is essential to link performance reward and promotion to ethical behavior so that employees are encouraged to do the right thing for their organization. Similarly organizations must ensure that they are hiring the appropriate employees who display a value system congruent with that of the organization. Finally, there should be zero tolerance for unethical behavior and any violation should be very firmly dealt with whatever the level of the employee concerned. The effort should be maintained over time to, fourth, ensure that the necessary principles and values become embedded in the culture and systems of the organization.

In conclusion:
1. Ethics is fundamental to enterprise risk management, and hence ethical culture objectives should be central to an effective ERM program.
2. Leading standards and regulations have recognized the centrality of ethics and have explicitly integrated ethics into the elements of effective enterprise risk management.
3. Organizations that are serious about implementing ethical principles and practices will not only protect their organization against damaging crises but also create tremendous benefits. A demonstrated corporate culture that supports and provides appropriate norms and incentives for professional and responsible behavior is an essential foundation of good governance, sustainable growth and profitability.

References and Bibliography

How Leeson broke the bank. (1999, June 22). BBC News Online http://news.bbc.co.uk/2/hi/business/375259.stm

Enron scandal at-a-glance. (2002, August 22). BBC News Online http://news.bbc.co.uk/2/hi/business/1780075.stm

Marsh & McLennan accused of price fixing, collusion. (2004, October 15). *USA Today* http://usatoday30.usatoday.com/money/industries/insurance/2004-10-15-spitzer-insurance_x.htm

Musgrove, M. (2010, February 06). BAE Systems pays $450 million to settle bribery scandal charges. *The Washington Post* http://articles.washingtonpost.com/2010-02-06/business/36873514_1_bae-systems-top-contractor-defense-contractor

Lyall, S. (2007, September 12). Anita Roddick, Body Shop Founder, Dies at 64. *The New York Times.* http://www.nytimes.com/2007/09/12/world/europe/12roddick.html?_r=0

COSO (2004), Enterprise Risk Management – Integrated Framework, Committee of Sponsoring Organizations of the Treadway Commission, AICPA, Jersey City, NJ.

ISO 31000, 2009, Guidelines on Risk Management Implementation, International Organization for Standardization.

Power, M. (2004). *The Risk Management of Everything: Rethinking the Politics of Uncertainty.* UK: Demos.

Citigroup's Chuck Prince wants to keep dancing, and can you really blame him? (2007, July 10). *The Business Times* http://business.time.com/2007/07/10/citigroups_chuck_prince_wants

Smith, G. (2012, March 14). Why I Am Leaving Goldman Sachs. *The New York Times.* http://www.nytimes.com/2012/03/14/opinion/why-i-am-leaving-goldman-sachs.html

4.2   GOVERNANCE, RISK, COMPLIANCE: THE NEW PARADIGM OF RISK MANAGEMENT

Jean-Paul Louisot

Formerly Université Paris 1 Panthéon-Sorbonne, Directeur pédagogique du CARM Institute, Paris, France

No one can deny the depth of the financial and economic crisis the world continues to experience in 2013 after the near collapse of the finance industry in 2008. The combined efforts of twenty heads of state and changes made to financial regulation and the identification of systemic risks created by large institutions may not be adequate to restore the value that was lost. It remains to be seen who will suffer most and, unfortunately, once again the poor populations in emerging countries may be the first human victims, even if Africa did not suffer as badly as was feared at the beginning thanks to its new economic link with the BRICS[1] countries.

This economic crisis has profoundly and permanently changed the context in which most organizations operate and strategy, tactics and operations must especially take into account the increased scrutiny of all stakeholders, which has been enhanced through the explosion of social media.

However, at the level of institutions and organizations, the main victim might well prove to be the deregulation that took place at the end of the twentieth century, even in spite of its latest attempt at surviving through the *Sarbanes-Oxley Act* in the USA and the "tick the box" model named COSO 2, invented by the auditors to offer a quick fix to frightened executives. Obviously, it is still tempting for governments to appease their citizens' fears through the enactment of layers upon layers of regulation to corset the economic actors. Could there be

---

[1] BRICS – Brazil, Russia, India, China, & South Africa.

a miracle remedy, a panacea? Most certainly it will prove to be just another temporary fix, unless it starts at the root of the problem – not only the greed of too many, but more deeply the systemic failure of the current "accounting standards" to reconcile the "real" economy with the "virtual" economy. What we experience currently is literally a choking of the former by the latter, covered by a thick foam of non-productive financial assets.

The rating agencies who at best did not see the debacle coming and at worst encouraged it by inappropriately rating some of the so called "toxic assets", had to reinvent themselves and now operate under a much closer scrutiny by government and industry. It seems that the rating agencies that were at the heart of the trust issue as they gave a "pass", including triple A rating, to the financial products that failed so abysmally, seem to have discovered ERM as a way to regain the public trust and confidence. To be totally fair, they had started to grasp the importance of a global and integrated approach to risk management and in May 2008, Standard & Poor's announced that it would incorporate an "evaluation of ERM" in its ratings for non-financial companies beginning in late 2008.

However, in times of high volatility, symbols are important and the investment community and the public at large must be reassured and new tightened regulations will probably change their perception of risk, especially as some encompass the interdiction of golden parachutes, a limitation of compensation packages for executives and a consolidation of the real estate market. Access to decent housing for all may be a right, but it is high time that governments realize that it may not mean that all citizens should own their house. But let us not delude ourselves, regulations will not be enough, the cure will require a change of mind, a return to basics and fundamental values; solidarity should remind us that we will either succeed together or sink. And this is true at the level of the organization, at the level of local authorities, the nation and even the world.

Indeed, only governments could curb the excesses of a liberal economy, and the financial crisis has opened a window of opportunity. This, of course is an opportunity, if and only if leaders have the courage to transcend national egoisms to build a "new international order" through which the short-term interests of everyone are aligned with the long-term interest of society. But is this not the true "sustainable development"? It remains to be seen if the agreement signed at the G20 meeting in Washington in 2011 (see box) will be transformed into working documents to offer an international framework for controlling financial activities.

Under these circumstances, the "golden triangle" developed by risk management professionals could prove to be the cornerstone for this reconstruction. In truth, the new risk managers' mantra is GRC, which stands for *Governance-Risk-Compliance*. In fact, woven in these three words lies what most of the professionals of the world have come to call ERM, from the American acronym for a global and integrated approach to managing risks.

The G20 Washington communiqué: "We, the Finance Ministers and Central Bank Governors of the G20, are committed to a strong and coordinated international response to address the renewed challenges facing the global economy, notably heightened downside risks from sovereign stresses, financial system fragility, market turbulence, weak economic growth and unacceptably high unemployment.

We are taking strong actions to maintain financial stability, restore confidence and support growth. In Europe, Euro area countries have taken major actions to ensure the sustainability of public finances, and are implementing the decisions taken by Euro area Leaders on 21 July 2011. Specifically, the euro area will have implemented by the time of our next meeting the necessary actions to increase the flexibility of the EFSF and to maximize its impact in order to address contagion.

The U.S. has put forward a significant package to strengthen growth and employment through public investments, tax incentives and targeted job measures, combined with fiscal reforms designed to restore fiscal sustainability over the medium term.

Japan is implementing substantial fiscal measures for reconstruction from the earthquake while ensuring the commitment to medium-term fiscal consolidation. Heightened downside risks have also made the economic environment for emerging markets and developing economies more challenging and they are adjusting their macroeconomic policies accordingly to maintain stability and sustain growth. The contribution of the emerging market economies to global growth will increase as these economies as a whole move toward more domestic-led growth, including through structural reforms and enhanced exchange rate flexibility to reflect economic fundamentals. We reiterate that excess volatility and disorderly movements in exchange rates have adverse implications for economic and financial stability.

We are committed to supporting growth, implementing credible fiscal consolidation plans, and ensuring strong, sustainable and balanced growth. This will require a collective and bold action plan, with everyone doing their part. We are working together to put in place for the Cannes Summit such an action plan of coordinated policies with both short-term decisions and a medium-long-term perspective.

We commit to take all necessary actions to preserve the stability of banking systems and financial markets as required. We will ensure that banks are adequately capitalized and have sufficient access to funding to deal with current risks and that they fully implement Basel III along the agreed timelines.

Central Banks will continue to stand ready to provide liquidity to banks as required. Monetary policies will maintain price stability and continue to support economic recovery.

We will review progress made in implementing the commitments made today at our next meeting" Communiqué of Finance Ministers and Central Bank Governors of the G-20, Washington D.C., USA, 22nd September 2011. http://www.g20.org/Communique/index _2.html

---

The challenge is the same, whatever the acronym, GRC or ERM, and it could be summarized in this illustration: "In a compliance culture, if you come to a pedestrian traffic light flashing red you would stop and not cross the road. In a risk management culture, you would look at the light, check the road to see if any cars are coming, and if not, you cross it."[2]

As a matter of fact, some regulators went one step further in coining the expression "Risk Governance"[3] and envisioning risk mitigation and transparency lies at the heart of any governance exercise. However, it remains true that the traditional GRC process promoted by auditors still is a "ticking boxes" exercise.

In contrast, the GRC approach that will be advocated in this article is rooted in the management system of the organization and in complete congruence with the ISO 31000 principles, framework and process. At the heart of the proposed understanding of the GRC triangle is its weaving into the *culture, mission, values, and strategy of the organization*. In other words,

---

[2] Jeanette Ward, Primary Credit Analyst at Standard & Poor's in *The Analyst* number 1, 2007 p.6 published by AON Australia, www.aon.com.au

[3] South Africa following the KING 3 report suggestions on governance.

following the GRC model will not in itself ensure ethical behavior. It is essential to understand that compliance is limited and even compromised if it is not ethics driven. Therefore, each point of the triangle contributes to the proper management of any organization: whereas governance ensures that a transparent and objective decision process is in place, compliance is necessary to guarantee the legality of all actions, and risk management provides long-term vision to ensure resiliency and sustainable development.

The triangle developed by some risk management professionals could become the cornerstone for modern risk management reconstruction. In truth, the risk managers' new mantra must be GRC, *Governance-Risk-Compliance,* and their goal to achieve measureable GRC performance goals. ERM is woven into the central position of these three words, and GRC success requires a global and integrated approach to managing risks.

In November 2007, before the deteriorating financial sector became a crisis, at the RMIA[4] conference in Australia, Marianne Robinson[5] gave a clear explanation on why the three GRC concepts are fundamentally intertwined:

> "Regulatory reform around the world the last 5 years has resulted in enormous changes to public and private sector entities as they attempt to manage the risks associated with overlapping regulation and reform on an unprecedented level."

The reforms have already driven changes to the concept of corporate governance and the profile of risk management as organizations struggle to accommodate the new legal compliance and corporate governance frameworks imposed by codes of conduct, prudential standards, government and regulators within and outside Australia.

Risk management has been elevated within organizations but often under the guise of compliance and governance. Governance, and legal and regulatory risk, issues have created awareness at director level that was often lacking in the past. Boards are playing a greater role in the monitoring of risk-related issues but there is a price paid for this new level of awareness. Many directors are so concerned with how the business deals with legal risk and their own personal liability that they have become risk adverse. Too many enterprises are still bogged down in time consuming but often ineffective "tick the box" compliance programs. Too many directors and managers are diverted from business decisions that involve innovation, and strategic policy and opportunities.

Another challenge facing both private and public sector organizations is how to manage legal risk and how to implement effective compliance and governance programs without creating a risk adverse environment where the core business comes to a standstill. Many organizations have yet to determine their level of risk appetite while others worry that district attorneys worldwide might be lurking in the background threatening organizations with legal exposures for conduct that was once acceptable but suddenly no longer meets community expectations of what is acceptable.

GRC must become the new mantra for public and private sector entities as they look for an integrated solution and a common enterprise-wide philosophy to underpin three quite different but at the same time similar frameworks (see Figure 4.3), thus they maintain their "social license to operate". This is why it is essential to consider the enterprise information relationships between governance, compliance and risk management. Senior management must examine how legal risk varies from other forms of risk and look at the relationships between the

---

[4] RMIA is the Risk Management Institution of Australasia.
[5] "Why is governance suddenly so popular with risk managers?"; RMIA Conference, November 25, 2007.

risk management teams and the compliance teams where training and background are often very different. The open question is whether there is a new type of hybrid risk professional emerging – someone who combines traditional risk expertise with a legal compliance and governance background and what boards need from GRC reporting.

Figure 4.3   The GRC triangle.

The understandable failure of traditional risk management to prevent the global economic meltdown of 2008 makes the comment above even more important for the development of ERM. However, not all practitioners share that vision on GRC and Michael Moody wrote:

> "A recent organizational trend has been to integrate risk management with compliance and governance. This fusion is frequently called 'governance, risk, and compliance (GRC)', but it often leads to companies relying too heavily on the 'checklist mentality'.[6]

This fusion has led boards to raise objections related to compliance-related challenges. Many directors are worried that the executives in their organizations are devoting too many resources to compliance issues and not enough efforts to competitive business initiatives. Some analysts have implied that a GRC approach that includes risk management in a wider framework is not sustainable over the long term. Therefore, the question remains open to envision risk management as an exercise separate from compliance and oversight.

Although the potential pitfall stressed by Michael Moody and his followers cannot be underestimated, there remain major drivers for an integrated approach to the three sides of the GRC triangle and they explain while this trend seems to be prevailing today:

1   The Intrinsic Relationship Between Governance and Risk

An organization's exposure space comprises all the types of risks; a number of them may potentially affect the achievement of its objectives. Some of those risks stem directly from the governance. The governance philosophy of the company (as embodied in the organization's governance framework, policies, practices and the implementation of these policies) may not support the organization in the pursuit of its goals.

---

[6] Moody, Michael J. (06/09) *Rough Notes* Vol. 152, No. 6, p. 46.

But conversely, the governance framework of an organization is also a risk management tool adopted by the board, as it is clearly the board's responsibility if they agree on its empowerment by the stakeholders.

2   The Elements of a Typical Governance Framework

There are many governance frameworks that can apply to an organization's compliance mandates. Each organization must develop its own hybrid framework to fit its purposes. The governance framework will reflect regulatory oversight and market performance expectations. An effective governance model should be based on the premise that corporate governance:

- Is not just about regulation and legislation, it is about doing what is right for the stakeholders.
- Is broader than boards and committees; it extends throughout the organization, and includes internal controls and compliance functions such as risk management and internal audit and external audit.
- Requires transparency of disclosure, effective communication, and proper measurement and accountability as essential elements for good governance.

The foundation of an effective governance model is the corporate structure that includes the owners of the business in the form of the shareholders, who appoint a number of trustees, in the form of a board of directors, to oversee their interests in the business and who in turn hire a chief executive to develop business strategies, employ resources, build and operate processes, generate profits, and increase the value for the shareholders.

3   The Impact of Culture on Governance and Risk Management; and the New Ethics Frontier

In the past few years, organizations have focused much energy on developing robust governance and risk management infrastructure. Despite this focus on getting the cultural design right, many organizations still find that the governance and risk management balance is not working properly. In a recent survey of the world's leading global mining companies,[7] the majority of respondents nominated the embedding of risk management into their culture as the key future challenge for their organizations.

So it would appear that for many organizations struggling with embedding governance and risk management in their culture, the answer may lie in aligning enterprise risk management goals and assessment practices at the top of their organization.

Defining the enterprise risk management culture of an organization rests on developing the necessary competencies of all staff and should provide insight on why things are the way they are. For example, is it acceptable to circumvent a particular policy or control without clear accountability for decision making? For the "risk management culture" defining the tone at the top is vital as top management can influence that culture through measureable policies linked to management reporting practices. Culture may be an intangible but we can introduce tangible measures to impact it, like recruitment processes, whistle blowers provisions, etc. This is what is required to influence behavior and confirm governance alignment with risk management performance goals. However, it is important to remember that truly changing culture is usually a slow process; it is not typically a quick fix.

---

[7] Ernst & Young, Attitudes to risk in the Global Mining Sector, 2007.

Among the spheres of activity defined in the Cindynics[8] approach (see *Brief overview of the Cindynics*) combining several of the five dimensions of the description of an individual perception of risks, the three-dimensional space regrouping objectives, norms and values is the sphere of ethics "in action". If one is to judge only by the volume of academic publications, professional articles and conferences, ethics plays a growing role in development on organizations' management at any level, private and public entities, NGOs and healthcare institutions, as well as governments. Managers, as well as elected officials, cannot limit themselves to an "efficient stewardship of the means", but need to question the ends; in other words they must revisit the goals and missions, redefine the norms and analyze the values that guide their leadership. This emergence of ethics as a management topic has become embedded in the culture of many organizations but there is still a long way to go. Could it be that reviving ethics was made necessary when the free economy model lost its counter-model, communism, and thus lost its counterbalance and mirror?[9]

Whatever the origin of this trend, it becomes clearer every day that standards and best practices cannot be limited to the pursuit of profit and the creation of value only for the shareholders. The allocation of colossal heaps of resources, often more than the GDP of "middle-sized nations", by private economic operators puts on the shoulders of those making these decisions the responsibility to question the ends which these means are serving. This is precisely why not only the executives of global companies, but also the leaders of local entities, the mayors, the county chairs, the state officials as well as healthcare managers must revise their objectives and missions, redefine their norms and establish their values, taking into account all the components of the society and the expectations and fears of all their stakeholders to ensure that there is value creation for all.

Under this new paradigm every leader must rethink his/her strategy in the context of the society's mission to its members, now and tomorrow. Ensuring that all behave "ethically" supposes that values are clearly defined, obeyed by all and that the "ethical frontier" is understood by all, and never to be transgressed without consequences.

If all issues were black or white, choosing the "right" solution would be easy. However, most ethical issues are grey and the level of grey may depend on the set of values for any given individual or any given organization. Therefore, whereas there is a minefield beyond the "ethical boundary" for everyone, the boundary differs from one entity to another, one period to the next. The ethical boundary, or set of values, is an integral part of what is often referred to as "corporate culture". It results from the "living and growing together", and the role of top management is essential in attracting and retaining employees that will fit into the culture and feel the bond to work together: the "affectio societatis".

As a matter of fact, as the recent developments on the financial institutions illustrate too clearly, the question that each member of staff must ponder with each decision is not so much "Could I?" that is the compliance question, but rather "Should I?" that is, is it in accordance with my own principles and values, with the values of my organization? Put in blunt terms: If the media published the consequences of my decision, if my children knew it, my spouse, my friends . . . could I still look at myself in a mirror without shame, even with pride?

---

[8] Cindynics the science of Danger, from the Greek Kindynos for hazard, was funded in France in 1987 to offer a conceptual framework to approach the understanding of risk, the enhancement of opportunities and the curbing of threats.

[9] Ethics of Transition from Communism, by Alejandro A. Chafuen (Lecture-speech delivered at the 1st International Conference-Workshop "Ethical Foundations of Economy", Krakow Oct. 14, 2003).

To summarize, the ethics dilemma could be summarized in a simple question that the G20 leaders should ask themselves: "Is it not time simply to refocus the economic system on the essential, make it its core mission to ensure humanity's well-being, rather than the accumulation of wealth?"

Beyond compliance, it is ethics that is at the core of reputation creation, with risk management and governance, i.e. the patient building of trust in all stakeholders, the strategic ingredient of resilience in the time of trials and ruptures; trust is undoubtedly the ultimate survival kit in a society so geared towards image, and reputation.

Too often, good intentions do not transform into good actions. The code emanating from the Orange Book issued by Her Majesty's Treasury stipulates that local authorities in the UK must conform to six principles of good governance that could serve as a model precisely at the time when the world leaders are searching for a new fuel to jumpstart the world economy engine:

- The efforts and means of the organizations must be allocated solely to the fulfilment of users' and citizens' needs.
- Each member of staff must work efficiently within clearly defined missions and roles.
- The good governance values defined by the organization must be publicly disclosed and adhered to by all involved in the organization's operations.
- All decisions must be informed and transparent, taking into account all the risks involved.
- Leaders (appointed as well as elected) must be trained to possess the competencies and skills needed for the efficient performance of their missions.
- Communication and consultation must be established with all stakeholders, and all must be accountable for the results obtained.

These principles are rooted in a key element, trust – the trust essential in any economic system short of bartering. Will the leaders of all countries, developed, the BRIC[10] countries, or BRICS if South Africa is included, and emerging countries finally find the courage to develop a vision, beyond egoistic interests, to redress or rebuild the global economic structure on firm principles? Time is of the essence. And risk management professionals should be called to play a key role; however, the GRC triangle, the golden triangle for the profession, seems to have become a Bermuda triangle for industry if risk managers hesitate too long to deploy it.

---

[10] BRIC = Brazil, Russia, India, China.

Communicate and Consult

Communication is an essential element in all aspects of risk management. While it is considered a step in the ERM framework it is one that is articulated with all phases of the risk management process. Without good communication that is relevant to the stakeholder, the understanding of issues and solutions may be muddled, leading to disastrous results. The second important piece of this step of the risk management process is consultation. The risk manager is an internal consultant and coach. The job of the risk manager includes helping those without technical experience in risk management to acquire the expertise necessary for risk owners and others to accomplish their risk optimization goals and objectives.

5.1 COMMUNICATION AS A RISK MITIGATION TOOL

Jean-Paul Louisot

Formerly Université Paris 1 Panthéon-Sorbonne, Directeur pédagogique du CARM Institute, Paris, France

5.1.1 Risks Perception and Reality: Communication of Risks

Risk management, both as a profession and as a discipline, has experienced an accelerated pace of evolution since the beginning of the twenty-first century due to the sudden request for additional "security" in all stakeholders segments. Physical security was brought to high priority since the terrorist attacks in the USA on 9/11/01 and maintained thereafter by the repeats in Madrid and London. It seems that since the tsunamis at the end of 2004, natural disasters have increased in visibility, if not in frequency and intensity, and are even more devastating in poor countries or neighborhoods. In addition, financial security has been highlighted since the Enron and WorldCom debacles, not to mention Parmalat in Italy.

Food and health security are a continuing problem with issues like the AIDS pandemic in Africa, the GM (genetically modified organisms) debate and the famine in so many "emerging" countries; and more recently in Europe, the horse meat sold as beef. Many governments have beefed up security, specifically in airports and entry points to their national territories. Western governments have enacted legislation to improve accounting transparency, for example, the *Sarbanes-Oxley Act* in the USA, and LSF *(loi sur la sécurité financière)* in France. There has even been a revision made to the French constitution to introduce a "general principle of precaution". Even the security of future generations is at stake with the new buzz expression: "sustainable development".

For more than four decades, risk management has been a technical job mainly focusing on financing the negative consequences of threats to the organization. It is now blossoming into a discipline on par with finance or marketing as the "management of uncertainties", which requires the development of a sound conceptual framework including the scientific skills needed to quantify the various impacts of uncertain events. Risks are both opportunities and threats, and risk management should ensure that risks are included and identified for analysis and treatment in all decision-making processes, at the strategic, tactical, and operational levels. This necessity is commonly called "risk appropriation by all risk owners", i.e. the operational managers who are at the source of many risks that can be best controlled at their level.

The explosion of information through both global networks and private channels based on computers, like websites and "blogs", provides new pathways for the rapid spreading of rumors, sometimes with ill intentions, sometimes not. Social media also creates open forums where the average citizen, not necessarily properly informed or educated, can express his/her perception of risks rather than an objective measure developed by qualified "experts". The irony is that specialists have initiated research to tackle the difficult task of quantifying and assessing risks through new methodologies made possible by the recent scientific developments, like the chaos theory, "bringing order to chaos and complexity".[1] Financial institutions, banks complying with Basel 2, and insurance and reinsurance companies battling with Solvency 2 have even found ways to get round the absence of historical data in operational risks thanks to expert opinions and the use of Bayesian networks.

Social acceptability of projects and innovation is greatly enhanced if the public is made aware of what is at stake, understands the medium- and long-term benefits and is convinced that those in charge try their best to reduce the possible negative impact. Even the famous NIMBY (not in my back yard) position can be mitigated with proper communication. But this will require a true and honest effort of engaging the stakeholders to manage their initial perception of risks and gain their trust so that they are ready at best to engage in the project, at least to tolerate it in their "back yard".

This brief introduction to the environment of risks leads to an essential conclusion: communication on risks and risk management efforts is becoming an integral part of any efficient global risk management, whatever the organization involved, state, public, private, or healthcare. As a matter of fact the experts who developed the ISO 31000:2009 standard on risk management were so aware of the need for interaction with the stakeholders that they call for "communication and consultation" with key stakeholders throughout the risk management process.

5.1.2   Conditions and Objectives of the Communication of Risks

Too often communication on risk is left to "public relations specialists" whose understanding of the mission is limited to polishing communiqués, at best radio or television interviews, for internal or external audiences so that the organization, and sometimes mostly its CEO, will appear in the best possible light. Public relations specialists may engage in exchanges with stockholders and the financial community, but for most of them it is a one-way street. However, the Latin root of communication, "to share" should remind the managers that the process calls for a two-way street, in this case establishing a continuous process of exchanges and dialogue with all the stakeholders in a given project or risk. The Australian Risk Management Guidelines Handbook (HB 436/2004) appropriately stated: *"Communication is an interactive process of exchanges of information and opinion involving multiple messages about the nature of risk and risk management."*

---

[1] John Gribbin, *Deep Simplicity: Bringing order to chaos and complexity*. Random House, USA 2004.

This communication clearly calls for a two-way vertical movement of information and action:

- First, top down, there must be a "risk champion" in the executive team so that managing risks is clearly understood as a boardroom mandate.
- Second, bottom up, the information on risks must be consolidated so that risks are managed according to what is called in the EU the principle of "subsidiarity" to provide the board with the "reasonable assurance" that all risks are managed at the appropriate level.

However, while all the risks must be entered into the risk register, the board must not be inundated with information on risks that should be handled at the operational level. The consolidation process sends to higher echelons only those risks that cannot be efficiently treated at a lower level, because of lack of perspective or means. Thus, the board receives a risk register limited to the exposures that may have strategic implications at the company level.

The risk management process developed at all levels in the organization allows the board, the CEO, the CFO and the audit committee to sign off on documents that ensure stakeholders that the objectives or mission of the organization will be met in as economically efficient and socially acceptable a fashion as possible.

It follows that the executive team must maintain a good connection with all stakeholders, both internal and external. One key element to build and protect their trust is to prove that those in command are able to conduct the necessary modifications and remain ahead of the change process even in time of accelerated evolution in the context of the organization that could result in rupture. In most cases, it is only in the time of turbulences that this capacity can be really tested, but it would be preferable to be able to assess the organization's resilience in quiet times. And it is precisely the board's and executives' understanding that uncertainties, threats as well as opportunities, must be taken into account in all decision processes within the organization that builds the trust of all stakeholders that the organizations is "responsible". Thus all who have a stake in the organization gain the assurance that their varied and sometimes conflicting interests are assessed and valued; it is that trust and confidence that builds and maintains an organization's reputation.

Good communication on risk management can only rest on effective sound risk management throughout the organization. Indeed, the task is to "nest" risk management in all staff and management as a result of an ongoing learning process whereby all concerned acquire an automatic sense of risks that may stem from their activities. In a complex system, where components are intertwined, it falls on each unit and operational manager to be the risk manager of the entity he/she is in charge of. Risk management is no longer some esoteric process at headquarters with stressing demands adding to the daily workload; it has become an essential part of the daily routine of any manager, indeed any employee. This new reality must now be reflected in the job description of all in managerial positions, and bonuses should also take into account the risk management performance of all.

However, good "in house" risk management is not enough anymore. The complex system itself is hooked to an increasingly complex web of relationships with outside partners, both upstream (sub-contractors and suppliers) and downstream (customers). Therefore, good risk management practices must be embedded in all economic partners. In the case of a public entity, in some instances, the whole population leaving or working in the area must be engaged in the learning process. For instance, in the case of a hospital or any healthcare provider, clearly patients as well as relatives and visitors are essential stakeholders that must be actively involved in the risk management process.

Fulfiling the conditions stipulated above is necessary if the organization's leadership wants to be able to face any situation and react rapidly not only to pre-identify risks but also when unexpected developments take place, the unknown-unknowns. Indeed, stakeholders demand that the executives prove they are able to cope when confronted with surprises, unpleasant as they may be. The leader is expected to set the example that will ensure the organization's survival.

The question any decision maker will ask at this stage concerns the benefits that the organization can draw from sound communication on risk management. This really means: Shall we get our money's worth? The eight benefits here are derived from those mentioned for reputation management:

- Creates an environment more favorable for investments, with better access to capital markets as potential investors are reassured, especially pensions funds and other institutional investors.
- Improves trust and confidence in dealing with stockholders and other stakeholders.
- Facilitates recruitment and retention of talented staff whose ethics and values agree with those expressed and practiced within the organization.
- Attracts the best possible economic partners.
- Upstream (reputation with sub-contractors and suppliers).
- Downstream (reputation with customers).
- Lowers barriers to entry into new markets, especially those where the public is actively involved in policy making.
- Commands premium prices for goods or services as the organization offers a higher level of procurement safety (especially in case of "just in time" and project management) and/or more sustainable development ("green" and equitable markets).
- Limits threats of legal proceedings or more stringent regulations (sometimes this will require a collective effort at the industry level).
- Limits the potential for crisis, in part thanks to the efficient communication tools developed in time of peace.

5.1.3   Basic Principles for Efficient Communication on Risks

Whereas sound risk management practices are a prerequisite for good communication, it is not enough and some rules must be followed to ensure the efficiency of the communication on risk management:

- Promote a sense of "specificity" in all stakeholders' minds (concerted efforts to take into account all perspectives on risks).
- Focus on a "central" theme (the mind is set to ensure security and safety for all).
- Ensure "coherence" in all communication (all concerned segments of the public receive the information they need within a coherent framework).
- Stick to "integrity and authenticity" in all dealings (in particular in the exchange process with the different stakeholders).
- Commit to "transparency" (it is the foundation of all financial and social performance sustainable in the long run through constructive dialogue, win-win situation, with the stakeholders).

- Be cautious when perceptions are based on impressions as opposed to the knowledge and understanding of the issues in a particular situation.
- Develop in contacts a conscience of danger without creating an anxiety prone society.
- Avoid approaching risk management on a "good feelings" basis as this will not give a real sense of direction to the activity deployed by the organization.
- Be specific in the description on modes and criteria of decision making and arbitraging options.
- Avoid jargon or unnecessary esoteric language, without losing track of the need for precise vocabulary.
- Develop validation instruments to measure the adhesion of the different stakeholders to choices made by the organization.
- Transcend individual interests to promote a "collective or societal" evaluation of risks.
- Use ordinary risk situations, confronted and managed by most, especially when communicating with large segments of the population (risk in the daily life of any household, purchasing insurance for the family, etc.).

All this can be summarized simply; it is all about conducting an adult dialogue with stakeholders on the key questions:

- What is at stake (opportunities and threats)?
- What is the proper balance between individual and collective interests?
- Can there be a licence to operate at best until the dialogue can reach the proper level of balance (between "consenting adults")?

In any event, the different risk communication tools are to be used to propose solutions and not to be an additional source of problems and fears for the many targets (stakeholders). This can be achieved so long as for each of those target stakeholder groups the organization strives to:

- Analyze their problems when confronted with uncertainties or necessary changes:
  - ✓ Avoid generating additional problems for them.
  - ✓ Enter an empathy mode to understand their way of thinking.
  - ✓ Decipher the challenges they are to meet.
  - ✓ Evaluate whether they are in survival mode or still in a fighting mood.
- Make sure to be seen as a provider of solutions:
  - ✓ Be perceived as a resource.
  - ✓ Share all possible solutions.
  - ✓ Help them see the benefits for them through the risks.
- Speak their language:
  - ✓ Understand and use stakeholders' own specific language, or vocabulary, for each "customer" segment when addressing them.
  - ✓ Listen to the "targets" (listening quality is essential).
  - ✓ Refer to key words in their vocabulary.
  - ✓ Cultivate empathy more than intrinsic content.
- Take into account their expectations through clear and transparent rules for dialogue:
  - ✓ Purpose of the meeting with the "contact group".
  - ✓ Modus operandi.
  - ✓ Timetable.
  - ✓ Negotiation points.

✓ Methods to overcome difficulties and dead ends.
✓ Beware of ambiguities *(in case of "agreement" do not hesitate to interpret more in favor of the stakeholders)*.
✓ Develop a critical approach to the fears expressed as well as to any proposed solution.
✓ Informal conversations may prove useful to enhance trust.
✓ Transparency means expressing things as they are (not always only to please the spectator).
✓ All critiques must offer a proposal (no negative comments without a counter-offer).
✓ Feed a dynamic dialogue.

The suggestions listed here could be applied to communication on any subject. However, communication on risk and the way it is mitigated has a very significant specificity: it must be efficient, particularly in times of turbulence. Therefore, it is essential to distinguish clearly communication:

• Under normal circumstances, both within and without the organization.
• In a time of a crisis, or immediately thereafter.

5.1.4   Which Stakeholders Need to Be Informed of Risks?

It would be cumbersome to try to provide an all-encompassing list that would include all stakeholders for any type of organization worldwide. However, the list below summarizes the main groups to be informed on risks under most circumstances, and practical tips are included in Section 5.1.5 for dealing with each of them.

Internal Stakeholders

For each of the targets identified, their main centres of interests are listed:

• Board of directors (beware of the specific needs of non-executive or "independent" board members):
  ✓ Strategic exposures *(as a rule of thumb there should be no more than ten)*.
  ✓ Evaluation of risk impact on stakeholders' trust and confidence.
  ✓ Crisis management and strategic redeployment options.
• Members of the executive team:
  ✓ Same as board members.
  ✓ Evaluation of their performance by the board.
• Unit and operational managers:
  ✓ Exposures within their control.
  ✓ Performance indicators.
• Floor managers and all staff members:
  ✓ Personal safety issues.
  ✓ Responsibility for individual risks.
  ✓ Understanding of the extent of their "risk management" mission.

External Stakeholders

For the external stakeholders, it will be a matter of providing answers to their fears and worries, while fulfiling their expectations. Who are they?

- Economic partners (up and downstream).
- Elected officials in the local authorities.
- Central (federal) government representatives.
- Local associations and special interests groups.
- Neighbors *(those that can be affected by risks while receiving benefits from them, or not)*.
- Media (press, television and radio).
- "The greens" and other environment protection groups, etc.

5.1.5   Tips for Communicating Risks to the Major Group of Stakeholders

One key to effective risk communication is to focus on the expectation and fears of each given group: they are not all expecting the same level of detail and they may not have the same right to inside information. However, it is essential for long-term credibility that all the communications are consistent and transparent as the different targets may have interaction, for example, through social media. The tips that follow take into account these considerations to help design the proper risk communication grid and follow the usual pattern of questioning that a journalist follows when writing an article for a newspaper.

- Communication with the board of directors:
    - ✓ When – keep channels of communication open at all times, regular RM report (no less than quarterly).
    - ✓ Who – the risk manager, or his/her boss if he/she does not have access to the board.
    - ✓ Content – strategic exposures only and progress on cost of risk and risk mapping exercises. Non-executive members will be mostly interested in governance issues and long-term resilience.
    - ✓ Format – one or two page presentation with two or three slides to draw attention.
- Communication with stockholders (if public corporation is subject to disclosure rules):
    - ✓ When – annual report and occasional if needed (profit warning).
    - ✓ Who – the CEO, prepared by the risk manager.
    - ✓ Content – major trends and strategic exposures and impact on the profit + communication on pending claims – check local and international legal requirements. Special stress on resilience and continued growth.
    - ✓ Format – depending on countries format may be 1 to 3 pages on the annual report. Messages may be needed in case of major events happening between reports.
- Communication with operational managers (risk owners):
    - ✓ When – ongoing and specifically for risk mapping and continuity planning.
    - ✓ Who – risk manager and his team and correspondent in the business units.
    - ✓ Content – assistance throughout the implementation of the risk-mapping exercise and risk-control measures (specifically BIA (business impact analysis) and BCP (business continuity planning)).
    - ✓ Format – notes, email, Internet and training session, coaching.
- Communication with personnel:
    - ✓ When – channels of communication should be open at all times, but there must at least be regularly scheduled RM reports to establish and maintain risk culture.
    - ✓ Who – RM professionals relayed by "risk owners" for reinforcement and human resources department.
    - ✓ Content – explanations on potential impact on work site, working conditions and own life, including "job safety".
    - ✓ Format – Internet, intranet, posters, training, etc.

- Communication with economic partners:
  - ✓ When – special emphasis at the initial stage of cooperation and follow-up through the contractual life.
  - ✓ Who – risk management team, purchase and procurement, marketing and sales, and communication department (PR).
  - ✓ Content – all shared exposures with the given partner, including resilience of relationship. Special attentions when consumer goods delivered to public.
  - ✓ Format – (will vary depending on the information needed to address the partner's concern directly, but it should be short and to the point).
- Communication with local authorities:
  - ✓ When – keep channels of communication open at all times to ensure proper interaction in time of need.
  - ✓ Who – RM professionals and compliance officer (when appropriate), PR personnel and local risk owners (plant managers).
  - ✓ Content – special emphasis on public health and safety issues and sustainable development commitment.
  - ✓ Format – filing official compulsory forms and requirements, and personal contact with elected officials and civil servants.
- Communication with media:
  - ✓ When – maintain regular contact *(line of communication should be open at all times)*.
  - ✓ Who – PR personnel or executives with the assistance of RM professional and risk-owners.
  - ✓ Content – mostly health and safety issues, CSR (corporate social responsibility) challenges, but do not forget "financial press" as this is really addressed to the stockholders.
  - ✓ Format – press releases and interviews depending on nature – see further for time of crisis.
- Communication with pressure groups:
  - ✓ When – selectively when necessary, if group interest at stake, but need to be proactive.
  - ✓ Who – PR personnel and/or executives, with RM professional support.
  - ✓ Content – stress exposures and risk control on areas of interest to the group.
  - ✓ Format – communication will include visits and discussion groups to get members feedback and "subjective perception of risks".
- Communication with the general public:
  - ✓ When – keep channels of communication open at all times to reassure and respond to preoccupation *(beware of social media)*.
  - ✓ Who – PR personnel and/or executives, with RM professional support.
  - ✓ Content – stress exposures and risk control on areas of interest to the public (health and safety, environment, sustainability, etc.).
  - ✓ Format – communication will include visits and discussion groups to get members' feedback and "subjective perception of risks", especially for "high risk" units.

Part II
Case Studies

6
Case Study Protocol

The individual case studies were conducted with the most senior risk officer in the organization. A series of questions (Appendix A) was put together before any of the interviews took place. These were intended as a guide. Depending upon the extent of the ERM implementation, some questions were not asked. In other instances interviewers asked additional questions to gain further insight into the issues risk managers have been facing.

Interviews were conducted either in person or by telephone. The interviewer wrote up the case study from interview notes and the case study was triangulated back to the interviewee for concurrence. In some cases the interviewee had others in the organization read the material for additional observations or changes. Case studies were approved by the interviewees for inclusion in the book.

This practice was not followed for the two case studies, *Risk Management Implementation in China*, which was written by the author of this case. *Agreeing Upon The Scope of the Project and the Job of the ERM Risk Manager* was based upon an interview with the authors of this book and considered only one facet of the ERM process – negotiating the scope of the job and ERM project.

APPENDIX A – CASE STUDY INTERVIEW QUESTIONS

Question Categories

1. **What is the organization?**
   (a) Legal entity: corporation, public, private, etc.?
   (b) If government institution, services provided and revenue sources?
   (c) If a business or not-for-profit, demographics: industry segment, major products, number of employees, total revenue, geographic markets, distribution channels?
   (d) Competitive issues: e.g., emerging market, mature market, commodity, oligarchy, etc.?
   (e) Important stakeholders (segments)?
   (f) Mission and vision and social license to operate?
   (g) Other information important to help understand the business (acquisitions, environmental, leadership style, etc.)?
2. **What is the identified need for ERM?**
   (a) When?
   (b) Why?
   (c) Scope (including threats and opportunities – extended to partners and external dependencies)?
   (d) Who made the decision?
   (e) What are the regulatory or rating agency compliance issues (if not identified)?
   (f) Other?
3. **What has been the process of implementing ERM?**
   (a) Who is in charge of the ERM initiative?
   (b) What is the project of ERM implementation?

   (c) What is your role/your education and background?

   (d) What is the hierarchy of those involved in ERM?

   (e) What is the support of management and board?

   (f) What strategic changes have been required?

   (g) What organizational changes have been required?

   (h) Other changes, e.g., systems, accounting, etc. (including data quality and adequacy to make informed decisions)?

   (i) What were the tools developed: dashboards, etc.?

   (j) What is the assurance process?

   (k) What are or have been other implementation issues?

4. **What are the critical risks associated with ERM?**

   (a) What critical risks were identified (prompt if necessary: operational, strategic, financial, reputation, other risks)?

   (b) How were critical risks identified (SWOT, etc.)?

   (c) What risk management tools are being used to treat critical risks?

   (d) What surprise risks were identified, and/or what were the unexpected challenges associated with critical risks?

   (e) Disruption planning: what are plans to deal with unanticipated disruptions; plans for resiliency in the event of major disruption?

   (f) Describe other issues associated with risks.

5. **What are the benefits of ERM / cost & benefit analysis?**

   (a) What are the metrics used?

   (b) How do you measure success?

   (c) What are the economic indicators important to your business?

   (d) What are the incentives for management/others?

   (e) What are the costs associated with ERM?

   (f) What have been the surprise benefits?

   (g) Other?

6. **What are the problems or challenges associated with ERM?**

   (a) Implementation issues?

   (b) Sustaining ERM over time?

   (c) Engaging employees/management?

   (d) Business model conflicts?

   (e) Quantification of results?

   (f) Learning curve?

   (g) Strategic integration?

   (h) Supply chain?

   (i) Other?

7. **What other surprises have come from your ERM experience?**

8. **What are the recommendations for others seeking to implement ERM?**

   (a) What to do?

   (b) What not to do?

   (c) What to avoid?

   (d) What would you do/have done differently if given the opportunity?

   (e) Under what conditions would you not recommend an organization begin an ERM implementation?

   (f) Other?

7

Case Study: Risk Management Implementation in China

Duojia (Doug) Lu

Chairman, First Huida Risk Management, Beijing, China

Risk management has been developing fast in the People's Republic of China in recent years. This article gives an overview of the Chinese market for risk management, highlights some of the prominent recent developments in the market, and presents a couple of cases of risk management implementation, which are typically seen in this field.

7.1 MARKET BACKGROUND

It is well known that China is a large country with a big market. As of recent statistics, China's population is over 1.3 billion people. China also has a large business community. In 2012, there were about 11 million registered for-profit companies in China, and about 36 million registered sole proprietors. By 2012, more than 2,300 Chinese companies were listed in domestic stock exchanges in Shanghai and Shenzhen along with a couple of hundred Chinese companies listed overseas.

China has a vibrant economy. Over the last twenty years, China's economic growth has averaged an annual growth rate of 9.8%, triple the world average. Right now China is the second largest economy in the world with an RMB[1] 51.9 trillion ($8.33 trillion dollar) GDP. China's economy is especially heavy in manufacturing, which accounts for 45% of GDP (2012) and produces anything from cars and machinery to airplanes and electronics. For example, in 2012, China produced over 19 million cars and light trucks, and sold about the same number domestically, ranking China the first in the world in both production and sales.

As the saying goes, "no risk, no return". The high growth in China's economy is inevitably accompanied by high risk. As a result, China's economy is showing signs of imbalances. China's currency has risen significantly in the last few years and is still under pressure to further increase. Domestically, the income gap is big as China's Gini coefficient[2] of 0.48; food safety problems have frequently made headlines and the pollution is dreadful. Internationally, China frequently engages in arguments over trade with its major trading partners. All of these issues continue to exist while China faces the difficult transition from an export and investment oriented economy to a more balanced one.

Within businesses there are different risk concerns. A recent survey of large SOEs (State Owned Enterprises) showed that investment, government policy, human resources, market fluctuation, and work safety were the top risks that concern the Chinese executives.

---

[1] RMB = Renminbi or the official currency of The People's Republic of China

[2] A distribution of national income. A Gini coefficient of 1.0 would indicate that all wealth in a country is owned by one person. The Gini coefficient for China is an estimate because the Chinese Government has not released this information for many years.

7.2   CHINA'S SOEs AND SASAC

For risk management implementation, the Chinese enterprises can be divided into three sectors of different characteristics.

The first sector consists of all financial industries, including banks, insurance companies, brokerages, mutual funds, etc. The risk management in these companies fundamentally follows international protocols such as Basel II and Solvency II under the supervision of respective regulators.

The second sector consists of the privately owned companies in the non-financial industries. The majority of 11 million for-profit Chinese companies are in this group; they are diverse and most of them are small or midsize companies. Certain reports claim that, on average, these companies have a brief lifespan of less than three years. Risk management in these companies at the moment is composed mostly of contingency and crisis management.

The third sector consists of about 150,000 State Owned Enterprises (SOEs). Generally, these companies are large and concentrated in a few industries including energy, telecom, aerospace, utilities, defense and transportation; they are the likes of China Mobile, Petro China, Sinopec, AVIC, Shenhua, and State Grid. The (non-financial) SOEs have been regulated and supervised under three levels of State Asset Supervision and Administration Commission (SASAC) since 2003: State Council SASAC (SC SASAC), provincial SASACs, and city SASACs. SC SASAC supervises the largest SOEs. The 116 SOEs under SC SASAC hold more than RMB 32 trillion in assets and control 100% of China's oil, gas, telecom, ocean shipping, power grid, nuclear power and defense. They also control 90% of China's airlines, 55% of China's electrical power, and 48% of China's auto industries. In 2012, 73 Chinese companies were in *Fortune 500*, 68 of which are SOEs. Among *China 100 2012*, 80 were non-financial SOEs, 68 of which were under SC SASAC's supervision. SOEs' revenue altogether accounts for 81% of China's GDP, while the 116 SOEs under SC SASAC accounts for 43% (2012).

SC SASAC acts as the shareholder of SOEs on behalf of the Chinese government. SC SASAC is required by law to "protect and enhance the value of SOEs". Since its establishment in 2003, SC SASAC has been keen on risk management. It learned from past experiences that the only way to "protect and enhance the value of SOEs" is to take proactive risk management measures. Soon after its establishment, SC SASAC started the *Enterprise Risk Management for SOEs* project. After three years of research and trial, SC SASAC issued *Enterprise Risk Management Guidelines for SC SOEs* in 2006, requiring all SC SOEs to implement risk management accordingly. *Enterprise Risk Management Guidelines for SC SOEs* by SC SASAC is a complete risk management standard very similar to ISO 31000 (see appendix A for this Author's Translation of the ERM Guidelines for SC SOEs). These guidelines use the same definitions for basic concepts like risk. The guidelines also describe a generic risk management process and define a comprehensive risk management framework, both of which are aligned with that of ISO 31000. Due to SC SASAC's continual prodding and insistence, SC SOEs have become the most active and advanced implementers of enterprise risk management in China. These SOEs embody enterprise risk management in China. Therefore, this article focuses on these non-financial SOEs.

7.3   CURRENT DEVELOPMENT

Besides SC SASAC's *Enterprise Risk Management Guidelines for SC SOEs,* there are several other regulatory documents recently published in China regarding risk management. The ones most relevant to the non-financial SOEs are the standard for internal control and corresponding implementation guidelines (2008, 2010), jointly issued by the Ministry of Finance and four other government agencies. These guidelines consist of an *Enterprise Internal Control Standard,* issued in 2008, and twenty detailed implementation guidelines, issued in 2010. *Enterprise Internal Control Standard* features an internal control structure similar to the COSO internal control framework of 1992. Eighteen of the twenty detailed implementation guidelines are set for the implementation of internal control in specific business and management areas such as financial reporting, fund management, budgeting, and contract management. There are also the *Internal Control Assessment Guidelines* for self-assessment purposes, and the *Internal Control Audit Guidelines* for external auditors to audit the internal control for overall effectiveness. All SC SOEs and public companies are currently required to maintain an internal control framework accordingly. Effective January 1st, 2012, all public companies listed on the two domestic stock exchanges must implement internal control according to the *Enterprise Internal Control Standard* and the implementation guidelines, disclose internal control self-assessment results in annual reporting, and allow external auditors to give their opinions on the companies' internal control on financial reporting and report on other "material weaknesses".

In 2007, China Standardization Administration Commission (CSAC) established the national technical committee in risk management, TC310. In December 2009, TC310 published the first national standard in risk management, GB/T 24353 2009, ***Risk management – Principles and guidelines on implementation.*** GB/T 24353 2009 is the Chinese version of the international standard ISO 31000. It was adapted from ISO 31000 with the same structure and definitions of basic terms of risk management but with a few minor changes for improvement. Similar to ISO 31000, GB/T 24353 2009 is not mandatory and is not made for certification purposes. Based on GB/T 24353 2009, a series of national risk management standards applicable to various specific areas were made, such as:

- Guidelines on Enterprise Legal Risk Management;
- Supply Chain Risk Management Guidelines; and
- Guidelines on Corporate Governance Risk Management.

Because the national standard GB/T 24353 2009 is not mandatory, most SOEs regard it as a mere benchmark. But since SOEs are under the supervision of SASAC, they follow the SC SASAC *Enterprise Risk Management Guidelines for SC SOEs* more rigidly. Though SC SASAC has not given a clear deadline for its implementation completion, some of the requirements in *Enterprise Risk Management Guidelines for SC SOEs* have become mandatory since its publication. For example, SC SASAC requires that all SOEs under its supervision carry out an annual risk management assessment and file a corresponding report using a pre-designed template by SASAC, which varies yearly to reflect SASAC's current concerns. In 2013, SC SASAC issued the *Risk Management Implementation Benchmark*, and planned to push forward in the next 3–5 years for the completion of enterprise risk management implementation.

Currently, most of the SOEs under SC SASAC have already started enterprise risk management implementation, meaning, they already have a multi-year implementation plan and build the framework accordingly. The majority of SC SOEs have already set up a risk management subcommittee within their boards, and most of SOEs have appointed an executive at headquarters level in charge of risk management implementation. Several have even appointed corporate CROs. The majority of SOEs have established a risk management department or similar functions in their headquarters. Some SOEs have further carried the integration of risk management into their business processes such as legal affairs, planning, procurement, sales, customer relationship, and trading. In doing so, more and more SOEs now use quantitative tools such as Monte Carlo simulation for risk modeling. Some SOEs have implemented risk management information systems, drawing data from their existing ERP (enterprise resource planning) and MIS (management information systems), and integrating them with OA (operations analysis). Risk management has become a regular course on the corporate training menu due to the influx of SOEs who have begun to realize their needs for talent in this area.

7.4 IMPLEMENTATION CASE STUDY

Unlike the implementation of internal control, for which all companies in China follow pretty much the same basic pattern, risk management implementation takes a variety of paths. Risk management implementation patterns vary in terms of parameters such as *Who, Where, When, What and How.* For instance, both top-down and bottom-up approaches are used by large SOEs of similar governance structures with no noticeable difference in terms of overall efficiency. Some SOEs start with building an overall framework and then embed risk management into different business areas, while others embed risk management in those specific areas first and then build a company-wide framework for integration. Some SOEs tackle risk management with an all-risk included risk assessment first and then focus on specific risk areas of their concerns, while others implement individual risk management systems first and then start integrating risk management practices with a unified company standard.

Three cases of risk management implementation representing three different approaches will be summarized. These cases are composite examples from the author's own experiences of implementing risk management in China.

7.4.1 Implementation Case I

Case I represents the most common type of implementation in recent years among large SOEs in China. At least 70 large SOEs, such as Shenhua, Aviation Industry Corporation of China, and China Eastern Airlines, started their enterprise risk management this way.

This type of implementation represents the top-down approach. It occurs in companies that have not done any company-wide formal risk management plan or process. The implementation typically starts with a board decision to go into enterprise risk management. It is considered the basic implementation that takes less than a year to complete. The implementation usually follows this series of steps:

1. The company's Board of Directors decides to do enterprise risk management. The decision is made, most likely due to external pressure from SASAC requirements because SASAC's **Enterprise Risk Management Guidelines for SC SOEs** requires the company's board be accountable for the effectiveness of the company's risk management. In other cases, the board's decision may have been stimulated by internal factors such as the review of recent loss events. The company's CEO will implement the board's decision.
2. The CEO delegates the responsibility to a vice president, sets up a risk management function within one of the existing departments, and puts said function in charge of any risk management implementation planning. Occasionally, the CEO himself/herself is in charge of the implementation directly.

3. As the company would have had no prior experiences in formal risk management framework, the risk management function contracts an external consultancy to do the work. They plan to finish the basic implementation by the end of year, so that the board can get the risk assessment report in time for the annual adjustment of the business plan. Given the size of the company and the complex nature of the job, the experience rather than the size of the consultancy is considered a vital success factor for the implementation.

4. The risk management function and the consultancy put forward a detailed work plan with a scope and methods for approval by senior executives. In this plan, the business case for risk management is made in order to get the commitment from the senior executives.

5. After the approval of the work plan, the consultancy directs the company's staff to carry out a company-wide risk assessment. The risk assessment follows a pre-designed process that is most effective with intensive training sessions for the company's staff. It usually combines qualitative methods such as brainstorming and the Delphi method with quantitative methods such as PRA (probabilistic risk analysis) and event tree analysis that draw data from the historical records. After all risks are identified, the top risks are confirmed by the senior management. The results of the risk management are put into a company risk database for future use.

6. The consultancy and the function design the risk management system together. This system has organizational arrangements such as risk management policy, risk management function, annual risk assessment procedure, and reporting. These arrangements are placed together into a company risk management handbook.

7. The Board and senior executives approve the risk management handbook, confirming the risk map with top-level risk criteria and the risk management policy statement.

After the first year of basic implementation, the companies will continue according to their long-term implementation plan. Although their first actions are similar, companies most likely branch off into different paths and approaches afterward.

7.4.2 Implementation Case II

This case, based on Sinopec and SinoChem's similar experiences, exemplifies a situation where the company wants to integrate risk management into its business areas. These business areas could be anything from quality control to inventory management. In the description below, the example of commodity trading as such a business area is used. The situation may occur in all types of companies whether or not they have implemented a formal risk management framework.

The implementation usually follows this series of steps:

1. The company decides to embed risk management into its commodity trading practice. The overall objective is to reduce the likelihood of big losses while maintaining a high level of profitability. These big losses need to be further broken down into manageable losses.

2. The company assigns the responsibility to a risk management function, which is set to assist the business units involved to accomplish the goal within a nine-month period. As the risk management function surveys the situation, it finds an insufficient amount of internal human resource for the job. Hence, it decides to seek help from a consultancy.

3. The risk management function and the consultancy work out a plan with a scope and a timetable after consulting with the business functions. The scope is confirmed by listing the business processes involved and people responsible for the processes.

4. The risk management function and the consultancy clarify the business process by formalizing all procedures using tools such as process charts and a control matrix.
5. The risk management function and the consultancy identify all risks from these processes related to the objectives in three categories: financial, operational, and legal compliance.
6. The risk management function and the consultancy analyze the risks identified by likelihood, consequence, and suddenness. They then put these risks into a risk map amongst other charts.
7. The risk management function and the consultancy set up integrated risk criteria embracing suddenness.
8. With the new risk criteria, the risk management function and the consultancy choose the top risks to be treated.
9. The business functions, with help from the consultancy and the risk management function, implement controls to treat risks with expected goals and a monitoring mechanism. They then send reports to different levels of executives in the company.
10. Together with the business functions, the risk management function and the consultancy set up a schedule to review annually the effectiveness of the risk management policy and its practices. Based on the review results, the risk management policy is adjusted accordingly.

The process described here is virtually duplicable to any specific business areas with adjustment made to risk criteria and metrics used for measuring risks.

It is important that the business functions are fully involved in the integration process for the risk management to be effective. After all, it is the business functions that are responsible for executing risk controls daily.

7.4.3 Implementation Case III

Implementation case III describes the risk management implementation for a situation where the company wants to focus its implementation of risk management for a single specific risk across all business areas. This example shows a company like China Mobile focusing specifically on legal risk.

The implementation usually follows this series of steps:

1. The company decides to implement a legal risk management system company wide in 3 years' time based on the new regulatory requirements and the national standard GB/T 27914.
2. The company's legal department is assigned to lead the project to accomplish the goal with help from a consultancy and all business units.
3. The legal department and the consultancy work out a more detailed plan with a scope and a timetable after consulting with business units. The plan outlines a system implemented at the company's headquarters first, and then extended to provincial business units in the subsequent years.
4. The legal risk management system is implemented in the company's headquarters in a similar way to that described above in Implementation case II.
5. Based on the implementation experience of the company's headquarters, the company-wide legal risk management handbook is written and the implementation specifications for provincial business units are designed. The legal department specifies the performance and maintenance standards for review of business unit implementation, legal risk management information system requirements, and technical specs.

6. The provincial business units, in turn, implement the legal risk management systems and corresponding IT systems.

From experience, it can be said that for a large corporation with a multi-level structure, all risk management systems for a single risk can be implemented similarly to the case described here. For instance, several Chinese SOEs carried out similar implementations for work safety and credit risk management. Most of the implementations were top-down (like in this example). However, there are cases where the implementation was first carried out in the business unit level. It is from the successful trial implementation that the company-wide specifications and work plan are rolled out to all business units throughout the company.

7.5 LESSONS LEARNED

Some important lessons have been learned from the implementation of enterprise risk management in recent years in China. These lessons are deduced from real life experiences of implementing risk management in large companies. Since the risk management implementation in China's SOEs was initiated from SASAC for all large SOEs, it had an unprecedented scale and strong character of enterprise risk management in style. Meanwhile, the sheer size and complexity of China's SOEs produced great diversity in risk management implementation. These characteristics of China's risk management implementation have made the lessons gathered from experiences especially worthwhile for large companies looking to engage in enterprise risk management.

Five lessons are listed below that we think are most important for enterprise risk management implementation in large companies:

1. Enterprise risk management implementation is a journey that takes years to shape up. For enterprise risk management to be mature, a multi-phase approach is required with each phase of implementation iterative in terms of the basic risk management process and its continuous framework improvement for better overall performance.
2. Commitment from the board/top executives for enterprise risk management implementation is actually to a plan with clearly defined objectives within an acceptable timeframe and an operational road map to achieve the objectives. Without such a plan, it is unlikely that the commitment from the top management becomes materialized.
3. For enterprise risk management to be sustainable beyond compliance, its objectives must be tangible on KPIs (key performance indicators) of the organizations sooner or later. Without impact on the company's KPIs, the risk management will be reduced to formality and the commitment from the top management will fade.
4. Each implementation is tailored to suit the unique characteristics and the needs of the organization; no single approach fits all. This is especially true after the establishment of the basic risk management framework. The specific approaches taken by the organizations depend on the context.
5. In all cases, the implementations integrate both framework and process components. The risk management process is effected by the risk management framework. In other words, the framework is the enabler of the process. Without an appropriate internal risk management framework, the risk management process is not sustainable. The framework itself also becomes more effective and completes itself through the process. One cannot build a complete framework for a large company without iterative execution of the risk management process.

The enterprise risk management for China's SOEs currently continues every day. SC SASAC still pushes for more risk management success, as it just published a new *risk management implementation benchmark* in early 2013. So, there will be more cases to observe and more lessons to learn from China's large SOEs. Stay tuned.

7.6   QUESTIONS FOR STUDENTS AND PRACTITIONERS

1. For each of the implementation categories discussed in this case identify the critical risks associated with the ERM implementation process as described. How would you suggest modifying the process so that these critical risks are addressed? Indicate how you might go about making these changes, keeping in mind the scope issues your recommended changes may require and the culture and business need of the organization(s) that utilized the method in question.
2. How do the risk management practices for state-owned enterprises in China differ from enterprise risk management practices utilized in private industry and non-state owned enterprises in your country?
3. Obtain a copy of the ISO 31000 risk management framework and compare it with the Enterprise Risk Management Guidelines for Central Enterprises in this case study's Appendix A. What are the similarities; what are the differences? Offer suggestions to both frameworks on how they might adopt one or more features of the other framework that will improve the framework. Explain why these changes would benefit the framework.
4. China has a strong central government and many state-owned enterprises. However, there are many independent businesses in China, some owned completely by Chinese interests and some are foreign owned or owned jointly by foreign and local investors. Assume that Chinese leaders want to continue their significant GDP growth going forward. Assume that they have identified risk management as a key to that growth strategy. If you were consulted on how to help China enable a culture of risk management in all industries, outline the strategy you would recommend and include a timeline and penalties for non-compliance (if that is to be part of the plan).
5. Other than restricting entry of others into particular categories of business, what other strategic risks do state-owned enterprises create or could create for private businesses?
6. All governments have "state-owned" enterprises of one form or another whether it is healthcare, bridges, roads, or schools and universities. Identify one of the local "state owned" enterprises in your area and identify the critical risks that can affect that enterprise.

APPENDIX A

Note: This is a translation by the author of this article. It is not the official translation of the Chinese government. Reference to the official Chinese version should be consulted wherever possible at these links: SASAC: www.sasac.gov.cn, and Ministry of Finance: www.mof.gov.cn

Enterprise Risk Management Guidelines for Central Enterprises (2006. 6.6)

Chapter I General Provisions

Article 1 The Enterprise Risk Management Guidelines for Central Enterprises (hereinafter referred to as the Guidelines) are formulated, in accordance with the Company Law of the

People's Republic of China, the Interim Regulations on Supervision and Management of State-owned Assets of Enterprises, and other related laws and regulations, for the purpose of directing the Central Enterprises (hereinafter also referred to as the enterprises), for which the State-owned Assets Supervision and Administration Commission of the State Council (hereinafter referred to as SASAC) performs the investor responsibility, on enterprise risk management, so as to enhance core competencies, to improve return on investment, and to promote sustainable, healthy, and stable growth.

Article 2 The Central Enterprises should implement the Guidelines based on their own specific conditions. For those central enterprises that are state wholly-owned, the board of directors is responsible for supervising and guiding the implementation of the Guidelines. For those enterprises that are state controlled, SASAC and the SASAC nominated directors, via the shareholder meeting and the board of directors in accordance with all statutory procedures, are responsible for supervising and guiding the implementation of the Guidelines.

Article 3 The term "enterprise risk" or "risk" in the Guidelines means the effect of the future uncertainty on the enterprise's objectives. The enterprise risks can be generally classified as strategic risks, financial risks, market risks, operational risks, and compliance (with laws, regulatory rules and internal policies) risks. Risks can also be classified as pure risks (meaning no gains possible) and speculative risks (meaning both gains and losses possible).

Article 4 The term "enterprise risk management" in the Guidelines means the process, together with the methodology, in which an enterprise, in order to achieve the enterprise's overall business objectives, carries out the basic process of the risk management through all management activities and business operations, cultivates sound risk culture, establishes and maintains the enterprise risk management system which includes the risk management strategy, risk financing, risk management organizational structure, risk management information system and internal control system, so as to provide reasonable assurance for reaching the integrated goals of enterprise risk management.

Article 5 The term "basic process of the risk management" in the Guidelines means the execution of the following five main steps:

1. Establish the context information.
2. Assess risks.
3. Establish the risk management strategy.
4. Design and implement the risk management solutions.
5. Monitor and improve.

Article 6 The term "internal control system" in the Guidelines means the system consisting of internal policies, structures, processes, and procedures, designed and implemented through the basic process of the risk management, for the business and management processes including strategic planning, product research and development, investment, fund raising, marketing, financial management, internal auditing, legal affairs management, human resource management, procurement, manufacturing and servicing, sales, inventory, distribution logistics, quality management, safety assurance, and environmental protection, etc.

Article 7 The integrated goals of the enterprise risk management are:

1. To ensure the enterprise risks are compatible with the enterprise's strategic objectives and are tolerable.

2. To ensure the communications among all parties, especially between the enterprise and its shareholders, are reliable, that include providing reliable financial reports.
3. To ensure the compliance.
4. To ensure the effective execution of the policies and other important measures of the enterprise and efficient management, enhance the effectiveness and efficiency of the operations, and reduce the uncertainty in reaching the business goals.
5. To ensure the enterprise has the proper contingency plan with respect to significant risks, protecting the enterprise from great losses caused by disasters and human errors.

Article 8 Enterprises, when working on enterprise risk management, should stress the importance of preventing and controlling the loss and damage that might result from risks. Meanwhile, enterprises should manage speculative risks, by viewing them as resources of a special kind, to create value and achieve business objectives.

Article 9 Enterprises should, while stressing the practicality and end-results, approach enterprise risk management proactively, and focus on major risks, material events (meaning major risk events), and the internal controls of important business processes. The enterprises who are ready should push forward all-round and establish the enterprise risk management system as soon as possible; other enterprises should make general plans for fulfilment of enterprise risk management, where the enterprises may first select one or more areas of business activities, such as strategic planning, capital investment and acquisition, financial reporting, internal auditing, derivative trading, legal affairs, safety, and account receivable, to establish internal control systems for gaining experiences and development of talents, effecting fulfilment of the enterprise risk management system step-by-step.

Article 10 Enterprises should integrate enterprise risk management with their overall management, embedding risk management requirements into all business and management processes. The enterprises that are ready may establish "three lines of defense" for risk management, with the various functional departments and business units as the "first line", the risk management function department and the risk management committee of the Board as the "second line", and the internal audit department and the audit committee of the Board as the "third line".

Chapter II Context Information of Risk Management

Article 11 For the execution of enterprise risk management, enterprises should collect continuously a wide range of context information that relates to the risks and risk management of the enterprises from internal and external sources, including historical data and forecast. Enterprises should assign the responsibility of context information collection to all functions and business units.

Article 12 With respect to the strategic risks, enterprises should collect widely the domestic and international cases, where firms suffered losses from strategic risks, and at least the following important information that relates to the enterprises:

1. International and domestic macroeconomic conditions and policies, the industry conditions, and the government industrial policies.
2. Information on related scientific progresses and technical innovations.
3. Market demand for the enterprises' own products and services.
4. Strategic alliances, and the possibility of forming strategic partnerships.

5. Information relevant to major customers, suppliers, and competitors.
6. The enterprises' strengths and the gap in comparison with the major competitors.
7. The enterprises' own and business plan, plan for investment and fund raising, annual operational goals, overall business strategy, together with the data used in the strategies, plans, goals, etc.
8. The business processes or activities that are mistake laden or error prone in the enterprises' processes for outside investment.

Article 13 With respect to the financial risks, enterprises should collect widely the domestic and international cases, where financial risks resulted in firm crisis, and at least the following important information that relates to the enterprises (including industry benchmarks when available):

1. Liability, contingent liability, debt ratio, solvency.
2. Cash flow, account receivable and its percentage of sales, working capital turnover.
3. Inventory and its percentage of cost of sales, account payable and its percentage of total purchasing.
4. Manufacturing overheads, G&A expenses, financial expenses, operational expenses.
5. Profitability.
6. Mistake laden or error prone processes in cost accounting and treasury management cycles.
7. Industrial accounting policy, accounting estimation, gaps and adjustments with IFRS (such as for pension and deferred tax treatments).

Article 14 With respect to the market risks, enterprises should collect widely the domestic and international cases, where firms suffered losses from ignoring the market risks or lacking of proper responses, and at least the following important information that relates to the enterprises:

1. Change in prices and supply–demand relation for the enterprises' products and services.
2. Sufficiency, stability for supplies of such as energy, raw materials, and parts and change in prices.
3. Credit reports of major customers and major suppliers.
4. Change in tax laws, interest rates, currency exchange rates, and stock indexes.
5. Potential competitors, competitors and their major products and substitute products.

Article 15 With respect to the operational risks, enterprises should collect at least the following important information that relates to the enterprises and the enterprises' industries:

1. Product structure and new product development.
2. New market development, marketing strategy involving product and service pricing and distribution channels, and market environment.
3. Organizational effectiveness, existing management practices, corporate culture, knowledge structures and experiences of senior and middle management and employees in the important business processes.
4. Mistake laden and error prone business processes or activities involving trading of futures and other derivatives.
5. Mistake laden and error prone business processes or activities with regard to quality, safety, environmental protection, and information security management.

6. Losses or business control malfunctions caused by unethical behaviors of internal and external personnel.
7. Natural disasters that caused losses, and other pure risks besides the situations above.
8. Capability of supervising, operation assessment and continuous improvement of the existing business processes and information system operation.
9. Current conditions and capability of enterprises' risk management.

Article 16 With respect to the compliance risks, enterprises should collect widely the domestic and international cases where firms suffered losses from ignoring the compliance risks or lacking proper responses, and at least the following important information that relates to the enterprises:

1. Domestic and international political and legal environment.
2. New laws, regulations and policies that may impact the enterprises.
3. Employees' ethical compliance.
4. Important agreements and trade contracts signed.
5. Intellectual properties of the enterprises and their competitors.

Article 17 Enterprises should go through the necessary steps of selection, reconciliation, comparison, classification, and confirmation of the context information for the purpose of risk assessment.

Chapter III Risk Assessment

Article 18 Enterprises should carry out risk assessment for their important businesses and the corresponding important processes with the risk management context information collected. Risk assessment consists of three steps as risk identification, risk analysis, and risk evaluation.

Article 19 Enterprises' risk assessment may be carried out by their internal function departments and business units, and assisted by professional consultancies in risk management that are qualified, reputable, and capable.

Article 20 Risk identification means to see if there are risks in the business units, important business activities and important business processes, and what risks are there. Risk analysis means to define clearly the identified risks and their characteristics, analyze and describe the possibilities and the conditions for the risk event occurrences. Risk evaluation is to estimate the impact of the risks on the enterprises' objectives, and the value of the risks.

Article 21 Enterprises should combine the qualitative and quantitative methods in risk identification, risk analysis, and risk evaluation. The qualitative methods include questionnaires, facilitated workshops, expert opinions, scenario analysis, policy analysis, industry benchmarking, management interview, and onsite inspection, etc. The quantitative methods include statistical analysis (e.g. trend analysis), computer simulation (e.g. Monte Carlo method), failure mode and effect analysis, and event tree analysis, etc.

Article 22 Enterprises should, for quantitative risk assessment, decide on the risk metrics and the risk models consistently across the enterprises, and, via various testing methods, make sure the assumptions made, the parameters chosen, the data sources, and the procedures for the quantitative assessment processes are valid and accurate. Enterprises should review, adjust, and improve the assumptions and the parameters periodically or based on the changes of the environment as well as the results from the comparison of the estimates of the assessment system to the real data.

Article 23 Risk analysis should cover the relationship between the risks to uncover the risk portfolio effects such as natural hedges and off-setting risk events so that all risks may be managed with an integrated strategy.

Article 24 Enterprises may, when assessing more than one risk, compare the risks by mapping them to a coordinate system with the possibility of risk event occurrence as one dimension and the impact of the risk event as the other, so as to set the priority and determine the corresponding management strategies.

Article 25 Enterprises should treat risk management information dynamically, following through the steps of risk identification, risk analysis and risk evaluation periodically or non-periodically to refresh the information on new risks and changes of the existing risks.

Chapter IV Risk Strategy

Article 26 The term "Risk strategy" in the Guidelines means the integrated strategy that, based on the enterprises' overall business strategy, their own conditions and the external environment, consists of the enterprises' risk appetite, risk tolerance, criteria for effective risk management, the choices of risk management tactics including risk acceptance, risk avoidance, risk transform, risk hedging, risk compensation, and risk control, and the corresponding principles for allocation of necessary human and financial resources.

Article 27 In general, for strategic risks, financial risks, operational risks, and compliance risks, the available strategies include risk acceptance, risk avoidance, risk transform action, and risk control. For risks that may be managed by risk financing methods such as insurance, futures, and hedging, one may adopt strategies including risk transfer, risk hedging, and risk compensation.

Article 28 Enterprises should determine their risk appetite and risk tolerance level consistently based on the characteristics of their businesses, that is, to determine what risks they are willing to accept as well as accordingly the upper and lower limits for the tolerance of those risks, and to determine the early warning indicators and the responses correspondingly. To determine the risk appetite and the risk tolerance, one should balance the risks and the rewards, avoiding the tendencies: one is pursuing the profit without properly taking risk factors like circumstances into considerations, usually indicated by incorrect emphasis on the risk part of the notion of more risk implying more rewards, the other is preventing risks at all costs, causing loss of opportunities of development.

Article 29 Enterprises should determine, based on the principle of balancing risk and reward as well as the positions of the risks on the risk map, the priority of risk management, the capital budget for the risk management expenses, and the overall arrangements in organizational structure, human resources and the risk responses.

Article 30 Enterprises should periodically review and analyze the effectiveness and the justification of the existing risk strategies, and improve the risk strategies continuously to the perfection. The enterprise should emphasize the review of the real effect of implementation based on the risk appetite, the risk tolerance, and the risk early-warning indicators for controls, and define qualitatively or quantitatively the criteria for the effectiveness.

Chapter V Risk Management Solutions

Article 31 Enterprises should design solutions for all risks or every significant risk in accordance with the risk management strategy. The solutions should in general consist of objectives, organizational leadership, business and management processes and procedures involved, resources needed, concrete responses before, in the middle of, and after the occurrence of the risk event, as well as risk management tools such as Key Risk Indicator Management and Loss Event Management.

Article 32 Enterprises should, while outsourcing the risk management solutions, pay attention to the balance of risk and reward, the quality of the outsourcing job, the protection of the business secret, and take steps correspondingly to control and to prevent from the risk of unhealthy reliance on the outsourcers for the risk solutions.

Article 33 Enterprises should satisfy the laws and regulations when establishing a risk management internal control system, be consistent with business strategy and risk management strategy, balance risk control with operational efficiency and effectiveness, aim at each management process and operation flow related to the significant risks, establish entire process flow control measurement, control the key points and adopt the corresponding control measurements to operational flows related to other risks.

Article 34 Enterprises should consider the following criteria when establishing internal control system:

1. Establishment of internal control position authorization system. Clearly define objects, terms, range and limits of each internal control position, any organizations or individuals should not make any risky decisions beyond authorization.
2. Establishment of internal reporting system. Clearly define the reporters and reportees, time, contents, frequency, information transfer route, and organization or individual who is responsible for managing the report.
3. Establishment of internal control approval system: for all internal control related material events, clearly define the procedure, terms, range, limit, necessary document of the approval, and regulate the responsibilities of the approval department or individuals.
4. Establishment of internal control duty system. Comply with the principle of consolidation between right, obligation and duty, and clearly define the duty and reward scheme for each related departments, business units and individuals.
5. Establishment of internal control audit system. Integrating with the requirement, methodology, standard and procedure of the internal control, clearly define the object, content, method of the audit and related department who is responsible for the audit.
6. Establishment of internal control assessment system. Qualified enterprises should integrate their internal control performance with related salary management.
7. Establishment of significant risk warning system. Constant supervision on the significant risk, timely risk reporting, proper contingent plan in respect to significant risk and adjustment of the control method regarding different circumstances.
8. Establishment of power balancing system. Clearly regulate the segregation of duties, this mainly includes: authorization approval, operation, accounting record, asset safekeeping and audit. Consider having two personnel responsible for one important position and restrict each other; clearly define the superior department or individuals of the position, related supervision measure and supervision responsibility; make this position the key point of the internal audit.

Article 35 Enterprises should seriously implement the risk management solution in terms of duty divisions between each department and business unit, to ensure each step is completed smoothly.

Chapter VI Monitoring and Improvement

Article 36 Enterprise should focus on significant risks, material events, important management and business processes, supervise initial information, risk assessment, risk management strategy, key control activity and the implementation of risk management solution. Enterprise should use stress testing, back testing, work-through testing and self-assessment on risk control to test the validity risk management, and improve in time when situation changes and limitation realized.

Article 37 Enterprises should establish the proper information exchange channel regarding risk management through the whole basic risk management process, as to communicate within all functional department and business units, and ensure that the information could be transferred timely, accurately and completely, which is the foundation of risk management monitoring and improvement.

Article 38 The related departments and business units should examine and assess risk management system periodically in order to find flaws and improve risk management timely. The assessment reports should be submitted to risk management departments in a timely manner.

Article 39 Risk management departments should constantly check the implementation status and efficiency of risk management in functional departments and business units, assess risk management strategy in accordance with Article 30 in the guidelines, evaluate risk management solutions across functional departments and business units, issue comments regarding adjustment or improvement, issue valuation and recommendation report regarding current risk management system, and timely submit reports to general manager of the enterprise or any other senior managers who are responsible for risk management.

Article 40 The internal audit department should monitor and evaluate risk management department, other related departments and business units, in terms of the implementation and validity of risk management work at least once per year, and the report should be delivered to the board of directors or risk management committee and audit committee. This project could be implemented in line with annual audit, term audit or special audit.

Article 41 Enterprises could engage some professional consultancies in risk management that are qualified, reputable, and capable to carry out current risk management assessment of the enterprises and provide risk management assessment report with advices for improvement. Generally, the report should contain situation of implementation, existing deficiency and improvement suggestions of the following aspects:

1. Basic risk management process and risk management strategy.
2. Risk management of the significant risks, material events, important management and business processes in the enterprise and the establishment of the internal control system.
3. Risk management organizational structure and information system.
4. The integrated goals of enterprise risk management.

Chapter VII Risk Management Organizational Structure

Article 42 Enterprises should establish and maintain the risk management organizational structure, which includes the standardized corporate governance structure, the risk management function and internal auditing departments, and management organizational structure and responsibility of other related function departments and business units.

Article 43 Enterprises should establish and maintain the standardized corporate governance structure. The shareholder meeting (for the state wholly-owned companies or the state wholly-owned enterprises, it means SASAC, hereinafter with the same meaning), the board of directors, the board of supervisors and managers should perform their responsibilities according to the laws, so as to form the monitoring mechanism that is efficient in functioning and effectively balanced.

Article 44 State-wholly-owned and state-controlled enterprises should establish external director or independent director system; the number of external directors or independent directors should exceed half of the board, in order to guarantee the board of directors can make independent judgment and choice beside management on important decision-making and significant risk management.

Article 45 The board of directors is responsible for the shareholder meeting according to the effectiveness of the overall risk management work. The board of directors mainly implements the following responsibilities in the aspects of the overall risk management:

1. Deliberate and submit yearly working reports of the enterprise overall risk management to the shareholder meeting.
2. Ensure the overall objectives, risk appetite and risk endurance of the enterprise's risk management and authorize the risk management strategy and momentous risk management solutions.
3. Know and master each significant risk faced by enterprises and its management status, make effective risk controlling decisions.
4. Authorize judgment standards or judgment mechanisms of the important decision-makings, significant risks, material events and important operational processes.
5. Authorize the risk assessment report of important decision-makings.
6. Authorize the risk management supervisory auditing report submitted by the internal auditing department.
7. Authorize the setting and responsibility solutions of the risk management organization.
8. Authorize risk management measures, correct and deal with risk decision behaviors that violate risk management rules made by any organization or individual.
9. Supervise the cultivation of enterprise's risk management culture, overall risk management and other important proceedings.

Article 46 In enterprises with good qualifications, the board of directors can establish the risk management committee. The committee caller should be the chairman of the board who meanwhile is not the general manager; the caller should be an external director or independent director if the chairman of the board is meanwhile the general manager. In the committee, there should be directors who are familiar with important management, operational flow and processes of the enterprise, or directors who have risk management and monitoring knowledge or experience, and certain knowledge of law.

Article 47 Risk management committee is responsible to the board of directors, and performs the following responsibilities:

1. Submit annual enterprise risk management report.
2. Deliberate risk management policy and important risk management solution.
3. Deliberate judgmental standard or judgmental mechanism on important judgments, significant risk, material events and important operational processes, and risk assessment report on important judgments.
4. Deliberate risk management supervision and evaluation audit integration report submitted by internal audit department.
5. Deliberate risk management organizational structure settings and responsibility solutions.
6. Transact other proceedings on enterprise risk management authorized by the board of directors.

Article 48 The general manager of the enterprises should be responsible for the validity of enterprise risk management and report to the board of directors. The general manager or the senior manager nominated by general manager should take charge of the routines of ERM, draw out the organizational structure settings and responsibilities scheme of ERM.

Article 49 The enterprise should establish full time department or ensure related functional departments to perform the responsibility of enterprise risk management. This department should be responsible to general manager or nominated senior managers, and perform the following responsibilities:

1. Research and propose enterprise risk management reports.
2. Research and propose judgmental standard or judgmental mechanism across functional departments on important judgment, significant risk, material event and important operational process.
3. Research and propose risk assessment report on important judgment across functional departments.
4. Research and propose risk management strategy and cross-functional departments solution on significant risk management, and be responsible for the implementation of the solution and daily monitoring of the risk.
5. Be responsible to evaluate the effectiveness of enterprise risk management, and propose improvement solution on enterprise risk management.
6. Be responsible to establish a Risk Management Information System.
7. Be responsible to coordinate daily enterprise risk management work.
8. Be responsible to supervise and monitor functional departments, business units, wholly-owned subsidiaries and controlled subsidiaries to develop enterprise risk management.
9. Manage other works related to risk management.

Article 50 Enterprises should establish an Audit Committee under the board of directors. The internal audit department should be responsible to the Audit Committee. The responsibilities of Audit Committee and internal audit department should comply the related regulations in "Interim Measures for Internal Audit Management of Central Enterprises" (Decree of SASAC No.8). In risk management field, the internal audit department is responsible for researching and developing the risk management Monitoring and Reviewing System, designing related procedures, conducting monitoring and reviewing and preparing auditing reports.

Article 51 Other functional departments and business units of the enterprise should accept the arrangement, coordination, guidance and supervision conducted by risk management department and internal audit department. Their main responsibilities are as follows:

1. Implement basic risk management processes.
2. Research and develop the criteria or mechanisms for judging significant decisions, risks, events and business process within own functional department or business unit.
3. Prepare risk assessment report of significant decisions within their own functional department or business unit.
4. Perform the tasks of establishing risk management information system within own functional department or business unit.
5. Perform the task of building risk culture.
6. Establish and improve the internal risk control system within own functional department or business unit.
7. Undertake other tasks related to risk management.

Article 52 Enterprises should direct and supervise their wholly-owned subsidiary companies and controlled subsidiary companies to establish their risk management organizational structure through legal processes. The establishment should correspond with parent enterprise, or be highly effective related to the characteristics of the subsidiaries.

Chapter VIII Risk Management Information System

Article 53 The enterprise should apply information technology to all tasks related to risk management, establish a risk management information system that covers basic risk management process and all steps of internal control system, including information collection, information storage, information process, information analysis, information test, information delivery, information report, information disclosure, etc.

Article 54 The enterprise should adopt controls to ensure the consistency, accuracy, timeliness, accountability, completeness between risk management information system input data and quantitative risk values. Input data to information system should not be altered without authorization.

Article 55 The risk management information system should include all kinds of risk measurements, quantitative analysis and quantitative test; be able to reflect risk metrics, sort frequency, supervision state of significant risk and important business process in real time; carry out information alarm when significant risk exceeds its risk acceptable range, and satisfy the requirements of internal information reporting system of risk management and external information disclosure regulation.

Article 56 The risk management information system should enable integration and sharing of information within departments and business segments. Risk management information system should meet not only the requirements of single risk management task, but also the synthesized risk management requirements from overall enterprise, cross-functional departments and business segments.

Article 57 The enterprise should ensure the stability and security of the risk management information system, and improve and update it continuously.

Article 58 Enterprises that have established or just established an Enterprise Management Information System, should complement, regulate and update its existing management processes and management procedures, and establish a matured Risk Management Information System. Enterprises that have not yet established an Enterprise Management Information System, should unify the risk management system with enterprise management processes and management software, to plan, design, implement and run them simultaneously.

Chapter IX Risk Culture

Article 59 Enterprises should strive to establish a corporate culture that is risk conscious, to enhance employees' awareness of risks and risk management, so as to assure the achievement of the risk management objectives of the enterprises.

Article 60 Cultivation of risk management culture should be embedded into the overall process of cultivation of corporate culture. Enterprises should cultivate a sound risk culture, establish the correct risk management philosophy, and enhance the awareness across the enterprises, in order to transform the risk management into the common understanding and conscious actions of the employees and to promote the risk management mechanism that is systematic, normal and highly effective.

Article 61 The enterprise should engage to build its risk management culture environment at different corporate levels. The board of directors should pay great attention to the cultivation of risk management culture, and the general manager is responsible for the daily work of cultivation of risk management culture. The director and senior management personnel should demonstrate and lead in cultivation of risk management culture. The management and operations personnel who are responsible for key management processes, key business processes and risk control points should be the main forces of cultivation of risk management culture.

Article 62 Enterprises should establish the employee code of conduct, in order to foster a risk culture in that everyone conducts ethically and compliantly. Enterprises should punish seriously those employees who violated the laws, regulations, or the corporate policies, and who committed fraud and corruption.

Article 63 The staff of the enterprise, especially the managerial staff and the operating staff, should endeavor to promulgate the enterprise risk management idea through many kinds of forms and cultivate the sound enterprise risk management culture. The culture must emphasize that the risk is ubiquitous, the risk is ever-present and everyone must control the pure risks strictly, handle the speculative risks prudently and take the post responsibilities of risk management seriously.

Article 64 The cultivation of the risk management culture should be integrated with the salary policy and the human resources policy, as to enhance the risk awareness of managerial personnel, especially senior managers, and prevent behaviors like blind expansion, one-sided pursuit of performance and risk neglect.

Article 65 Enterprises should establish a risk management training program for the personnel in charge of important management and business processes, key business activities and risk controls. Enterprises should adopt various methods to enhance the risk awareness, to intensify the training on knowledge of related processes and controls, to nurture the internal talents on risk management, and to cultivate the risk culture.

Chapter X Supplementary Provisions

Article 66 For those central enterprises that are state wholly-owned and have not yet formed the board of directors, the executive management meeting of the enterprises should take over the responsibility that is assigned to the board of directors in the Guidelines, and the general manager should be responsible for the implementation of the Guidelines. Other state-owned or state-controlled enterprises may implement the Guidelines accordingly.

Article 67 The documents supplementary to the Guidelines for the risk management of the enterprises with respect to investing, financial reporting and derivative trading are published separately.

Article 68 The SASAC shall have the power of the interpretation of the Guidelines.

Article 69 The Guidelines shall become effective on the date of promulgation.

Case Study: Agreeing Upon the Scope of the Project and the Job of the ERM Risk Manager

Christopher Ketcham

Ph.D., CPCU, CRM, CIC, CFP®, Formerly Visiting Assistant Professor, University of Houston Downtown, Houston, Texas; Garnet Valley, Pennsylvania

This expository is based on an interview and commentary from veteran Risk Manager, Franck Baron, and his recent experience of negotiating the scope of his responsibilities during and after the hiring process as General Manager, Risk Management with the leaders of the privately owned company he is working for now. He recounts his experiences from pre-hire negotiations into the identification phase of the organization's ERM project. He offers suggestions on how to negotiate the job and set the stage for ERM with senior leadership. The views expressed here result from a sharing of experience with the authors of the book and do not represent the views of Mr. Franck's current employer.

8.1 SCOPE OF THE PROJECT

When an organization determines that it is ready to explore an ERM enterprise-wide risk management initiative there are a number of items that must be considered. First, the change from traditional risk management to ERM is more than a phase change – it is a re-learning process about the nature of risk. The organization's strategy is the cornerstone of ERM. Organizations that do not have a robust strategic plan and consistent strategic message, goals, and objectives will need to develop these first, involving RM in the process in order to determine critical risks to strategy. Identifying, assessing, managing, and monitoring risks with impacts on strategy is the central task of ERM. To accomplish this requires a recasting of the organization's mindset towards risk and the selection of a capable risk manager who is attuned to the process of ERM, understands what is required for a successful ERM implementation, and is familiar with issues associated with sustaining ERM over time. This process begins even before the ERM initiative leader accepts the responsibility and accountability for the job.

Many who become chief risk officers will not be employees of the organization when interviewing for the job to build an ERM initiative. The CRO candidate will need to make it clear that the chosen CRO will need to have a better understanding of where the organization wants to go with ERM before any program can be implemented. Whether the candidate to run the ERM project is an employee or a new hire or whether the firm is public, private, or not-for-profit, that candidate must have a candid conversation with senior executives to make sure that all have a common understanding of what the ERM project will achieve. If the organization says yes to the ERM project, leadership must understand what has to happen and what the commitments are to the project. The ERM initiative leader must get agreement from senior management on the project's goals. At the same time, while there are ERM protocols, maturity models and other tools to help the risk manager begin an implementation, there is no one-size-fits all protocol, process, or solution for an ERM initiative. The person in charge of the ERM initiative first must take time to learn – to begin to understand the company and its history.

One of the concerns with any ERM implementation is that it may have been initiated because management understands that the seriousness of one or more issues affecting the organization requires a rethinking of the risk management process. There will be pressure to solve this (these) problems first as quickly as possible. Executives may lose interest in ERM after these situations are addressed, when what is needed is a more thorough understanding of the organization's strategy, its risk appetite, and its leadership capabilities towards the understanding of and management of risk to strategy. It is a very real possibility that the organization's culture and leadership may not be tuned towards understanding risk to strategy in the most fundamental sense. There may be real problems that need to be addressed immediately in the nascent ERM project. However, there must be an understanding within the organization that for the ERM initiative to be sustained the organization must be tuned towards the strategic and the identification, assessment, management, and monitoring of critical risks that can affect the strategic goals and objectives of the organization.

Candidates from outside the company may find it easier to ask these tough questions than internal candidates. If the ERM initiative leader candidate is internal, that person must have or develop a relationship with senior officers to ask the tough questions, even tough questions that extend far beyond the realm of responsibilities the employee now has. Whoever the person selected to run the ERM initiative is, that person must have the authority to consider the organization from a position outside of the hierarchy – to speak truth to power. Towards this end the ERM initiative leader needs to understand that on the route to learning "everything about the organization" there will be reluctance by proprietary owners or other leaders to share some information that heretofore has been privileged. It is the job of the risk manager to obtain the necessary information about risk to determine how the ERM initiative can best manage the risk. Without the transparency of information critical risks may be overlooked, underestimated, or ignored.

8.2   JOB DESCRIPTION FOR ERM

There are specific competencies that a good ERM initiative leader must possess. First, the CRO (or equivalent) must take the time to learn – to understand the company and how it runs – all aspects of the company. The leader must be interested and show initiative towards this end. The leader must possess strong project management skills. This includes how to ask the right questions and how to communicate to all employee levels whether blue collar, professional, or field or office workers. This communication process includes the message to others, "I don't know and I am here to listen." The initiative leader by the same token must be a good listener who does not have pre-conceived or prepared answers. The initiative leader must be innately curious and have the ability to ask questions even when inconvenient to executives and others.

To avoid having ERM become a checkbox exercise, or a compliance issue, the initiative leader needs to be able to identify and assess situations or processes which may not have been scrutinized to any great extent in the past and ask questions that may not have been asked before. The aim of any ERM program must not be to administratively manage risk but strategically manage risk and the risk manager must be prepared to think strategically.

Therefore, it is the responsibility of each person in the organization to manage risks. The CRO must see the job partly as a consultant to risk managers. A good CRO does not want managers to view the CRO as managing risk. Risk owners manage risk. The risk manager's job is to facilitate the process and coach risk owners.

However, if the CRO is to be successful local risk managers and risk owners must provide him/her with appropriate information. One of the CRO's challenges is how to structure the performance review and incentives so that risk management is part of the responsibility. At the same time the RM professional must understand that a certain amount of risk is good for any organization, so leadership will need to build a performance incentive program that comports with the company's risk appetite, so that the incentive programs do not create risk-averse risk managers. Ultimately some risk is good because it provides opportunities.

One issue that is critically important for ERM: there is a need for the risk management community to better understand how people make decisions under uncertainty. More research is needed on how people think; how to help people learn how to make good risk decisions.

Second, the risk management community must do a better job at explaining how to sustain an ERM initiative over time. There is now a good body of literature on starting a project and success stories in beginning ERM, but there is an obvious lack of articles about success stories in sustaining ERM. In too many situations ERM becomes a compliance checkbox and is never integrated within strategy. In these situations, it is all too frequent that ERM develops its own bureaucracy but never is truly grafted onto strategy nor is it deeply embedded into the culture of the organization. To deliver the full value it can, a true ERM initiative should help an organization developing risk agility and not just compliance. The ERM leader supports the business and should be the catalyst for the business (not its conscience).

8.3   QUESTIONS FOR STUDENTS AND PRACTITIONERS

1. The case asks the risk management community to do a better job explaining how to sustain an ERM initiative over time. List what you believe are the critical requirements to sustain an ERM initiative over time.
2. Scenario: The current operational risk manager probably is not be the right candidate to become chief risk officer but that operational risk manager is very good at his/her job and knows the company well. You will become the company's first CRO. What role do you see this operational risk manager having in an ERM installation and what would be your plan to retain this person (if you will retain the person) and train this person for operating in an ERM environment?
3. Do a "Google Scholar" search of "Decision Making Under Uncertainty". Identify key research articles in this area of research and provide a brief summary of the issues and the empirical data that are part of this research paradigm to date.
4. The board of directors has just hired you as a consultant to analyze the company to see whether it is ready to commence an ERM implementation. What circumstances or conditions in a business or enterprise would cause you to recommend that the company NOT pursue an ERM implementation at this time?
5. Develop a template for building a job description for a chief risk officer in a for-profit enterprise. This should include a list of questions that must be answered and a list of critical skills that must be a part of every CRO's job. Also include questions that will identify competencies required for the particular industry and business that the CRO job description will be designed for.

9

Case Study: Wellcome Trust

Interviewee: Fiona Davidge, Enterprise Risk Manager for Wellcome Trust, London, England

Interviewer: Professor Jean-Paul Louisot, Formerly Université Paris 1 Panthéon-Sorbonne, Directeur Pédagogique du CARM Institute, Paris, France

Date: February 4, 2013

9.1 GENERALITIES AND PRESENTATION

The Wellcome Trust is a charitable endowment fund, registered with the UK Charity Commission. The Wellcome Trust was established in 1936 under the will of Henry Wellcome, founder of the Wellcome pharmaceutical company. Initially the Trust was funded from company profits as it owned shares of the company and received dividends. In 1992, the shares were sold thus severing direct links with the pharmaceutical industry. The money raised was invested in an endowment fund with the sole purpose of providing income for the Wellcome Trust. That endowment is now worth over £14 billion and provides an income annually of £600–700 million.

Despite its not-for-profit status and being a charity, the Trust is still among the top 100 companies paying taxes to the UK government, mainly VAT (value added tax) and transaction tax on the investment portfolio.

The Wellcome Trust funds research in universities and other educational institutions in the field of bio-medical research for humans and animals. It also funds a public engagement program to promote understanding of science. It has recently created a new subsidiary, Syncona, endowed with £200 million in funds, which will invest in companies in the bio industry – start-up or small companies – in order to ensure practical adaptation of the science for end users.

Academic institutions apply for funding directly to the Trust, where an internal team of scientists creates a shortlist. Final selection is made by expert committees from across the world, chosen for their expertise. The Trust has a staff comprising 2000 employees. Half of these work at the Trust headquarters or at the adjoining Museum, and half work in Cambridge, England at the Sanger Institute, a wholly-owned not-for-profit subsidiary of the Institute devoted to genome research. The Trust also funds research outside of the UK through academic institutions in Malawi, Kenya, South Africa, Vietnam and Thailand. Funding overseas is cost effective and the work increases the level of science and research competencies in those countries.

The Trust also partners with other charity, governmental and not-for-profit institutions that could be seen as competition but in reality work cooperatively. These institutions include universities, the Gates Foundation and the Howard Hughes Foundation.

The major stakeholders are:

- Charity commission (a charter needs to be complied with).
- UK government – encouraging a culture of sciences (Education, Health).
- NHS – National Health Service in the UK.
- European Union authorities (policy influencing, animal research, stem cell research, etc.).
- Animal protection groups (not high on their list but still be aware of very limited action).
- University community, especially in the UK.
- Medical Research Council (GOV) and Cancer Research UK (Charity).

The institute's mission statement clearly defines its purpose: "To achieve extraordinary improvements in human and animal health. In pursuit of this, we support the brightest minds in biomedical research and the medical humanities."

However, beyond research grants, the Institutes operate in different directions to improve the public understanding and knowledge of the biomedical science and advances, and that includes:

- A robust public engagement to inform the public through the Wellcome Collection (exhibits collected by Henry Wellcome which are all linked to health and medicine) and visiting exhibitions – one held in early 2013 was about "Death": art related to death. Exhibitions are planned to be controversial and ask the viewer to question science and medicine. The current exhibition includes paintings from disabled and psychiatric patients in Japan.
- Education in schools (Darwin, etc.).
- Improvement of science teaching in schools (funding of residential courses for teachers).

9.2   THE ERM PROGRAM

In 2008, a risk professional was hired to understand and promote risk management in the investment portfolio. The risk manager embarked on a journey to raise the need of the organization for a global and integrated approach to risk management far beyond the limited scope of the investment portfolio. The ERM responsibility now covers all other areas of Trust activity.

Contrary to many organizations, no adverse event prompted top management to move towards ERM, but the environment and the context were opportune.

The scope of the ERM implementation for Wellcome is clearly defined. In principle it leads a process for the management of all risks except those in the investment portfolio. While there is a connection through a strategic risk identified with the investment portfolio, the ERM program deliberately has no direct involvement in investments. The ERM manager also manages the insurance portfolio but not health and safety, which has its own professional manager. The two managers do interact and share information.

The executive board and the board of trustees endorsed the establishment of the ERM program and made the original decision to hire a risk management professional. There is no legal or regulatory obligation for the trust to set up the function. The ERM manager reports to the COO who is part of the executive board (comprising of eight members). Internal audit reports to the COO and the audit program is largely delivered by Deloitte but supervised by one direct Trust employee.

Fiona Davidge, the incumbent risk manager, assumed the position in 2012. She holds a law degree, a diploma in RM and is a FIRM and M-BCI. She has 14 years' experience in risk management but had not been directly involved with insurance purchasing until joining

Wellcome. She found that her experience in managing risks helped her to understand the scope of the job and she did not find a huge challenge in tending to the insurance portfolio thanks to the assistance of a broker – Aon. Wellcome has global exposures requiring a broker with a worldwide expertise.

The COO chairs the risk committee, which has four members of the executive team (involved in rotation), the two risk professionals, head of finance and a member of the investment team as permanent attendees. Each main department has a risk champion – a senior manager – who is in charge of the periodic review with risk owners. Davidge feels that she has the full support of the executive teams and has adequate resources.

The organization has a clear strategic plan and an operational plan (clearly articulated objectives) and set up regular meetings to ensure involvement of RM in the process. In the risk register, the link between strategic objectives and risk is identified and managed.

The risk register is held as a Word document and there is no specific software as it is not needed. The risk committee provides full papers to the whole executive and the board of trustees. Minutes are available to all staff on the intranet. Specialists are invited as required to the risk committee to examine specific issues (such as IT resilience, health and safety, business continuity). The periodic review is well accepted by risk owners who view it as an opportunity to enhance their performance.

When she arrived at Wellcome, Fiona had these goals:

- "Tidy up" the risk register that contained "non risks" and "risk controls" instead of just active risks. Reduce the number of risks (from 32 to 18) and bring more focus on risk mitigation.
- Develop an annex for key risk controls. The annex requires an annual review unless the risk control owner feels it has to be reviewed sooner.
- Make sure that systematic project RM is in place for major projects like the one currently in progress to refurbish the exhibition building next door to the Wellcome Institute headquarters in London.

The heat map reproduced in Figure 9.1 provides an evaluation based on impact and probability. The main issues considered are cash flows, investments, health and safety issues, and reputation. Wellcome controls the grantees as they look into the reality of research results. Wellcome leadership is especially keen on verifying the reality of the research results and must remain beware of the risks of falsified result claims used to justify funding.

While the investment department has developed its own controls, the ERM had shied away from complex approaches and adopted the "KISS" motto (Keep it simple stupid) and has traditional controls that reflect the ISO 31000:2009 terminology.

So far, the Institute has not identified any surprise challenges for critical risks. As it is not a large organization, it is felt that most risks have been identified. What risk management has brought is a more systematic approach to risk management, which is presumed to be more efficient. However, there can be surprises overseas, for example, when the money does not find its way to the end users *(not necessarily fraud but lack of competence)*.

The following processes and procedures related to disruption planning and reinforcement for the institute resilience have been developed:

1. Business continuity in place at London headquarters and at Sanger.
2. Auditing funding programs.

		A	B	C	D	E
Almost certain Very high, may occur more than once per year (80% per year)	5	Medium	High	High	High	High
Likely High, may arise about once per year (50%-<80% per year)	4	Medium	Medium	High	High	High
Possible Possible, may arise at least once in a 1–10 year period (10%-<50% per year)	3	Low	Medium	Medium	High	High
Unlikely Not impossible, likely to occur in the next 10–50 years (2%-<10% per year)	2	Low	Low	Medium	Medium	High
Rare Very low, very unlikely during the next 50 years (Less than 2%)	1	Low	Low	Low	Medium	Medium
		A	B	C	D	E
Impact categories		Minor	Moderate	Major	**Critical**	**Catastrophic**

Likelihood (vertical axis label)

Figure 9.1 Wellcome Trust Corporate Risk Matrix (edited September 2010). Reproduced by permission of the copyright holder. (*Continued*)

3. Generic response plans with a crisis management procedure. Activation route will depend on the nature of the potential crisis. Communication is then assessed and implemented.
4. Evacuation plans.
5. Business continuity plans exercised twice a year.
6. All members of staff have business continuity information card and know what to do in an emergency.

	Impact				
Financial loss over 1 year	Loss of up to £100,000	Loss of >£100,000 to £1 million	Loss of >£1 million to £10 million	Loss of >£10 million to £50 million	Loss of more than £50 million
Reputation	Private criticism by key stakeholders	Public criticism by key stakeholders	Criticism by key stakeholders in media	Outrage expressed by key stakeholders	Boycott by key stakeholders
Investment loss over 1 year	Loss of up to 3% of the endowment	Loss of 3% to <8% of the endowment	Loss of 8% to <15% of the endowment	Loss of 15% to <30% of the endowment	Loss of over 30% of the endowment
Regulatory or legal damage	Provoke informal questions from Charity Commission to HMRC	Provoke letter from Charity Commission or HMRC asking for further information	Provoke prolonged attention from Charity Commission or HMRC; Serious consideration of formal inquiry	Charity Commission Section 8 inquiry or equivalent HMRC formal inquiry	Charity Commission Section 18 action to suspend Trustee; prosecution, punitive fines
Health & safety	Minimal harm to 1–20 people	Minimal harm to >20 people, multiple short-term injuries	Permanent or long-term injury	Single fatality	Multiple fatalities

Figure 9.1   (*Continued*)

9.3   THE BENEFITS OF ERM: COST AND BENEFIT ANALYSIS

The heat impact map is mostly assessed in financial terms (for investment in percentage of portfolio) but the impact on Wellcome's reputation cannot be ignored as it might result mostly in a challenge to its charitable status. Also the loss of scientific credibility could jeopardize the very existence of the Institute. Health and safety are also taken into account. However, there is no performance indicator as such due to the specific activities involved in health and safety.

Success is measured by how "uncertainty" becomes part of the natural way of doing business. The only measure is linked to return on investment (there are ceilings to the percentage of investment at risk in decision making). The endowment must generate the money needed but this can be difficult in certain economic conditions like the recent great recession. The only "no-no" investment area is the tobacco industry (others may be debated).

The managers have no direct incentive to participate in the risk management effort. There is presently no direct incentive in the "bonus equation" – and with the not-for-profit culture bonuses are very limited *(small bonuses are in place for the investment team but their size is limited compared to an investment banking or hedge fund)*. One important note is that the time horizon for investment is much longer than in commercially driven funds so Wellcome is able to take a longer-term investment view.

The costs associated with ERM consist mostly in salary and related expenses: one full time person and one in "investment". Insurance premiums are part of cost but are carefully managed. Being a risk champion is part of each manager's job. The main benefits gained from how risk management is organized are efficiency gains and focus on the essential, but this is not easily translated into financial terms.

9.4   THE PROBLEMS OR CHALLENGES ASSOCIATED WITH ERM

One of the major challenges is to maintain the attention of all involved, to keep the risk management process afloat and relevant to objectives, and to prevent it from being linked to the view that it is only about events/accidents.

In management meetings, risks are managed but not necessarily consciously and systematically – this is the added benefit of a formalized risk management approach. However, sustaining ERM over time does not come naturally and requires a strong personal engagement, and engagement of everyone, especially the new employees.

The quantification of results, or lack thereof, is not really an issue at Wellcome Trust as RM has become a natural way of doing business.

However, Wellcome understands it still is in the learning curve for ERM:

- New hires are educated during the induction process (seminar); and
- The intranet is being realigned to better explain ERM to employees.

The 3-year strategic plan is reviewed with RM in attendance and remarks are expected, but there is still room to identify more clearly the risks that could potentially impact strategic goals. Also, the procurement process is reviewed and RM is checked with the tender offer process (mostly IT due to the specific activity). Davidge has found that on the whole the executive level is more aligned with RM issues than what she experienced at a previous employer.

9.5   RECOMMENDATIONS FOR OTHERS SEEKING TO IMPLEMENT ERM

For those organizations and professionals engaging in the development and the implementation of an ERM programs, Davidge has the following advice: Work on clear objectives otherwise it does not go beyond "emergency" management. Strategic objectives are at the heart of the RM process.

Davidge suggested that there are two pitfalls to avoid in risk management:

- One size fits all (i.e. in a smaller organization, personal interaction matters more and in larger need of proper structure).
- Be wary of heavy methodology for light structure (risk management information system, business information system or analytics).

More specifically it is essential to avoid unnecessarily complex procedures that would duplicate existing management systems.

At a previous job Davidge explained that disbanding the RM committee proved a bad idea, as its replacement did not materialize. She suggested that this might be considered only when risk management maturity is such that risk management is actually totally woven in the management process and culture. No organization today can afford not to invest in a robust risk management framework but top management active involvement is essential.

Davidge must coach all managers on keeping the RM viable everywhere and this includes taking an active part in the project risk management exercises for major investment projects, such as the exhibition building that is being refurbished.

Fiona is a member of the group of international experts that is in charge of writing the Risk Management Standards for the International Standard Organization (WG 262) currently working on the implementation guide for the ISO 31000:2009 (ISO 31004). She is also active with the IRM (Institute of Risk Management in London) and recommends such involvement to her peers as she finds that sharing experience with other professionals is a key to successful ERM implementation in one's own organization.

9.6   QUESTIONS FOR STUDENTS AND PRACTITIONERS

1. Use the Wellcome Trust Corporate Risk Matrix to identify critical risks for a company of your choosing or one that your instructor provides.
   (a) Relate these critical risks to the strategies and strategic plan of the organization.
   (b) Define the impact of these critical risks to the organization and develop a risk management strategy for each.
2. Identify potential risks to reputation that could affect an organization like Wellcome Trust.
3. In this case it was determined that the horizon for investments in ERM is longer than other measures used to incentivize managers. Develop an incentive program for executives and managers of the Wellcome Trust that will be in sync with a longer investment horizon for ERM.
4. Not-for-profit enterprises do not produce profits. Traditional measures used to assess the value, and change in value, of publicly traded organizations are not appropriate to evaluate the ERM initiative.
   (a) What measures would you recommend that not-for-profit organizations use to assess the value of their ERM implementation?
   (b) How can the not-for-profit enterprise provide evidence that their ERM activities are producing the value and not other activities or influences?
5. What are the characteristics of a good athletic coach? Translate these characteristics into the characteristics for being a good risk management coach. Would you add additional characteristics or competencies, if so, what and why?

10

Case Study: Large Health Insurer
in the US

This case is derived from a conversation with a risk
manager for a large health insurer in the United States who wanted
to remain anonymous. The interview was conducted by
Christopher Ketcham, Ph.D., CPCU, CRM, CIC, CFP®, Formerly Visiting
Assistant Professor, University of Houston Downtown, Houston, Texas;
Garnet Valley, Pennsylvania
Date: July 9, 2012

10.1 THE LARGE HEALTH INSURER TODAY

This is a large not-for-profit health insurer in the USA that has been in business for more
than seventy years. Presently it has more than 10,000 employees. At the time of this writing
(September, 2012), the company had an A.M. Best financial size rating of XV.[1] The organization's principal business is to provide health insurance for individuals and organizations in a
defined geographical area. The organization provides traditional healthcare products, including
products associated with the US Affordable Healthcare Act for which the first major changes
will be implemented late 2013 and 2014. Beyond traditional health insurance the insurer
offers Preferred Provider Organization (PPO) products, Health Maintenance Organization
(HMO) products, and the Federal Health insurance program for seniors called Medicare.

10.2 IMPLICATIONS OF THE AFFORDABLE CARE ACT

The Affordable Care Act passed by Congress in March 2010 will have major implications
for how health insurers will do business in the US beginning in late 2013. Approximately
forty million uninsured persons are expected to be eligible for coverage, expanding the market
approximately 13% (of 300 million US residents) for all insurers. Expanded eligibility rules
will make some who were previously uninsurable for various reasons eligible to purchase
coverage. Those who do not purchase health insurance and who are not otherwise exempted
will pay a fee (tax) of a few hundred dollars early in the program's rollout. This fee or tax
will increase in later years. How the influx of new customers will affect this insurer or other
insurer loss ratios is unknown.

New rules also mandate minimum loss ratios. Depending upon the type of customer, insurers
will have to demonstrate that they have paid out at least 80–85% of premiums in claims. This
leaves health insurers only 15%–20% of premiums (before investment income) to pay for all,
underwriting, and marketing overhead expenses. As a not-for-profit business, this insurer does

---

[1] A.M. Best Company, Inc. specializes in rating insurers. A Financial size of XV is two billion dollars or greater.

not have the same requirements for shareholder value as for-profit competitors, but on the other hand it cannot raise capital in the equity markets. However, this insurer will be challenged to maintain a low expense structure in the years to come in order to meet new government loss ratio requirements.

The federal mandate of 80–85% claims payment combined with health insurance exchanges where individuals can go to a virtual market space to obtain quotes on insurance, will change the market dynamic for insurance sales. First, health insurers will be forced to compete on price which means operating at as low an expense ratio as possible. Second, the product benefits in the exchanges have been standardized by healthcare reform. The end result is that health insurance available from exchanges is likely to become a highly commoditized business where price and reputation will be the only differentiators.

There will still be traditional HMO and PPO insurance products and services for those who are employed by companies who will maintain their group insurance products and will not purchase insurance from the exchanges. Exchanges are expected to provide different plan options in terms of deductibles and co-payments for services rendered. The coverage, however, will be the same in all cases. The exchanges will likely be used by those who were once uninsured (taking advantage of government subsidies) and by those who have traditionally purchased individual or family policies. These exchanges may also include individuals who work for small companies or companies who choose not to provide insurance for employees.

The mandate of the Affordable Healthcare Act does not extend to all of this insurer's product lines. Fee products such as TPA services are not affected by the mandate. Medicare and Medicaid services are subject to other federal and state requirements. Health insurers are likely to look for product and business diversification opportunities to offset the higher loss ratios and lower expense ratios that the Affordable Healthcare Act mandates. There are likely to be consolidations in the marketplace as less cost-efficient health insurers or those without the resources to prepare for the exchange environment are acquired by larger, more cost-efficient insurers.

10.3   WHY ERM FOR THIS INSURER

In the 1990s a series of lawsuits for errors and omissions against health insurers were settled for multiple million dollar rewards in the US. New legal theories gave plaintiffs access to the "deep pockets" of the health insurer.[2]

Plaintiff lawyers introduced new legal concepts, one of which was that an insurer had some measure of control over how the doctors and hospitals practiced medicine through their coverage restrictions and claims handling/payment practices. RICO (racketeering and conspiracy) accusations against insurers were also on the rise, because the relationships between providers and payer were created by contract and could be interpreted as conspiratorial by a jury. To address this issue head on this insurer asked the risk manager to look beyond traditional risk management for answers.

Risk management has been practiced for decades around the world. However, increasing court judgments, regulations, rating company requirements, globalization, and the impact of catastrophes, whether natural or economic, have forced large companies and organizations to reconsider their risk management practices. The predecessor term to ERM was IRM or integrated risk management. From the beginning of the international debate to expand risk management from operational to organizational, the concern was that organizations faced more

---

[2] For an example of such a case consult: Fox v. Health Net, Civ. No. 21962, Riverside County Super. Ct., Cal., Dec. 28, 1993.

than hazard risk, the traditional risk that most risk managers focused upon. Prior to IRM and ERM, the job of many risk managers was insurance procurement and hazard risk control of operations. Understanding and managing strategic, financial and other risks the organization faced was not part of the risk manager's responsibility.

When the risk manager for this insurer began the process of rethinking risk management there was limited information and literature about how one might consider and manage all of the critical risks an organization does or could face. While the acute problem of these large vicarious lawsuits in the industry has substantially been mitigated by state reform, the enterprise risk management initiative has evolved over time as the external and internal risk profile changed. The maturation of this insurer's ERM program has been a dynamic process. Processes or reporting structures have been implemented only to have them changed or eliminated as reporting structures or company processes changed. However, even though there have been rough spots and learning curves, this insurer has been working within an ERM framework for more than a decade.

10.4 ERM REPORTING STRUCTURE AND ERM DEPARTMENT STRUCTURE

After beginning the IRM conversation in the mid-1990s the organization realized that it needed to better understand the risks that the organization faced. However, there was not a structure in the organization to accomplish this task.

Throughout the years of the ERM initiative, the risk management department has focused on a business capability to help the organization to identify, evaluate and manage risk. The majority of activities are conducted in the context of making the insurer's projects, products and process changes successful by removing obstacles from the paths of project sponsors. Early on in the initiative, risk management invited itself to functional meetings to summarize the insurer's risk management process and explain the benefits of using risk coaches in the identification and assessment of risk. Over time departments have become amenable to risk management assistance because the coaching and process helps managers feel more comfortable that they have identified, evaluated and treated the critical risks so that unexpected consequences are much less likely to result.

Within eighteen months of beginning the conversation with risk management, the legal counsel's office brought risk management, legal services, internal audit, compliance SIU (Special Investigative Units[3]) together as one department. Bringing these units together not only provided the insurer with valuable information after events occurred but also allowed greater integration of disparate risk management functions to identify and manage potential issues before they turned into events or losses.

Where the risk management department reports to in the organization can have considerable impact upon the tasks the risk manager and team are asked to perform. In many organizations risk management reports up through the CFO (Chief Financial Officer), the place where insurance was traditionally purchased in many companies. In other organizations risk management reports to human resources. This is often the case in organizations where workers compensation is the significant operational cost of risk driver. In technology companies, some risk managers report up through the CTO (Chief Technology Officer) where data integrity and security are of prime importance.

---

[3] SIU units investigate questionable and possibly fraudulent claims. Arson, malingering, false claims, inflated injuries, fraudulent claims practices, physician, chiropractor, and legal practices that inflate claims without cause are the types of activities that SIU units investigate. Often SIU units are staffed by former police officers or FBI agents.

Table 10.1   ERM Program Components

Governance	Reporting	Processes	Tools and Support
Corporate policy	Risk council	Annual risk assessment	Risk assessment program
Board oversight	Board and committees	Oversight of mitigation plans	Risk evaluation tool
Senior Management risk ownership and accountability	Core process risk profiles	Risk Coaching Annual Strategic Risk Assessment	Computer base training
Risk council	Quarterly Reporting	Integration with audit and other functions	Templates
		Program benchmarking	Expertise

There are some advantages for having the risk management department report up through the chief legal officer for a health insurer. The principal product of an insurer is an insurance contract and the service provided in the majority of its healthcare business is to pay a claim. In other divisions (e.g. TPA – Third Party Administrative Services) fee income is generated. Both ends of this insurer's business spectrum involve contracts which require legal scrutiny. Additionally, litigation along with claim payment trends provide valuable information concerning emerging risks. Audit, compliance, and risk management services reporting up through legal services also provides additional information about how well the company's internal controls are working and where changes need to be made. Finally, the insurer has acquired business. Acquisitions require significant legal, risk, compliance, and audit scrutiny before any deal is consummated.

Yet there are also disadvantages in an ERM initiative where the risk management and similar risk identification services report up through one member of the executive committee. The principal disadvantage is that the risk management team may not have direct access to the business units run by other executives.

There are those who suggest that the CRO (chief risk officer) should report directly to the board. However this is organized, it is important that ERM is at least perceived as an enterprise-wide initiative and at best becomes part of the strategy and culture of the entire organization.

However, there are methodologies for grafting ERM onto a company's strategy and culture even when risk management is not a position on the executive committee. This insurer's ERM program has evolved over time to provide services to the many departments and divisions that report up through all executive committee members, not just legal services. Table 10.1 provides an overview of the ERM program and the components associated with its tools, process, management and administration.

10.5   THE ERM INITIATIVE TODAY

Today this insurer's risk management department reports up through to the chief legal counsel. The risk management department has a director, program managers, and risk finance and insurance procurement professionals. In addition to managing the ERM initiative, risk management staff serve as risk coaches – sources of expert guidance to departments, managers and executives on the organization's efforts to optimize risk taking decisions in support of corporate directives. Towards this end, the risk management department has developed tools and methodologies to help other units of the company to understand and evaluate the risks they face. These tools have been developed in consideration of the risk appetite and strategic vision of the company and have been reviewed, approved, and published by the executive committee as company policy. The risk tools and risk assessment process associated with change and project management are covered later in this case study.

The risk management department has its own mission and vision statements which are aligned with the corporate mission and vision statements. The risk management mission statements are associated with its three main responsibilities: ERM, risk financing and business continuity.

- The ERM mission is to provide corporate leadership, methodology and tools to support operational and strategic management with their responsibility to optimize risk taking decisions.
- Risk Financing's mission is to support corporate objectives by sharing optimal design and cost effectiveness of the risk financing program including corporation insurance retention and transference of risk.
- Business continuity's mission is to lead the company to an appropriate level of resilience through expert guidance to operational areas within the established business continuity program.

From this mission, this insurer's ERM program has identified specific goals (see Table 10.2).

Table 10.2   ERM Program Goals

Governance	Provide a strong risk governance structure to manage risks at all levels; establish risk tolerance of the company and board of directors
Assessment and Monitoring	Embed a structured risk management process; establish risk ownership and accountability; build mechanisms to proactively address emerging risks; develop monitoring and evaluation activities
Culture	Build an organizational competency of forecasting the environment to understand current and future significant threats, including financial, market, compliance, reputation, and security risks; build risk training and education programs that improve management's ability to make risk intelligent decisions

While the ERM mission statement supports operational management this has changed with the growing business diversity efforts of the company, its increased appetite for acquisitions and partnerships, and the need to adapt processes and practices in advance of the Affordable Healthcare Act's legislated changes. This means that today the risk management team is spending more time on strategic issues than on operational issues.

Certain risks such as unintended release of private information and sexual harassment have established processes to both prevent and mitigate events. Also risk management does get involved with risk management of data security and similar risks when assessing risks associated with new ventures, joint ventures, product and process change projects.

Business continuity does not just prepare for a weather or earthquake event but any event that could cripple infrastructure or otherwise make operations in its territory less than optimal or even impossible. The event-centric approach is more flexible than the peril-centric (e.g. hurricane plan) approach for it can be used in many situations i.e. fire, earthquake, flood, windstorm, lockdown or other events that require coordination, evacuation, in-situ patient care and reallocation of resources to areas not affected by the event. Resiliency and business continuity concerns do not involve only owned organizations. With certain outsourced functions such as claims handling, this insurer must also have partners who have the same ability to maintain and adjust operations to meet customer needs after what could otherwise be crippling events.

This insurer is vertically integrated with a centralized management structure. The risk management department is also centralized within the organization which is consistent with the organizational structure of the organization. However, the message from the risk management department to executives and employees alike has been that regardless of the centralized management nature and function the individual employee is also a risk manager. Everyone manages risk – risk management is distributed in the broadest manner possible. What the risk management department at this insurer has worked towards is developing a "risk taking competency" to support leadership, management, and project teams when they are faced with change, acquisition, or new projects that require new thinking about critical risks or when they face new risks or risks the organization has not contemplated previously. Part of developing this competency is to provide active risk coaching and consultancy within the organization.

Although the ERM concept is supported by the CEO and senior executives, no edict or mandate to use the ERM discipline has been issued by either. This requires the risk management team to sell the need for its services within the organization. This is not a simple task and has taken time for the risk management team to be "automatically" engaged by project sponsors when new processes, procedures, and acquisitions are initiated.

The risk management team has gained respect from many departments in the organization through the application of risk management services and tools. First and foremost, the job of the risk management coach is to support the leader of the project, acquisition, or partnership initiative. This means that the risk coach's job is to help assure that the sponsor and the team have a successful project or initiative. This means not only identifying risks and obstacles towards facilitating a successful result so they can be proactively addressed but also means giving the leaders and teams credit for their successful result. Second, there is a viral component in the organization that results from successful risk coaching. Managers talk with managers, they and executive sponsors recommend to new project managers that they consult with the risk management team. Finally, specific corporate mandates require that project managers or acquisition leaders consult with risk coaches for acquisitions or process or procedural change. Projects involving certain critical risks also must engage a formal risk assessment process. Subtle reminders to project sponsors may be necessary to begin this effort.

While risk coaching requires knowledgeable risk professionals, the process of identifying, analyzing, and categorizing risks must be simple and intuitive to those who are not risk professionals. Risk management understands that not only the process must be simple, but the end product produced must be simplified so that it is understandable to all stakeholders of the project, process change or acquisition or joint partnership initiative. The results of the risk assessment process including mitigation plans are incorporated into the project team's ongoing reporting process.

The objective of the risk assessment process is to help the assessment team understand the risks associated with the project, assess the impact of vulnerability, likelihood, and timing of these risks, develop risk mitigation strategies, and determine which of these risks are critical and require attention of the project team and/or senior leadership (see Table 10.3). The risk analysis report is passed along to those who will manage the implemented process or new venture so that these risks, their impact, and treatment can be monitored and changes made

Figure 10.1   The ERM process as applied to enterprise risks, project risks and functional risks

where necessary. In this process risk management becomes part of the project impact and efficacy statement. At the same time and since these projects represent strategic as well as operational initiatives for this insurer, they help to align risk and strategy within the project itself which, if the project is approved for implementation, becomes integrated with strategy of the company. The approach of the risk management team has been honed over many years into a process that is remarkably simple in its concept and implementation but effective in its results. Figure 10.1 provides an overview of the typical steps found in many ERM plans.

10.6   THE RISK MANAGEMENT PROCESS

Risk management gets involved with most significant projects, changes, new processes, acquisitions, and new ventures, and new joint ventures in various ways. Project sponsors and others request assistance directly from the risk management department. In other situations the process is mandated by company policy. In other cases, the risk management team learns of a new process or project and "invites themselves" to the team meetings.

A testament to the success of the process is the fact that the risk management department is often called back to conduct a new risk assessment when things change over time. For example, risk management has been consulted in all of the four iterations of the project to analyze outsourcing risk. As outsourcing evolved over time, new project teams were formed to reconsider the outsourcing process and risk identification and assessment has become integral to that evolving process.

Over time, corporate policy has evolved to define and embrace ERM standards and tools. As the company has rapidly evolved in recent years through change and acquisition the need to use the risk identification and assessment process has accelerated. As a result ERM and corporate ERM practices have become part of the culture to the extent that employees and leadership are aware of the standards, even though some may not have participated in a project where these tools were deployed.

The risk assessment process has the following iterative steps. See the Project/Committee Risk Assessment Users guide Appendix A for more details.

First, when a department initiates a new project, risk management recommends to the department head or project sponsor that a risk assessment should be conducted. In other cases, where the process has been incorporated into department culture, the project sponsor or manager contacts the risk management department to conduct the assessment.

The risk assessment itself is facilitated by the risk management department, generally in a two hour window of time. However, before the assessment is conducted, risk management meets with the project sponsor to determine together who should participate in the assessment. Most assessment participants are not project team members. Instead assessment participants are selected from areas of the company that will be affected by the change, new process, acquisition, or new venture. This might include someone from the legal department when contracts are part of the process or information technology when processes change and/or there are confidential data issues at stake. If the project involves reputational issues, a public relations representative is included. Other typical participants include those from affected departments, compliance, finance, and audit.

Prior to the assessment meeting the sponsor is asked to develop a brief but encompassing scope statement of what is to be assessed during the meeting. Risk management understands that the simpler this statement is the better it will be understood and embraced by the assessment team.

The assessment meeting date is chosen and is held in a room that has adequate technology to support the use of a computer interface and projection on a large screen or monitor. The information is recorded real time so all participants can see and agree with what is being documented.

Facilitated by the risk management representative, the first five minutes of the assessment is the review of the assessment scope statement and the consensus that this should be the scope. During the next thirty minutes or so, the risk management facilitator and recording assistant ask the assessment team to identify the risks that this project will have and how it will manifest itself in the company (e.g., reputation problems, affect upon net income, customer dissatisfaction, etc.) – limited, of course, to the scope statement agreed to at the beginning of the session. The facilitator must be skilled in gaining clarification and drilling down further where necessary. Often this is the first time that stakeholder participants in this meeting have heard that this project or process change is being conducted. The added benefit of this process and the inclusion of stakeholders is that this gives the insurer institutional notice that the project is being conducted and starts to socialize the need for the project and the intended outcomes.

After the initial brainstorming effort, the facilitator leads the group in a twenty minute discussion to consolidate these identified risks into six to ten critical risks.

After the critical risk list is developed, most of the second hour of the assessment is devoted to further assessment and evaluation of the six to ten critical risks using the ERM Risk Evaluation Tool. See Appendix B for details. The assessment team first considers the impact of the risk to various risk factors and aspects of this insurer's business for each of the six to ten identified risks. The impact portion of the tool assumes that the risk has not been controlled in any way. Impact assessments range from insignificant to catastrophic, even to the extent that an event could lead to impairment of the organization as a going concern. This is a multi-dimensional impact assessment, considering affected operations, reputation, privacy, compliance, and complexity of the project itself. By considering multiple dimensions of impact the assessment team can evaluate the degree of impact to each stakeholder of the project. Cumulative impact to the insurer is also considered and evaluated. For example a change in claims data reporting might have a slight risk to reputation but the complexity risk could be very high which may have a serious impact on compliance with state statutes.

After assessing impact for each of the six to ten risk factors, the team assesses the likelihood of a risk event actually occurring (see Table 10.4). The assessment for each risk can range from extremely unlikely to highly likely. This controls the bias of very conservative organizations to inappropriately assess the importance of specific risks and consider them all as "Black Swan" risks which causes them to misapply corporate resources.

Finally, the assessment team considers whether effective risk mitigation measures are in place or reasonably expected to be in place. The efficiency of these measures is rated using the tool guidance. The range here runs from effective to ineffective or ad hoc. Each level of effectiveness is defined by the tool so that assessment participants can identify categorical risk control techniques and measures that could or should be applied. At the same time the team considers how effective these controls might be both from the position of the technique itself and the organization's ability to implement and manage the control.

After the risk has been assessed using the ERM Risk Evaluation tool (see Appendix B), a risk index is created by multiplying the rates for each of the three risk aspects together. The list of risks is then reordered according to the index value to determine the top risks associated with the project or the process change being assessed. The higher the score, the more critical the risk is to the organization. The company has mandated that any risk that exceeds a certain composite score must have a documented risk mitigation plan. Other factors such as very worrisome impact and significant compliance risk also merit special treatment. Composite scores and other risk indices that exceed a specific threshold require review by increasing levels of authority.

After scoring and ranking the risks, the assessment team determines a cut line. Those above the cut line will require significant attention by the project team and the other affected stakeholders. While the risks below the cut line may not merit special attention, the fact that these near-critical risks exist may warrant review and evaluation periodically should things change.

The advantages to this risk assessment process are manifold. First, risk identification and assessment are assessed by stakeholders who would be involved with or impacted by the change or new process that is the intended outcome of the project. Second, the scope of the assessment is narrowly focused to the project or initiative at hand and is simply written for all to understand. Third, the risk identification and assessment process takes two hours, not months. Fourth, a company agreed upon ranking and scoring methodology is used to prioritize risks according to impact, likelihood, and controllability. This allows everyone in the organization to think consistently about risk and how it is evaluated. The assessment process also has built in vetting with higher levels of authority which serves to alert the organization to criticality of risk associated with the project. Ultimately this process serves the organization by identifying critical risks prior to any change that is implemented as a result of the project team's work.

The final step in the risk assessment meeting process is to make sure that there is consensus with all participants. After the meeting, the risk management facilitator produces a summary of the discussion, including the ranked critical risks, the cut score and other information obtained at the meeting. This report is sent to participants for review and approval. Participants are not permitted after the meeting to change the results or ranking, only to correct inaccuracies.

Following the assessment team approval process, the risk management facilitator vets the information with the business area sponsor or risk owner (usually a senior executive) to review the results. The owner is usually not a participant in the assessment meeting. The advantage of this is that the assessment team of stakeholders can speak more freely at the meeting and add their local expertise to the discussion. The disadvantage to not inviting the project sponsor to the meeting is that the sponsor may have a completely different assessment of the risks associated with the projects. Sometimes sponsors have identified risks not considered critical by the assessment team as being most critical to the project. In other cases the sponsor may suggest a re-ordering of the risks based upon his/her understanding of the project and its risks. There could be many reasons for this difference of opinion. One, of course, is that senior executives may have a greater (or possibly lower) appetite for certain risks than those chosen for the assessment team. Sometimes the risk category is something that has the attention of senior executives at the moment which may color the executive's thinking. Other possible reasons include experience differences, better data, or discussions at senior levels to which others are not privy. Although rare, changes made by the senior risk owner are considered by the risk management team, internal audit and other areas as appropriate. Changes are negotiated and reconciled until an agreed upon list of evaluated risks is developed.

A caveat. This risk assessment process may not identify every critical risk. Practitioner assessment team members or the risk management staff may have little or no experience in the process or change being investigated and may, as a result, miss critical risks. Missing critical risks becomes more probable the less experienced team members are with the subject of the project. For example, the organization may be assessing a completely new product, process or acquisition that currently has no peer within the existing organization. In a situation like this, the risk assessment team may want to consider hiring outside experts to assist in the assessment process.

An advantage in this process is that during the assessment the original members of the project team are augmented with individuals from finance, IT, legal, audit and compliance. As the project evolves over the course of its mission, risks that were considered not critical may become critical due to changes in project scope or external environment. Factors such as new laws or changing market conditions may make insignificant risks significant. Part of the risk assessment process is monitoring results. This includes monitoring the project team's process and its eventual deliverables.

Success can also produce risk. A limitation that the risk management department faces is the significant increase in demand for its services especially for its project risk assessment process. With its limited resources the department risks being stretched too thin.

10.7 SURPRISES

Although the risk management team currently enjoys strong support for ERM, direct support for ERM can change as organizational leadership changes. While the major ERM frameworks (ISO 31000, COSO) and others emphatically point to the need for support for ERM from senior executives, these guidelines provide little guidance to ERM managers on how to navigate the inevitable cyclicality of support and the labyrinth of internal cultural challenges necessary for ERM to be fully blended into the organization. The risk management team understands that despite the lack of a "thou must" mandate from the C-suite, ERM and the risk assessment process is becoming more organically ingrained into the culture of this insurer. In many departments the assessment process has been inculcated into process. One of the reasons for this inculcation, which was mentioned before, is that risk management's mission in the assessment process is to support the person who asked for and sponsored the assessment in order to make him/her successful in the project. If the risk management team can do this, likely they will be called upon again to assist the sponsor in future projects. Risk management believes that this socialization of the ERM processes has been one of the biggest benefits of the ERM initiative.

10.8   HOW CAN AN ORGANIZATION SUSTAIN AN ERM INITIATIVE OVER TIME?

ERM practitioners have complained of organizational fatigue that makes it difficult to sustain ERM initiatives. One reason for this is that ERM may have been engaged to solve a particular problem. Once solved executives lose interest and the initiative loses critical support from the top. In other cases practitioners complain that the initiative turns into a compliance score card, a check-box process where once the items are completed, the initiative is shelved until it is time to produce the next scorecard.

This insurer has sustained its ERM initiative for more than a decade. Risk management explained why their program has endured. First, while the ERM initiative is involved in both strategic and operational projects, the assessment process risk management uses can be applied with near universality to all organizational projects. Second, while the C-suite has not always had ERM at the top of its attention list, the risk assessment process was agreed upon and approved by the executive committee and codified into company practices, procedures and a corporate ERM policy. Third, the tool produces a metric which is simple and easily understood by all stakeholders in the organization. Thresholds require additional consultation which helps inform the entire organization from top to bottom of critical risks this insurer faces and how (or whether) they can be controlled.

Within this insurer's risk management approach is a recognition of the difference between operational risk and strategic risk. Each requires risk management but within different time frames. At the strategic level and three to five year time horizon, it's about managing risks to provide strategic advantage (strategy formation) and "straightening the path" for strategic implementation. Sizeable opportunities present themselves more at the strategic level than the operational level. At the operational risk level the effort is about managing within tolerance levels in the present to eighteen month time frame. While operational changes do not often provide sizeable opportunities there are times when changes in process or more efficient uses of resources can be opportunistic in nature and may even serve to offset some of the cost of risk of the operation itself. In between the strategic and operational levels are intermediary risk themes. These can include managing risks for a major business process that are both operational and strategic in substance and in time horizon. The focus at this level could also be on intermediate-term trends that may impact the organization such as a mild recession or an improving economy. It is also the space where emerging (and potentially critical) risks are reviewed and discussed by officers for possible acceleration to a strategic discussion at the board and senior vice president level or returned to the operations level to be addressed there.

Next, the mantra of the risk management department is simplicity. This insurer's risk management team has boiled down the risk management process into four simple steps: identify, evaluate, mitigate or find the opportunity, and monitor. This simplified approach makes it easy for all employees to understand and remember.

There is a distinct difference in this insurer's risk management approach that is not often noted in other risk management process methodologies: mitigate or find the opportunity. What this insurer wants to understand is not only what the risk is but whether this risk has a positive opportunity to increase profitability, productivity, reputation or other valuable corporate assets. This subtle emphasis on the positive possibilities of risk can help alter the perception that risk management is all about pointing out the bad to the exclusion of the good. With this approach, project sponsors and others understand that efforts will be made in the assessment process to identify positive opportunities from the existence of risk that can be exploited.

The risk assessment process and tools have been simplified and improved over time and reports from risk assessment meetings are written for the average person, not a risk management specialist. The risk management team is also aware that it provides a coaching and consultative service that can command only limited amounts of time from busy employees and executives. The streamlined two hour assessment meeting is an example of this. At the same time the risk management team helps the assessment team, project team, executives and other stakeholders focus on critical risks – another simplification process.

Complexity has been a major stumbling block for other ERM initiatives. Consultants and others in early ERM initiatives tried to develop processes to identify every risk. The developed and deployed sophisticated analytical tools and instruments to sort, quantify, and assess impact and criticality. Often risk managers and executives became frustrated with the pace of the risk assessment process and/or the amount of time that individuals in the organization had to spend in risk assessment meetings answering surveys or providing more and more data to the risk consultants or risk management department.

Risk management at this insurer explained the assessment process with this analogy: it gets us to the right zip code, not to the street address. Rather than try to identify all the risks that face the organization, the risk management team concentrates on critical risks. This also means that if there is a need for sophisticated analysis this can be done on a small number of risks. A smaller number of critical risks makes it easier to consider how these correlate with each other which may increase occurrence probabilities or impact effects.

The risk management department is not distributed among business segments. The disadvantage is that the risk management team may not have specialists who have in-depth knowledge of the processes and procedures and products of the division. That said the annual companywide operational risk assessment by the risk management team is used to develop an annual audit plan which informs the compliance department and is used to drive new initiatives. However, the process that the risk management team has developed uses the expertise of the organization to understand risks and how to treat them. After all, the operational areas own the risks and are responsible for managing them. They are the ultimate risk managers and the ERM processes, including the risk assessment process and risk coaching, have served to make many participants better risk managers as a result.

An advantage of the centrality of risk management is that individuals have participated in most of the change projects and have a central risk database that they can use to determine whether there are risks of one project that could adversely impact other projects or produce correlated risks that might be detrimental to the organization.

The insurer has developed an ERM timeline that involves the different levels of risk ownership over the course of one year. Maintaining a consistent set of activities is important for many reasons. First, it allocates responsibilities and authorities to appropriate levels within the annual calendar. Second it provides temporal benchmarks for when certain reports or other results must be reported or meetings conducted to further the ERM discussion. To accomplish this objective the ERM program schedule is synched with the "rhythm" of the business and its tasks have been made part of the company's schedule of prescribed activities. Third, the ERM Program Timeline provides a framework for the ERM department to manage the ERM process and identify places where the process is being engaged and places where progress is slipping.

10.9   HOW DOES THIS INSURER RISK MANAGEMENT PROGRAM MEASURE ERM SUCCESS?

The persistent dilemma that all risk managers face is how to measure success. Success is preventing risks from producing problems and losses in the first place. Although there are some methods like comparing lawsuit or loss data to previous periods, it is difficult to measure what didn't happen. However, this insurer conducts regular employee surveys which include risk management questions that provide the risk management department with information on how well its acculturation efforts are working and how effective its processes are in identifying and assessing risk. ERM is embedded in most planning processes, in project management, internal audit, compliance and legal. Often it is key employees and executives who now deliver the message of why it is important to use the risk assessment process rather than the risk management department. Risk management has identified that one of the most critical measures of success is the increase in numbers of project managers and others who call the department when new projects or processes are being considered.

10.10   QUESTIONS FOR STUDENTS AND PRACTITIONERS

1. Even if coverage grants will not differ between one insurer and another in the Health Insurance Exchanges mandated by the Affordable Healthcare Act, no participating insurer can predict its cost of goods sold in advance because it cannot know the frequency and severity of its claims costs during the coverage period. Thus the premium charged for a year is only an estimate of claim payments, reserves, and adjustment expenses plus underwriting expenses and a provision for profit. With other commodities such as grains, oils, and the like, the cost of goods sold is known at the time the product is sold.
   (a) Speculate on how this difference in the health insurance commodity product might affect the marketplace for health insurance coverage in the exchanges.
   (b) Consider also what impacts this difference might have on theories of supply and demand as it relates to commodity products.
2. Company leaders change. Often new leaders bring new ideas and sometimes lead the organization in new directions. While ERM is flexible conceptually, and techniques and critical risks can be adjusted with strategy changes, a change in leadership and/or strategy can move ERM either in or out of what leaders spend time thinking about or managing.
   (a) Consider what techniques or steps that the risk manager can take to inculcate the ERM program into the culture of the organization so that it can continue to thrive even during the extremes of leadership and strategic changes with minimal disruption (proactive).
   (b) Next, consider this scenario: there has not been time to inculcate ERM into the culture of the organization. There is a change in leadership where ERM becomes important to management. How can the risk manager optimize the ERM program in this environment (reactive)?
   (c) Finally, consider the reverse: ERM is not important or much less important to the new leadership. How can the risk manager maintain a viable and productive ERM program in this environment (reactive)?
3. One issue with the success of an ERM initiative is something that this insurer is facing and others may face – having the risk management staff become stretched too thin. This could reduce the efficacy of the risk management initiative and as a consequence the ERM project may lose momentum over time which it may never get back again. One solution, of course, is to hire additional risk management staff to maintain the levels of service required.

What other solutions could you offer this insurer or other organizations when faced with this dilemma?

4. There can be differences within the organization in people's appetite for risk. This insurer indicated that some senior leaders assessed the impact and criticality of risks differently from risk assessment team members. Differences in risk perception and appetite are likely inevitable between persons hired to take risks and persons with little appetite for risk who see themselves as protecting the assets of the organization from risks. However, this disconnect between stakeholders in an organization can lead not only to conflicting messages but missed opportunities or risks taken that could have been better managed.
   (a) How would you identify and provide a metric that defines the target risk appetite of the organization?
   (b) How would you assess the risk appetite across the levels of the organization?
   (c) What techniques, processes, or activities would you recommend that an organization consider deploying that could produce an optimal consensus of the risk appetite throughout the enterprise?

5. Consider the risk assessment tool that this insurer has developed. As risk manager or consultant you want to adapt this tool for your organization, your client organization, or some other target organization.
   (a) How would you begin this process? Who would you consult?
   (b) What team of persons would you want to develop this tool?
   (c) From what you know about this organization today: assess the risk appetite of the organization.
   (d) After assessing risk appetite, modify the tool to meet the needs of that organization.
   (e) Then, identify the risk score and/or situations where risk assessment must be elevated to increasingly higher levels of management.
   (f) Finally, explain how you might influence the organization to adopt this tool and the circumstances under which this tool should be or must be used.

6. Organizations outsource critical services or processes and have critical suppliers. These suppliers and service providers are part of the extended enterprise of the organization. However, should critical suppliers or services be disrupted for any reason, critical services to customers of the enterprise may be interrupted which may be damaging to the enterprise's operations and reputation. Consider your organization, your client organization, or some other target organization.
   (a) Define what a critical supplier or product or service delivery partner is for this organization.
   (b) Identify critical suppliers and product or service delivery partners.
   (c) Develop a plan to influence and/or mandate that critical suppliers or product or service delivery partners have a business continuity plan that is in synch with that of the organization.

7. Develop a simple but complete explanation/illustration of risk and the risk management process for your organization that can be understood by all employees. Consider that a significant percentage of employees speak English as a second language and may not have learned to read English.

8. This insurer has a centralized management structure and a centralized risk management department. Consider how you might construct an effective ERM initiative in a company:
   (a) Where management is department driven and where there are business silos.
   (b) Where the company is split into self-contained product or service divisions whose senior executives are members of the senior leadership team.

(c) In a matrix organization where individual division heads may report up through multiple senior executives.

APPENDIX A

Project/Committee Risk Assessment – User Guide

The _____ department within the _____ group, is responsible for providing the governance, methodology, and overall oversight of the ERM Program at _____. Part of that responsibility includes the development of process tools like this Project/Committee Risk Assessment process.

This user guide provides an overview of the following areas:

- Purpose of the Enterprise Risk Management Program and how the Project/Committee Risk Assessment process supports the Program.
- Project/Committee Risk Assessment Process.
- Roles & Responsibilities related to the Project/Committee Risk Assessment (see Table 10.5).

PURPOSE

The purpose of Enterprise Risk Management (ERM) is to help reduce uncertainty associated with risk taking activities by providing a disciplined process and methodology to sustain stakeholder value and improve operational efficiency and effectiveness through better decision-making, thereby improving company value.

The Project/Committee Risk Assessment (PCRA) process is a tool in the ********* ERM program to help ensure efficient achievement of management's goals through a better understanding of significant risks and development of pro-active mitigation plans within a specific context (e.g., new product, significant project, "blue-printing" of entire subsidiaries, or process re-design).

PROJECT/COMMITTEE RISK ASSESSMENT PROCESS

Preparation

1. Assessment Sponsor identifies the need for a PCRA due to a significant change/addition of product, system and/or process.
2. Assessment Sponsor contacts ****** to identify a *** Facilitator for the PCRA.
3. *** Facilitator works with the Assessment Sponsor to identify needed participants. A person to capture the assessment information on an EXCEL file (real-time, on screen) is identified.
4. Assessment Sponsor schedules the PCRA for a 2-hour session in a room that has network connectivity and the wall space for a projector (*** may be able to schedule the session in *******, which contains all the needed technology).
5. Assessment Sponsor prepares a synopsis for the PCRA participants that includes the subject of the assessment to help set the context of the discussion. The synopsis should indicate any impacted products, systems, processes, and a time period.
6. Assessment Sponsor emails the synopsis and this PCRA User Guide to meeting participants ahead of the scheduled PCRA.

Assessment – Risk Identification and Evaluation

1. *** Personnel and the assessment sponsor confirm that all PCRA materials are ready and the technology is set up for the session.

Table 10.3 Risk impact

Risk Impact

(DO NOT consider existing controls or mitigating strategies or how often the impact may occur)

Impact Categories	(A) Financial Impact	(B)* *********	(C) ********	(D) **********	(E) **********	(F) *********	(G) **********	(H) **********	(I) **********	(J) *********
(1-2)	Insignificant	Insignificant	None	None	None	None	Consistent	Critical functions not impaired	Consistent	Relatively straight forward
(3-4)	Up to 10%	Inconvenient	Easily resolved/ Minor penalties	Small and temporary	None.	None	Consistent	Plan alterations required	Consistent	Low complexity
(5-6)	10-25%	Significant	Significant	Significant	Significant	Rating ********	Significantly inconsistent	Significant	Somewhat inconsistent	Moderately complex
(7-8)	25-50%	Serious, long-term	Serious	Serious, long-term	Serious	***** rating drop	Seriously inconsistent	Serious	Significantly inconsistent	Very complex
(9-10)	50-100%	Long-term impairment of **** functions	*****seize control	Catastrophic deterioration of ****	Going concern status impact	Drastically revised ******	Catastrophic deterioration of ********	****** cannot be achieved	Seriously inconsistent	Extremely complex

*Categories B-J denote different risks and their impact on the organization. For example, one might be weather, another might be regulation, and a third might be litigation.

Table 10.4   Risk Likelihood

Risk Likelihood (how likely the impact is to occur at selected level above)			Risk Control/Mitigation	
Likelihood	**Description (Probability)**		**Ranking**	**Description**
(1-2) Extremely unlikely	• Almost inconceivable that event will occur • Activity or event that occurs intermittently	(Less than 10%)	**(1-2)**	Effective, documented controls in place. Control self-assessment or independent review (e.g., internal audit) within in the past two years
(3-4) Unlikely but possible	• Event or activity occurs intermittently, not likely but could happen • Not know if event has occurred	(10-33%)	**(3-4)**	Effective, documented controls in place, but controls have not been independently reviewed.
(5-6) About as likely as not	• Event sporadic in nature, potential for infrequent occurrence • Has occurred rarely	(34-66%)	**(5-6)**	Controls documented but not always effective
(7-8) Likely	• Likely to occur sometimes (occurred infrequently) • Will occur often if events follow normal patterns	(67-90%)	**(7-8)**	Controls are documented but are not effective. Significant deficiencies have been identified.
(9-10) Expected	• Likely to occur many times (occurred frequently) • Will be continuously experienced if no action is taken to change events.	(Over 90%)	**(9-10)**	Undocumented controls. New controls

2. The Assessment Sponsor provides copies of the synopsis and kicks off the session detailing the background of the topic under assessment.
3. The *** facilitator will start the assessment session which includes:
   • 5–10 minute overview of ERM process.
   • 45–50 minutes of risk identification/brainstorming by PCRA participants.
   • 45–50 minutes or risk evaluation and ranking by PCRA participants.
   • 5–10 minute closing/next step discussion.

Post Assessment – Risk Mitigation and Monitoring

1. *** Facilitator emails the completed assessment to the PCRA participants. The assessment is in an Excel format and includes columns for mitigation plan information.
2. Assessment Sponsor is responsible for ensuring approved mitigation plans are identified for all significant risks and the updated assessment document is returned to the *** facilitator.

What is a significant risk?

1. Any scores above 200 require a Risk Mitigation plan
2. For a Project/Committee risk assessment, some type of mitigation/acceptance should be documented for the following scenarios:
   • Risks with Impact scores 7 and above.
   • Risks with Risk Indices 100 or above.
   • Any risk that has significant compliance implications.

Table 10.5   Summary – roles and responsibilities

Role	Responsibilities
Assessment Sponsor	1. Contact ***for a risk management facilitator. 2. Identify participants and schedule session. 3. Provide synopsis and this User Guide for participants ahead of the scheduled PCRA. 4. Obtain and/or develop mitigation plans for significant risks identified during the PCRA. Return mitigation plans to ***Facilitator.
PCRA participants	1. Be on time!! A 2-hour session is just enough time to complete an assessment. 2. Be prepared. Read the synopsis provided by the Meeting Host and ask preparatory questions if needed. 3. Be present mentally (don't reply to text messages and e-mails) and <u>actively participate</u>. Risk management is everyone's responsibility. As an identified Subject Matter Expert, the Meeting Host is relying on your input to help ensure potential/existing risks are identified and appropriately ranked.
***Facilitator	1. Provide the tools (technology, methodology) to host the PCRA. 2. Provide guidance throughout the PCRA related to ERM process/tools. 3. Provide oversight and governance of the ERM process to ensure that mitigation plans are provided timely and are reasonable for significant risks identified. 4. Be available for questions before, during and after the PCRA. 5. Follow-up on any risks with indices 200 or above.

APPENDIX B

Risk Evaluation Tool

PURPOSE	PROCESS
The purpose of Enterprise Risk Management (ERM) is to help reduce uncertainty associated with risk taking activities by providing a disciplined process and methodology to sustain stakeholder value and improve operational efficiency and effectiveness through better decision-making, thereby improving company value. The Project/Committee Risk Assessment (PCRA) process is a tool in the _____ ERM program to help ensure efficient achievement of management's goals through a better understanding of significant risks and development of pro-active mitigation plans within a specific context (e.g., new product, significant project, "blue-printing" of entire subsidiaries, or process re-design).	Assessment – Risk Identification and Evaluation 1. Project personnel and the assessment sponsor confirm that all PCRA materials are ready and the technology is set up for the session. 2. The Assessment Sponsor provides copies of the synopsis and kicks off the session detailing the background of the topic under assessment. 3. The facilitator will start the assessment session which includes: 1. 5–10 minute overview of ERM process 2. 45–50 minutes of risk identification/brainstorming by PCRA participants 3. 45–50 minutes or risk evaluation and ranking by PCRA participants 4. 5–10 minute closing/next step discussion

Case Study: Three Steps for Bringing Risk Management Back in House

Interviewee: Renee Reimer J.D., Chief Risk & Legal Operations Officer,
Memorial Hermann Health System

Interviewer: Christopher Ketcham, Ph.D., CPCU, CRM, CIC, CFP®,
Formerly Visiting Assistant Professor, University of Houston Downtown,
Houston, Texas; Garnet Valley, Pennsylvania
Date: November 30, 2012

11.1 MEMORIAL HERMANN

Memorial Hermann (MH) is a 107-year-old not-for-profit healthcare system in the greater Houston Texas community. The area served by MH today has a population base of 6.14 million, which is expected to grow to 6.71 million by 2016. MH is one of the largest not-for-profit healthcare system in the state of Texas and has a 23.5% market share [Note: using 2011 data] in the Expanded Greater Houston Metropolitan Service Area (MSA[1]) for inpatient services through 12 hospitals. MH also has other service operations in 171 locations. The MH package of services includes: inpatient hospital delivery services, outpatient ambulatory services, home health, drug rehabilitation and alcohol treatment, and retail services including diagnostic, laboratory, sports medicine, rehabilitation, and imaging. MH's trauma center is one of the nation's busiest. In addition MH operates one of the only air ambulance services in the region and has its own health insurance company providing health benefits for its employees and others.

The Federal government in the US requires hospitals to measure and report patient safety and other clinical indicators to show not only that hospitals comply with various standards, and regulations but also to provide consumers and others with comparative quality clinical outcomes data to make informed choices about medical care. Having excellent performance indicators is becoming critical to hospital accreditation and reputation. These measures of quality and patient safety are public information and are used by various governmental agencies and healthcare quality improvement organizations. MH has been recognized as a national leader in quality and patient safety. MH was awarded the 2012 Eisenberg Patient Safety Award by the National Quality Forum (NQF) and the Joint Commission. The award recognized MH as a national leader in delivering safe, effective healthcare with a patient-centered focus. Thompson Reuters recognized MH as one of America's top 5 Large Health Systems and also among the top 15 health systems in the nation in quality in 2012. The Delta Group recognized MH as America's number one quality hospital for overall care for the last two consecutive

---

[1] Includes Harris County (Houston) and eleven surrounding counties.

years. Seven years in a row MH has been cited as being one of healthcare's "100 Most Wired". MH is also classified as a distinguished healthcare system because of its clinical excellence. Four MH hospitals are listed among America's 50 Best Hospitals by HealthGrades®, ranking among the top 1 percent in the nation. Six MH hospitals are listed among America's 100 Top Hospitals® by Thompson Reuters.

Memorial Hermann is the result of a 1997 merger of two not-for-profit health systems in the Houston area. At the time of the merger each of the two systems had a risk management department. However, leadership at that time decided that it was prudent to outsource risk management to a third party administrator. This was the case until 2009 when Renee Reimer was hired as the chief risk officer, responsible for risk management and insurance services for the organization. Her boss, the chief legal officer, asked Reimer to study whether continuing to outsource risk management in whole or in part was still a good idea. This case is a summary of the process taken by Reimer and her team when it was determined that risk management should be brought back in house.

11.2   THE DECISION TO BRING RISK MANAGEMENT BACK IN HOUSE

MH's risk management function had been outsourced to a single TPA (third party administrator) firm for approximately ten years. The TPA managed the claims function and provided loss control and other services. There were TPA employees on site acting as a corporate risk management department for the health system and interfacing with a risk liaison in each hospital. Shortly before Reimer joined MH, the general counsel, known within MH as the chief legal officer, who had been with MH for almost three years when Reimer joined the organization, commissioned an independent assessment of the risk management function as he was uncertain whether the TPA model was an effective risk management structure for MH. When asked to study whether the existing model was the best way for MH to manage risk, Reimer not only reviewed the findings of that independent study from the outside firm but also did her own assessment. An attorney in the state of Texas, Reimer has almost 30 years of legal experience, with approximately half of those years spent specifically in healthcare.

The studies suggested that the circumstances that led to the initial outsourcing decision no longer existed. Second, MH had grown considerably in size and complexity to warrant both a high level of direct accountability by a senior leader and their own team, and a strategic approach to the management and mitigation of risks. A third critical factor that these studies uncovered was that the outsourcing model, while effective in handling claims, was less effective in proactive data mining and trend analysis that could be used to create actionable risk and quality initiatives to prevent or mitigate risk events in the future.

Reimer and MH began a three-step approach to re-establish a risk management function in the organization and create a strategic approach to management of risks. Step one was laying the groundwork or a design–build phase to create the foundation for a high functioning internal risk management department including adding the necessary business intelligence data structure. Step two was the introduction into the organization of an enterprise risk management (ERM) framework and the establishment of an enterprise risk council at the highest level of the organization. Step three, which was launched in 2011 and continues today, is focused on the maturation of the ERM approach to risk identification and management at a strategic level as well as the expansion of and integration of ERM principles throughout the organization. Work in 2013 will consider how to improve the quantification of the impact of various risks to MH in

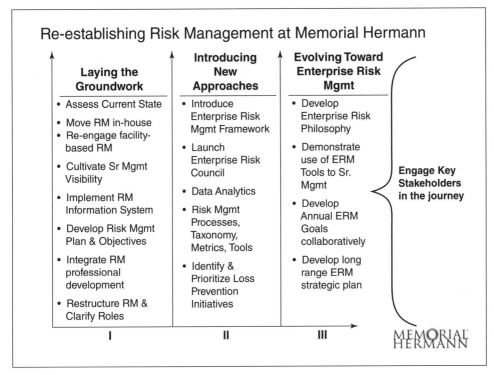

Figure 11.1 Re-establishing the Risk Management at Memorial Hermann. Reproduced by permission. Copyright © 2013 Memorial Hermann. All rights reserved.

order to move beyond a financial impact "score" and to a narrative description methodology for better articulation of the potential impact of key organizational risks. Figure 11.1 outlines the three-step approach Memorial Hermann has used to reestablish the risk management function and engage ERM.

11.3 STEP ONE – LAYING THE GROUNDWORK: RE-ESTABLISH RISK MANAGEMENT

Risk management had not disappeared from MH. Each hospital had talented and experienced registered nurse clinical risk liaisons focused primarily on working on the day-to-day patient safety clinical risk issues for their individual hospital. There was the centralized risk control function of the TPA and claims were being competently managed and resolved when turned over to the TPA, yet there was minimal interaction between the individual hospital-based risk liaisons or alignment of risk management initiatives across the health system. There was insufficient appreciation of the value of bringing the risk management staff together for professional development or collaborative work. Risk management had low visibility amongst senior leaders in the organization. The insurance services and risk transfer program, while managed competently by on-site TPA staff for many years, had also grown more complex requiring the expertise of more skilled and experienced insurance services professionals.

When the relationship with the TPA was terminated Reimer was still a new employee at MH. She turned to the vision, brand promise and cultural values espoused by the organization for guidance in how to proceed in re-establishing the risk management function within the organization to create the necessary alignment. MH had an aspirational vision to be "best of the best." MH values the whole over the individual parts of the system to advance health and deliver the best possible health solutions. Enterprise-wide thinking is a key consideration for any organization that wants to embark upon an enterprise risk strategy. If an organization continues to maintain independent risk silos then it will be difficult to build an approach that can be engaged throughout the organization.

Reimer saw that the key strategies of the company known as "Big Dots" would be a good place to begin the alignment of risk. This was also helpful because when she introduced ERM to the organization, what had been developed to date in the risk management function was consistent with what would be necessary to the development of a strong ERM program.

MH's "Big Dots" align with its current vision and brand promise as shown in Figure 11.2. Vision – be the pre-eminent health system in the US by advancing the health of those we serve through our physicians, employees and other partners to deliver best health solutions while we relentlessly pursue quality and value. Brand Promise – We advance health. Overall the structure of strategy is organized around three dimensions:

1. Care delivery.
2. Health solutions.
3. Physician integration.

The Big Dots are distributed into six categories:

1. Quality and Safety.
2. Patients.
3. Operational Excellence.
4. Growth.
5. People.
6. Physicians.

Some of the individual Big Dots include:

- High reliability patient care.
- Advancing inpatient quality and safety – the physician dimension.
- Employee safety culture – safe work environment.
- Patient, physician, employee and member satisfaction.
- Expand number of covered lives (members) in insurance program.
- Medicare improvement – reduction in Medicare opportunity days.
- In-network utilization – keeping customers within the MH system.
- Market share growth – care delivery.
- Medical Home expansion – expanding the primary care medical home network.

As with any good strategic plan, the Big Dots are reassessed each year but must align with the overall strategic plan.

When the risk management function was re-established it was determined that it would report up through the general counsel via the chief risk officer. Reimer is in charge of both the day-to-day operations of the system's legal department under the direction of the chief legal officer as well as responsible for the risk management department. There are fourteen

OUR BRAND COMPASS

Our Vision

Memorial Hermann will be the preeminent health system in the U.S. by advancing the health of those we serve through trusted partnerships with physicians, employees and others to deliver the best possible health solutions while relentlessly pursuing quality, quality and value.

Our Brand Promise

We advance health.

Our Culture

Innovative: We discover, develop and implement new ideas, technologies, partnerships and processes.

Accountable: We accept responsibility for our actions and decisions and the impact they have on those we serve.

Empowered: We create and embrace change, readily adapting to new situations and encouraging all to be part of the solution.

Collaborative: We build trusting relationships through open communication and productive teamwork integrating all parties to create the best solution.

Compassionate: We genuinely care about people. We are sensitive to the needs of others and strive to make a difference.

Results Oriented: We make timely decisions. We take an intentional approach, integrating data and evidence in all decision-making to achieve desired outcomes.

One Memorial Hermann: We value the whole over the individual parts of the System.

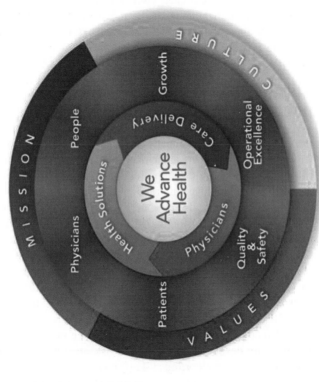

Figure 11.2 Brand compass outlining Memorial Hermann's vision, brand promise, and culture. Copyright © 2013 Memorial Hermann. All rights reserved.

people in RM in the corporate office responsible for five key functional areas: (1) claims and litigation management; (2) loss control and prevention; (3) risk data analytics; (4) insurance services and risk transfer; (5) emergency management; and (6) system policy and procedure governance. Thirteen risk managers are located "in the field" covering individual hospitals and the outpatient ambulatory care facilities and services. Further, three additional people devote a portion of their time as risk liaisons to be an additional set of "eyes and ears" or "boots on the ground" in the outpatient care areas. Field risk managers are RNs but unlike traditional hospital risk management departments their scope of responsibility is not just clinical but includes ERM.

Risk Management departments in many organizations have traditionally reported through finance. Reimer believes that for MH, risk management is more effective reporting through legal because so many of the issues associated with risk management at MH have a legal or regulatory dimension. From the beginning of the re-establishment of the risk management department it was determined that the chief risk officer (CRO) should be an attorney. In addition to the CRO, the RM department has three attorneys, including an RN-JD, and a paralegal. The senior leaders at MH are called chiefs. Reimer is also a chief and sits on the president's council. As a result, risk management is visible at the highest levels of the organization. Being involved at the highest level of the organization has helped to facilitate the re-establishment of the risk management program and made it possible for an ERM program to be implemented.

In addition to owning a health insurance company providing health benefits for its employees and external member customers, MH owns a Cayman incorporated captive insurance company through which it self-insures its healthcare professional liability (malpractice coverage), general liability, auto liability and employee injuries.

But that is today. When Reimer reestablished the risk management department her first objective was to obtain data for better decision making, clarify roles, fill leadership gaps, and implement key processes to ensure that the risk management function was operating effectively with regard to the basics of risk management (risk identification, loss control, claims analysis, and insurance/risk transfer). Reimer began by meeting with senior leaders from across the healthcare system to apprise the leaders of her assessment of the current state of RM, to provide them with a vision for the future, and to engage them in supporting the alignment of the field risk managers with the new re-established corporate RM function. In transitioning away from the TPA model, a new claims management information system was needed as well as replacement of an internally developed and designed risk identification variance system. The claims management and variance reporting systems now in place not only enable claims capture and payment but also produces relevant data reports for risk analysis and proactive risk mitigation initiatives.

MH had not utilized loss control in any structured way and its insurance needs were more complex so Reimer began a process of shoring up loss control and insurance services by bringing in new professionals to the organization. Reimer brought in data analysts to begin the process of analyzing incidents and claims for causes, outcomes, and prevention and mitigation opportunities. Field risk managers were brought together on a monthly basis with the corporate office risk management team for professional development, common risk issues discussion, and for alignment of risk objectives. The risk manager role was expanded beyond clinical risk management to encompass an ERM approach and new job descriptions developed. Reserve guidelines and risk management plans were also developed and documented and Reimer brought in more attorneys and RNs into the function.

Reimer established a Claims Authority Group (CAG). The CAG includes, the chief financial officer, chief risk officer, chief legal officer, and chief medical officer. CAG meets on an ad hoc basis to discuss only claims reserved above one million dollars. One of Reimer's attorneys is tasked with presenting an assessment of the case in a confidential written pre-trial or pre-mediation summary. During the review process, the attorney asks the CAG to make a decision on the claim and either authorize a settlement amount or direct that the case proceed to trial. The benefits of using a CAG are two-fold. First, the decision is made by a senior team of leaders who are most likely to appreciate the potential broader implications of the claim beyond its financial impact. Second, these large claims make senior leaders aware of the cumulative impact of risks to the organization and have served to raise the visibility of the risk management function and alert the organization to important risk mitigation opportunities.

Reimer reasons that leaders most often make decisions based on data and numbers. Therefore risk management began to show claims data to a broader audience of executives and tasked the in-house risk management attorneys to review all cases resolved in the concluding year and prepare and present a report for senior leadership at each of the business segments. The report included what the claim was about, the reserve, what was paid, and what was learned. The CEOs and senior leadership in the divisions had not seen this data before, but quickly learned how the information could be used to better manage risks in their areas of accountability. She explained how risk managers review and triage over seventeen thousand variance reports annually although very few ultimately result in claims or suits.

However, just having the basics of the risk management function operating effectively was not enough. Gathering and presenting data was not enough. Developing good risk management practices in the field was not enough. Reimer reasoned that there were risks that a traditional risk management department was not likely to be able to address at the operational level. She determined that an ERM approach at the highest strategic level was an important next step. Figure 11.3 demonstrates the risk management journey at Memorial Hermann and the three risk management approaches that are now in place.

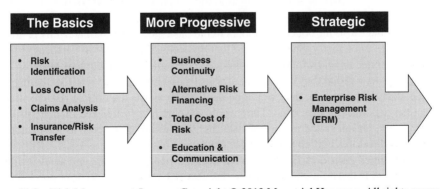

Figure 11.3 Risk Management Journey. Copyright © 2013 Memorial Hermann. All rights reserved.

11.4   SECOND STEP – INTRODUCING NEW APPROACHES: THE ERM COUNCIL

Even before establishing the ERM Council, Reimer began to introduce the concept of ERM to senior executives. MH did not have a forum to look across the organization to assess interrelated risks and potential impact on the organization or how multiple risks could correlate. She determined that an advisory group of executives should serve together as a coordinating body to look at diverse risks to the organization from whatever source. The advisory group is called the ERM Council and was chartered to look more expansively and from a strategic point of view at risks in order to understand the interrelatedness and cumulative impact on the organization. The council, formed in 2010, consists of executives who have a broad depth of knowledge and expertise in their own areas of accountability but also know the MH strategic objectives. They have the knowledge, authority and influence to be able to assess risks at a strategic level, prioritize the importance of a risk on the organization and assess the potential impact of such risks. Second, they have the ability to bring resources to strategic risk issues and focus the organization on key critical risks. The council includes the System's:

- Chief Medical Officer.
- Chief Financial Officer.
- Chief Legal Officer.
- Chief Operations Officer.
- Chief Information Officer.
- Strategic Planning Officer.
- Marketing & Communications Officer.
- Chief of Facilities.
- Chief Risk Officer.
- Community Benefits Officer.
- Internal Audit and Compliance Officer.
- CEO of the owned insurance company.
- 2 physician organization chiefs (physician network/ACO and employed physicians).
- 3 CEOs of the largest hospitals in the system.
- Chief Human Resources officer.

This council represents individuals who have the greatest influence and understanding of MH. The council meets three to four times each year.

The first meeting in 2010 was an introduction to the concept of ERM. Before the meeting Reimer sent seminal articles on enterprise risk management to the council to read. During that meeting Reimer also introduced members to the basic goals of risk management and the concept of risk as uncertainty. She explained that this council had a broad perspective of the organizational strategies and would have a unique understanding of the major business areas of the company. As a group they could look at risks from a big picture view. Combining their experience, data, and intuition, they would be the team to assess the critical risks to strategy that affect the organization over time. They would develop in a formalized manner, using an ERM framework, an integrated picture of risks and they would then serve as the champions of helping MH develop a unified approach for risk action planning.

The ERM Council considers ERM as both a decision making process and analytic framework. The council is tasked with considering business risks from an enterprise portfolio perspective. They use simple tools like an online survey tool to identify potential risks, facilitated group sessions to prioritize and rank risks, heat maps to identify the priorities, and facilitated small group meetings to fully articulate the identified risks, risk triggers, consequences, and current controls in place.

The committee's charter was clear: their focus was strategic. They needed to develop at the strategic level a common language and methodology for the identification and management of strategic business risks based on their collective perspectives of the risk tolerance of the organization in the context of the strategic objectives. They considered risks within a three-year horizon in order to concentrate their view and limit their attention on critical business risks that will affect the organization in the calculable future. In essence the committee is tasked with assessing: What are the risks to our organization achieving its strategic goals over the next three years?

11.5   THE THIRD STEP – EVOLVING TOWARDS ENTERPRISE RISK MANAGEMENT: NARRATIVE RISK DESCRIPTION

Part of the third step in MH's process to reinstitute the risk management program is the development of a narrative approach for expressing the potential impact of certain risks, which cannot be adequately or accurately reflected by a numeric or quantitative method. As this is a step that has just been embarked upon there are no results. However, the concept of a narrative approach to risk management may not be familiar to many risk managers.

Traditionally risk management has used a quantitative approach to defining risks, probability or likelihood and impact severity in terms of financial costs. Narrative knowledge has found its way into law, medicine and other professions and it deserves consideration in risk management. The narrative approach to medicine uses narrative to explain complex events (Charon, 2001a, 2001b, 2005, 2007). Medical events not only include the physical malady but also the person, their circumstances, and their environment. The need for narrative is no different in risk management. Events or incidents often require that the issues be put into context or have complex origins, which may have antecedents that may have contributed to the event or incident. Nor are all assets of an organization easily quantified. Reputation is a good example of a risk that is often viewed as an intangible and therefore difficult to quantify and best expressed through narrative reporting when numerical expression can be unreliable. For hospitals the narrative in risk management could be constructed similarly to that of medicine. First is active listening. The second is putting into writing what happened, beyond the basics of the incident. What was the environment at the time; were there emotional issues that surrounded the event or incident; and what happened in the days, weeks, or moments that led to the event? The third is sharing the narrative with those affected by it whether it is an individual or an entire organization.

Nor is the narrative just for ex post facto analysis of events. Narrative can be used to describe critical risks that the organization faces. This is important for multiple reasons. First, the narrative can more fully explain the problem and how it might produce loss. Second, many people are more attuned and responsive to stories because they help individuals to visualize the concept. Third, narratives more fully describe the circumstances of the organization and may lead management to understand risk more holistically in association with attitudes, aptitudes, and environment that may produce or exacerbate losses.

The narrative in risk management has received limited attention in the literature but is something that should be more fully researched and considered.

11.6   TANGIBLE RESULTS AT MH

The council initially identified sixty potential risks in operations, financial, reputation, hazard, environmental, legal, and regulatory areas. These 60 risks were prioritized by impact on the organization. As a result of the impact assessment the list was distilled down to 12 critical risks. After a facilitated process of fully articulating the critical risks, the council assigned a champion for each of the 12 risks and asked the champions and their teams to provide the council with a more in-depth view of each risk, current controls or risk mitigation efforts, and to develop an action plan designed to minimize the risk impact or likelihood.

One of the top strategic risks identified by the council was the significant and increasing uninsured population and the resulting impact on the healthcare system. Texas leads the nation in uninsured residents and only 53% of Texas employers provide health insurance for their employees. In the Houston area alone, more than 31% of the population does not have health insurance and 72% of the uninsured are employed by small employers who do not offer healthcare coverage, or whose coverage options are unaffordable. Many of the uninsured tend not to get healthcare on a routine basis to manage chronic conditions and more than half of all patients entering emergency centers are seeking care that could be provided in a community based clinic, overcrowding emergency facilities and delaying care for the truly critically ill. MH is a primary healthcare safety net in the Houston area communities for the uninsured but as their numbers increase, the safety net is stretched to its breaking point.

The assigned champion for the uninsured patient project developed a five-prong action plan. One of those initiatives was to expand an emergency center navigator pilot program in a hospital campus emergency center to help uninsured patients begin the process of obtaining a medical home for care of their future non-critical but chronic or acute illnesses more affordably and conveniently. The healthcare navigator connects them with lower-cost community healthcare providers who can provide a medical home for future healthcare concerns. The navigator follows up with each patient to ensure that they have used the referral and are satisfied with the care they received. As a part of this action plan, three hospitals created a primary care center next to each of their emergency centers to care for patients with non-critical care needs that could be appropriately treated in this care setting. One of the hospitals found in the first few months that 34 percent of patients presenting to their emergency center could be appropriately cared for in the primary care facility; and it was 43 percent at a second hospital. The three participating hospitals have experienced a combined 79 percent reduction in non-critical emergency room visits since the program began. This is a win–win for both the patient and the hospital. The patient receives appropriate high quality care and the hospital has a lower uninsured cost burden for non-critical care provided in the hospital emergency center.

Traditional operational risk management would not have considered the strategic business risk to the organization of the growing uninsured population nor would it have the authority or likely even the capability to propose options to mitigate this significant risk. While the uninsured initiatives cannot make the problem go away it is making the costs to the organization less significant. What is also important is that the ERM council is made up of key individuals who (1) understand the strategic direction of the enterprise, (2) represent most major segments in the enterprise, and (3) have significant decision-making and budgetary authority to make changes happen. They meet regularly not only to continually reassess the critical risks that face the medical system but also to report on progress in each of the initiatives that is associated with critical risk. Reimer periodically informs the system's board as well as the team of risk managers and others of the identified strategic critical risks and the projects in play to mitigate and manage the risks. As a result the council's work is distributed throughout the organization. The work of the ERM Council also highlights how an organization can accomplish risk mitigation without engaging in silo thinking. The uninsured problem solutions required the engagement of many different departments and disciplines both at the local and organizational level. The side-by-side emergency room–primary care concept required a reorganization of hospital services, new ways of screening, regulatory consideration, and reallocation of physician and nursing staff. Without silo thinking the organization was able to develop new procedures and programs in a very short period of time because affected parties worked together to put the enterprise first and turf second.

11.7   RECOMMENDATIONS FOR OTHER RISK MANAGERS

Reimer suggested that there is no cookie-cutter approach to risk management even to similar organizations in the same industry. Every enterprise is different in what it does, its approach to the business, and its culture. Therefore each risk management program will be unique.

Second, Reimer was new to the organization when she was asked to rebuild the risk management function. She could not learn the intricacies of MH in the short period of time she had on the job. Instead, she has had to engage people who know the organization well and her role has become to facilitate and to engage the organization's leadership to take ownership of the enterprise's strategic risks. She has worked to bring alignment to the work of the nurse risk managers so that collectively the risk management team looks beyond just clinical risk issues and considers a broader enterprise risk management approach to their work.

Reimer explained that the risk management group in any organization has to shine some light on what risk managers do, provide data to leaders, and engage leadership in a dialogue regarding strategic risks. When management is engaged on risk issues the organization's view towards risk management will change.

11.8   QUESTIONS FOR STUDENTS AND PRACTITIONERS

1. How could a narrative approach be used to better identify and assess risks that are not easily quantified?
2. MH identified one of its greatest risks as the cost of the growing uninsured population. In keeping with its mission of quality care it realigned its services to make these less costly. What other non-traditional strategic risks do you think that the ERM Council could have identified?
3. Outsourcing of services has its place in risk management. However, it may not be the total solution. What would be the circumstances under which an organization could consider to outsource some of its risk management function? What would be the controls and assurances that an organization should put in place to make sure that what has been outsourced meets the continuing needs of the organization and is consistent with its strategy, vision, and brand promise?

REFERENCES

Charon, R. (2001a). Narrative medicine. *JAMA: The Journal of the American Medical Association*, 286(15), p. 1897.

Charon, R. (2001b). Narrative medicine: form, function, and ethics. *Annals of Internal Medicine*, 134(1), p. 83.

Charon, R. (2005). Narrative medicine: Attention, representation, affiliation. *Narrative*, 13(3), pp. 261–270.

Charon, R. (2007). What to do with stories: the sciences of narrative medicine. *Canadian Family Physician*, 53(8), p. 1265.

Case Study: University of California

Interviewee: Grace Crickette, Chief Risk Officer, Office of Risk Services,
Office of the President, University of California, Oakland, California

Interviewer: Christopher Ketcham, Ph.D., CPCU, CRM, CIC, CFP®,
Formerly Visiting Assistant Professor, University of Houston Downtown,
Houston, Texas; Garnet Valley, Pennsylvania
Date: March 4, 2013

12.1 THE UNIVERSITY OF CALIFORNIA AND THE OFFICE OF RISK SERVICES

The University of California System is one public university system that is part of California's three-tier public higher education system under the State's Master Plan for Higher Education.[1] University of California campuses are located in: Berkeley, Davis, Irvine, Los Angeles, Merced, Riverside, San Diego, San Francisco, Santa Barbara, and Santa Cruz. The system, including university campuses and medical centers, has an operating budget of over twenty-three billion dollars, employs approximately 190,000 employees, and has 230,000 students. In addition to operations in California, the University has employees, students, and/or research facilities in most countries around the world. Some of these foreign operations may be as large as an institute, a semester abroad program, or the presence could be as small as an archaeological dig.

The Office of Risk Services was formed in 2004 and is part of the University of California Office of the President.[2] Grace Crickette, Chief Risk Officer (CRO), was hired in 2004 to develop the enterprise risk management (ERM) initiative at UC. She had previously served for 16 years as VP of Risk Services for United Rentals, a large commercial equipment and tool rental company. Today Crickette has 23 direct reports in various specialties from safety, business continuity, environment, health, risk financing, laboratory safety, construction, travel, general and auto liability, workers' compensation, employment practices and professional liability.

Unlike for-profit enterprises that develop strategic statements, many public universities and systems rely upon mission statements to guide their initiatives and frame their business model. The University's mission has remained the same since 1883:

"The distinctive mission of the University is to serve society as a center of higher learning, providing long-term societal benefits through transmitting advanced knowledge, discovering new

---

[1] The University of California System is separate from and has no authority over the California State University (CSU) system or the California Community Colleges system.

More information on California Higher Education can be found at:
http://en.wikipedia.org/wiki/University_of_California
http://en.wikipedia.org/wiki/California_State_University
http://en.wikipedia.org/wiki/California_Community_Colleges
http://en.wikipedia.org/wiki/California_Master_Plan_for_Higher_Education

[2] Website: http://ucop.edu/

knowledge, and functioning as an active working repository of organized knowledge. That obligation, more specifically, includes undergraduate education, graduate and professional education, research, and other kinds of public service, which are shaped and bounded by the central pervasive mission of discovering and advancing knowledge."

Each of the campuses in the system also has a mission statement, which helps to differentiate the institution for faculty, students, government, and the community. As with most public universities, the core mission of the University of California includes three basic components: education, community service, and research. For the University of California and its campuses, the largest source of funding is not tuitions, state allocations, or private donations but research grants. UC also manages several countrywide research grant programs.[3]

12.2 WHY ERM?

In the mid-1990s the control and financial management groups (now the CFO division[4]) became interested in the COSO framework that had just been developed by the Treadway Commission and PricewaterhouseCoopers. An early ERM initiative, it was developed by the accounting profession to better define financial controls, audits, and assurance against risk. In 1995 the UC Board of Regents adopted the COSO framework. In 2004 Grace Crickette was hired to begin the ERM initiative and in 2011, the regents expanded their original endorsement of the COSO framework to formally adopt ERM for the system.

When Grace was hired she explained to management that she would need six months to visit campuses and speak to individual departments to better understand the risks, operations, culture, and needs of the university system. It quickly became apparent that data was the most critical issue for the organization. Data collection, aggregation and management were decentralized and there was no clear data taxonomy that could be applied across the system. Crickette and management realized that in order to monitor operations they would need advanced tools to extract and analyze large quantities of disparate data. They soon purchased the COGNOS business intelligence system and adapted it to their need, establishing the first Safety Index dashboard. As the information from this dashboard was analyzed, new key performance indicators were developed that led to the birth of the university's Enterprise Risk Management Information System (ERMIS), a collection of dashboards, reports and modeling tools that help decision makers focus scarce resources.

A few months after her hiring, in February 2005, Crickette conducted the first UC Risk Summit for one hundred individuals involved in risk management at the various campuses and locations. By 2012 the annual Risk Summit attendance exceeded eight hundred. The Risk Summit is a three-day conference devoted to workshops, planning, and awards. In fact, the Risk Summit is the largest conference that is conducted by the University. In addition to educational sessions, awards are presented to campuses and operations that achieve the best results according to system-wide key performance indicators (KPIs). Campuses and operations compete for these coveted awards, which are prominently displayed in each chancellor's office. Awards include excellence in ERM, insurance programs, risk treatment, business continuity and emergency management, loss control, and healthcare and patient safety.

---

[3] UC Office of Risk Services website: http://www.ucop.edu/enterprise-risk-management/index.html
[4] Website: http://ucop.edu/finance-office/index.html

12.3 CRITICAL STRATEGIC RISKS

The University is funded through a variety of sources including federal and state/local government, private industry, research, clinical funding (medical centers) and student fees. Campuses' budgets often must direct these funds to the appropriate earmarks. Grant money, for example, must fulfil the specific requirements and rules. Unlike private sector funds where revenue can be put into a general fund and dedicated to strategic initiatives, universities must accede to targeted accounts funding. In contrast with businesses, general revenue represents a small portion of the system's overall operating budget. For UC the number one risk for the past three years has been budget impairment, meaning the overall budget is impaired because a significant amount of money cannot be used for general purposes because it is allocated towards specific projects, research, activities, or special purposes. Because of this and other reasons traditional strategic planning is not appropriate.

Crickette explained the different levels of strategy associated with the system. At the highest level, the State of California has a Master Plan, begun in 1960 for higher education, which includes goals for the 10 campuses of the University of California, 23 California State University campuses, and 108 campuses for the California Community College System. The Master Plan created a framework by which the California public higher education schools could establish courses of study (majors and minors) as well as allocation of funded research dollars, and university and community college matriculation and graduation goals. The governor appoints regents at the UC level and the regents are tasked with shared governance over the university's strategy.

Campuses focus strategy using long-term development plans that include campus footprint, buildings and infrastructure, and outreach. For example UC Santa Cruz determined there was a need to develop a mini-campus in Silicon Valley in order to build a stronger relationship with the university and high tech firms in the area. UC Riverside saw that there was a need for a medical school in the Riverside community because of the dearth of medical professionals and facilities in the area. Typically the long-term development plans are five years, sometimes longer. ERM is an integral part of these major long-term initiatives from the planning through the implementation stages. Risk identification, control and transfer, and monitoring become part of these long-term projects as they become campuses themselves or part of another institution.

Crickette emphasized that at UC, ERM integrates with large projects such as the medical school in Riverside. Also ERM has been instrumental as the system begins to migrate from a decentralized payroll system to a system-wide payroll system. ERM tools are also appropriately applied when a new initiative is proposed for a foreign country. Crickette suggested that long-term planning is the level where ERM has had the most success. In such projects,[5] one or more senior executives will request an ERM review.

Smaller initiatives that hit the radar also conduct an ERM review but Crickette is pragmatic that not all projects receive such risk management attention. Often an ERM review is engaged when a scientist, administrator, or local risk management professional contacts the Office of Risk Services for advice to solve a problem. The key strategy at this level for the Office of Risk Services is to treat the problem as an opportunity, asking the question, "How do we get to yes?" After the problem is presented as an opportunity and analyzed as such, solutions are explored that often make what seemed like an impossible risk scenario a plausible and feasible opportunity.

---

[5] See office of the president organizational chart: http://ucop.edu/business-operations/_files/opchart.pdf

At the next level are the grant programs, which are generally applied for by professors, departments, or schools. Grant recipients are involved with planning as they apply for and obtain funding. Generally an ERM review is not conducted at this level with risks associated with obtaining grants nor is it involved in the grant process itself. However the risk of the project or research funded by the grant are often the subject of an ERM review at the local campus level, sometimes with consultation from the Office of Risk Services. Researchers are required to gain permission from IRB (Institutional Review Boards) for any human subject research. ERM reviews are conducted for new laboratories, sites, experiments or other operations associated with the grant project. The Office of Risk Services provides tools that help people in various operations and disciplines identify, mitigate/prevent, finance, and monitor their inherent project and grant risks. Education and a wide variety of treatment options are available, depending upon the project. New tools and risk management processes have been developed for grants and projects that have unique risk opportunities and exposures to loss. When projects are implemented they are monitored using system-wide and institution-specific dashboards. The ERMIS draws data from systems at all the campuses and medical centers, and all campuses and medical centers have authorized users who are able to view and run reports on their data.

As previously mentioned, universities do not have traditional strategic plans. In addition to helping local campuses provide a strong ERM framework for their continuing operations, the ERM initiative also provides strategic planning tools for novel new initiatives. Project teams examine the risks of new initiatives. Enterprise risk management: identification, assessment, treatment and monitoring, become part of the project business plan. In effect, instead of assessing risk to strategy, strategic planning is embedded in the risk management process.

Universities in most states are facing shrinking state and direct federal governmental funding. They actively search for opportunities from grants, patents, commercial enterprises and services, and other alternative sources for operating revenue. The risks of not having adequate resources can impact community, teaching, and research activities and exacerbate crumbling infrastructure issues. It would be valuable for universities and others in the risk management and business communities to come together to evaluate the proposition that higher education is a business. This includes the entrepreneurial but competitive process of obtaining grants. Considering the university in business terms will raise many questions of ethics, community service obligations, conflicts of interest, freedom of speech, and other issues that may compromise university missions if not properly accounted for and controlled. However, the specter of a university system as large as California's without meaningful state financial support is a very real scenario.

12.4 ERM ACCOMPLISHMENTS

The UC ERM Panel in 2008 developed their ERM maturity model based on the COSO framework and Standard and Poor's methodology. As a result of the maturity model initiative UC in 2010 was recognized by S&P for its ERM program, the first non-financial institution to be so acknowledged.

The 2011–2012 Annual Report of Risk Services recorded that the cost of risk had fallen from a high of $18.46 per $1,000 operating revenue in FY 2003–2004 to its current level, which is estimated at $12.30 per $1,000 operating revenue for FY 2011–2012. This represents cost avoidance of over $716 million over the last eight years.

In light of shrinking budgets, UC has embarked upon the Working Smarter initiative, a five-year plan to redirect $500 million in administrative budget dollars to academic and research missions. In 2011–2012 the Office of Risk Services calculated that its efforts had produced $88.4 million in cost savings that year alone through various initiatives and projects, including the continuing efforts to build a more robust ERMIS.

In a recent project the ERM team and UC campus police departments developed a streamlined reporting structure for incidents in the police function. UC police were required to report to federal, state and local government agencies, which required additional man-hours. The reporting framework removed six figures from the overall police budget and allowed campuses to redirect resources to focus on reducing crime rates on campus. This centralized reporting yielded an additional benefit by allowing the police greater visibility to essential information on campuses and within the system.

Study abroad program safety and the security of researchers in the field are of paramount concern. In a recent project in Israel, UC developed relationships with knowledgeable security organizations that provide students, faculty and others with information that is critical for avoiding dangerous situations in country, lowering the risks for all. Similar services are provided worldwide for university faculty, staff, and students, wherever they travel on university business.

The Office of Risk Services has implemented campus risk assessments that roll up to a system-wide assessment. System-wide key performance indicators are measured along with local performance indicators. The Risk Management Leadership Council, a system-wide group, meets twice a year in person and holds monthly meetings online to review KPIs, and share best practices for programs and mitigations. Other groups involved in risk management such as emergency management services, controllers, risk managers and their teams, and others also meet regularly throughout the year to do the same assessments and reviews.

As new initiatives are proposed by schools, professors, and others, the Office of Risk Services works with project leaders and risk practitioners to build out initiative-specific assessment tools, which can often be applied to future initiatives. In effect, enterprise risk management becomes part of project analysis, assessing risk of the venture at the scope and operational level. ERM helps project planners decide whether to conduct the project or not, or discovers or devises alternatives or additional resources that will be necessary to make the program successful.

Not every project gets an ERM review – that is a fact of life. However, ERM reviews are available to all. When the Office of Risk Services discovers new initiatives they reach out to the team to recommend an ERM review. Often teams do their own review or ask for assistance from the Office of Risk Services. The Office of Risk Services does not micromanage local campuses nor are campuses required to report their ERM review results to the system.

As with any large business or university system there are changes in leadership and key risk management personnel. The annual Risk Summit serves as a major gathering point for new and experienced risk owners to learn new things and get up to speed on current initiatives. Also, the Office of Risk Services provides ad hoc training and development for new employees who are associated with the risk management function at the campus and system level. Training includes videos, website tool orientation and meetings with key risk personnel at local campuses. New risk management personnel also receive training at the Office of Risk Services and at monthly risk management meetings.

12.5   ERM PROGRESS OVER TIME

The university had a systemic need for data quality improvement. The new ERMIS initiative combined data from over 30 separate systems and has educated risk owners about business intelligence at campus level and medical center level, including new ways of looking at old information. As the ERMIS was rolled out there were many questions at the local level about quality of data and not unexpected surprises about performance that either did not meet or exceeded commonly held beliefs about performance. One major issue was the need to develop a common taxonomy so that data could be properly calibrated and compared. While the data initiatives and other ERM processes did not uncover many surprising or new or novel risks, information about trends began to drive changes in risk treatment and mitigation strategies. Non-performing strategies were altered or replaced. Better data led to better risk understanding and identification and also produced changes in risk treatment, and mitigation that produced behavioral changes across the system.

While the core KPI measures have been consistent over time, the bar is raised every year and top performers continue to be awarded at the annual Risk Summit. However, as the ERM initiative has matured and more new initiatives have developed ERM strategies, new KPIs have been developed or refined. For example, the executive director for the Research Grants Program Office oversees large grant programs for the entire nation. The problem was that the executive director had experienced only the downside of risk and not upside. Because the Office of Risk Services had become known as a "problem solver" the executive director asked Crickette and her team for help. What the Office of Risk Services and the executive director discovered was that the grant programs had major administrative and infrastructure problems that required additional IT solutions to mitigate. Together with IT the Office of Risk Services and the executive director deployed tools to identify, mitigate and monitor risks to help mitigate the research data problem. As a result of the success of this initiative the executive director has agreed to visit campuses to explain how all can leverage the ERMIS to help them operate more efficiently.

12.6   THE "UPSIDE OF RISK"

Many in the global risk management community struggle with defining scenarios that might be considered upside risks. UC has had success in identifying and capitalizing on upside risk opportunities.

The ERM initiative at UC is deployed in the context of creating a culture of *yes*. For example, as mentioned previously, budget impairment is a major risk to UC campuses and operations. The ERM *budget changes worksheet and analysis tool* was designed not only to help campuses determine the risks of budget cuts but also includes questions related to opportunities that could increase revenue or produce alternative revenue-generating opportunities.

Many of the ERM tools also analyze processes to determine where things are over-controlled. By eliminating duplication, introducing mechanizing processes, and streamlining operations, resources can be shifted from one area to another to increase opportunities.

The ERM initiative and tools are widely understood as a resource that can help a new venture determine how to develop a successful program and outcome. In a recent example, a scientist at a campus without a medical school wanted to develop more robust medical services without building the extensive infrastructure required for a full medical school. The scientist and local risk management team worked with the Office of Risk Services to develop a hybrid plan that did not involve developing a complete set of hospital services. The team was able to identify risks, resources, and available campus resources to create a viable plan.

Another case involves turning a liability expense into a profitable revenue-producing venture. The University of California, Davis has thousands of olive trees on campus. The problem is that olives fall on people and property and cause injury and damage. Olives on the ground also represent trip and fall hazards and sanitary issues. One local facilities person approached risk management with the idea that these olive trees could be harvested for their fruit to make into olive oil. At first the idea seemed far-fetched to all but the facilities manager. After an ERM review, the facilities manager approached a local olive oil company about the prospect of producing an actual product from the tree. The olive oil company took on the challenge and not only harvests the olives and processes the fruit into oil but is partnering with the university on a private labeled line of olive oil products that produces revenue for both the university and the olive oil company. While the net benefit of this project to the university has not yet been calculated, this endeavor represents a situation where what was considered to be a net-loss risk scenario was managed into something that not only mitigated the risk of loss but turned the risk into opportunity that could be exploited for its value-add to the organization and its stakeholders. As a byproduct the operation also provides a useful product from a renewable resource. This venture enhances the reputation of the university as an environmentally friendly community partner. For more information on this program see this Olive Center fact sheet: http://olivecenter.ucdavis.edu/news-events/news/files/Three%20Years%20of%20Achievement%202011.pdf

The olive tree also is a symbol of the University of California, Irvine. It has become a symbol for students from many faiths, cultures and political views who have come together to understand the Palestine–Israel conflict. For more information on the Olive Tree Initiative see the online video: http://www.uci.edu/video/olivetree/. One of the lessons learned from the olive trees on UC Irvine is that brand and reputation are not always tied to a slogan or vision but to an environment as symbolized by a tree, location, or other physical space. Nor are environmental factors the only non-verbal aspect of the image and branding associated with a company. Understanding the nature of the brand of any organization and how it is manifested for stakeholders is basic to the understanding of how the organization's value is understood by and transformed for its stakeholders.

12.7   CHALLENGES FACING HIGHER EDUCATION AND THE UNIVERSITY OF CALIFORNIA

Research risk has become and will continue to be a major enterprise risk for universities. In general, researchers feel their projects and endeavors have been over-controlled; those not in research feel that projects and endeavors are under-controlled. The challenge for UC and other universities is to develop tools that will optimize controls that streamline processes for researchers and provide adequate control measures and greater transparency for other stakeholders.

Another problem facing universities and UC is deferred maintenance. For example, the State of California will often budget for new projects but not provide resources for needed infrastructure maintenance.

Also, universities are for the most part open campuses. General safety and security has become a heightened concern in the wake of recent events at other campuses and schools.

Finally, leadership changes are always an issue. Grace is preparing to welcome the university's third president since she joined the university in 2004. Fortunately the shared governance of regents and university presidents has a good understanding of ERM and there has been little disruption associated with leadership changes. Since the writing of this case study, Crickette herself has left the University.

12.8   RECOMMENDATIONS FOR OTHERS ENGAGED WITH ERM

For those new to ERM or who have been hired into an organization beginning an ERM project or have been appointed from within a company to lead an ERM initiative, Crickette provides the following advice. Even if you are a tenured employee with the company, spend the first few months visiting the operations of the organization to discover what type of ERM program would be appropriate for the organization to develop at this time. An outsider when she was hired, Crickette told management that she would need to spend her first six months on the job visiting campuses and medical centers and interviewing key personnel to determine what flavor of ERM would be appropriate for UC. Crickette took heed from her former boss at United Rentals who said, "Your desk is a dangerous place to do your job".

Instead of asking "What keeps you up at night?", she recommended that new enterprise risk officers ask these two questions: "What information do you need to be able to know you are operating at optimum?" and "What does success look like?" Naturally the persons interviewed will try to turn the conversation to risks they face, but Crickette suggested that the risk manager eventually steer the conversation towards understanding, "How do you know whether you are doing well or not?", and "What are the results you want to see?" For example, one issue that Crickette discovered when she interviewed human resources was that there was limited analysis from data on the retention of new employees after the first 90 days of hire. The question that needed to be asked was, "What does a new hire need to do to be considered a successful hire?", or; "What does successful hire's performance look like?"

In her first conversation with campuses she asked, "Do you have accurate and timely data that shows whether you are doing well or not?" The answers she received uncovered the need for a robust system-wide ERMIS solution.

There are many ERM initiatives that have stalled in other organizations. ERM leaders complain of ERM fatigue. Fatigue can come from many sources: the original problems or pains have been mitigated, there are more pressing issues, new leadership has a new agenda, or the ERM team cannot articulate the value of the program in a meaningful way. The question is how does the organization sustain its ERM program long term? Crickette said that the UC ERM initiative remains strong eight years out. She explained that a major reason for this is that the initiative is in a continuous improvement mode. This means that her team and local risk managers are always looking for ways of improving risk management practices at the local level and at the department level. New tools are being developed, assessed, and strengthened all the time for issues such as security, medical safety, and fiscal controls. As new projects are envisioned tools are developed for these projects and what is learned in one project is often transferred to other projects. In a continually learning environment it is not likely that initiatives, tools or metrics will become stale.

At the same time the ERM initiative has become solutions focused and is the go-to facility to provide ideas, tools, and strategies for getting even complex or unique projects to yes. Rather than being *the* risk management department, the Office of Risk Services has worked hard with local campuses and operations to develop their own self-sustaining efforts in ERM. The annual Risk Summit goes a long way in articulating value through its awards program and system-wide key performance indicators which are now well understood and have become part of the accountability equation at all levels of the organization.

Crickette speculated that one reason why ERM programs become fatigued or stale is that many just focus on risk assessment, risk inventory analysis, and treatment. Identified risk owners come into risk boards and report and go back to their respective operations. Crickette suggested that this is not sustainable over time. While there needs to be a core identification, management, and monitoring function in place, the ERM initiative needs to continually look inside the organization for opportunities to tailor ERM processes to specific operation. What this means is that the initiative must work to improve the tools and build new ones for each segment of the operation. The CRO and team must help individual risk owners identify risks on their own and come up with their own risk treatments, and where necessary, work with the ERM team to develop new tools or other alternatives. In the end, this culture of yes enables the organization to understand risk and even increases the capabilities of the enterprise to take more risk – a greater but more understood risk appetite.

The ability to articulate value is critical to the long-term success of any ERM initiative. Crickette said that one of her major initiatives in articulating value is the cost of borrowing. The university has 10 billion dollars of debt, which means that even a few basis points of increase in borrowing cost can add millions of dollars of expense that could have been spent in other areas. The ERMIS reduces redundancy in IT systems – it is a flexible system that can be applied to numerous programs, departments, divisions and campuses in ways that reduce the cost of data aggregation, analysis and reporting and creates processes for new ventures and long-term projects.

But sometimes an ERM initiative goes off the rails or new leadership wants things done a different way. Crickette suggested that if the ERM program is experiencing fatigue, get up from your desk and tailor – reinvent the program. Ask new questions. Look for immediate wins at the operational level. Pick a department and work hard to get wins – partner with business partners – show on the ground value. Crickette said that if UC determined that a new approach to ERM was warranted, she would treat this as a completely new initiative and go on the road again to visit campuses to understand better the needs of the organization related to this change in thinking.

12.9   WHERE FURTHER RESEARCH AND ANALYSIS IS NEEDED

Medical schools have initiated programs to help new physicians develop a caring and empathetic bedside manner while remaining consummate professionals. These initiatives have also found their way into hospital programs and continuing education for tenured physicians. Crickette would like to see a similar initiative engaged with faculty, students, and higher education in general. She suggested that emotional intelligence and the concept of care in the educational endeavor could be improved.

Forces are amassing on all sides, pulling universities in many directions: towards vocational education to serve employers today, more quality research that can serve humanity in all areas, and stronger pedagogy to help students become better problem solvers and decision makers. Society wants universities to be effective community players who are instrumental in resolving persistent societal issues such as poverty and discrimination. In the world arena universities are called upon to serve as leaders in ecology, political science, and human rights. The role that higher educational institutions play in this new century will in part be promulgated by faculty, students and administrators. If faculty and administration can learn one thing from colleagues in medicine it is the importance of "bedside manner" – the development of a professional but caring relationship with those with whom they serve and interact. The gruff doctor and curmudgeonly professor have become relics of a bygone age. To capitalize on the opportunities for the future, both medicine and the university require continuous improvement in emotional intelligence and bedside manner.

APPENDIX A: UC ENTERPRISE RISK MANAGEMENT TOOLS

UC has and continues to develop enterprise risk identification, assessment, treatment, and monitoring tools. As the ERM program evolves additional tools and methodologies will be developed.

At the beginning of the ERM process, individual campuses and organizations within the University are tasked with identifying goals and objectives within the strategic mission of their organization:

> "The UC ERM Program uses the term 'Goals' to mean general statements of long-term outcomes in support of the campus/unit mission; goals are broad in scope. 'Objectives' are statements of short-term outcomes generally achievable in one year or less. The best objectives are measurable with an achievable end state indicating that the objective has been achieved."

These tools and documents were available on the UC Office of Risk Services website as of 3/6/13. http://www.ucop.edu/enterprise-risk-management/index.html. These documents are freely available to adapt to your needs but are not available for commercial sale. Please reference "University of California Office of Risk Services" as the original source.

- COSO Framework.
- Balanced scorecard.
- Campus charter committee worksheet and invitation letter.
- Medical center charter.
- Dashboard description.
- Risk planning tool.
- Budget changes worksheet and analysis tool.
- Protected health information analysis tool.
- Risk control structures assessment tool.
- Program risk review tool.
- Higher Ed risk assessment tool.
- Risk ranking tool.
- Risk inventory.
- Control self-assessment tool.
- IT assessment tool.
- Hazard vulnerability assessment tool.
- Sample ERM case study.
- ERM maturity levels framework and associated tools.
- ERMIS (ERM information system) tools, information, and guidelines.
- UC Tracker: compliance with SAS 112/115.
- UC Ready: business continuity planning tool.
- New initiative risk workbook.
- Library collections risk model.
- UC Action: risk control monitoring tool.
- Risk assessment toolbox.
- Unit risk workbook: campus level.
- Risk management leadership council: structure and duties.
- Risk summit: description.
- ERM bulletins, panel report on status of ERM at UC, webinars, sample ERM documentation.

QUESTIONS FOR STUDENTS AND PRACTITIONERS

1. If you were to develop a preliminary set of specifications for a request for proposal for an ERMIS, what would be the questions you might ask? If you have a particular organization in mind, what enterprise-specific questions would you add?
2. In what areas of relationships between universities, students and the community could the "bedside manner" or communication between stakeholders be improved? If you were assigned the initiative for improving communication, how would you begin the process, and what resources would you engage?
3. Go to the Office of Risk Services Website at UC – see the URL in Appendix A – and download the COSO framework document. Explain in layperson's terms what this framework could mean to an organization that embarks upon a new ERM initiative.
4. UC has demonstrated how an organization can capitalize on "the upside of risk". Provide two other examples from industry, government, or academe of such risk transformations.
5. Pick another university. Review the information on the website, including mission statements, academics, administration, risk management and develop a set of preliminary key performance indicators that you believe might be appropriate to discuss with the leadership and others at the university. If the university has developed and publicly provides key performance indicators, critique these metrics for their understandability, applicability, measurability, and long-term viability.
6. The annual Risk Summit is a cornerstone of the UC ERM plan. Develop a proposal for senior leadership to create such a forum for a for-profit organization. Consider all stakeholders and list the benefits for each. Estimate the value of such a program over time, both quantitatively and qualitatively.
7. Universities are open campuses but recent events have made that proposition difficult to manage. Research and report what universities have done in recent years to balance safety and security with the needs for an open and accessible university campus. Be specific and also indicate how these practices could also be transferred to other than university settings.

13

Case Study: Managing Risk at the OPAC du Rhône

Interviewee: Samiha Viand, Directeur Gestion des Risques et Assurances,
The OPAC du Rhône

Interviewer: Professor Jean-Paul Louisot, Formerly Université Paris 1
Panthéon-Sorbonne, Directeur Pédagogique du CARM Institute, Paris, France
Date: August 10, 2013

13.1 THE ORGANIZATION

13.1.1 Context

The OPAC[1] du Rhône, later OPAC, is the public housing office related to the local authority in charge of the department (*Conseil Général du Rhône*[2]); it operates under the statutes of public establishment with commercial and industrial activity (EPIC[3]), meaning it is a not-for-profit entity in France.

Therefore, the OPAC has a public service mission, to provide social housing, and it is the first social lessor in the department. It is currently managing 42,570 housing units after having sold all the units outside of the department (the French equivalent of a county in the USA).

13.2 ACTIVITY

The OPAC is engaged in three main activities:

- Builder and Developer:
  - Housing for the public.
  - Specialized housing for the elderly, the handicapped, students, and young workers, including assisted living housings that are rented to management associations.
  - Public equipment like sports venues, media centers, and nurseries. For these, the OPAC acts as project manager on behalf of the final owner.

---

[1] Office Public de l'Habitat du département du Rhône.
[2] The "Conseil Général" (general council) in France is the equivalent of a County Board of Supervisors in the USA, although the responsibilities are not exactly the same.
[3] An "EPIC" – Etablissement public Industriel & Commercial – Is a specific statute in France for public entities who play in a competitive market that contains mostly private players.

- *Lessor*: Managing family housing and commercial premises.
- *Planning and urban renewal*: Interventions in assistance to local authorities for the development of new commercial and habitation zones.

In addition to these main activities, the OPAC conducts many real estate rehabilitation projects.

OPAC acts as a managing company for condominiums for mixed property.

OPAC also sells housing units:

- Either through transactions of social home (new home sales to first-time buyers); or
- As part of the sale to tenants of existing assets; the sale of assets HLM[4] is part of a legal obligation: social landlords have to sell 1% of their family housing of more than 10 years in age.

13.3   TURNOVER AND COMPETITION

The OPAC and its staff number 990 associates. OPAC 2012 revenue was 178 million euros – rent income. Housing units are rarely empty, except for repairs, as there is a constant flow of request for housing and a waiting list. However, since the beginning of the economic crisis, the number of families who have difficulty paying their rent has increased. As far as competition is concerned, there are other "social lessors" in the same region but with a smaller number of housing units.

13.4   MAIN STAKEHOLDERS

Because of its intervention in the social housing sector, the OPAC has many stakeholders. Principal stakeholders are:

- Local authorities – and state representatives.
- Elected officials.
- Lessees/tenants.
- Associations for the tenants.

13.5   VISION AND SOCIAL LICENSE TO OPERATE

The housing policies are highly sensitive to the public and there is a ministry of the government in charge of housing. Therefore the local authorities are in charge of making sure that these national policies are implemented at the local level. The OPAC is a key player in this implementation so it is highly dependent on current policies.

---

[4] HLM – Habitation à Loyer Modéré – Social Housing with moderate rents.

OPAC may have to adapt decisions when the policies change with the election of a new government, a new mayor, a new county chair. The rules and amount of subsidies and aids may be substantially impacted.

The future will bring the creation of a major metropolis in Lyon, which will change the context in which the OPAC operates, including the membership of its board of directors.

13.6   THE IDENTIFIED NEED FOR ERM

The ERM process is still in the first stage of implementation. The concept of a global approach to risk management has been introduced with the insurance portfolio as a starting point. In fact, with the activities in which OPAC is involved, the insurance budget is important and many of the main exposures linked with real estate, construction, maintenance and management, are insurable.

The main task of the director of insurance to ensure the executive commitment to an ERM program was to stress the first step, risk mapping, so that the initial investment is limited and the advantage, even at the level of the insurance budget, should appear as the underwriters would have a better understanding of the risks and feel secure by the effort.

Furthermore the approach would allow getting the operational entities "on board" since the beginning of the process as they would be handed a tool to better manage their own risks.

It is for this dual purpose that the director of insurance developed the proposal for initiating an ERM program using Table 13.1 to initiate the discussion at the executive committee level.

The table approach is in line with the way the executive committee discusses and makes decision in an objective and transparent fashion. Table 13.1 summarizes the executive committee main questions to be answered for the implementation of the ERM process and stresses the creation of value the implementation would bring.

Approved by the top management, it becomes the roadmap for the risk-manager to initiate implementation throughout the organization as summarized in Table 13.2.

13.7   SUMMARY

As illustrated above, the ERM program is still at the first stage of implementation at OPAC and the road ahead is still long before the process will reach maturity. However, in many medium size organizations convincing top management of the need for an ERM program and getting on board the operational managers will often prove the two potentially key factors in the successful implementation. Therefore, the tables included could help any organization in the process of developing and implementing an ERM program, recognizing that risk mapping is often the initial stumbling block.

Table 13.1 OPAC Risk mapping process. Reproduced by permission.

N°	Step	Modus Operandi	Objectives	Actors	Time	Agenda	Sentinel points
Step 1	Defining a methodology	Proposal for the Members of the Executive committee	Validate the process and the criteria defined that all risk owners will have to appropriate for risk-management purposes. Take into account executives' remarks and advice.	Members of the Executive committee			A key is to define a common language, to use the appropriate pedagogy, and to ensure that the proper "risk culture" is grafted at all levels in the organization in a climate of open cooperation.
Step 2	IDENTIFICATION Assessment	Individual interview: On the basis of a declaration by "risk owners" during the course of an interview based on a pre-established questionnaire allowing for changes		Who should be involved? *This is one of the questions that the RM opened to debate with the Exec Committee*			Information gathered must be checked and validated, data must be cross-examined to ensure a transversal and coherent vision shared by all risk owners within the organization.
		TOP DOWN The initiative must start with the CEO and the members of the Executive Committee and then their deputies and so on: max two levels depending on the size of the department	1. Identify risks to list those of strategic implications for the organization, the major risks and also those that are significant. 2. Evaluate risks to determine a first approach to their probability and potential financial impact.	Persons to be "individually" interviewed			• Cross examining processes will allow to gather a maximum of information but the risks criteria defined must be kept in mind at all times.
		BOTTOM UP In the same time the ascending process will start with the Operational Agencies and territories	1. Detect risks or set up a risk register for the organization, define the risks in concrete terms *"Catalogue des risques de l'OPAC du Rhône"* 2. Evaluate risks to determine a first approach to their probability and potential financial impact	Persons to be "individually" interviewed:			• It is essential that the risk-owner provides his/her own evaluation of the risk therefore both probability (P) and impact/severity (S) scales must be relevant for all departments within the organization.
		Additional individual interviews	*Should the need appear, the identification process may be pursued to complete or improve the list of identified risks.				

Step 3 EVALUATION:	"Risk Evaluation Workshop" In project mode	1. Exchanges and sharing about risk and discuss the evaluation 2. Develop objective criteria to evaluate risks within a global and transversal vision.	"Risk Evaluation" Workshops 1- Pilot: 2- Sponsor: 3- 4- 5- 6- 7- 8-
Step 4 CLASSIFICATION Summary	Development of the base program directives for the Risk Management Dept	1. Set-up risk sheet for each exposure identified in the risk identification process 2. Set up the risk register that will have to be regularly updated. 3. Develop a provisional risk classification grid to be validated by the executive committee.	Risk Manager
Step 5 HIERARCHIZATION	"Risk Vision" Workshop In project mode	1. Discussion on risk categories and sources of risks 2. Discussion on the major risks and priority risks 3. Draw the first risk map	"Risk Vision" Workshops 1- Pilot: 2- Sponsor: 3- 4- 5- 6- 7- 8-
Step 6 Project MAPPING	Risk Mapping workshop In project mode	1. Discussion on the first iteration of the Risk map 2. Revisit risk categories: major risks & high priority risks (heat map)	Risk Mapping workshops 1- 2- 3- 4- 5- 6-
Step 7 Presentation of the MAPPING	Executive committee	• Validate risk mapping • Provide instructions to the next step with the mapping first iteration	Members of the Executive committee

Table 13.2 OPAC ERM final process. Reproduced by permission.

Questions	Answers	Benefit for the Organization	Sentinel Points	Impacts
What is risk management about?	To put in place a process to IDENTIFY, EVALUATE, TREAT and MONITOR RISKS	1. Limit the human, legal and financial consequences of risk. 2. Avoid crisis for the organization 3. Enhance the organization's image, its reputation 4. Enhance the organization's capacity to anticipate competitive move and improve its performance	1. For the success of such a mission, the will and support of the CEO and the executive committee are essential. 2. Instill & develop a risk culture within the organization in a serene climate. 3. Manage the project by associating staff of all levels in the organization so as to secure and maintain the adhesion of all to the project. 4. Be careful in choosing a vocabulary that all in the organization can understand and own.	**Take into account impact on governance and strategy:** • To fill the mission and be more effective in offering social housing. • To provide excellent service for the tenants, and the elected officials. • To enhance development and remain a major player in social housing.
What tools are needed to initiate the RM process?	RISK MAPPING Constitute the cornerstone of an efficient Risk Management exercise	1. Organize transversal exchange of information 2. Prioritize risks to highlight major risks, those that the organization must pay attention to immediately. 3. Offer a shared vision of risks in the organization. 4. Enhance decision making process and assist in strategic orientation and governance issues. 5. Facilitate a homogeneous iterative approach to update the program regularly?	1. The interview step must be conducted with judiciously chosen staff so that risks can be consolidated at all levels in the organization. 2. Take into account predefined criteria to prioritize risks.	**Operational dimension:** • Impact on human resources through empowerment, implication & cohesion of all the actors in the organization. • Impact on the organization through fluid processes, resources optimization, return on information system investments.
What are the limits of Risk Management?	Beyond a shared vision, risk management must lead to optimizing risk taking through the search for systemic solutions, the development of action plans with implementation follow-up	Identify those risks that are transferable and those that are not	Analyze with each concerned actor the appropriate transfer solutions	

QUESTIONS FOR STUDENTS AND PRACTITIONERS

1. Public, quasi-public and some private enterprises can be subject to radical changes in policy by government mandate. Legislative changes may take years to develop but sometimes administrative rule changes can be implemented very quickly. How does an organization in such an environment, especially when its operation is subject to governmental control, prepare for such contingencies?

2. If risk mapping were often a stumbling block for an organization, what would you do as the project leader for ERM to help the organization prepare for the risk mapping exercise? How would you establish the risk mapping process so that it can capture changes in the organization's risk profile over time?

3. The social license to operate OPAC is derived not only by its mandate from public authorities but also by its service to society. It is required to support the elderly, the poor and others who need assistance in housing and other services. OPAC also faces competition in this sector. OPAC must walk a fine line between meeting the exacting requirements of the public authority and the needs of its customer stakeholders. For example, it may not be able to disburse funds beyond that which the law requires even if there is evidence that the need for such additional funds would resolve certain social issues. If you were the executives at OPAC, how would you develop a strategic statement that expresses the organization's social license to operate?

4. OPAC is in the first stage of its ERM initiative. What do you see are the immediate next steps in its process of integrating ERM into the enterprise?

QUESTIONS FOR STUDENTS AND PRACTITIONERS

ERM References for Practitioners

The ERM field is expanding rapidly and there are new resources for risk management practitioners and others that are becoming available all the time. The references in this list are of publications since 2005 or more seminal books that the authors of this text felt might be important to ERM practitioners. They do not represent a complete list of references for ERM but will provide the ERM practitioner with ideas on some of the more recent developments in ERM. Risk associations in many countries now have sections and material devoted to ERM that should be regularly consulted. The insurance and risk management trade press continues to publish articles on ERM developments. Brokers, insurers, consultants, and other service providers continue to develop and post white papers for customers, members, clients, and interested practitioners. Online book vendors can often be searched for new texts on ERM on a regular basis. Many regulators, standards organizations, and ratings organizations have developed criteria, legislation, and other standards associated with ERM that apply to specific industries or more broadly and should be regularly consulted as they apply to the scope of any organization's geographical or operational footprint.

Albouy, F.X. (2002) *Le temps des catastrophes*. Paris: Descartes & Compagnie.

Apgar, D. (2006) Risk Intelligent: Learning to manage what we don't know. Boston, MA: Harvard Business School Press.

Auerswald, P.E., Branscomb, L.M., La Porte, T.M., and Michel-Kerjan, E. O. (Eds) (2006) *Seeds of Disaster, Roots of Response – How private action can reduce public vulnerability*. New York: Cambridge Press.

Barrett, D.A., Lentz, D.G., and Torpey, D.T. (2004) *The Business Interruption Book*. Erlanger KY-USA: The National Underwriter Company.

Benard, A. and Fontan, A-L. (1994) *La gestion des risques dans l'entreprise*. Paris: Eyrolles.

Berndt, A. and Anurag, G. (2009) Moral hazard and adverse selection in the originate-to-distribute model of bank credit. *Journal of Monetary Economics*, 56, pp. 725–743.

Bernstein, P.L. (1996) *Against the Gods. The remarkable story of risk*. New York: John Wiley & Sons.

Bland, D.E. (2000) *Treasury risk*. London: Witherby & Co.

Boisselier, J. (1979) *Prévention des risques industriels*. Paris: édition Organisation de l'entreprise.

Boultwood, B. (2012) Risk in boardroom; GARPS RISK NEWS and resource newsletter, December 2012.

Bradshaw, W.A. (1998) *Learning about risk. Choices, connections and competencies*. Toronto: The Canadian Institute of Chartered Accountants.

Briggs, R. Companies: Tackling the risk of kidnapping. *Guild of Security Controllers Newsletter*. Spring edition.

Brodeur, J.P. (2006) Air transport and risk management. *Canadian Journal of Criminology and Criminal Justice*, 48(3).

Business Insurance White Papers (new ones appear regularly). There is a charge for these white papers whether a member or not: http://www.businessinsurance.com/section/white-papers#

Cendrowski, H. and Mair William, G. (2009) *Enterprise Risk Management & COSO*. New York: John Wiley & Sons.

Chapman, C. and Ward, S. (2003) *Project Risk Management*. 2nd edn. Chichester: John Wiley & Sons.

Chapman, R.J. (2011) *Simple tools and techniques for Enterprise Risk Management*. 2nd edn. Chichester: John Wiley & Sons.

Charbonnier, J. (1983) *La pratique du risk management*. L'Argus de l'assurance.

Charbonnier, J. (1985) *Le risk management européen*, L'Argus de l'assurance.

Chevalier, A. and Hirsh, G. (1982) *Le risk management*. Paris: Entreprise Moderne.

Condamin, L., Louisot, J-P. and Naïm, P. (2006) *Risk Quantification*. Chichester: John Wiley & Sons.

Donaldson, T. and Dunfee, T.W. (1999) *Ties that bind (a social contracts approach to business ethics)*. Boston: Harvard Business School Press.

Douglas, K.Y., de Kempenner, M. and Vandenborre, S. *Systemic approach in real time*. Athena, n°54

Drucker, P.F. (1995) *Managing in a time of great change*. New York: Truman Talley Books/Dutton.

Duckert, G.H. (2011) *Practical Enterprise Risk Management: A business process approach*. New York: John Wiley & Sons.

Dupuy, J-P. (2002) *Pour un catastrophisme éclairé. Quand l'impossible est certain*. Paris: éditions du Seuil, 2002, Coll. La couleur des Idées.

Elliott, M. (2000) *ARM 56. Risk Financing*, Malvern, PA: Insurance Institute of America.

Elliott, M. (2000) *Risk Financing*. 1st edn. Malvern, PA,: Insurance Institute of America.

Elms, D. (1998) *Owning the future. Integrated risk management in practice*. Christchurch, New Zealand: Center for Advanced Engineering – University of Canterbury Christchurch.

Evans, D. (2012) *Risk Intelligence*. New York: Simon & Schuster.

Fournier, A., Guitton, C., Kervern, G-Y. and Monroy, M. (1997) *Le risque psychologique majeur*. Paris: Éditions ESKA (1997).

Fraser, J. and Simkins, B. (2011) *Enterprise Risk Management: Today's Leading Research and Best Practices for Tomorrow's Executives*. (Kolb Series) New York: John Wiley & Sons.

Gaultier-Gaillard, S. and Louisot, J-P. (2004) *Diagnostic des risques*. Paris: AFNOR.

Glynn, D. (2005) *BI Cover issues – Business Interruption*. Reading, UK: Cunningham Lindsey.

Gray, J. (2002) *Mars and Venus in the workplace*. New York: Harper Business.

Guide des assurances du maire, Paris, France: Association des Maires de France.

Guilhou, X. and Lagadec, P. (2002) *La fin du risque zéro*. Paris: Eyrolles Éditeur, Coll. Tendances.

Guinier, D. (1995) *Catastrophe et management (informatique)*. Paris: Masson.

Hampton, J.H. (2009) *Fundamentals of Enterprise Risk Management*. New York: AMACOM.

Harrington, S.E. and Niehaus, G.R. (1999) *Risk management and insurance*. 8th edn. New York: Irwin & McGraw-Hill.

Head, G. (1995) *Essential of risk control*. 3rd edn. Malvern, PA: Insurance Institute of America.

Head, G. and Horn II, S. (1997) *Essentials of risk management*. 3rd edn. Malvern, PA: Insurance Institute of America.

d'Herbemont, O. and Bruno, C. (1996) *La stratégie du projet latéral*, Paris: Dunod.

Hoffman, D.G. (2002) *Managing Operational Risk: 20 firm-wide best practice strategies*. New York: John Wiley & Sons.

Hong, H. and Marcin, K. (2009) The price of sin: The effect of social norms on markets. *Journal of Financial Economics*, 93, pp. 15–36.

Jorissen, R.E. and Stallen, P.J.M. (eds) (1998) *Quantified societal risk and policy making*. Australia: Kluwer Academic Publishers.

Jutte, B. (2013) 10 Golden rules of project risk management. Project smart. http://www.projectsmart.co.uk/10-golden-rules-of-project-risk-management.html

Kaplan, R. and Amette, M. (2012) Managing risk: A new framework. *The Magazine*, June 2012.

Katz, D. and McIntosh, L. (Wachtell Lipton, Rosen & Katz) (2009) Boards play a leading role in risk management oversight. *New York Journal*, Thursday 8th October 2009 at 9:02 am.

Kauf, E. (1986) *Évolution de la gestion des risques*. Paris: Réalisations éditoriales pédagogiques.

Kauf, E. (1982) *Guide du risk management*. Paris: Diffusion CCL.

Kauf, E. (1978) *La maîtrise des risques*. Paris: Éditions Sécuritas.

Kervern, G-Y. (1995) Éléments fondamentaux des cindyniques. *Économica*.

Kervern, G-Y. (1993) *La Culture réseau (éthique et écologie de l'entreprise)*. Paris: Éditions ESKA.

Kervern, G-Y. (1994) Latest advances in cindynics. *Économica*.

Kervern, G-Y. and Boulenger, P. (2007) Cindyniques – Concepts et Mode d'emploi. *Économica*.

Kervern, G-Y. and Rubise, P. (1991) L'archipel du danger. Introduction aux cindyniques. *Économica*.

Klewes, J. and Wreschniok, R. (Eds.) (2009) *Reputation Capital*. Germany: Springer PLEON.

Kloman, F. (2008) *The Fantods of Risk – Essays on Risk Management*, Lyme, CT: Seawrack Press.

Kumor, A. (2009) Who gambles in the stock market. *The Journal of Finance*, August 2009, 6:4, pp. 1889–1933.

La gestion de crise, Cahiers de la sécurité intérieure, La documentation française, 1991, n° 6.

La gestion de crise, La Revue Risques, 1992, n° 9, pp. 85–90.

La PME face aux risques, Travaux et recherches de l'IAE de Toulouse, 1985, n° 33.

Laeuen, L. and Levine, R. (2009) Bank governance, regulations and risk taking. *Journal of Financial Economics*, 93, pp. 259–275.

Lagadec, P. (1988) *États d'urgence. Défaillances technologiques et déstabilisation sociale*. Paris: Le seuil, coll. « science ouverte ».

Lagadec, P. (1981) *La civilisation du risque. Catastrophes technologiques et responsabilisé sociale*. Paris: Le Seuil, coll. « science ouverte ».

Lagadec, P. (1991) *La gestion des crises. Outils de réflexion à l'usage des décideurs*, Paris: McGraw-Hill.

Lagadec, P. (1981) *Le risque technologique majeur. Politique, risque et processus de développement*. Paris: Pergamon Press, coll. "Futuribles".

Lagadec, P. (2000) *Ruptures créatrices*, Paris: Éditions d'Organisation, coll. Tendances.

Lamand, G. (1993) *La maîtrise des risques dans les contrats de vente*, Paris: AFNOR.

Lamere, J-M. and Torly, J. et al. (CLUSIF) (1989) *Comment gérer les risques de l'entreprise. Méthode AROME*. Paris: Dunod Entreprises – Bordas.

Lange, S.K., Davis, J.K. and Jaye, D. et al. (2000) *E-risk: liabilities in a wired world*. Cincinnati: The National Underwriter Company.

Larkin, J. (2003) *Strategic Reputation Risk Management*. New York: Palgrave MacMillan.

Les accidents technologiques, Paris (France): CNPP & AFNOR, 1988.

Linck, J.S., Metter, J.M. and Young, T. (2009) The effects and unintended consequences of the Sarbanes –Oxley Act of the supply and demand for directors. *The Review of Financial Studies*. 22:8, pp. 3287–3328.

Lookman, A.A. (2009) Bank borrowing and corporate risk management. *Journal of Financial Intermediation*, 18, pp. 632–649.

Louisot, J-P. Trois études de Jean-Paul Louisot: *Managing reputational risk – A cindynic approach; Managing reputational risk – Case studies; Managing reputational risk – From theory to practice, pp. 115–178.*

Louisot, J-P. (2005) 100 questions pour comprendre la gestion des risques. – Paris: Collection 100 questions, AFNOR.

Louisot, J-P. and Ketcham, C. (Eds) (2009) *Enterprise-wide Risk Management: Developing and Implementing*. Malvern: The Institutes.

Lynch, G.S. (2009) *Single Point of Failure – The Essential Laws of Supply Chain Risk Management*. New York: John Wiley & Sons.

Maîtrise des risques. Prévention et principe de précaution, Actes du Colloque du 6 novembre 2001, INRS, 2002.

Maquet, Y. (1978) *Le contrôle économique des accidents dans l'entreprise*. Bruxelles: Bruylant.

Maquet, Y. (1991) *Des primes d'assurance au financement des risques*. Bruxelles: Bruylant.

Maquet, Y (1994) *Le risk management des PME*. Bruxelles: Bruylant.

Marchelli, A.M. (2012) *Enterprise Risk Management best practices*. New York: John Wiley & Sons.

Marmuse, C. and Montaigne, X. (1989) *Management du risque*. Paris: Vuibert.

Merna, T. and Al Thani, F.F. (2008) *Corporate Risk Management*. 2nd edn. Chichester. John Wiley & Sons.

Midol, A. (1988) *Crises agressions conflits*. Paris: CNPP & AFNOR.

Moeller, R.M. (2007) *Coso Enterprise Risk Management*. 2nd edn. New York: John Wiley & Sons.

Monahan, G. (2008) *Enterprise Risk Management: a methodology for achieving strategic goals*, New York: John Wiley & Sons.

Monroy, M. (2000) *La Violence de l'excellence (Pressions et contraintes en entreprise)*, *Hommes & Perspectives*. France: Martin Média.

Morel, C. (2002) *Les décisions absurdes (sociologie des erreurs radicales et persistantes)*. Paris: Gallimard.

Morel, C. (2012) *Les Décisions Absurdes Tome 2: comment les éviter*. Paris: Gallimard.

Neuhauser, P.C. (1988) *Tribal Warfare in Organizations*. New York: Harper Business.

OCEG, *red book – GRC capability Model*, Version 2.1, New York (USA), 2012.

Patton, A.J (2009) Are market neutral hedge funds really market neutral? *Review of Financial Studies*, 22:7, pp. 2495–2536.

Quels avenirs pour nos villes? Dossier du bulletin d'information des cadres, 1996, n° 32.

Rayner, J. (2003) *Managing Reputational Risk: leveraging opportunities, curbing threats*. Chichester: John Wiley & Sons.

Reuvid, J. (Ed.) (2007) *Managing Business Risk – a practical guide to protecting your business*. 3rd Edn. London (UK) and Philadelphia (USA): Kogan Page.

Risques et assurances des PME/PMI, Paris: Dunod & L'Argus, 1990.

Sanjeev, B., Hribar, P., Picconi, M. and McInnis, J. (2009) Making sense of cents: an examination of firms that marginally miss or beat analyst forecast. *The Journal of Finance*, October 2009, 64:5, pp. 2361–2388.

Schwartz, P. and Gibb, B. (1999) *When good companies do bad things*. New York: John Wiley & Sons.

Segal, S. (2011) *Corporate Value of Enterprise Risk Management*. New York: John Wiley & Sons.

Shiller, R.J. (2003) *The New Financial Order (Risk in the 21st Century)*. Princeton, NJ: Princeton University Press.

Shimell, P. (2002) *The universe of risk. How top business leaders control risk and achieve success*. Harlow (UK): Pearson Education.

Steinberg, R.M. (2011) *Governance, Risk Management & Compliance*. New York: John Wiley & Sons.

Stephenson, C. (2010) The role of leadership in managing risk. *Ivey Business Journal*, December 2010.

Taleb, N.N. (2007) *The Black Swan*. New York: Random House.

Tixier, Maud et al. (1991) *La communication de crise. Enjeux et stratégies*, Paris: McGraw-Hill.

Trieschmann, J.S. and Gustavson, S.G. (1998) *Risk management and insurance*. 10th edn. Mason, OH: South-Western College Publishing.

Widmer, L. (2012) Risk management makeover. *Risk Management,* Article pp. 19–24, April 2012, RIMS.

Widner, L. (2012) The supply chain balancing act. *Risk Management*, Article pp. 37–44, April 2012, RIMS.

Williams, A.C., Smith, M.L. and Young, P.C. (1998) *Risk management and insurance*. 8th edn. New York: Irwin & McGraw Hill.

Wybo, Jean-Luc et al. (1998) *Introduction aux cindyniques*. Paris: ESKA.

Yazdanah, M., Zamani, G., Stiglerr, S.H., Monfarred, N. and Yaghoubi, J. (2013) Measuring satisfaction of crop insurance a modified American customer satisfaction model approach applied to Iranian farmers. *International Journal of Disaster Reduction*, 24th April 2013.

Young, P.C. and Fone, M. (2001) *Public Sector Risk Management*. Oxford: Butterworth Heinemann.

Young, P.C. and Tippins, S.C. (2001) *Managing business risk. An organization-wide approach to risk management*. New York: Amacom.

Further Reading

Beasley, M.S., Clune, R. and Hermanson, D.R. (2005) Enterprise risk management: An empirical analysis of factors associated with the extent of implementation. *Journal of Accounting and Public Policy*, 24(6), pp. 521–531.

Chen, C.R., Steiner, T.L. and Whyte, A. (1998) Risk-taking behavior and management ownership in depository institutions, *Journal of Finance Research*, 21(1), pp. 1–16.

Knight, F.H. (2009) *Risk, Uncertainty and Profit*. 1st edn, pp. 315. Boston: Signalman Publishing.

Liebenberg, A.P. and Hoyt, R.E. (2003) The determinants of enterprise risk management: evidence from the appointment of chief risk officers. *Risk Management and Insurance Review*, 6(1), pp. 37–52.

Low, A. (2006) Managerial risk-taking behavior and equity-based compensation. *Journal of Financial Economics*, 92(3), pp. 470–90.

Martin, R. (1993) Changing the mind of the corporation. *Harvard Business Review*, November, pp. 81–94.

Tversky, A. and Kahneman, D. (1991) Loss aversion and riskless choice: a reference dependent model. *Quarterly Journal of Economics*, 106(4), pp. 1039–1061.

White, R.W. (1959) Motivation reconsidered: the concept of competence. *Psychological Review*, 66(5), pp. 297–333.

Wynne, B. (1992) in Ansell, J. and Wharton, F. (eds) *Risk: Analysis, Assessment and Management*. Chichester: John Wiley & Sons.

Index